# Canada, the Congo Crisis, and UN Peacekeeping, 1960-64

*Kevin A. Spooner*

# Canada, the Congo Crisis, and UN Peacekeeping, 1960-64

**UBC**Press · Vancouver · Toronto

17 16 15 14 13 12 11 10 09     5 4 3 2 1

Printed in Canada with vegetable-based inks on FSC-certified ancient-forest-free paper (100% post-consumer recycled) that is processed chlorine- and acid-free.

**Library and Archives Canada Cataloguing in Publication**

Spooner, Kevin A. (Kevin Alexander), 1968-
  Canada, the Congo Crisis, and UN Peacekeeping, 1960-64 / by Kevin A. Spooner.

Includes bibliographical references and index.
ISBN 978-0-7748-1636-6 (bound)
ISBN 978-0-7748-1637-3 (pbk.)
ISBN 978-0-7748-1638-0 (e-book)

   1. United Nations – Peacekeeping forces – Congo (Democratic Republic) – History.
2. Canada – Armed Forces – Congo (Democratic Republic) – History. 3. Congo
(Democratic Republic) – History – Civil War, 1960-1965. I. Title.

DT658.22.S65 2009                    967.5103                    C2008-907953-1

Canadä

UBC Press gratefully acknowledges the financial support for our publishing program of the Government of Canada through the Book Publishing Industry Development Program (BPIDP), and of the Canada Council for the Arts, and the British Columbia Arts Council.

This book has been published with the help of a grant from the Canadian Federation for the Humanities and Social Sciences, through the Aid to Scholarly Publications Programme, using funds provided by the Social Sciences and Humanities Research Council of Canada.

Printed and bound in Canada by Friesens
Set in Stone by Artegraphica Design Co. Ltd.
Copy editor: Judy Phillips
Proofreader: Jenna Newman
Indexer: Natalie Boon
Cartographer: Eric Leinberger

UBC Press
The University of British Columbia
2029 West Mall
Vancouver, BC V6T 1Z2
604-822-5959 / Fax: 604-822-6083
www.ubcpress.ca

*For Bina, Nikesh, and Prem*

# Contents

Acknowledgments / ix

List of Abbreviations / xiii

Introduction / 1

**1** Prelude to Crisis: Setting the Stage for Canadian Involvement / 12

**2** Decision Time: Diefenbaker and the Dispatch of Peacekeepers / 31

**3** Deployment: Trials and Tribulations in ONUC's Early Days / 63

**4** Constitutional Crisis: Peacekeeping in a Political Vacuum / 94

**5** Continued Chaos: Balancing Peacekeeping and Politics / 134

**6** The Challenge of Katanga: Peacekeeping and the Use of Force / 162

**7** Preparing for Withdrawal: ONUC's Final Months / 201

Conclusion / 214

Notes / 223

Bibliography / 259

Index / 268

# Acknowledgments

This book can trace its beginnings to my graduate work, so I am particularly grateful for the financial assistance I received while completing my MA and PhD. In addition to Carleton University funding, I benefited from scholarships named in honour of Lester B. Pearson, David and Rachel Epstein, and Sydney Wise. While at Carleton, I held a Department of National Defence Master's Scholarship and a Social Sciences and Humanities Research Council Doctoral Fellowship, funding that was essential to carry out my research. This book has been published with the help of a grant from the Canadian Federation for the Humanities and Social Sciences, through the Aid to Scholarly Publications Program, using funds provided by the Social Sciences and Humanities Research Council of Canada. I would also like to acknowledge the generous book preparation grant provided by the Wilfred Laurier University Research Office.

Dependent as this book is on primary archival material, it owes much to the unfailing advice and expertise of many archivists. Paulette Dozois at Library and Archives Canada and Joan Champ at the Diefenbaker Centre for the Study of Canada were exceptionally helpful. In New York, the staff at the United Nations Archives exceeded all my expectations with their guidance and support. Staff at the Canadian Communications and Electronics Museum, at Canadian Forces Base Kingston, were most welcoming and generous in sharing their collection and knowledge. In the Directorate of History and Heritage at National Defence, Yves Tremblay and Isabel Campbell gave excellent advice, steering me in the direction of very useful files and sources. Valoise Armstrong and John Vernon, at the Dwight D. Eisenhower Library and the National Archives and Records Administration respectively, responded most efficiently to my queries and requests for documents.

While working on this project, I never ceased to be amazed by the number of people I encountered who knew of individuals who had served as peacekeepers in the Congo. Though this book is not strictly a military history of Canadian peacekeeping in the Congo, as an historian, I was most grateful for the chance to learn from the many people who shared their recollections and even mementos of service in the Opération des Nations Unies au Congo. In particular, I would like to thank Ivan Burch, Bill Carr, Lloyd Carr, E. Foubert, Brian Hanly, Ian Hetman, Wally Pokotylo, Ken Smith, Bob Terry, Edward Thornhill, and Thomas White. Similarly, I benefited from wonderful opportunities to meet and interview former officials with the Department of External Affairs. William Barton, Gary Harman, and Geoffrey Murray were generous with their time and kindly responded to my many, repeated questions. Their views and memories particularly helped to shape and colour my sense of how policy was formulated and communicated within the Department of External Affairs. H. Basil Robinson was also especially helpful in clarifying some of the details relating to Prime Minister John Diefenbaker's early views of the Congo crisis.

At various stages of writing, I was fortunate to receive advice on my manuscript from individuals who not only wisely saved me from making certain errors in fact or interpretation but also made suggestions for improvements that undoubtedly resulted in a much better book. I would particularly like to acknowledge John English, Fen Hampson, Blair Neatby, Stephen Harris, and Douglas Anglin. I could not have asked for a more eminent and respected group of scholars to serve as my PhD dissertation examiners. Each provided advice that I remembered, considered carefully, and very much took into account as the dissertation evolved into the book over a number of years. The anonymous reviewers selected by UBC Press perceptively identified several opportunities to strengthen the manuscript; I hope they will recognize that much of what they had to say has indeed shaped this book. Greg Donaghy provided wise advice and words of encouragement at just the right moment. I am grateful to John Hilliker for sharing both his considerable knowledge of the Diefenbaker years and his contacts. Emily Andrew, Ann Macklem, Judy Phillips, and Randy Schmidt steered the manuscript through the publication process with great skill and efficiency. One could not ask for better editors.

While working on this book, my academic life took me from Carleton University to Trent University and finally to Wilfrid Laurier University. In each of these places, I happily encountered people who helped me in so many ways. In Peterborough and at Trent, I received much support and encouragement from Joëlle Favreau, Margaret Doxey, Martin Boyne, John Jennings, Jim Struthers, and John Wadland. At Laurier, my colleagues in North American Studies certainly deserve mention, Debora Van Nijnatten and Lucy Luccisano in particular. Brian Tanguay and Katherine Roberts verified my understanding of French-language sources and kindly listened as I often rambled on about this project. Finally, I sincerely thank Norman Hillmer. In the years I have now known him, he has proven himself over and over again to be the best teacher, supervisor, mentor, and friend. I will be forever grateful for the confidence he has shown in me.

I must also thank members of my family: Cecilia, Ken, Gloria, Tracy, Ramesh, Hansa, and Krishan. Writing this book has taken up much time that otherwise might have been spent with them. This has entailed considerable sacrifice, particularly by my partner, Bina, and I recognize a debt of gratitude to her for years of unconditional support that I will never be able to repay. Dedicating this book to her and our sons, Nikesh and Prem, is but a first, small step in this direction.

Clearly, many people have helped to make publication of this book a possibility. That said, any errors remain entirely my own.

# Abbreviations

| | |
|---|---|
| ABAKO | Association Culturelle des Ressortissants du Bas-Congo |
| AHQ | Army Headquarters |
| Air Comm. | Air Commodore |
| AMED | African and Middle Eastern Divison |
| ANC | Armée Nationale Congolaise |
| Brig. | Brigadier |
| CANARMY | Canadian Army |
| CANDELNY | Canadian Delegation in New York |
| Capt. | Captain |
| CCEM | Canadian Communications and Electronics Museum |
| CCOS | chairman, chiefs of staff |
| CENCOM | Central Command |
| CGS | chief of the general staff |
| CO | commanding officer |
| Col. | Colonel |
| CONAKAT | Confédération des Associations du Katanga |
| C Pro C | Canadian Provost Corps |
| DCC | Diefenbaker Canada Centre |
| DGPO | director-general of plans and operations |
| DHH | Directorate of History and Heritage, Department of National Defence |
| DL | Defence Liaison |
| DMI | Director of Military Intelligence |
| DMOP | Directorate of Military Operations and Plans |
| DRC | Democratic Republic of Congo |
| External | External Affairs |

| | |
|---|---|
| *FRUS* | *Foreign Relations of the United States* |
| Gen. | General |
| Grp. Capt. | Group Captain |
| LAC | Library and Archives Canada |
| Lt. Col. | Lieutenant Colonel |
| Lt. Gen. | Lieutenant General |
| Maj. | Major |
| Maj. Gen. | Major General |
| MDND | minister of the department of national defence |
| MP | Member of Parliament |
| NATO | North Atlantic Treaty Organization |
| NCO | non-commissioned officer |
| ONUC | Opération des Nations Unies au Congo |
| PERMISNY | Permanent Mission, New York |
| RCAF | Royal Canadian Air Force |
| SSEA | secretary of state for external affairs |
| UAR | United Arab Republic |
| UN | United Nations |
| UNA | United Nations Archives |
| UNEF | United Nations Emergency Force |
| UNTSO | United Nations Truce Supervisory Organization |
| USSEA | undersecretary of state for external affairs |
| V. Adm. | Vice Admiral |
| VCGS | vice chief of the general staff |
| WASHDC | Washington, DC |
| Wing Com. | Wing Commander |

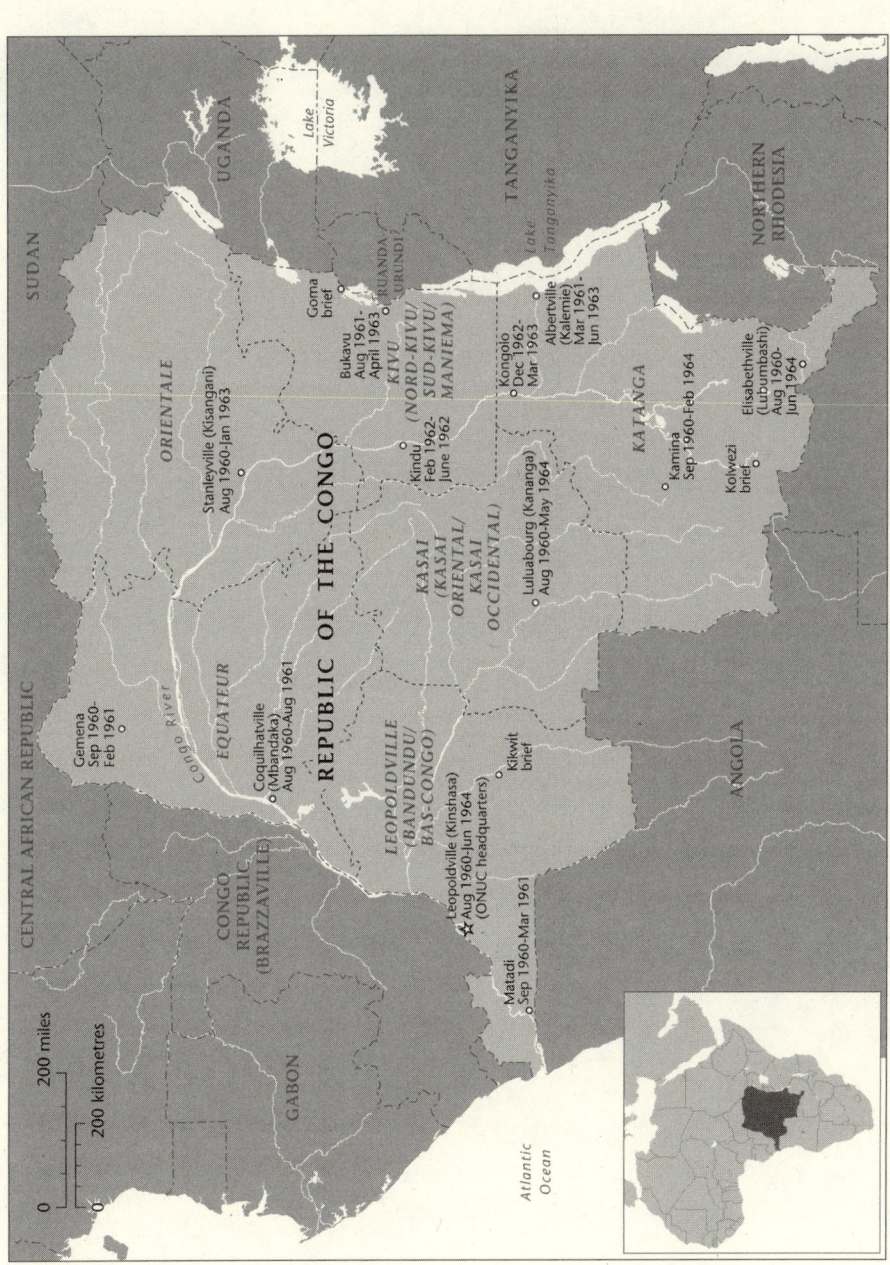

Republic of the Congo (1960), with dates and locations of Canadian deployments

# Introduction

The late 1950s was a remarkable period in Canadian political history. In 1957, having brought to an end more than two decades of Liberal government in an upset election victory against Prime Minister Louis St. Laurent, John Diefenbaker's Progressive Conservative Party formed a minority government and laid in wait for the opportunity to strengthen its hold on the reins of power. As it happened, Diefenbaker and his party would not have to wait long. After his defeat at the polls, St. Laurent was encouraged to see the wisdom of stepping down as Liberal Party leader and was replaced by Lester Pearson. After a long and impressive career in the Department of External Affairs, Pearson had transitioned from the civil service into government to serve as secretary of state for external affairs. Canada's most gifted diplomat found political leadership challenging, however. Lacking in political acumen, Pearson's early strategic missteps as party leader opened the door to another election in March 1958, a contest that saw Diefenbaker's government returned to power with a landslide majority.

John Diefenbaker, first elected as a Member of Parliament from Saskatchewan in 1940, fancied himself a Prairie populist. While he was not consistently successful in his early political career, by 1956 he had been chosen as party leader and his electioneering abilities had become, without question, singularly impressive. His oratorical skills, whether they were used on the campaign hustings to inspire ordinary Canadians or in the House of Commons to vehemently attack his political opponents, were honed during years of practice as a well-respected and successful defence attorney. His tremendous election triumph held out the promise of a sea change in Canada's political landscape; voters had turned their backs on the Liberals, who had become arrogant in their belief that they were Canada's "natural" governing party. Emboldened by his win – in fact, one of his ministers would later say it contributed to a case of megalomania – Diefenbaker was keen to govern and to leave his mark. On the world stage, his personal style of politics translated into a decision to embark in the autumn of 1958 on an ambitious six-week, fourteen-country world tour through Europe and Asia. His travels abroad were also, undoubtedly, part of an attempt to mould a distinctive foreign policy in the shadow of Pearson's exceptional success as an international statesman.

Even though Diefenbaker was prime minister at a critical time in the Cold War and when tremendous change characterized the global community, primarily as a result of decolonization, ultimately the course of Canadian foreign policy was not significantly altered during his time in office. His government certainly addressed numerous important international issues (e.g., continental defence and nuclear weapons, South African membership in the Commonwealth, trade with the United Kingdom), yet Diefenbaker's foreign policy legacy is mostly unremarkable. Basil Robinson, who served as the prime minister's liaison with the Department of External Affairs, has written: "It is perhaps not surprising that he left the foreign policy scene without having significantly altered the values, the priorities, or the continuing threads which he inherited from his predecessors."[1] Particularly from 1960 onward, Diefenbaker's government increasingly struggled with decisions related to continental defence. Serious divisions within his cabinet compounded the effects of the prime minister's own indecisiveness, and in the end the seeds of his government's demise were partly sown in foreign and defence policies.

The Congo crisis of 1960 is a useful historical case study, not only because it was a noteworthy international event but because the Diefenbaker government's Congo policy exemplifies the continuities of many of the issues associated with the study of Canadian foreign policy generally: peacekeeping, multilateralism, Canadian-American-British relations, middlepowership, quiet diplomacy. But if these speak to methodology, the evolution of Diefenbaker's Congo policy was more reaction to foreign policy circumstance than to theories about what Canada was or would like to have been in international politics. The government carefully weighed its options when the United Nations formally requested Canadian participation in a peacekeeping mission planned for the newly independent Congo. Canadian officials were especially concerned for the safety of peacekeepers; there were fears French-speaking Canadian soldiers might be mistaken for Belgians, the former colonial authorities. Nevertheless, the government gradually increased its support of the Opération des Nations Unies au Congo (ONUC). At first, aid and aerial support were provided. Once the UN was in a position to identify its particular needs, Canadian signal personnel were also sent. Canadian forces remained in the Congo until June 1964, when the mission ended. Significantly, the entire episode reveals a more reasoned and effective response than is typically associated with the Diefenbaker government's handling of foreign and defence policies, dominated as they were by difficulties over nuclear weapons.

The Democratic Republic of Congo has endured a turbulent and violent history. A brutal colonial legacy of forced labour gave way to an intense period of post-independence turmoil, which gave way to the dictatorship of Mobutu Sese Seko, which by the late 1990s gave way to a civil war that is reported to have claimed the lives of some three million Congolese. Although the DRC gained its independence from Belgium in 1960, it would take another four decades for full and free elections to take place; a journalist for the *London Observer,* reporting from the independence ceremonies, alluded to the potentially tortuous path that lay ahead. The Palais de la Nation, home of the Congo's first parliament and setting for the celebrations, was at first sight a structure replete with lofty lobbies, airy stonework, and a garden rolling toward the river. On closer inspection, journalist George Clay noted that curtains obscured considerable unfinished construction; the scene came to resemble a hastily built film set.[2] The veneer of government did not last. Within days of independence, the new country's armed forces, the Force Publique, mutinied. During the ensuing civil disorder, Belgium invaded to secure the safety of nationals who had decided to remain. Many in the international community condemned Belgium, and the Congolese leadership formally requested assistance from the United Nations. In response, the UN established ONUC, initially tasking it with the restoration of order and the supervision of the withdrawal of all foreign nationals from Congolese territory.

UN peacekeeping was not new in 1960. It emerged in the immediate postwar period when it became apparent that the collective security provisions enshrined in the Charter of the United Nations would not function as envisaged. With the unique exception of Korea, the UN Security Council was too often paralyzed by the rivalry of the permanent members and, consequently, the use of their right of veto. Provisions within the charter for the development of an effective, international force to be used by the UN were never realized. Peacekeeping, then, developed as a de facto alternative to inaction; it served as a mechanism to defuse and stabilize international situations, primarily in regions where the interests of the great powers were indirectly threatened. By the time of the Congo crisis, peacekeeping had already been used numerous times in the Middle East and along the border between India and Pakistan.

Yet, peacekeeping was encumbered by constitutional and operational ambiguity. The UN Charter, for instance, does not define peacekeeping. Its legal basis is found in Chapter 6 ("Pacific Settlement of Disputes") more often than in Chapter 7 ("Action with Respect to Threats to the Peace, Breaches of the Peace, and Acts of Aggression"), though it might be most accurate to say it falls somewhere between the two. Written in the mid-1940s, the UN Charter embodies several assumptions later challenged by postwar international relations. Its authors expected the new institution not to field peacekeeping operations but to enforce measures for collective security, even by the use of military force as a last resort. In contrast, peacekeeping was based on the principle that force should be used only in self-defence.

The principle of consent was also embedded in early UN peacekeeping. Under the charter, only the Security Council can legally authorize a United Nations military operation to take enforcement action against a nation. Only when all five permanent members of the council are in agreement or at least when each agrees not to use its power of veto, a feat typically achieved through compromise and consensus, is it possible to impose a UN peace-keeping mission on parties to an international dispute. When it proved impossible to reach such a consensus during the Suez Crisis in 1956, the Uniting for Peace Resolution was used to transfer the matter to the General Assembly, where the UN's first major peacekeeping force, the United Nations Emergency Force (UNEF), was ultimately approved. The General Assembly, however, could not legally force the parties to that dispute to accept UNEF, nor could it authorize the peacekeepers to use force to achieve a settlement. Instead, the General Assembly relied on the disputants to consent to the force's presence, without powers of enforcement. Later, when the Security Council approved subsequent UN peacekeeping missions during the Cold War, it typically followed this precedent with passive, consensual operations. Of course, this is not to suggest that other forms of international peacekeep-ing could not be or were not used outside the aegis of the UN, as in Indochina with the International Commission for Supervision and Control and the International Commission of Control and Supervision, and in the Middle East with the Multinational Force and Observers.

By the time of the Congo crisis, still other precedents had been established by the UN's experience with UNEF. Neutrality was perhaps the most import-ant of these. In practice, this required that peacekeeping forces not intervene in the domestic affairs of disputants or influence the outcome of a conflict. The need for neutrality also meant that peacekeepers normally had to be recruited from nations other than the permanent members of the Security Council. This last point had clear significance for middle or non-aligned powers, such as Canada. It has been suggested that while the great powers had to permit the UN to play a neutral role, the powers that were least aligned in the Cold War enabled the UN to appear neutral.[3]

Finally, peacekeeping in its earliest manifestations was used as a tool in conflicts between states. This was in keeping with a UN charter that was written to address hostilities between nation states, all but ignoring civil wars. In fact, the charter prohibits any involvement in the domestic affairs of a state, primarily by Article 2, paragraph 7, and by the emphasis placed on "international" peace and security in Article 24.

ONUC, as one of the earliest UN peacekeeping operations, was significant primarily because it challenged most of these formative principles. Put bluntly, ONUC broke all of these early rules. The Congo crisis was essentially domestic, yet interference in the domestic affairs of a state was prohibited under the UN's charter. Secretary-General Dag Hammarskjöld justified intervention on the grounds that a serious threat to international peace and security would be averted if the superpower rivalry of the Cold War was prevented from exploding in the Congo. There was no mistaking that Cold War politics would play a role in the outcome of the crisis. To observers at the time, events in the Congo "seemed at one moment to pose the risk of a direct Soviet-American confrontation, initially in Africa but eventually elsewhere."[4] The practicalities and logistics of an actual intervention in the Congo by the forces of either the Soviet Union or the United States aside (and the difficulties that would have been inherent in any such intervention should not be underestimated), the potential for the Congo crisis to escalate tensions between the superpowers and to lead to increased internal strife if rival factions could openly seek military support from the East and West, free from the scrutiny of an international presence, was real. But, with the dispatch of ONUC, the UN entered uncharted territory. As the crisis wore on and it seemed as though the secessionist movement in the province of Katanga might jeopardize the territorial integrity and viability of the new country, the UN abandoned a passive approach to peacekeeping in favour of a more forceful one. Through their efforts to expel foreign mercenaries from Katanga and to prevent civil war, the peacekeepers became a party to the conflict, compromising the neutrality principle.

ONUC stretched not only the definition of peacekeeping but also the UN itself. At its height, ONUC consisted of almost twenty thousand personnel and eventually cost the UN US$400 million. In its size, cost, and mandate, ONUC was a precursor to the type of peacekeeping missions increasingly undertaken by the UN in the post-Cold War period. Because of its tremendous political and financial stake in ONUC, the fate of the UN was perceived by many at the time to be inextricably linked to the outcome of this mission. Indeed, Alan James, a leading peacekeeping and Congo crisis scholar, has described the mission as "a watershed in the development of international peacekeeping."[5]

By 1960, Canadians had already served in peacekeeping operations in the Middle East, in the disputed Kashmir region between India and Pakistan, and outside a UN framework in the former French colonies in Indochina as part of the International Commission for Supervision and Control. In addition to carrying out peacekeeping duties, Canada made notable contributions to the diplomacy of peacekeeping. In 1956, it was Lester Pearson, then secretary of state for external affairs, who had urged the UN to send peacekeepers to resolve the Suez Crisis. Before this, peacekeeping typically involved a limited number of soldiers, used as observers to monitor peace agreements. UNEF was a significant development in the history of peacekeeping, and

Pearson was awarded the Nobel Peace Prize for the role he played. Historian Norman Hillmer has noted that this "contributed mightily to Ottawa's and the public's proprietorial interest in peacekeeping."[6] By the late 1950s, the Canadian government considered peacekeeping sufficiently important to warrant earmarking an army battalion for standby service with the UN.

This study examines Canada's foreign policy during the Congo crisis and its participation in ONUC, recounting and assessing significant issues and events between 1960 and 1964. Within a chronological framework, several themes are addressed: the politics of decolonization in the Canadian and international responses to the collapse of "order" within the Congo, and Canadian efforts to bridge political differences between developed and developing nations in particular; the impact of the Cold War on Canadian and UN involvement in the Congo; the increasingly interventionist nature of ONUC's mandate and official views on the use of force; the inter- and intra-departmental dynamics of Canada's peacekeeping policy development; and the motivations and objectives behind Canadian participation in ONUC.

At the time of the Congolese request, relations between states at the United Nations were shaped by two significant political developments: decolonization and the Cold War. As a result of decolonization, the United Nations was at a critical turning point in its evolution. Although the Western states had enjoyed a strong position in the early years of the UN, by 1960 this position of strength was in decline. Some five years earlier, it was Paul Martin who had in fact set this train in motion, as the chair of Canada's delegation to the tenth session of the General Assembly. Martin had worked earnestly, and in the face of considerable and at times vehement opposition from the United States and United Kingdom, to break a political deadlock that prevented the admission of new members to the UN. The Canadian efforts resulted in sixteen new members.[7] Membership subsequently surged, as African and Asian states at the UN increased from 22 percent in 1946 to 51 percent by 1964. Beginning in the fifteenth General Assembly, African and Asian states found it much easier to obtain a two-thirds majority, while the Western states found it increasingly difficult to garner sufficient support to block a vote.[8] And it was not uncommon for the Western states themselves to be divided by the politics of decolonization. In order to appeal to a majority of UN members, the United States was often at odds with its European allies on colonial issues. Unlike the United States, Britain and even more so France were reluctant to take positions during the Congo crisis that would limit freedom of action in their own African colonies.

Although Western states may have been divided at the UN by decolonization, the Cold War usually served to unify the West, especially when confronted by Soviet opposition. Initially, both superpowers identified a common interest in using a UN peacekeeping mission to address the potentially explosive situation in the Congo. Later, tensions re-escalated after ONUC itself was exploited to maximize political gain.[9] John Holmes, former Canadian diplomat and expert on Canadian foreign policy, has argued that Canada "more assiduously" worked for compromise on colonial questions than on Cold War issues but added, "Canada usually joined the Scandinavians in NATO to oppose the rigidities of the great powers in their attitudes both to the Communist states and the neutralists." Canadians, it seems, developed a "reputation for objectivity and independence, if not neutrality."[10] Holmes's assessment is confirmed by Geoffrey Murray, head of the UN Division at External Affairs during the Congo crisis, who believes Canada was certainly part of a moderate wing in NATO, working closely with the Norwegians and Danes.[11] Although Canadian governments sometimes shared the political objectives of their Cold War allies during the Congo crisis, they were content to allow others to shoulder the West's ideological burden, in order to preserve this reputation for independence and objectivity.

Attempting to account for a certain style in Canadian diplomacy, Holmes suggests Canada's "reputation for independence and objectivity had to be reflected in endeavours to establish bridges between the blocs, to find compromise solutions."[12] As will be seen, building bridges was a complex task for Canadian diplomats when it came to the Congo crisis: an international problem that divided both North from South, and East from West. Canada was keen to curry favour with the newly independent states. Geoffrey Pearson attributes Canada's sympathy with developing nations to "the common experience of 'colony to nation' experience which includes the political economy of resource development and foreign ownership."[13] Diefenbaker's secretary of state for external affairs during the Congo crisis, Howard Green, was certainly well disposed to the idea that Canada should play an active role at the UN and cultivate new relationships with developing nations. He was clearly taken with the idea that Canada could play a constructive, "helpful fixer" role in the international community, even when this annoyed our allies. The American secretary of state, Dean Rusk, went so far as to suggest President Kennedy raise Green's "neutralist tendencies" with Diefenbaker. Rusk bemoaned Green's preoccupation with Canada's "great peace-making role," though he acknowledged that Green's view seemed to be largely supported by Canadian public opinion.[14] Faced with the constraint of being allied to NATO colonial powers and others in the alliance that were more ideologically committed, quiet (at times silent), constructive diplomacy was often the order of the day for Canada.

The level of force ultimately used by ONUC seriously tested the notion that peacekeeping should be passive. In the post-Cold War period, muscular interventions in Somalia and the former Yugoslavia challenged the international community and scholars alike to redefine what was meant by "peacekeeping." Terms such as "peace enforcement," "peacemaking," and "mandate enforcement" were used to distinguish this supposedly new kind of multinational military operation from the earlier forms of peacekeeping. In many ways, however, ONUC was a precursor of the later form of active, interventionist peacekeeping. While not entering into the debate surrounding definitions of peacekeeping or the legality of what ONUC did in the Congo, I do document the Canadian government's reaction to ONUC's creeping mandate that edged the mission ever closer to confrontation in Katanga. It is clear that the Diefenbaker government was not keen to see ONUC depart from the precedents of neutrality and passivity.

The development of government policy during the Congo crisis is a primary focus of this book. For decades, the planning and conduct of Canada's international relations were in the hands of a small group of elected officials and civil servants. This was still true in the period under examination here. In Canadian diplomatic history, the paramount decision-making role played by this political and bureaucratic elite has been acknowledged. Kim Richard Nossal has suggested that they are given considerable licence to conduct foreign relations, subject only to very wide parameters set by civil society.[15] Similarly, D.W. Middlemiss and J.J. Sokolsky have drawn comparable conclusions about Canadian defence policy. They suggest that "on the whole, Canadian governments have not been greatly swayed by public opinion in formulating and implementing defence policy."[16] This view has been contradicted by one of the most noted scholars of Canadian peacekeeping. Historian J.L. Granatstein has argued that when it comes to peacekeeping, public opinion has been a very important determinant in Canadian foreign and defence policies.[17] I believe, however, that Canada's experience with ONUC demonstrates that, in this early period, the significance of public opinion as a factor in the development of Canadian peacekeeping policy has been overstated.[18]

Canada's Congo policy differed little from foreign policy generally: it was motivated by self-interest. Support for the United Nations, an institutional cornerstone in Canada's multilateral approach to foreign policy, was the foremost reason Canada became involved and maintained its commitment to ONUC. There was no shortage of additional concrete, though sometimes contradictory, considerations in Canada's Congo policy: preventing the Soviet Union from gaining a foothold in Africa, averting open conflict between the two superpowers within the Congo, reaffirming respect for the sovereignty and self-determination of nations, mitigating the friction between Belgium and the United Nations, and garnering influence among the Afro-Asian states.

Finally, I hope this book will help fill a remarkable gap in the literature on Canada and peacekeeping. For decades, Canadians and their governments have consistently emphasized the importance of international peacekeeping, yet there are surprisingly few histories of Canadian involvement in specific peacekeeping missions. My final objective, then, is to provide a more detailed account of the experiences and challenges faced by Canadian peacekeepers serving in ONUC. While this study does not pretend to be an exhaustive military history of the Canadian contingent in ONUC, it does discuss important incidents, issues, and events that affected the 57th Canadian Signal Unit and Royal Canadian Air Force personnel stationed in the Congo.

Before proceeding, it is worth sketching the key personalities and administrative structures that played important roles in the formulation and implementation of Canadian Congo policy. John Diefenbaker was prime minister until April 1963, for most of the time ONUC was in the Congo. Diefenbaker took a keen and involved interest in Canadian foreign policy. The prime minister also served as secretary of state for external affairs briefly in 1957, until he named Sidney Smith to the post. When Smith died suddenly, Diefenbaker became acting secretary of state for external affairs for three months, until Howard Green was selected to replace Smith in June 1959. Partly because of his political rival Lester Pearson's close association with External Affairs, the prime minister was more than a little anxious about the loyalties of his foreign service, the "Pearsonalities" as he rather derisively called them.[19] Throughout the Congo crisis, Diefenbaker developed his own views and interpretations of events and, at times, forcefully presented these during cabinet meetings. Whenever a decision relating to the Congo could have serious political repercussions, the prime minister was sure to have it discussed in cabinet. Lester Pearson became prime minister in April 1963, only after the secession of Katanga was at an end and the important questions remaining related to retraining the Congolese army and the timing of ONUC's withdrawal.

Howard Green, as secretary of state for external affairs, played a critical role in shaping Canadian policy during the Congo crisis. A veteran of the First World War, Green was first elected to the House of Commons in 1935. Before assuming the post at External Affairs, he had proven to be a very able minister of public works. John Hilliker and Donald Barry note that he had a close relationship with the prime minister and "was known to be a man of firm resolve, a quality ... that Diefenbaker could rely on to prevent him from becoming a captive of his officials in External Affairs."[20] Geoffrey Murray, head of the UN Division at External Affairs at the time, recalls that Green had an overwhelming interest in United Nations Affairs, so much so that during Green's tenure as minister the UN Division reported directly to the undersecretary of state for external affairs, bypassing the usual intermediary of an assistant undersecretary. The number two official at Canada's mission to the UN beginning in the fall of 1961, William Barton, remembers that

Green expected daily updates on the status of UN resolutions and always wanted to know what the developing countries were going to do.[21] Green's paramount foreign policy concern was disarmament, and this partly accounts for the significance he attached to the United Nations, a forum where he took important initiatives on this issue. It also explains why Green and Douglas Harkness, Diefenbaker's minister of national defence and a strong advocate in favour of Canada's acquisition of nuclear weapons, infamously deadlocked cabinet on issues relating to continental defence. There was little evidence of this ministerial rivalry, however, when it came to decisions relating to peacekeeping in the Congo.

Harkness was a decorated veteran of the Second World War, first elected as a Member of Parliament in 1945. He served as minister of agriculture and minister of northern affairs and national resources before becoming minister of national defence in October 1960. He was chosen by Diefenbaker to replace George Pearkes, who was minister in the early months of the Congo crisis but was then named by the prime minister to be lieutenant-governor of British Columbia. At National Defence, Harkness was advised by the chairman, chiefs of staff, Air Chief Marshal F.R. Miller. Miller, in turn, was advised by the chief of the general staff (Lt. Gen. S.F. Clark, then Lt. Gen. G. Walsh), chief of the naval staff (V. Adm. H.G. DeWolf, then V. Adm. H.S. Rayner), and the chief of the air staff (A/M H.L. Campbell, then A/M C.R. Dunlap). Miller continued as chairman, chiefs of staff, after the Liberals returned to power in 1963, to advise Prime Minister Pearson's minister of national defence, Paul Hellyer.

While National Defence assessed the military's capability to meet UN requests for peacekeeping assistance, it fell to External Affairs to consider their politico-strategic implications. At External, several divisions contributed to the development of Congo policy: the UN Division, the African and Middle Eastern Division, the European Division, and the Defence Liaison Division. Norman Robertson, the undersecretary of state for external affairs, was ultimately responsible for communicating departmental views to other departments and to the secretary of state for external affairs. Robertson was a seasoned diplomat, having earlier served as undersecretary during the Second World War, high commissioner to the United Kingdom, and ambassador to the United States. During Diefenbaker's time in office, it was not uncommon for Robertson to communicate directly with the Prime Minister's Office, where Basil Robinson liaised for the department. At the United Nations, Canadian diplomacy was in the very capable hands of ambassadors Charles Ritchie until February 1962 and Pierre Tremblay thereafter.

At the United Nations, Canadian diplomats and politicians worked with two secretaries-general during the Congo Crisis: Dag Hammarskjöld and U Thant. Hammarskjöld, a respected Swedish diplomat, was chosen to be secretary-general in 1953. He played a critical role in launching and overseeing ONUC until September 1961, when he died in a plane crash while on his way to negotiate with provincial authorities from Katanga. U Thant, who had been serving as Burma's permanent representative to the UN, became acting secretary-general from November 1961 until November 1962, when appointed secretary-general. Other important figures in the UN Secretariat also influenced and implemented Congo policy: Ralph Bunche, undersecretary for special political affairs and special representative of the secretary-general in the Congo from July to August 1960; Indar Jit Rikhye, military adviser to the secretary-general; and Brian Urquhart, who served as an assistant to Ralph Bunche and later the UN representative in Katanga.

For the sake of historical consistency, I have chosen to use names in common usage at the time of the events discussed. Beginning in the mid-1960s, after seizing power in a coup and appointing himself head of state in the Congo, Mobutu Sese Seko (formerly Joseph Mobutu) began renaming cities. Leopoldville, for example, became Kinshasa. The country was itself renamed the Republic of Zaire. A map has been provided to help readers, with current placenames indicated in parentheses (see page xv). I have also chosen to use "Department of External Affairs," "secretary of state for external affairs," and "undersecretary of state for external affairs," as these terms were in use during the period addressed here, even though the department, for example, is now known as Foreign Affairs and International Trade Canada. The peacekeeping mission sent to the Congo in 1960 is known variously as the United Nations Operation in the Congo, Organisation des Nations Unies au Congo, and Opération des Nations Unies au Congo (ONUC). I have chosen to use the latter.

# 1
# Prelude to Crisis: Setting the Stage for Canadian Involvement

Belgium's association with the Congo began in the late 1800s, when King Leopold II, the reigning monarch, hired the explorer Henry Stanley to establish trading posts in Central Africa. Stanley's success led to an African sphere of influence for the Belgian king. Britain, France, Italy, Germany, Portugal, and the Netherlands all competed for African territories, but Leopold shrewdly played each power against the others and in the end retained control over the Congo. In light of his humanitarian pronouncements on the region's economic development, Leopold's claim was officially recognized at the Berlin Conference of 1884-85. More to the point, he was willing to maintain the Congo as an African free-trade area, and this appealed to the economic interests of each of the European states. Under Leopold, the Congo Free State quickly became a hotbed of commercial activity and colonial exploitation. Huge tracts of land were leased to private companies in order to raise money, and railroad development was encouraged through a system of land grants. The Anglo-Belgian-Indian Rubber Company was one of the largest commercial enterprises in the Congo, but Leopold's Domaine de la Couronne remained the largest concession. Covering an area the size of Poland, this region exclusively enriched the Belgian royal family. Private enterprises benefited from a state-imposed labour tax that forced the Congolese to spend much of their time collecting rubber and ivory. Historian Adam Hochschild's frightening accounts of the systematic practice of hostage-taking as yet another means to achieve rubber quotas are further evidence of the brutality of colonization in the Congo.[1]

The region of Katanga, in the southeast corner of the Congo, remained largely unexplored until Leopold began to fear its annexation by the British. To develop the province, he leased land and resource rights to private companies, as he had done in the rest of the colony, but in Katanga this reciprocal relationship of development and exploitation reached new heights. In the early twentieth century, numerous companies were created to develop Katangan resources. Copper and diamonds were mined by the Union Minière du Haut Katanga and the Société Internationale Forestière et Minière du Congo (FORMINIERE) respectively, and each of these major companies was owned in part by the Société Générale de Belgique, a company that was closely linked to King Leopold.[2] In Katanga, more than in any other Congolese region, private enterprise played a dominant economic and administrative role. This arrangement was a critical factor in the secession crisis that followed soon after independence.

By the turn of the nineteenth century, there were growing international protests over the horrendous living conditions endured by the Congolese. In Europe and North America, suggests Hochschild, activists and reformers such as Edmund Morel and organizations such as the Congo Reform Association effectively raised public awareness of the atrocities associated with Congolese slave labour. By 1903, the British House of Commons had debated the issue. In Canada, both the Ottawa and Victoria Ministerial Associations forwarded resolutions to Prime Minister Wilfrid Laurier condemning the cruelties endured by the Congolese and urging British authorities to "secure to the people of the Congo Free State due protection and justice."[3] Ultimately, this growing outcry forced Leopold to relinquish control of the Congo to the Belgian government in 1908, but not before his reign left a horrific legacy. A 1919 Belgian government report concluded the Congolese population was reduced by half during Leopold's rule, and oral tradition in the Congo maintained that the rubber policy was more murderous than sleeping sickness or smallpox.[4] And although conditions in the Congo generally improved following the transition in its governance to the Belgian state, there remained disturbing parallels with the earlier period that continued into the 1940s, particularly in the practices of corporal punishment and forced labour.[5] For the Congolese, even Belgian rule was certainly seen as much less than a mixed blessing. In a speech delivered during the Congolese independence ceremonies, the new prime minister, Patrice Lumumba, denounced the brutal and painful colonial legacy of his new country as one filled with "ironies, insults, blows which we had to endure morning, noon, and night because we were 'Negroes.'"[6]

## Canada and the Belgian Congo

Relative to the European colonial powers, Canada's interest in Africa was modest at best. Both in terms of foreign and economic relations, Canada lagged behind most other developed nations in the establishment of links with the African continent and its newly independent states. In the early twentieth century, missionaries accounted for the earliest and most consistent Canadian presence in Africa. At the time of the Congo crisis, for instance, the vast majority of Canadians living there were missionaries. In 1959, 49 Roman Catholic and 275 Protestant missionaries were living in Congo, Angola, and Mozambique. In the Congo, these were predominantly

Mennonites.[7] Although the relationship between Africa and Canada was limited in scope, Prime Minister John Diefenbaker and his secretary of state for external affairs, Howard Green, were well disposed to the idea that Canada might play a greater role in that part of the world. Diefenbaker took the initiative at the Commonwealth Prime Ministers' Conference of May 1960 to expand development assistance to include not only the Asian Commonwealth countries that had benefited from the Colombo Plan but also African Commonwealth countries. By September of that year, Canada pledged $10.5 million to establish the Special Commonwealth African Assistance Plan. To a degree, Diefenbaker was motivated to do this by his fear that developing nations might be susceptible to Soviet overtures if the West did not meet their needs for assistance. This concern ultimately became an important consideration in the prime minister's foreign policy decisions relating to the Congo.

Early Canadian relations with African nations were usually with other members of the Commonwealth. The African states, however, often knew little of Canada except that it was not a great power and that it did not have colonies. Both of these considerations greatly enhanced its image relative to other Western countries. Yet, Canada's appeal as a potential friend stemmed also from its access to the powerful democracies – particularly the United States. Diefenbaker perceived an opportunity for Canada to enhance its international image by formulating constructive policies toward Africa in order to increase Canada's influence with the developing and non-aligned nations, though Canada was clearly industrialized and Western-aligned. This goal was not easy to achieve and met with mixed results. In the UN General Assembly, Canada was sometimes reluctant to vote with African nations on issues important to them. This did not go unnoticed. Canadians were sometimes perceived as "unsympathetic to African aspirations," and members of the Canadian delegation came to be known as the "total abstainers" because they often avoided taking a stand on significant votes.[8]

Although the government professed a concern and interest in Africa, in reality Canada was sorely under-represented by diplomatic missions there, and few resources at the Department of External Affairs were devoted exclusively to Africa. The Commonwealth Division at External was responsible for all of Africa south of the Sahara, and it was not until 1956 that a single desk officer in that division was appointed to cover African affairs. By 1959, three officers staffed an African section and consideration was given to the establishment of a full-fledged African division. By comparison, the United States was far ahead of Canada in the development of a diplomatic corps specializing in Africa. While a single Canadian desk officer struggled to keep up with the frantic pace of events during the Congo crisis, and was still responsible for all the rest of Africa south of the Sahara, there was in the United States a Bureau of African Affairs, with a staff of more than seventy that was headed by an assistant secretary of state.[9] It should come as no surprise that the Americans, given their greater interests, would naturally have more diplomats and officials to serve and study Africa, but the vast difference between the two countries is even larger than might be expected. And yet, the Belgian Congo was served relatively well by Canadian officials. In 1960, at the time of the Congo crisis, there were only five Canadian diplomatic posts in all of Africa. The Congo was among the five, with a consulate general, and was the only one of the five posts located in a country that was not a Commonwealth nation; before the Canadian consulate general in Leopoldville was established, the Congo had been the location of one of only three trade commissions in Africa since 1946.

In spite of sustained interest and repeated attempts to develop trade between Canada and the Congo in the decades leading to the Congo crisis, by 1960 Canadian exports to the Congo had reached only $1.3 million. As early as the 1920s, the Canadian trade commissioner in South Africa, G.R. Stevens, had gathered information on opportunities for Canadian trade in the Congo. His travels revealed the central role of Katangan resources in the Congo's economy but also the limited prospects for Canada because traders relied heavily upon established sources of supplies in Britain and Belgium. Although Canadian businesses managed to increase trade marginally during the 1920s, in the 1930s the Great Depression and increased competition from Belgium and Japan combined to end this development. Little changed until 1939, when the outbreak of hostilities in Europe significantly affected Congolese trading patterns.

Virtually cut off from Europe during the Second World War, Congolese trade shifted toward North America. The United States principally benefited from this, but Canada also temporarily experienced an increase in trade. In August 1940, Max Horn, counsellor of the Belgian government to the Belgian Ministry of Colonies, toured Canada and the United States to discuss Congo trade issues. The Belgian government had already concluded an agreement with the British, by which Britain agreed to import from Belgian colonies a fair share of colonial produce, relative to its own colonies. Horn was interested in a similar arrangement with Canada and managed to negotiate a tentative agreement on trade concessions with Canadian authorities. The Canadian agreement, in effect, placed the Congo on the same footing as parts of the British Empire, in terms of Imperial preferential rates of duty and the war exchange tax. Trade and Commerce officials believed the Congo stood to gain more from the agreement than did Canada but felt justified in suggesting its approval because it enabled Canada to purchase Congolese goods in sterling and because the Congo was an active participant in the war. The minister of trade and commerce, James MacKinnon, gave preliminary approval to the idea, which was then forwarded to External Affairs for consultation with Britain. At this point, the agreement ran into difficulty, when the British objected to it on the grounds that it undermined the very principle of Imperial preference. This, they felt, would cause serious difficulties not only within the Empire but also with other nations. Much to Horn's disappointment, the Canadian government chose not to follow through on the tentative agreement. Nevertheless, by the end of the war, 70 percent of Congo imports came from either the United States or Canada.[10]

In hopes of retaining and enlarging its share of the Congolese market in the postwar period, Canada opened a trade mission in October 1946, and MacKinnon visited the colony the following year. While it is difficult to precisely determine Canada's position relative to other countries trading with the Congo, it seems that Canada remained a top twelve trading partner until the early 1950s, when exports to the Congo fell because of competition and periodic downturns in the Congolese economy.[11] Canadian efforts to retain the market share it achieved during the war were, therefore, only partially successful. Canadian exports never fell to prewar levels but could not be sustained at the heights they achieved during the early 1950s. Overall, Canadian economic interest in Africa was limited – less than 1.5 percent of total Canadian exports and less than 0.5 percent of imports. Only twenty Canadian companies operated in Africa, and most were quite small. Three companies accounted for two-thirds of total investment; the largest was Aluminum Limited, with African holdings totalling $30 million.[12]

In the mid-1950s, Aluminum Limited became involved in a hydroelectricity project that sought to harness the energy of the Congo River. A two-hundred-mile stretch of river between the capital of Leopoldville and the seaport of Matadi, known as the Inga site, was considered a promising location for a massive power installation. In April 1955, the Belgian minister of colonies announced that Canadian and American specialists had toured the area to evaluate its potential – much to the dismay of Aluminum Limited officials, who anxiously preferred to remain discreet about their interest in Inga so as not to arouse Belgian nationalist sentiments or to antagonize Belgian business interests. The company's intentions, however, were clear: to get control over the project's construction and future direction of Inga's power supply.[13] These objectives ran counter to the views of both the Belgian public and the Société Générale. The Canadian ambassador in Belgium, Charles Hébert, quietly met with Aluminum Limited's representative, and in Ottawa his reports were forwarded to keenly interested officials at the International Joint Commission and the Atomic Energy Control Board. While information he obtained was useful to Ottawa, the ambassador was nonetheless urged not to compromise relations between the embassy and Belgian authorities. The Canadian government was interested by the possibility of Canadian investment in the Congo, but this was tempered by its desire not to offend or to undermine Belgian colonial sentiments. Proportionately,

American trade and investment with Africa was far greater. The one instance of considerable Canadian involvement and potential investment in a venture in the Belgian Congo was met with interest, but circumspect caution. Although it appears that Canadian trade with the Belgian Congo was important for a time, it was never sufficiently significant to become a factor in decisions relating to Canadian participation in ONUC or to Canada's approach to the Congo crisis.

First and foremost, relations with its mother country influenced Canadian relations with the Belgian Congo during this colonial period. Canada was reluctant to jeopardize its relations with Belgium, as evidenced by the Inga project; yet, Canadian officials in Ottawa and Leopoldville were sometimes critical of Belgium's colonial policies. It was a balancing act. The Congo contributed greatly to Belgium's economic well-being but was significant to Belgium for less tangible reasons as well – it was a source of pride. William Turgeon, the Canadian ambassador to Brussels in 1945, drew this to the attention of External Affairs, noting that Belgium's crushing defeat within days of the German thrust westward in May 1940 did nothing to foster the impression that Belgium had been able to contribute meaningfully and proportionately to the Allied war effort. Worse yet, the ambassador added, Belgians were further embarrassed when their resources were subsequently used by Germany against the Allies. These humiliating events and circumstances were offset by Belgian pride in the Congo's valuable economic and strategic role in the war. For example, critical Congolese mineral resources, including uranium, were made available to the Allied war effort. Still, the Belgians watched increased British and American wartime involvement with their colony with suspicion, and the Canadian ambassador warned that they would be uneasy about US and UK intentions when postwar colonial arrangements were addressed.[14]

Opinion at External Affairs on Belgian colonial policy was divided, revealing a more general difference in views of decolonization. Belgium's goal was to attain a partnership between Europeans and Africans, but the time frame for achieving this goal was unclear. Other colonial powers concentrated on developing a general social awareness that would result in increased political responsibility. Belgium, on the other hand, paternalistically placed emphasis on the economic well-being of the Congolese and avoided measures that might lead to the development of an elite. For example, primary and secondary school education was far more common in the Congo than in other African colonies, yet university education was rare because Belgian authorities almost never permitted Congolese to study in Belgium and not at all in other countries. To the Belgians, it seemed that the approach taken by the other colonial powers too often developed an elite that lacked judgment and political maturity. They encouraged the development of a stable Congolese middle class and gradually dispensed limited political rights to vote in established urban areas when not to do so might result in demands for an even greater political role.[15]

An interesting exchange of views in April 1957 between Escott Reid, high commissioner to India, and Ambassador Hébert demonstrates the opposing views within External Affairs toward decolonization, and Belgian policy in the Congo in particular. In preparation for a visit to Ottawa by Indian prime minister Jawaharlal Nehru, Reid had written a memorandum on colonialism in which he suggested that the colonial powers in Africa place their non-self-governing territories under the aegis of the UN and fix a date by which self-government for each territory be achieved. He believed the African decolonization process should take no longer than twenty years. Hébert disagreed. He argued that the Congo was an "inchoate mass" that a century of Belgian administration had been unable to mould into a uniform society. Belgian achievements and motives were assessed largely in positive terms:

> The Congo ... is inhabited by very backward peoples few of whom can have any conception of government ... In the circumstances it is inconceivable that, twenty years from now, these peoples should be asked to assume the direction of their own affairs through a grant of self-government ... Belgium's reluctance to make any such grant on her own initiative and her resistance to UN pressure cannot be said to stem entirely from imperial ambitions supported by vested economic interests.
>
> ... Belgium's achievements in the Congo do her credit ... Despite this progress however it is perhaps asking a great deal to expect a transition in three generations (from 1890 to 1980) from tribal warfare and cannibalism to twentieth century standards of justice, political development, orderly and responsible government.
>
> If, in spite of the existing situation, Belgium is forced to yield to UN pressures and grant to the Congolese self-determination in twenty years [sic] time, the consequences are not difficult to imagine ... the resultant regime would be far from stable economically or politically and would soon be in the hands of semi-trained Congolese who would either exploit their fellows for their own benefit or for the benefit of some other foreign power, possibly the USSR. In either case UN help would probably be rejected on the grounds of infringement of sovereignty and interference in domestic affairs.[16]

In some ways, Hébert's views are prophetic. He anticipated some of the important issues associated with the Congo crisis, including fear of Soviet penetration and the legal difficulties that could arise should the UN consider involvement in a crisis that was essentially a matter of domestic jurisdiction.

Escott Reid, by this time a senior diplomat well recognized within External Affairs for his ability to produce insightful analyses of Canada's foreign policy interests, countered Hébert's perspective in what had become his typically sardonic, effective style. Reid conceded that it might take thirty years before independence could be granted, instead of the twenty years he had previously stated. Using the example of India, he argued that it was not impossible for a diverse society to still achieve independence. The Congolese, he noted, were on average in a better economic position than were Indians at a similar stage in that country's development. Finally, he took issue with the idea that the Congolese could not meet twentieth-century standards of justice, political development, and orderly and responsible government. He cited a long list of leading twentieth-century political figures who failed to meet these same standards, including Joseph Stalin, Adolf Hitler, Benito Mussolini, and Francisco Franco.[17] In subsequent years, as we will see, most Canadian officials held the Belgians partially responsible for the Congo crisis for not having enough faith in the Congolese to assist them fully in preparing for independence. They questioned the Belgian position that it was a favour to the Africans to withhold independence until such time as they had sufficiently developed a responsible political consciousness. In this sense, later views and attitudes had more in common with Reid than Hébert.

## Colonial Turmoil

The slow pace of progress toward independence in the Congo eventually contributed to deteriorating race relations there. By the 1950s, increased industrialization caused the Congolese to migrate from rural to urban areas. This concentration of people, combined with a cyclical economy that resulted in labour shortages and then unemployment, aggravated an already tense situation. Apartheid was not a legal fact in the Congo, but in economic and social terms its impact was every bit as real there as in South Africa. In April 1951, Royal Canadian Air Force (RCAF) Wing Commander R.F. Douglas, serving in Brussels as an air attaché, went to the Congo to report on conditions. He was received well by Belgian officials and submitted a detailed report covering everything from the history of the colony to its geography and military installations. On the subject of race relations, he described the living and work conditions of the Congolese who served within the Force Publique:

Training natives requires tremendous patience, and the officers of the Armed Forces in the Congo possess this to a very great degree. The result is a happy situation among the native soldiers, and I believe the same applies to most of the civilian organizations. In general, the native who goes to work for the white man immediately enjoys a far better life than he knows in his native village. The natives seem to realize this. There is a complete colour bar in the Congo, and the natives have nothing approaching the rights of white men. It is common practice in the cities to have the native quarter and to ensure that the natives are in there by 9 p.m. There are separate railway cars, waiting rooms, restaurants and sometimes stores, for the natives. The natives have no voice in the Government. At present and for a long time to come, this system seems to be the only practical one.[18]

Douglas' interpretation of relations between whites and the Congolese was simplistic in its optimism but does provide a provocative snapshot of Congolese living conditions. The Congolese perceived the situation Douglas described as happy quite differently. The discriminatory working conditions and condescending attitudes of Belgian officers would ultimately lead to the revolt of soldiers in the Force Publique within days of independence.

But Douglas was not alone in underestimating the deleterious effects of the persistent racism and discrimination that characterized Congolese society. A.B. Brodie, the Canadian trade commissioner, held favourable views of Belgium's colonial policies. He believed that the Belgians had no desire to suppress the Africans but, rather, were interested in elevating them to become "healthier and more useful citizen[s]."[19] Official policy was meant to be benevolently paternalistic, and while it is possible that Belgian colonial administrators believed that they were sincerely assisting in the development of a new nation, the racist views and practices of the "non-official European" were strengthened and given credence by this notion of the need to "civilize the savage." In their decision to focus on the colony's long-term political goals, the Belgians failed to appreciate that the seeds of discontent were being sown in segregated quarters of the cities.

When riots broke out with some frequency in 1959, it became apparent that race relations were not as rosy as had been thought. European families resented the incorporation of the subject of African culture into the school curriculum, for both white and black students. K. Nyenhuis, the Canadian trade commissioner at the time, concurred with the Europeans. In a report to External Affairs he suggested, "Better subjects could be found since savagery is still very near the surface in most of the natives." In addition, incidents between individual Congolese and whites assumed a new intensity of racial hatred and prominence. In late May, for example, two cars driven by whites were demolished and the occupants seriously injured in retribution for the death of a Congolese woman involved in a car accident earlier in the day.[20]

Such stories of racially motivated violence contributed to a growing sense of hysteria. In the fall, Nyenhuis toured the Eastern Congo and found tensions rising there, too. He noted that most violence was between rival tribes but that the rising level of violence left many whites concerned:

Although no white people had suffered bodily or materially during the rioting, there was, nevertheless, the uneasy feeling that it would only take the
slightest provocation, real or presumed, to unleash the latent hatred against
the whites with the most abominable consequences ... Therefore, the large
majority of white citizens have heavily armed themselves ...

The general behaviour of many blacks in Luluabourg was sufficient indication that the respect for the white man is disappearing. Whatever animosities
the blacks may foster amongst themselves, they would be united in taking
bloody revenge for having been treated as inferiors, if not worse, for many
years.[21]

In a report filed the previous month, Nyenhuis noted that many urban
Congolese expected to take over the Europeans' possessions once independence was granted but that those living in rural areas had not changed their
attitude toward whites. The Europeans believed that minor political concessions to the Congolese caused the racial difficulties and that everything
would be solved if the unemployment problem was addressed.[22] Even as the
colony edged closer and closer to the breaking point, the European residents
still failed to appreciate the root causes of native discontent – paternalistic
colonial policies and demeaning living conditions. Trade Commissioner
Nyenhuis was equally late coming to this realization and seemed to share
the views of other whites living in the Congo.

Indeed, the Belgian Congo was often seen as a model colony. The Congolese standard of living was said to be among the highest of all colonized
Africans. Improvements in economic well-being, however, were not accompanied by an evolution in political rights. A governor-general and six provincial governors ruled the colony, and each of these officials was responsible
to the Colonial Ministry in Brussels. Political parties appeared for the first
time in 1957, during the first elections ever held in the colony. Voting was
permitted in Leopoldville, Elisabethville, and Jadotville to choose local officials. Membership in political parties was usually based on tribal allegiances.
In spite of local reforms, there were no concrete plans for decolonization as
late as 1959.

Then, quite suddenly in 1959 and early 1960, the Congolese independence
movement was ignited. In January 1959, riots erupted in Leopoldville during
a rally of the Association Culturelle des Ressortissants du Bas-Congo (ABAKO),
a political party headed by Joseph Kasavubu. At first the crowd was small
and orderly, but soon there were shouts for immediate independence. The
police began to panic and their *commissaire* was knocked over while trying
to arrest the party leaders. Police started to shoot in an effort to clear the
crowd, and pandemonium resulted. The crowds rampaged, looting stores
in both African and European neighbourhoods. Reinforcements from the

Force Publique tried to cordon off the affected areas, but by nightfall disorder had spread throughout the segregated quarter of the city. The Canadian trade commissioner in Leopoldville later reported that "all white people walking or driving through the native City and the outskirts of Leopoldville were attacked with stones, iron bars, and anything handy, their cars smashed and burnt, some women disrobed." Police arrested more than two hundred people, including Kasavubu, and some fifty Africans were killed. High unemployment was said to be one of the causes of the riot, but dissatisfaction with the level of political independence from Belgium was also a crucial factor.[23]

After the international community soundly criticized Belgium for its brutal suppression of the riots, the Belgian government unveiled its plan for Congolese self-determination in fall 1959. The plan called for complete independence by 1964, with various stages of political development in the interim. This pace was unacceptable to the Congolese and, fearing widespread riots, the Belgians agreed to discuss matters further at a February 1960 conference, where a much faster schedule of reform was drafted. The conference also produced an interim constitution (the *loi fondamentale*), which identified the political institutions of the new state. General elections were scheduled for May, and independence was to be granted on 30 June 1960. A spectacular pace of political reform had replaced Belgian intransigence. Yet, in their new haste to concede independence, the Belgians failed to adequately prepare the colony. The Congo completely lacked a native, effective administrative and political structure because of the Belgian decision to limit the number of Congolese permitted to pursue post-secondary education. This was to have serious consequences for the first Congolese government as it prepared to govern the vast territory the Congolese had regained.[24] One explanation for this critical shortcoming is that Belgium fully expected to continue to play a role in the administration of the Congo, even after independence.

The two politicians who would ultimately become the central figures in the Congo crisis were already prominent by the late 1950s. ABAKO president Joseph Kasavubu, arrested during the January riots, was educated in Catholic seminaries and, after working as a teacher and in administration, elected mayor of Dendale (in the segregated quarter of Leopoldville) in the local elections of 1958. Trade Commissioner Nyenhuis reported that the most significant political event in May 1959 was Kasavubu's return from Belgium, where he had been sent by colonial officials following his brief detention and removal from local office. His political supporters heralded his return "as the beginning of the millennium" and gave him a new light blue Cadillac convertible to mark the occasion.[25] During the February 1960 independence negotiations in Belgium, Kasavubu was the acknowledged head of the Congolese delegation. He was not popular with the Belgian authorities, who regarded him as a "separatist and an intriguer."[26] Above all, however,

Kasavubu was a federalist whose support rested upon traditional, tribal loyalties.

Patrice Lumumba was the other key figure. Born in Kasai and educated in Stanleyville, Lumumba eventually moved to Leopoldville, where he became a sales manager for a brewery. He was prominent in the Mouvement National Congolais, the only political party that could ever truly claim to be national in membership in the early years of the Congo's independence. Independence movements in other African countries influenced Lumumba's nationalism; unlike Kasavubu, he opposed tribalism and federalism in favour of a centralized, socialist, and unitary state similar to Ghana. Although once jailed for his political activities, Lumumba did attend the Round Table Conference in Belgium, and it was there that he came to prominence as the leading Congolese political figure. At first he attempted to ease fears that the Congolese would repudiate Belgium and confiscate white property, so initially he was seen as a trustworthy moderate who the Belgian authorities preferred over Kasavubu. After the May elections, he increasingly attacked Belgium. As a consequence, both official and public Belgian opinion shifted: Lumumba came to be characterized as unstable and likely to turn to Communist states for assistance.[27]

The Canadian ambassador in Belgium, Sydney Pierce, did not wholeheartedly accept this Belgian view. Embassy staff assessed Lumumba as

> a born politician and the most astute of the Congolese political leaders. He has chameleon-like characteristics which enable him to change his position suddenly and without worrying too much about being consistent. Lumumba is energetic, self-centred and very ambitious ... Lumumba's chief drawback is his apparent inability to get along with people who work with him ... Another drawback is that he is disliked and distrusted by most of the other Congolese leaders ... they suspect him of dictatorial tendencies ... In our view Lumumba is basically an opportunist and we doubt if he would let the fact that he got financial support from a certain quarter [Communists] influence his policy.

The American ambassador in Belgium echoed, almost exactly, his Canadian counterpart's assessment of the likelihood of Lumumba's potential allegiance to Communist quarters. Following a February 1960 meeting with Lumumba, Ambassador William Burden reported to the State Department that if Lumumba was receiving support from the Communists, he was "perfectly prepared to betray these supporters to the fullest extent that suits his purposes."[28] The Belgian government would, from time to time, raise the issue of Communist involvement to rally NATO support for its policies in the Congo. At this early stage in Lumumba's career, it is likely that they were overreacting and that the Canadian and American assessments of the future

Congolese prime minister are more accurate. Later, once the Congo began to descend into anarchy and Lumumba sought external support, his willingness to accept assistance from the Soviets needed to be more closely examined.

In December 1949, a news story appeared in the Paris edition of the New York *Herald Tribune* calling attention to the threat Communism posed to the Belgian Congo. Because the story was riddled with inaccuracies, in and of itself it is relatively unimportant, but the reaction it received and the diplomatic correspondence it spawned is interesting as a demonstration of the views of Canadian diplomats on the seriousness of the threat of Soviet penetration in the Congo. The article, entitled "Red Danger Reported in Congo," purported to be based on a Belgian state security report written by a state security officer. Among other things, the article suggested that the Soviets had sent sixty native Congolese to Moscow in order to take a special course in modern witchcraft. Apparently, they then returned to rural areas of the Congo to inculcate witch doctors with the slogan "The Soviets are going to come and liberate Africa and return its old tribal chiefs and sorcerers. You have been elected. When, with your support we have ousted the white oppressors, your ancient powers will return."[29]

In conversation with British officials at their Belgian embassy, Canadian diplomats discovered that a certain Captain Freddy, an individual of questionable background, had written the report. The British considered some parts of the story to be "utter nonsense" and discovered that it was not at all an official report of the Belgian government. L.H. Ausman, the Canadian trade commissioner in Leopoldville at the time, also considered the news story "extremely inaccurate." Ausman was moderate in his views. He acknowledged that some Communist ideology had penetrated into the Congo but maintained that activities along the lines reported in Freddy's account simply did not happen. He noted that the local Belgian authorities took the Communist threat seriously and had recently adopted measures to limit, as much as possible, the spread of Communist ideals. A year later, W. Gibson-Smith, who succeeded Ausman as trade commissioner, reported that the commanding general of the Force Publique was unconcerned about the spread of Communism because he considered the ideology to require more discipline than was to be found among the Congolese. In the early 1950s, when political conditions were relatively calm and stable, Canadian officials believed that there was little need to be worried about Communism in the Congo. Belgium took the threat more seriously, but even its officials remained relatively unconcerned until it became obvious that independence would need to be granted much earlier than anticipated. By June 1960, Canadian officials also acknowledged that the Eastern European countries could pose a serious threat if they became involved in the political development of an independent Congo.[30]

## Toward Independence

In the months before the Congo's independence, Canada considered upgrading Canadian representation in the Belgian Congo from a trade commission to a consulate general. The Canadian embassy in Belgium first raised this idea in July 1959, but the suggestion received a cool reception at External Affairs, where the Commonwealth Division considered it unwise to "take an isolated plunge into the question in Black Africa." The European Division also expressed the concern that such a change might imply tacit recognition of an independent Congo at a time when the Belgian government and Congolese leaders were still trying to negotiate the political future of the colony. The idea was set aside until the following year, when the undersecretary of state for external affairs, Norman Robertson, raised it again. He argued that developments in the Congo would have an important bearing on the political evolution of surrounding African territories and noted the advantage of having first-hand political reports from the area. Concern for the safety of Canadians in the potentially unstable weeks that would follow independence was also an important consideration. Howard Green was unsure that cabinet would approve the change, particularly if it was not clear that there would be trade advantages to doing so. The idea was shelved again until June, when Green agreed to take a joint proposal to cabinet, together with Gordon Churchill, minister of trade and commerce. There the idea once again ran into opposition, this time from Treasury Board officials who argued that the cost was not warranted because Congolese officials had in the past recognized the trade commissioner as an official Canadian trade representative. Cabinet overruled these concerns, visions of greater wheat sales to a growing African market turning the decision-making tide.[31]

In the weeks before independence, the Belgian ambassador to Canada called upon Howard Green to see what, if any, assistance Canada could provide to a newly independent Congo. Before the meeting, officials at External Affairs prepared a memorandum, in which they surmised there would be a great need for material aid and technical guidance in the Congo. They argued, however, that Canada was not in a position to offer any assistance. Canada provided no direct capital aid to Africa, and technical assistance and scholarships were given only to countries within the Commonwealth. Nevertheless, Green seems to have given the Belgian ambassador the impression that some help might be expected from Canada. The ambassador was especially interested in contributions to the field of education or technical assistance by French-speaking Canadians.[32]

The linguistic aspect of the Belgian ambassador's request does raise an important issue: francophone directions in Canada's foreign policy during the 1960s. John Schlegel has argued that "prior to 1965 biculturalism had not been a fundamental element in the elaboration and management of Canadian international policies."[33] In support of this view, Schlegel notes that, from 1950 to 1964, less than 0.0004 percent of the aid budget directed by the Department of External Affairs' External Aid Office was spent in French language areas – a statistic well explained by the memo prepared for Green, which makes clear that aid to Africa was minimal and, such as it was, exclusively limited within the Commonwealth. The Diefenbaker government did take some initiatives in forging relations with French Africa: Pierre Dupuy, the Canadian ambassador to France, toured French Africa in the fall of 1960; new programs were approved to provide educational assistance to newly independent former French colonies; and diplomatic representation with French-speaking African states was established. Despite these endeavours, however, Schlegel still concludes, "with the return of the Liberal Government in April 1963, Canada's policy toward French Africa continued as under the Conservatives – as a small, even insignificant policy which appeared as an adjunct to the Government's major concentration in Commonwealth Africa."[34] Belgium's request for assistance for its colony appears to have arrived just at the cusp of growing Canadian interest in French Africa, but also at a time when there were no established programs in place to provide such assistance.

Dag Hammarskjöld, the UN secretary-general, had visited the Congo in January 1960. He believed that the Congolese would need considerable technical assistance after independence and was aware there might be political difficulties. Practicing "preventative diplomacy," the secretary-general hoped the UN might insulate a post-colonial Congo from the Cold War and provide additional stability.[35] To this end, Ralph J. Bunche, UN undersecretary for special political affairs, was present at the independence ceremonies. Bunche was assigned the task of meeting with the new government to determine how the UN could be of assistance. Subsequent events, however, found the UN playing a far greater role than was earlier imagined.

Within a week of independence, Prime Minister Patrice Lumumba's government was on the verge of collapse, and the new country was descending into anarchy. The twenty-eight-thousand strong Force Publique mutinied on 5 July in Leopoldville. Mutineers attacked Belgians and other Europeans, reportedly committing rape and other atrocities. The Congolese soldiers were upset by the continued presence of Belgians in the force. Indeed, a Belgian, Lt. Gen. Emile Janssens, commanded the military, and the officer corps remained exclusively Belgian. Congolese soldiers wanted greater opportunity for promotion and advancement, but Janssens was unwilling to compromise on this issue. He believed little should change once the Congo achieved independence and was vocal about this. Moreover, on the day of the mutiny, Janssens wrote to Prime Minister Lumumba to admonish him for delivering "irresponsible speeches and announcements" that he believed had a demoralizing effect upon the soldiers in the force. He warned, "As I am not in the habit either of changing my mind or of repeating myself, I would be grateful if you would take this as a final and solemn warning." Later in the day, Janssens met with force officers and scrawled on the blackboard the words "before independence = after independence."[36] He personified the disagreeable effects of Belgian colonialism and paternalism; his actions and words in the days that followed independence propelled Congolese members of the Force Publique toward mutiny. Janssens was typical of many Belgians who fully expected that little, if anything, would be changed by independence. In the days and weeks ahead, events demonstrated just cause for the new Congolese leaders to be suspicious of Belgian motives.

The mutiny quickly spread to other centres within the country, and Europeans began to flee to neighbouring states. There was a mass exodus across the Congo River into Brazzaville. As the Europeans fled, the infrastructure and essential services fell into disarray. On 8 July, in consultation with the British ambassador, the Canadian acting trade commissioner, Roger Bull, decided to evacuate women and children associated with the Trade Commission to Brazzaville and Belgium. Approximately 240 to 260 Canadians were present in the Congo, but the majority were missionaries who chose to remain, until the situation worsened during the second week of July.[37] Bull found that the situation in Leopoldville, relative to other regions of the country, remained calm. He reported that the Force Publique mutineers in Leopoldville had been rough, but he saw no evidence that they had severely injured anyone; indeed, their main purpose for stopping people seemed to be to plead with them not to run away. At roadblocks, simply identifying oneself as Canadian or English, and at least not Flemish, usually resulted in nothing more than a quick search of cars for arms.[38] However, in various locations outside the capital, as the mutiny widened, crises erupted. In the port city of Matadi, Europeans were held hostage and looting was rampant. In Luluabourg and the provincial capital of Katanga, Elisabethville, Europeans withdrew in the face of rampaging mutineers. Canadian newspapers carried front-page coverage of the events. The *Chronicle-Herald* exclaimed, "Revolt in Congo Spreads; Mutineer Troops on Rampage," while the *Toronto Daily Star* featured the dramatic headline "Panic-Stricken Europeans Flee Congo Troop Bayonets; Report Assaults on Girls, Nuns."[39] Thousands of Belgians fled the Congo, and their stories of violence were said to have been "considerably exaggerated" by the world press. Brian Urquhart, a senior official in the UN Secretariat at the time, noted that, from this point, the crisis took on "strong racial overtones ... [and] no amount of idealism, sincerity, or disinterestedness would keep the UN operation immune from them."[40] Prime Minister Lumumba and President Kasavubu flew from location to location trying to quell the riots, but their absence from the capital made it more difficult for the Congolese government to take concerted action. Nonetheless, the Congolese cabinet met with Ralph Bunche on 10 July and Hammarskjöld was subsequently advised of a Congolese request for a team of technical assistance personnel capable of providing military advice to the new government.

The following day, Belgium ordered its forces to enter the Congo to protect its civilians and interests. The Belgian paratroopers landed in Leopoldville and Matadi in Leopoldville province, Luluabourg in Kasai, and Elisabethville in Katanga. This move by the Belgians aggravated an already complicated situation. The Belgian aim may simply have been to provide protection for Europeans living in the Congo. Certainly many European residents hoped the Belgian government would intervene, but to the Congolese the arrival of paratroopers was tantamount to a reversal of decolonization. Whatever the intent, Belgian intervention led to a serious deterioration in relations between whites and Congolese. Skirmishes between Belgian and Congolese forces occurred throughout the country. After the Belgians bombarded the port city of Matadi, killing nineteen Congolese, the American ambassador reported that some Belgian forces "have become completely irrational and in many instances have behaved worse than the worst Congolese."[41] Roger Bull was similarly critical of Belgium. He considered the invasion of Leopoldville unnecessary and suggested that Belgian policy was "ill-conceived, ill-executed and, in the deepest sense, irresponsible ... Popular opinion among Europeans here is that the Belgian government has been cowardly, vacillating and stupid." He also noted that Belgian military officers were inconsistent in their interpretation and application of the premise on which their intervention was based. Bull said of Gen. C.P. Cumont, sent by Belgian authorities to take command of its military forces in the Congo, that he knew "little about the Congo and cares even less for the welfare of its citizens. He has behaved throughout in a childish and vindictive manner ... treating army intervention as an exercise." He concluded that the Belgian invasion "completely obliterated any element of black/white cooperation or sympathy in the Congo. A most unpleasant xenophobia is now present."[42] Regardless of Bull's private views, the Canadian government did not publicly criticize Belgium. But aside from Belgium's NATO allies, the international community was virtually unanimous in condemning its actions in the Congo. The Soviet bloc was quick to exploit the situation, calling it an act of Western colonial imperialism.

This chaotic situation was only made worse on 11 July when the provincial president of Katanga, Moïse Tshombé, declared independence. Tshombé, born in southwestern Katanga and educated by Methodist missionaries, had been largely unsuccessful as a businessman before entering the political fray. He helped to create and subsequently became the chairman of the Confédération des Associations du Katanga (CONAKAT), a political movement that favoured Katangan autonomy and the maintenance of close ties with Belgium. His decision that Katanga secede within two weeks of independence had serious implications because the viability of the entire country was placed in question once its richest province declared its intention to leave the federation. Katanga's many economic and political connections with Belgium, combined with the political support Tshombé received from white settlers in the province, also cast a larger shadow of doubt on the motives behind that country's intervention. Some have said this doubt was warranted; by July, it appeared that Belgium had reversed its policy of fostering a united Congo in order to support breakaway provinces that chose not to stay within a Congo unified under the leadership of Lumumba.[43]

On 12 July, Lumumba and Kasavubu cabled the secretary-general from Luluabourg requesting UN military assistance. They emphasized that this aid was "to protect the national territory of the Congo against the present external aggression which is a threat to international peace."[44] It was now clear that the Congolese hoped not only for UN technical assistance to restore internal order but also for a large-scale UN military intervention that would protect Congolese interests in the face of Belgian aggression. Earlier that day in Leopoldville, the vice-premier, Antoine Gizenga, had approached the American ambassador to ask for similar bilateral military assistance. President Dwight Eisenhower and Secretary of State Christian Herter discussed the Congolese request and, noting that Hammarskjöld was working with the African ambassadors at the UN to develop a force that would not require white troops, the president concluded that no Western troops should go. Eisenhower thought Turkish or Pakistani troops might be used if there were an insufficient number of African soldiers available. The Americans tactfully declined the request, suggesting the Congolese redirect their inquiries to the UN.[45] Partly to clarify the conflicting requests originating in Leopoldville and Luluabourg, Kasavubu and Lumumba cabled the secretary-general again on 13 July. They stressed that the purpose of UN intervention would not be to "restore the internal situation in Congo but rather to protect the national territory against acts of aggression committed by Belgian metropolitan troops." They also expected that the UN force would consist of military personnel from "neutral countries and not from the United States."[46]

Thus, by mid-July, the stage was set for the international community to intervene, in hopes of restoring order and setting the Congo back on a sound footing. Whether Canada would be drawn into this effort was about to be seen. On the one hand, Canada clearly had few economic interests in the Congo. Moreover, Africa had not featured prominently in the minds of those responsible for Canada's foreign relations; unlike a number of its NATO allies, Canada was not a colonial power and had few historic ties to the continent. And while the Belgians had begun to express concerns about the potential for Communist penetration in their former colony and about the political susceptibilities of Patrice Lumumba, Canadian officials were more circumspect – raising doubts as to the veracity of tales of Communist intrigue and suggesting Lumumba was more likely an opportunist than a Communist. On the other hand, the Congo was one of only a few countries in Africa with which Canada had diplomatic relations. Both the prime minister and the secretary of state for external affairs had demonstrated an interest in Africa and a willingness to incorporate Africa into Canada's aid programs. Howard Green, in particular, was keen about the United Nations and the place of developing countries within that organization. At this earliest stage in the Congo crisis, there were hardly any obvious, hard, pragmatic, or self-interested reasons to explain why Canada might contribute to an international effort to defuse the tense situation emerging in the heart of Africa. Yet, within days, the Diefenbaker government would begin to contemplate whether Canadian forces should be incorporated into a UN peacekeeping force for the Congo.

# 2
# Decision Time: Diefenbaker and the Dispatch of Peacekeepers

In Canada, the Congo crisis received considerable attention. Across the country, newspapers, including the *Globe and Mail, Toronto Daily Star, Chronicle-Herald, Winnipeg Free Press, Montreal Gazette,* and *Le Devoir,* followed the situation for weeks, often printing front-page stories. This might help to explain the results of a July 1960 poll, in which Canadians were asked, "Of all the trouble spots in the world – Russia, China, Cuba, or the Congo, which do you think is the most critical?" After Russia, the Congo was identified as the next most critical trouble spot, according to 21.2 percent of respondents, ahead of both China and Cuba.[1] The editorial pages of many of these papers were filled with commentaries calling for UN action. On 12 July, the *Globe* asked, "Where are the UN Police?" in an editorial that was essentially pro-Belgian, yet called for the dispatch of a UN armed force. In *Le Devoir*, editor-in-chief André Laurendeau also called for an international effort to assist the Congolese government. He warned, "Si l'ONU refuse d'assumer ce rôle, son prestige diminuera" (If the United Nations refuses to assume this role, its prestige will diminish).[2] In the House of Commons, Liberal critic Paul Martin asked the Progressive Conservative government of John Diefenbaker if it intended "to inform the secretary general of the United Nations that if United Nations police forces are required and requested for the preservation of order in the new Congo state, a Canadian contingent is ready, trained and available to be moved by air transport immediately."[3] Prime Minister Diefenbaker was evasive in his response, noting that Secretary-General Hammarskjöld was consulting with the African nations and that it was premature to offer assistance until these consultations were completed.

Meanwhile, officials at the Department of External Affairs met with J.W. MacNaughton of the Directorate of Military Operations and Plans, Department of National Defence. MacNaughton had been directed by the chairman, chiefs of staff, Air Chief Marshal Frank R. Miller, to consider the potential implications of a UN request for military assistance. If the UN decided to send peacekeepers to the Congo, National Defence assumed it might approach Canada for French-speaking personnel. MacNaughton considered it unlikely that peacekeepers would be used "in any combat capacity," so he expected the UN would ask for military advisers and not the standby battalion Canada had readily available for UN service (the 2nd Battalion, Royal Canadian Regiment). Nevertheless, he believed the Canadian military could meet most requests, noting that the army maintained a standby list of one hundred officers, including some who were bilingual and could be posted abroad on short notice. One of three French-Canadian battalions could be made available but would take longer to prepare than the English-speaking standby battalion. In the end, it was recognized that the secretary-general would decide what was "feasible and appropriate." The government would, in the meantime, continue to take the position that the matter was under study at the UN and that no requests had yet been made of UN members.[4]

In addition to its consultations with National Defence, External Affairs maintained close contact with diplomatic posts in Belgium, the United States, and the United Kingdom, and also with the Canadian permanent representative to the United Nations, Charles Ritchie. Ottawa was most fortunate to have Ritchie in New York. He was an experienced diplomat, having joined External Affairs in 1934 and served as assistant undersecretary and ambassador to Germany before his appointment as ambassador to the UN in 1958. In the months and years ahead, it would fall primarily on his shoulders to carry out the sometimes complicated and delicate task of communicating the Canadian government's views of the Congo crisis to his diplomatic counterparts and to the UN Secretariat.

At this early stage in the crisis, political differences between the United States and the United Kingdom became evident, particularly over the continued presence and role of Belgian forces in the Congo, a key issue confronted by the Security Council in the days ahead. Fearing intervention by either the United Arab Republic or Guinea, and the spread of pan-Africanism, the United Kingdom hoped that any international intervention would be "on the broadest possible basis of white, brown, yellow and black, including the Belgians, but omitting the Permanent Security Council members." Alan James adroitly identifies the British position: "Britain's consistent line at this period was that it was necessary for the Belgian troops to withdraw from the Congo, but that there was no need for them to be unduly harried."[5] In contrast, the Americans were more concerned by the Belgian military presence in the Congo. If outside help was required to resolve the developing crisis, they preferred non-African sources to be used only as a last resort. Accordingly, the State Department also considered, for the time being, that this meant there was "no scope for an initiative on the part of Canada."[6]

The secession of Katanga, led by Premier Moïse Tshombé, complicated both an already tense political situation in the Congo and any plans for intervention in the crisis. Unlike the central government, Tshombé sought to maintain close ties with Belgium. He not only welcomed the intervention of Belgian forces but also sought troops from Britain and neighbouring Rhodesia. Substantial British economic interests in Katanga, primarily in Union Minière and the Benguela Railroad, led one Canadian diplomat to conclude Britain "may have to make a hard decision on Katanga." At External Affairs, Katangan secession was discussed, and it was thought best to "do and say nothing to assist separatism in the Congo." While the Commonwealth Division favoured a united Congo, it did not recommend condemning the separatists publicly. It did question whether restraint might privately be urged upon both Belgian and Rhodesian authorities; this was rejected by Norman Robertson, the undersecretary of state for external affairs, who thought it unnecessary to take any position on the status of Katanga or to press what he considered to be a "pretty remote interest on the U.K." It was, nonetheless, clear to Robertson that the "revolt" had created "a situation of civil war in which there will be strong pressures on European powers to take sides."[7]

Because Belgium was already open to charges of neo-colonialism, there was fear that any further intervention by European powers might leave the Congolese central authorities susceptible to Communist influence. The Soviet leader, Nikita Khrushchev, in his first statement on the crisis, clearly characterized it in Cold War terms: NATO had sent troops "to suppress the peoples of the Congo by force of arms."[8] Ominously, the Canadian embassy in Brussels reported that Prime Minister Patrice Lumumba was unlikely to "let Katanga go without a struggle and since he has no [repeat] no forces of his own effective against trained European troops, he may turn elsewhere." These views contradicted initial Canadian assessments of Congolese political attitudes that had suggested the Congolese were likely to pursue a policy of pan-Africanism and positive neutrality. Before independence, Canadian military intelligence suggested that there was no evidence of Communist meddling, in spite of the presence in Leopoldville of a Czechoslovakian consul general considered to be a "most able and dangerous official." Now, however, the chaotic political situation and the threat of secession became worrisome, as they presented "an ideal breeding ground for Communism." Canadian analysts concluded that while either British or French forces could restore order in the Congo, the only practicable solution was assistance from the UN in the form of military advisers to the Force Publique, a UN military force, or a combination of the two.[9]

## The United Nations Responds

In New York, the UN Secretariat had to contend with the rapidly changing situation in the Congo as it contemplated a response to a number of Congolese requests for assistance. On 11 July, the secretary-general was in Geneva when he was contacted by Ralph Bunche, the UN undersecretary for special political affairs, with the first Congolese request for technical assistance in support of the Force Publique. Canadian diplomats in Geneva reported that Hammarskjöld seemed to have in mind "some fairly major operation which could help restore order and confidence." The secretary-general immediately returned to New York and met with representatives of the African states on the morning of 12 July to discuss the matter. He suggested the dispatch of UN technical personnel to the Congo to assist in restoring order and discipline within the armed forces; the African states accepted this in principle. Hans Wieschhoff, in the UN Secretariat, later advised the Canadian representative that the UN hoped to use suitable officers already stationed in the Middle East with the United Nations Truce Supervisory Organization (UNTSO) for service in the Congo, with the approval of the contributing countries. Hammarskjöld expected to fund this operation from the UN technical assistance budget and his own contingency fund. He did not intend to ask the Security Council to endorse his program; instead, he planned to explain his proposal to members of the Security Council at a luncheon the next day, and if there were no objections, simply put it into effect.[10]

It was at this point that a second Congolese request arrived, cabled directly to the secretary-general by President Joseph Kasavubu and Prime Minister Lumumba. The Congolese leaders asked for UN military forces to counter the Belgian intervention. Canadian diplomats in New York reported that Hammarskjöld "would have liked to keep this additional (and of course highly embarrassing) request quiet until his programme to meet the first request for technical assistance had been developed and could be made public." In fact, he hoped the second request would simply "fade quietly away" once the technical assistance took effect. In conversation with the UK representative, Hammarskjöld revealed that he expected to select French-speaking officers for service in the Congo immediately after his luncheon meeting with the Security Council and specifically mentioned Canada as a potential contributor. Ritchie understood, on the basis of a phone conversation with External Affairs, that he was to make no prior offer of Canadian assistance; in any case, he was able to assure Ottawa that no other nation had made such an offer. Any request from the Secretariat would be relayed immediately for urgent consideration.[11]

Events the next day forced Hammarskjöld to change his plans. On the morning of 13 July, yet another cable arrived from Kasavubu and Lumumba. In this telegram, the Congolese requested a UN force with personnel drawn not from the United States but from neutral countries. They also threatened to turn to the Bandung Treaty powers for assistance if the UN did not quickly meet their request. In Leopoldville, Ralph Bunche grew increasingly concerned with events in the Congo. Belgian paratroops arrived in the capital and forcibly took control of both the European area of the city and the airport. In response, Lumumba threatened to call upon Ghana to provide military assistance until UN forces arrived. The American ambassador, Clare Timberlake, urged his French counterpart to have troops in Brazzaville ready to intervene in the mounting crisis. Together, these events persuaded Bunche to reverse his previous position against the dispatch of a UN force. In a cable to Hammarskjöld, he concluded, "I believe [the] UN may be able to save this situation, chaotic as it is rapidly becoming, if some action is taken quickly enough ... Only some manifestation of a 'third presence' which definitely should be international, military, but not indispensably fighting men, can save the situation."[12] Convinced by Bunche's assessment, Hammarskjöld decided a larger UN military force should be sent, in addition to the technical assistance program he originally envisaged for the Congo. From informal discussions, Ritchie learned the secretary-general expected the force to consist of three or four "fully equipped units ... which he hoped to obtain from several Asian and African countries and from 'a trans-Atlantic French-speaking country.'" Ritchie noted that the later phrase could conceivably be a reference to Haiti; he was inclined to think that forces from NATO countries would not be asked to be a part of the larger force. That afternoon, Hammarskjöld informally met with Security Council members and presented a three-pronged approach to deal with the Congo crisis. First, he maintained that Lumumba's initial request for military, technical assistance was a long-term project that could be met by seconding officers from UNTSO in Palestine. He had in mind French-speaking officers from Canada and Scandinavia, though official requests had not yet been sent. Second, he proposed the UN send a military force sufficient in size to enable Belgian troops to withdraw. Finally, Hammarskjöld identified an urgent need for supplies and food aid.[13]

Once convinced of the need to send a peacekeeping force to the Congo, the secretary-general demonstrated considerable initiative in putting his plans into effect. Bunche later noted that ONUC was "mainly Hammarskjöld's in conception and reflected Hammarskjöld's boldness."[14] While he had played a critical role in the development of UNEF, with ONUC Hammarskjöld was more involved at the earliest stages of planning and took the lead in defining the proposed mission's mandate.[15] One observer even commented that although it would be "misleading to imply that Hammarskjöld welcomed the crisis ... he did accept the challenge with enthusiasm."[16] Using Article 99 of the Charter for the first time, Hammarskjöld requested a meeting of the Security Council to formally consider the Congo situation and his proposed response. When the council convened at 8:30 that evening, two issues became the focus of debate. Hammarskjöld hoped to sidestep the Congolese charge of aggression against Belgium by receiving assurances that Belgian forces would withdraw once ONUC was dispatched, as British and French forces had done soon after UNEF was deployed.[17] The first operative clause of a draft Tunisian resolution, however, clearly called upon Belgium to withdraw its forces from Congolese territory. While the Western powers believed Belgium was justified in its intervention and saw the clause as unnecessary, the African states insisted that this relatively mild rebuke be retained. Indeed, the Soviets were upset that the clause was not more forceful in condemning the actions of Belgium and suggested amendments to the resolution that called for the immediate, unconditional withdrawal of Belgian forces. When these amendments were voted down and Mongi Slim, the Tunisian representative, refused to make any changes to his resolution, the Western nations and the Soviets finally agreed to accept the clause as originally drafted.[18]

The council then debated the question of ONUC's composition. Arkadiy Sobolev, the Soviet representative, wanted the UN to use only African contingents. While acceptable to the African states, such a limitation contradicted Hammarskjöld's belief that, although ONUC should consist mainly of African troops to reflect the primary responsibility of the African states for the UN's efforts in the Congo, it should also include peacekeepers from elsewhere to mirror the UN's universal character.[19] Given the colonial context of the crisis, the secretary-general recognized the political necessity of a primarily African force, even though, as one scholar would later note, "it was impossible for a force so composed to be completely disinterested."[20] Ultimately, Sobolev's amendment was narrowly defeated, five votes against to four in favour, with two abstentions. For the moment, the issue of force composition was settled.

In the early hours of 14 July, the Tunisian resolution was approved by a vote of eight in favour, none against, and three abstentions.[21] In addition to calling upon Belgium to withdraw its forces from the Congo, the Security Council authorized the secretary-general, in consultation with the Congo government, to provide military and technical assistance until the Congolese armed forces could carry out their responsibilities. The resolution also requested the secretary-general to report to the Security Council as appropriate. This resolution, like many of the subsequent enabling resolutions related to ONUC, proved to be problematic. It was, for instance, deliberately vague on the question of Belgian withdrawal. In fact, when explaining their votes on this resolution, the Americans and Soviets maintained contradictory interpretations of the clause on Belgian withdrawal.[22] Significantly, the resolution failed to identify the charter provisions on which it was based. Because of these ambiguities, the secretary-general exercised considerable latitude when translating the decisions of the council into operating instructions for ONUC, filling what Peter Calvocoressi terms the "gap between resolution and action."[23] To a degree, this followed the pattern established by UNEF. During that peacekeeping mission, the General Assembly was content to leave the daily operations in the hands of the secretary-general; "Leave it to Dag" was a common refrain. Initially, this approach provided the Secretariat with greater flexibility in the implementation of ONUC, but later, as senior Secretariat official Brian Urquhart noted, the rather "Delphic" instructions of the Security Council became a political hazard.[24]

## Early Reaction in Ottawa

After Hammarskjöld's luncheon meeting with members of the Security Council earlier in the day, Canadian officials in Ottawa and New York began to assess the possibilities of Canadian participation in the UN efforts to deal with the Congo crisis. The undersecretary of state for external affairs, Norman Robertson, prepared a memorandum for the minister that provided details on all three of Hammarskjöld's proposed actions, in anticipation that a formal request from the UN could be forthcoming. J.W. MacNaughton at National Defence had already advised External Affairs officials that there was no military reason why Canada should not respond favourably if the secretary-general requested the secondment of French-speaking Canadian officers serving in UNTSO. Nor did Robertson see any political reason to turn down such a request, though there would be considerable personal risk for white officers serving in the Congo. But Robertson was cautious on the question of Canadian participation in the secretary-general's proposed UN peace force for the Congo. Because the force would be assigned the task of restoring order, he imagined it might become necessary for peacekeepers to fire on Congolese mutineers or even rowdy civilians. He remarked, "It is difficult to see any United Nations force in this role because in effect the United Nations would have taken up arms against citizens of a state in what was essentially a domestic situation." He sensed, however, that the secretary-general's earlier reference to a "trans-Atlantic French-speaking" country was intended to suggest Canada. He anticipated that Hammarskjöld would have a difficult time locating forces that were capable of providing logistic support to a mixed force, particularly given the problems posed by differences in language. He concluded,

> I believe that any white troops involved in the proposed law enforcement role of the United Nations would be in a most difficult situation, since it would be difficult to persuade the Congolese masses that the United Nations force was not another form of white domination. The administrative units of the force might not be required to coerce the Congolese in any way but they might have to protect themselves and the supplies and equipment of the force against Congolese attack. On balance, therefore, we should have to look very carefully at any request involving a Canadian contingent for the force and the Secretary-General should be made aware of our hesitation to become involved in this way.

Robertson's recommendation was a far cry from the Opposition's eager suggestion, put forward in Parliament just the day before, that Canada should approach the UN to offer the services of its standby battalion. This was a moot point. In New York, Charles Ritchie was in a better position to appreciate the political debate surrounding ONUC's composition. He reported, "There had been no question of supplying a Canadian contingent to the proposed Force," and that "the Canadian standby battalion (second RCR's) would not be suitable in any event." Robertson did recommend that cabinet consider the provision of foodstuffs or supplies, and the necessary air transportation to move these gifts to the Congo, to alleviate serious food shortages. He noted also that the UN had informally requested the use of two Canadian aircraft serving in UNEF, for the purpose of ferrying supplies and personnel to the Congo. The RCAF saw no objection to such service, and so Robertson suggested that Canada agree to provide the aircraft if the UN formally requested their use.[25]

Because the secretary of state for external affairs, Howard Green, was away from Ottawa at a joint conference of American and Canadian ministers on defence matters, the prime minister reviewed the Congo file himself. Basil Robinson, Diefenbaker's special assistant on foreign affairs, reported that the prime minister "shot out of his chair and told me to see that Hammarskjöld was told right away not to proceed with the idea of troops from Canada."[26] Robinson reported Diefenbaker's views to the undersecretary at once, advising Robertson that cabinet would likely approve the temporary transfer of Canadian officers in UNTSO and that serious consideration would be given to any UN requests for foodstuffs. The question of a Canadian contribution to the large peace force, on the other hand, was a different matter. Hammarskjöld was to be advised not to speak of a possible military contribution from a "trans-Atlantic French-speaking country." According to Robinson, Diefenbaker was "emphatic that he did not wish any expectation to be aroused that military assistance from Canada would be forthcoming."[27]

Initial discussion of a Canadian contribution to the larger peace force was focused on the prospect of Canada sending combat forces, the standby battalion in particular. News stories from 13 to 14 July, in various Canadian newspapers, noted the availability of the 2nd Battalion of the Royal Canadian Regiment but soon began to report that this unit would not be suitable for service as part of ONUC. On Wednesday the 13th, *Le Devoir* ran a story entitled "Bataillon Canadien prêt à partir à la demande de l'ONU." That same day, though, the *Montreal Gazette* and *Winnipeg Free Press* quoted supposedly reliable sources who suggested that the "standby battalion for United Nations duty is unlikely to be used in the Congo situation" because the "UN would be unlikely to want to use a white, English-speaking battalion in a black non-English-speaking country when troops from African and Asian nations presumably would be available." Indeed, the very next day, *Le Devoir* ran another story in which it was noted, "la nature de la contribution que le gouvernement canadien pourra apporter à la nouvelle République du

Congo, en proie à des difficultés internes considérables, dépendra des requêtes qui lui seront adressées par le secrétaire général des Nation Unies" (The nature of the contribution that the Canadian government could provide to the new Republic of the Congo, plagued as it is by considerable internal difficulties, depends on the requests addressed to the government by the United Nations secretary-general).[28]

In the press, the House of Commons, and at External Affairs, the spectre that Canada might send combat forces was raised repeatedly, in spite of Charles Ritchie's assessment from the outset that the UN would not request such forces from Canada. Diefenbaker's initial negative reaction also seems to have been based, in part, on his faulty assumption that the UN would want and request Canadian combat forces. Writing some years later, Basil Robinson suggests that Hammarskjöld "at first asked for a military unit from Canada" but that upon hearing of Diefenbaker's reaction, "settled for administrative and specialist personnel." In fact, Hammarskjöld initially asked Canada only for a small number of technical personnel and had no intention of asking for combat forces. Diefenbaker's approach was similarly reported to be to "avoid soliciting requests for help and to respond favourably to anything short of combat troops."[29] It would thus appear that a later request for non-combat, signal personnel was in line with what Diefenbaker and Hammarskjöld both considered an appropriate Canadian contribution. Mistaken assumptions aside, there may have been political reasons why Diefenbaker reacted as he did. Robinson later recalled that the prime minister was upset that Canada might be asked to assist the UN on the basis of its bilingualism. Ann Livingstone suggests, "He was not at all prepared for Canadian society to be viewed as divided into French-speaking and English-speaking segments. His 'one Canada' mindset determined that should requests be made for assistance, it would not be because Canada was bilingual." In his study of Canadian relations with French Africa, John Schlegel also asserts that Diefenbaker wanted to silence "all talk of hyphenated Canadians" but notes that this tendency, as it relates to furthering connections with French-speaking African countries, was tempered by Howard Green and his minister of justice, Davie Fulton.[30]

In the House of Commons, Diefenbaker was somewhat evasive, his responses to questions tending to obfuscate rather than explain the nature of any proposed Canadian participation in ONUC. In a question about Canada's role in the Congo crisis, Hazen Argue, MP for Assiniboia and parliamentary leader of the Co-operative Commonwealth Federation, remarked on Canadian popular support for peacekeeping activities and asked if the Canadian government was considering "an offer of needed technical and professional personnel, preferably through the United Nations, for use in the Congo?"[31] Diefenbaker somewhat muddied the issue when he suggested in his response that Argue was thinking of the secretary-general's technical assistance program and that Hammarskjöld was interested first in drawing personnel for this mission from the African states. The prime minister's response was inaccurate because Hammarskjöld planned to use African and Asian forces primarily for the larger peace force and fully expected that he would need to use personnel from non-African and non-Asian countries, who had some peacekeeping experience, for the smaller technical assistance program. Diefenbaker then confused matters further when he mentioned that officers might be seconded from UNTSO for this purpose, once permission from the Canadian government was granted. In the end, the prime minister's responses did little to clarify Canada's role. The *Globe and Mail* could almost be excused for printing a story that in one paragraph sweepingly stated, "Canada is prepared to fill any United Nations appeal for police troops for service in the Congo," but two paragraphs later added, "Canada hopes no request will come from UN Secretary-General Dag Hammarskjold for the battalion of troops which this country maintains on a twenty-four-hour alert for such international police action."[32] It seemed to be a case of peacekeeping if necessary, but not necessarily peacekeeping.

Before the Security Council meeting on the evening of 13 July, Charles Ritchie met with Hammarskjöld to discuss the secretary-general's plans. Earlier, External Affairs contacted Ritchie and requested that he speak to Hammarskjöld and express clearly the Canadian government's reluctance to become involved in the larger peacekeeping force that was being contemplated. Although mixed signals may have been given in Ottawa, the Canadian position was enunciated clearly and frequently in New York. Hammarskjöld assured Ritchie that "there was no [repeat] no question of making mention of a military contribution from [Canada]."[33] The secretary-general confirmed, however, that he intended to approach General Carl von Horn (chief of staff in Jerusalem) to see if French-speaking officers could be spared from UNTSO for the technical assistance program. He expected that this would involve both Canadians and Scandinavians. The larger peacekeeping force was to evolve in two stages. In the first stage, contingents from African states would be used to develop an atmosphere of confidence by demonstrating to the Congolese that the UN presence was designed to help maintain their independence. He suggested that it would be desirable to include non-African forces only after the first stage had been accomplished. The secretary-general added, "At the present time, however, there was no question of any request for a Canadian contingent. Press reports suggesting that the Secretary-General was looking to Canada for a contingent were entirely inaccurate and misleading."[34] On the morning of 14 July, Hammarskjöld and Ritchie spoke again. By this time, the Canadian representative had received yet another telegram from External Affairs exhorting him to discourage further any request from the Secretariat for military assistance. Ritchie once again expressed the government's concern. Hammarskjöld emphatically stated that the question did not even arise because offers of troops from African nations were more than sufficient to staff the force. He did take the opportunity to formally request the secondment of two Canadian officers from UNTSO for the technical assistance program.[35]

The Canadian cabinet addressed the Congo situation for the first time on 14 July. Diefenbaker explained that, in Green's absence, he had been asked by the Canadian delegation for instructions on how to respond to a UN request to send military units to the Congo. He noted his objections to Hammarskjöld's proposed announcement that troops for the Congo would be drawn from Africa, possibly Asia, and "French-speaking units from a trans-Atlantic country." Presuming the latter was a definite reference to Canada, Diefenbaker advised cabinet that he had told the delegation to advise Hammarskjöld not to label Canada in this way. Cabinet noted the prime minister's actions and the fact that the secretary-general had made no mention of Canadian units in his public statements, but no further discussion of the matter took place.[36] It would seem that cabinet came to share Diefenbaker's unwarranted concern that Canada might be asked to contribute combat forces.

Later that day, the Congo situation was raised in the House of Commons and Diefenbaker took the opportunity to outline the government's position. He argued that peacekeepers for a major UN force should be drawn primarily from neighbouring African states to avoid any misapprehension, on the part of the Congolese, that might otherwise result from the use of non-African forces. He stated that the government would look favourably on requests for technical advisers, food, or transportation and concluded, "The government is responding favourably to requests of this kind because it believes that this is the most useful contribution which Canada can make in the current situation. If there are additional requests of the same nature they will be considered seriously." Lester Pearson, the Liberal leader of the Opposition, agreed with the government's policy and actions but suggested that, if sufficient forces could not be mustered by the UN relying on African states alone, perhaps the government could advise the UN that a Canadian battalion would be readily available if required.[37]

In truth, the secretary-general was not inclined to request such combat forces from Canada. Just in case, the government took every opportunity to remind the Canadian representative at the UN to limit or head off any such requests. As Ritchie was informed of the government's approval of the UN's secondment of Lt. Col. J. Berthiaume and Maj. H. King from UNTSO to ONUC, he was again told, "We are aware that you have already informed the Secretary-General that the [government] does not wish any expectation to be aroused that military assistance from Canada would be forthcoming. You should continue to discourage any such request from the Secretariat."[38]

Nevertheless, the government *publicly* demonstrated that it was sensitive to expectations that Canada should play a peacekeeping role in the Congo. During debate in the House of Commons, Howard Green stated,

> We are continuing to be greatly interested in the peace-keeping machinery of the United Nations. Canada already plays as big a part as any other nation in the peace-keeping arrangements of the United Nations and the government is continuing that policy. It may be that some provision will have to be made for further support for the United Nations in this field. Certainly our minds are not closed and we are very much in favour of doing everything that Canada can do that is practical to help strengthen the peace-keeping machinery of the United Nations.[39]

As a middle power, Canada had played an important role in previous peace-keeping missions, and this only encouraged many to expect similar involvement in the Congo, as an editorial from the *Globe and Mail* amply demonstrates:

> Prime Minister Diefenbaker was asked in the Commons this week if he has offered this battalion to the UN for use in the Congo. He replied that the UN secretary-general, Mr. Dag Hammarskjold, had the Congo crisis under advisement; the question of Canadian assistance, military or otherwise, would not arise until Mr. Hammarskjold made a specific request to Canada.
>
> This is too passive, too negative. Canada should be playing an active, positive role on the side of peace. How better, at this time, could we play such a role than by helping to bring peace to the Congo? What greater contribution could we make to the world than by helping to put out flames which could spread through Africa? We have poured, still are pouring, billions of dollars into defense. This money would be more usefully spent on organizing a permanent Middle-Power police force than on maintaining our present subservient role in the North American Air Defense system ...
>
> With like-minded countries, we could build a force that would clear up trouble-spots, removing them from the area where they give the Great Powers an excuse to rattle rockets at one another.
>
> In the Congo today, the blood of Africans and Europeans is being spilled. If Canada stands for peace, this is Canada's business. As the darkness gathers in Africa, Canada should not be waiting to find out what, if anything, is expected of it by Mr. Hammarskjold. Canada should be stating clearly its will and wish to join other peaceful nations in going to Africa and restoring the peace.[40]

The Diefenbaker government did not want to answer this call to restore peace in Central Africa. Diefenbaker later wrote, "As Prime Minister, I believed that Canada should take an appropriate part in United Nations peacekeeping activities. But I never thought that this should be automatic; I think the idea ridiculous that Canada should perforce participate in every United Nations peacekeeping activity."[41] It is worth noting that at least one newspaper, in contrast with the *Globe and Mail,* echoed and appreciated Diefenbaker's more cautious approach. An editorial in the *Chronicle-Herald* perceptively drew the distinction between combat and technical or support troops, arguing that it was only the latter that Canada should contemplate as a contribution to ONUC. In support of the prime minister, the editorial declared, "Mr. Diefenbaker has rightly said that this country has no desire to be pulled as a nation into it [the Congo situation] by the sending of field troops."[42] Nonetheless, Diefenbaker was still aware of the political importance of participation in UN peacekeeping. In all probability, this influenced his Congo policy. The government felt compelled to support peacekeeping publicly, as it quietly placed limits on the nature of any possible commitments in the Congo.

### Belgium, NATO, and the Communist Threat

During the evening of 14 July, the NATO Council was called to a special meeting, at the request of the Belgian representative. Belgium attempted to rally support for its position in the Congo. Prior to independence, a treaty of friendship was negotiated between Belgium and the Congo that provided Belgium with two permanent military bases. The Belgians wanted to retain these installations after their forces were withdrawn in compliance with the UN Security Council resolution. They appealed to their NATO allies to support them on this issue. The other Western powers were reminded of the Congo's strategic importance, in terms of both geography and mineral resources, and were told that the actions of the Congolese authorities were being orchestrated by Communist sources outside the Congo. The Canadian representative, Jules Léger, was surprised by the Belgian assessment of events in the Congo.[43]

Léger may have been surprised to hear it suggested that Communists were behind the Congo crisis, but not officials at External Affairs. In Ottawa, the possible involvement of Communist provocateurs had been a topic of recent interest. From Pretoria, the department learned that the South African consul general in Leopoldville saw little evidence that Communists had helped bring about the collapse of the Congolese authorities. He did, however, think it quite probable that some Belgian Communists in the Congo would take advantage of the anarchy there. In Washington, the African Affairs Bureau was also studying the question of Communist infiltration. Robert Hennemeyer, of the West African Desk in the State Department, shared the American analysis with a number of diplomats, including staff from the Canadian embassy. Hennemeyer said that American officials were puzzled by the nature of the operations of the Force Publique's mutinous elements. They had expected the mutineers to participate in indiscriminate looting, other disorderly conduct, and the selfish acquisition of food and other valuable commodities. Instead, they seized control of municipal offices, telegraphic services, and air strips. State Department officials discerned a pattern in these circumstances that implied either internal or external guidance of the mutiny, likely the result of contact with Communist organizations. In a National Security Council meeting on 21 July, the director of Central Intelligence, Allen Dulles, had painted an incriminating picture of Lumumba, suggesting he was a "Castro or worse." Expanding on Dulles' comments, the secretary of defence, Thomas Gates, was concerned by the degree of synchronization in the Congolese disorders. In the end, in spite of these troubling aspects of the mutiny, the State Department concluded that there was little likelihood of serious Communist inspiration and noted they had no evidence to substantiate allegations Lumumba was a Communist or Communist sympathizer. The deputy assistant secretary for African Affairs argued that the Belgian military authorities were simply using the "spectre of communism" to rally support for their position.[44]

Although little evidence emerged to confirm the possibility that Communist agents may have played a role in the instigation of the Congo crisis, the Cold War implications of anarchy in the Congo were obvious to all and influenced both public perceptions of the crisis and policy making. For example, Canada was reluctant to publicly support Belgian claims to Congolese military bases because this might "give substance to charges of Western aggression ... [and] would seem calculated to create the worst possible impression among African and anti-colonial powers generally."[45] On 14 July, Kasavubu and Lumumba severed diplomatic relations with Belgium and sent a telegram to Khrushchev asking him to monitor the situation carefully in the event they found it necessary to ask the Soviets to intervene. The *Globe and Mail* informed Canadians that Khrushchev obliged with a threat to take "decisive measures to stop the aggression." In an editorial echoed in other newspapers, the *Globe* soundly criticized the Soviet leader for making a bad situation worse by promising military support "to every country or faction which is involved in trouble with any of the Western Powers, however remote the scene of action may be from Russia and its normal concerns." Cartoons appearing in the *Globe* on 19 and 23 July clearly portrayed a sinister side to Soviet motives. A *Toronto Daily Star* editorial headline simply summed up the situation this way: "Mr. K. Fuels the Cold War."[46]

On 20 July, the Belgian ambassador in Ottawa called on External Affairs, where he met with the deputy undersecretary of state for external affairs,

Marcel Cadieux. The two discussed various aspects of the situation in the Congo. In particular, the ambassador was concerned the Soviets would intervene if the West did not take a firm, public stand. The Belgian ambassador to the United States, Baron Louis Scheyven, had already made similar representations to the American secretary of state, Christian Herter. Cadieux acknowledged Belgian concerns and assured the ambassador that the Canadian government "was alive to the possibilities of a Soviet coup." He added that it would be helpful for the ambassador to forward any detailed information concerning Communist infiltration in the Congo. Cadieux noted that he had witnessed a Communist takeover in French Indochina and realized how upsetting this could be for the former colonial authorities, but he was sure the Belgian government would take into account the psychological shock that often attended the transfer of authority as they assessed Communist threats.[47] The ambassador also raised the issues of Katanga's secession and the role of ONUC. He was adamant that the UN should not become involved in the internal affairs of the Congo and that ONUC should focus its deployment in areas where order had not yet been restored. He was unequivocally against sending ONUC to Katanga. Cadieux diplomatically suggested that, in his view, such matters were best left to the judgment of the secretary-general. If the Belgian ambassador had hoped to find a sympathetic ear, he must have left External Affairs somewhat disappointed. His government's views were politely acknowledged but not wholeheartedly accepted. Cadieux, first and foremost, expressed faith in the UN and Hammarskjöld and, while accepting the possibility that Communists might take advantage of anarchy in the Congo, did not uncritically subscribe to the idea that the Soviets were plotting a takeover. On the one hand, Ottawa had to respect its NATO ally; on the other, it could not ignore the realities of decolonization and the impact of Belgian interests in the Congo on that country's policies.[48]

That same day, Amasasp Aroutunian, the Soviet ambassador to Canada, visited Norman Robertson. The undersecretary noted that remarks made by the ambassador demonstrated the wisdom of the Canadian government's decision not to send combat forces to the Congo. Aroutunian firmly stated his belief that combat troops from NATO countries should not be used in ONUC. NATO allies of Belgium, he argued, should refrain from playing any role in the UN's military operations in the Congo. Robertson took issue with this latter point and by the end of their conversation had persuaded Aroutunian to accept the possibility that support units from some NATO countries might have to be incorporated, in particular because of the difficulties posed by language. Although the Soviet Union objected to NATO nations participating in ONUC, the ambassador maintained that if the Congolese government requested military assistance from the Soviets, they would respond.[49]

In fact, radio reports that day announced Lumumba's intentions to turn to the Soviets for military assistance should the upcoming session of the Security Council fail to deliver the complete withdrawal of the Belgian military from Congolese territory. Aroutunian's comments, combined with these radio reports, must have made the possibility of Communist intervention that much more real – except that it would be achieved not as the takeover suggested by the Belgian ambassador but as part of an open invitation from the Congolese government. There may not have been a pre-existing Communist plot to infiltrate and influence the Congolese authorities, but in the early days of the crisis, circumstances certainly prevailed that made Communist penetration conceivable.[50]

Historian J.L. Granatstein has argued that public pressure forced the Diefenbaker government to increase Canada's contribution to the UN efforts in the Congo and that this public pressure sprang from a desire to fulfill a national self-image. He states, "None of the usual triggers for public response were there," and suggests, as an example, that "until a few months after the UN decision there were not even any Communists suspected of trying to usurp the government."[51] Public opinion did influence Diefenbaker's Congo policy, as noted earlier, but public opinion was not fashioned by national self-image alone. Canadian officials, as well as the public, were concerned that Communists might indeed capitalize on the chaotic situation in the Congo. Stephen Weissman examined American foreign policy in the Congo crisis and concluded, "Some feared that instability in the Congo would spread beyond its borders, creating golden opportunities for the Soviet bloc. All were concerned that a Communist victory in this large, centrally located state could create a base for the subversion of Central Africa."[52] Although one cannot always apply conclusions made about the attitudes of American officials to their Canadian counterparts, in the case of the Congo crisis it is possible to do so. On the issue of Communist penetration, Canadian and American officials were clear-minded enough not to believe the almost paranoid ravings of the Belgians. They made an important distinction: the crisis was not perceived as Communist-hatched. They did see the potential for Communists to exploit chaos in the Congo. It is significant that Diefenbaker provided an account of ONUC in his memoirs as an example of how his government acted to prevent Africa from becoming embroiled in the Cold War.[53]

### ONUC Takes Shape, and Canada Prepares to Contribute

ONUC began to take shape quickly. By 18 July, the secretary-general was in a position to submit to the Security Council his *First Report on Assistance to the Republic of the Congo*. The first half of the report enunciated the key principles by which ONUC was to operate. Hammarskjöld made it clear that, although the force was in the Congo to assist the government, the peace-keepers could act only on orders from the UN. The Congolese government would have no authority to command ONUC, and the peacekeepers were not to become involved in any internal conflicts. It was on this fundamental understanding that member nations contributed personnel and material for the mission. The UN and the Congolese government were expected to cooperate to ensure that ONUC would have the freedom of movement and access to communications necessary to carry out operations. Authority to decide on the composition of the force rested with the UN alone, but it was expected that Hammarskjöld would take into consideration the views of the Congolese government. ONUC would be entitled to use armed force in self-defence but was strictly prohibited from taking the initiative in its use.[54]

Expanding on the issue of force composition in the *First Report*, Hammarskjöld reiterated his plans to launch ONUC with a core of African units. To demonstrate an "element of universality," additional forces were to be drawn from three European, one Asian, and one Latin American country. Hammarskjöld was clearly trying to preclude any charges that ONUC could become an instrument of neo-colonialism. He argued, "It would be wholly unjustified to interpret the United Nations action in the sense that nations from outside the region step into the Congo situation, using the United Nations as their instrumentality, because of the incapability of the Congo and of the African states themselves to make the basic contribution to the solution of the problem." In his selection of European countries, he avoided NATO and Warsaw Pact member nations. Only Ireland, Sweden, and Yugoslavia were asked to provide combat forces; Norway and Denmark, members of NATO, were both asked only to provide non-combat, specialized logistics personnel. While the African states were able to provide infantry in adequate numbers to enable the initial deployment of ONUC, there remained key shortages in logistics, signals, material, aircraft, and specialized personnel, and so Hammarskjöld addressed requests to countries able to fulfill these needs quickly, without concern for geographical position. In particular, he noted that it had been difficult to locate signal personnel who knew both French and English. The politics of decolonization and the Cold War ensured that infantry for ONUC would be drawn first from non-aligned, and primarily African states. By necessity, Hammarskjöld broadened the list of acceptable contributors in order to find the specialized, technical, and non-combat elements of the force.[55]

Although Charles Ritchie repeatedly advised UN officials that Canada did not want to be asked to contribute forces to the military operation in the Congo, the shortage of technical personnel prompted Hammarskjöld, on 15 July, to ask Canadian authorities if they would be prepared to send logistics and communications personnel as part of ONUC. The United States was contributing equipment, and the UN hoped to employ technical personnel from the Scandinavian countries and Canada to operate and service it. Just the day before, in a conversation with Secretary of State Herter, Henry Cabot Lodge, the American representative at the UN, noted that France had recommended French-Canadian troops be used – a suggestion with which Herter concurred. From Canada, the UN specifically needed signal personnel and additional equipment, in roughly the same proportion as had been provided for UNEF, as well as quartermaster and maintenance personnel.[56] The request for Canadian assistance was exploratory. Specific details and requirements were not expected to be available until after the newly appointed ONUC commander, General Carl von Horn, had surveyed the situation in the Congo. Ritchie reminded the UN of the Canadian position on the provision of military assistance and emphasized that the government did not consider it appropriate to contribute troops to the UN force. He offered, nonetheless, to transmit the secretary-general's appeal.[57]

Basil Robinson was informed of the UN's need for Canadian peacekeepers in the early afternoon. He sent a memorandum to Diefenbaker outlining the secretary-general's new requests. In addition to the potentially controversial logistics and signal units, the UN asked the government to approve the secondment of three more officers from UNTSO. The Secretariat also requested assistance in the form of foodstuffs – flour, canned pork, and dried milk, as well as the necessary air transportation to send the supplies to the Congo. Robinson penciled some notes on the bottom of the memorandum to highlight that a contribution of logistics and signal personnel would be for the military force and not for the technical aid program. When he saw Diefenbaker later in the day, the prime minister approved the secondment of one of the three officers in question and indicated that the remaining requests would need to be raised in cabinet the next day. Robinson orally reiterated the significance of the request for communication and logistics experts, and while Diefenbaker did not give a positive reaction, his assistant was left "with the impression that his inclination might be to respond favourably if a specific request were received."[58] Diefenbaker was reluctant to agree to the UN request in principle because he thought the Secretariat might perceive this, in the words of J.L. Granatstein, as "a blanket commitment to supply technicians."[59]

The cabinet met on 16 July to consider the recent UN requests just as the first peacekeepers began to arrive in the Congo. Secondment of two additional UNTSO officers to serve as technical advisers to the Congolese government was approved. The government also agreed to provide twenty thousand pounds each of canned pork and whole milk powder, but only after considerable debate. Some cabinet ministers wondered if Canadians might not perceive the aid as a gift to "revolutionaries, rapists, looters, etc." Others expressed the view that surplus food supplies should be distributed as a priority to the Canadian unemployed rather than as international aid. In the end, the cabinet decided to send the supplies. Given that India provided gifts of food, an act of charity it could barely afford, it would have subsequently proved embarrassing if the Canadian government had turned down this request. As it was, the *Chronicle-Herald* chastised the government for not sending enough food. "Canada certainly can afford to give the thirteen million Congolese more and better food than the few tons of excess milk powder and canned pork it is now releasing from its bulging larder of excess stocks," argued the Halifax newspaper. A decision regarding ONUC logistics and signal personnel was postponed pending further examination by National Defence; Diefenbaker simply declined to discuss the question of providing additional Canadian troops when asked by reporters as he emerged from the cabinet meeting to announce the government's donation of food.[60]

The following day, the Permanent Mission in New York reported on the secretary-general's requests to Sweden, Yugoslavia, and Ireland. Yugoslavia and Sweden both agreed to provide aircraft, pilots, and maintenance personnel. Ireland agreed to provide a battalion, despite the strain it placed on its defence forces: the fourteen hundred Irish peacekeepers represented 20 percent of the regular Irish forces.[61] Hammarskjöld asked Haiti and Burma for smaller infantry contingents. Canadian diplomats recognized that, with the use of non-African forces, Hammarskjöld had launched the second phase of ONUC. They were aware that the secretary-general had opted for an exclusively Swedish battalion instead of a combined Scandinavian contingent that would have included combat forces from Denmark and Norway. This decision again confirmed Ritchie's original view that NATO countries would not be asked to contribute combat forces. The Secretariat, nevertheless, remained anxious for a reply to its appeal for French-speaking signal personnel.[62]

In Ottawa, National Defence studied the implications of a Canadian contribution of signal and logistics personnel. With few details available, its planning proceeded on the assumption that ONUC would likely consist of 6,000 peacekeepers, organized into eight major units or battalions. Provision of a brigade signal squadron, capable of supplying radio, line, and dispatch rider communications for the command and control of a force that size was estimated to involve 5 officers, 183 men, and $794,000 in equipment. If the UN expected Canada to provide internal communications within battalions, a further 8 officers, 416 men, and $728,000 worth of equipment would be required. A long-range circuit from the Congo to the UN in New York would need 2 officers, 50 men, and $200,000 in equipment. Provision of logistics involved considerably fewer resources. A supply organization and ordnance railhead could be staffed with 19 officers, 199 men, and $342,000 in equipment. Finally, a further 25 officers, 125 men, and $125,000 would be required to establish a Canadian headquarters in the field.[63]

The UN request was a difficult one. Canada was short on both signallers and equipment. To provide the long-range communications necessary within the Congo, mobile radio teletype stations (AN/GRC-26) could be used, but they were all committed to the National Survival plan. The provision of personnel could be met only through significant disruption of regiments in Canada and a reduced capability to fulfill the army's national survival role. The Directorate of Operations and Planning concluded that the Royal Canadian Corps of Signals was practically the least able corps in the Canadian Army to provide personnel and that some other form of a Canadian military contribution to ONUC would be preferable.[64] In the end, the chief of the general staff (CGS), Lieutenant General Clark, was reluctant to allow any sizable withdrawal of signallers for Congo service because of the difficulty involved in separating personnel without causing widespread disruption to other defence responsibilities. The army was in the process of training additional signal personnel, "but the demands of the National Survival plan, NATO, UNEF, and other regular commitments were outstripping the production of trained signallers." Defence officials believed that the withdrawal of any more than 150 signallers would disrupt their ongoing operations.[65]

When cabinet met on the 19th, it learned that the secretary-general had inquired anxiously the day before whether a decision on his request was forthcoming. While awaiting a Canadian decision, the secretary-general asked the Tunisian government to temporarily provide a small signal detachment. External Affairs had already asked Hammarskjöld for a more detailed assessment of the UN's needs, and the Secretariat had urgently forwarded this task to General von Horn when he arrived in Leopoldville. Until the cabinet received a specific list of von Horn's needs, the minister of national defence, George Pearkes, thought there was insufficient information on which to base a decision.[66] Pearkes advised cabinet of the need to inoculate personnel against tropical diseases, a process that would take three weeks. Canadian peacekeepers in UNEF had already been inoculated for tropical service, and the cabinet wondered if they might be used to first establish communications, even temporarily.[67]

The cabinet was asked to consider what help, if any, Canada could provide to assist the UN in its airlift of supplies for ONUC and other UN agencies operating in the Congo. Supplies were accumulating in a staging area established at Pisa, Italy, awaiting transport onward to Leopoldville. Four Canadian aircraft used to transport the gift of foodstuffs were in the area, and the minister of national defence had determined that the cost would be $9,000 per day per aircraft. The cabinet once again deferred a decision until more complete information could be obtained from the UN. Over the next two days, External Affairs communicated with the Secretariat, through the Permanent Mission in New York, to clarify details regarding the Pisa-

Leopoldville airlift. The UN envisioned an airlift shared equally between Italy and Canada, the arrangement was for thirty days, and the cost of the operation was to be reimbursed by the UN. It was made clear that this airlift was to provide logistic support for ONUC and was not at all related to the transport of gifts of supplies and foodstuffs. The assistant trade commissioner in Leopoldville wired Ottawa requesting that the government consider authorizing the aircraft to land at points within the Congo, in addition to Leopoldville.[68]

The UN request for signal and logistics personnel was also further clarified. External Affairs learned from the Permanent Mission in New York that the Secretariat was thinking of a signal squadron similar in size to that provided for UNEF. The government's concerns over committing signallers without a clear picture of the numbers required were allayed by assurances that an affirmative Canadian reply would not be seen as a blank cheque: it was entirely up to the Canadian government to determine the size of the contribution it was prepared to provide. UN officials quite tentatively suggested a ceiling of 150 personnel, with appropriate equipment, but then quickly added "or less if this should be the wish of the government." The UN was advised that it might take three weeks for Canadian soldiers to be immunized for service in the Congo and that this was true for both signal and logistics personnel. The idea of using an advance party of Canadian signallers from UNEF was raised with the UN, and the Secretariat indicated that it intended to consult with the UNEF commander to see if this was possible. The UN intimated that it required signals more than logistics personnel, so it was best for Canada to concentrate its efforts on that front.[69]

At a special meeting of the heads of branches of the Armed Forces, it became clear that planning should proceed on the basis of a much smaller signals contribution than was initially proposed. Plans now envisioned a brigade signal squadron without an accompanying regimental signal organization. 2 Brigade Signal Squadron was designated to provide a nucleus of personnel, and the immunization of the first battalion of the Royal 22e Regiment (the Van Doos) was stepped up. Consideration was given to how the time required for immunization might be shortened, particularly if the situation in the Congo became critical, but it was clear that a decision to send Canadian peacekeepers to the Congo without meeting normal medical requirements would be left to the government. Plans to send a liaison officer to New York were cancelled when it was learned that Gen. Henry T. Alexander, of the Ghanaian army, who had been acting as interim commander of ONUC, was on his way to the UN. Instead, the director-general of plans and operations, Brig. R.M. Bishop, and the director of signals, Col. J.B. Clement, were dispatched to meet with Alexander, the one person thought capable of providing a more precise picture of the UN's signal needs. Significantly, at this stage, the army thought it unlikely that forces other than signals would be required but still had not ruled out the possibility of providing "*infantry* and service elements."[70]

On the evening of 20 July, Bishop and Clement met with Alexander and UN undersecretary Henry Labouisse. They learned that ONUC force and divisional headquarters would likely be located in Leopoldville. In addition, four brigade headquarters were envisioned for Leopoldville, Luluabourg, Bukavu, and Stanleyville. The Canadians were needed to provide signals for the divisional headquarters (switchboard, signal office, wireless teleprinter network with cipher from divisional headquarters to each of the brigade headquarters), and for wireless-teleprinter links and ground-air links at each of the brigade headquarters. Communications within brigades and the rear communication link to the UN were to be provided by other sources. Clement estimated that eight officers and one hundred other ranks would be needed, though the distances between headquarters required equipment larger than the AN/GRC-26, the sets National Defence initially planned to use. Clement's request to consult with the United States on the availability of equipment was turned down, however. CGS Lieutenant General Clark noted, "I would not want this. It would look as if we wanted to take it on."[71] The UN remained hopeful that, in addition to the signal contingent, Canada might still provide logistics support to organize and supervise supply depots at each of the brigade headquarters. The bilingual capability of Canadian forces was a key factor in the UN request. UN officials stressed, "Canada had been selected despite being a NATO power" because of this. The UN did not expect an entire contingent of French-speaking peacekeepers but hoped as many as possible would be bilingual.[72]

At the 21 July meeting of cabinet, Howard Green recommended that cabinet assign four North Star aircraft and their crews to the Pisa-Leopoldville airlift, to transport ONUC supplies and equipment to and within the Congo. He further recommended that cabinet approve the provision of signal personnel and equipment once immunization had been completed. George Pearkes reported that a liaison officer was present in New York to discuss the UN's needs with the Secretariat. He anticipated that equipment for ONUC would cost $1 million and was anxious to replace the equipment in Canada immediately. He believed that as many as five hundred men would be needed to establish effective supply depots and communications. Cabinet approved the proposed use of Canadian North Stars in the Pisa-Leopoldville airlift and the immunization of the necessary signal, logistic, and administrative personnel of the Canadian army. Approval for actual participation in ONUC was withheld, but the cabinet wanted Armed Forces personnel to be prepared should it be subsequently granted.[73]

As National Defence and External Affairs laid the groundwork for Canada's additional contribution to ONUC, media reports were suggesting that more

Canadian peacekeepers would head to the Congo. A rather impatient editorial in the *Toronto Daily Star* chastised the minister of national defence: "It may be that the U.N.'s needs have not been made clear to Ottawa. But Mr. Pearkes's statement implied no alacrity about meeting them. Now would be a fine time to reaffirm our readiness to send troops – if, indeed, we are ready." On 20 July, when responding to public speculation, which was based partly on the rumours that had originated in Leopoldville with Ralph Bunche the previous week that Canadian troops would be part of ONUC, Howard Green was said to be "not anxious to comment on the report." He declined to say whether a Canadian contingent had been offered to the UN or if the UN had requested one. The minister briefly said, "I will deal with that when I am in a position to do so." Yet, the very next day, both the *Chronicle-Herald* and the *Winnipeg Free Press* quoted reliable sources in reports that the government was indeed considering the dispatch of supply and communications personnel to the Congo. "It is understood," the *Free Press* asserted, "that the UN has asked Canadian help because the Asian and African nations sending troops to the Congo are not particularly well equipped to handle supply and communications problems." The *Chronicle-Herald* added, "It is also understood that no Canadian combat troops will be sent to the Congo."[74]

Throughout the next week, consultations between External Affairs, National Defence, and the UN continued. The CGS asked the DGPO to work with External Affairs to prepare a joint submission to cabinet. Anticipating that cabinet would, in the end, decide to send signallers, Clark was anxious to have the authority to concentrate troops and equipment and to send a reconnaissance team to the Congo. After finally arriving in Leopoldville, General von Horn refined the UN request for assistance. A separate divisional headquarters seemed unlikely; instead, the force headquarters was expected to work directly with the brigades. The force commander hoped to use Canadians at the force headquarters to provide communications, including ground to air. Because von Horn had not received a firm commitment for signals from Canada, he had proceeded with the deployment of forces throughout the Congo, relying on civilian resources to provide the rear-link from brigade to division. Nonetheless, the UN still needed Canadians at brigade headquarters to provide ground-to-air communications and signals to the battalions. An independent signal company, similar to that deployed in UNEF, was considered by von Horn to be an appropriate model. Signals became the clear priority over logistics. The Permanent Mission suggested, "We can stand down on logistic depots for now."[75]

As the army proceeded with its consultations, the North Stars assigned to UN duty became embroiled in controversy. The cabinet understood that the planes were to be used exclusively to ferry supplies and equipment both to and within the Belgian Congo. Then the secretary-general approached the Canadian Permanent Mission in New York to request that the North Stars be used for transporting Belgian troops from Leopoldville to Katanga, as part of the troop movements agreed to by Brussels and New York in preparation for the withdrawal of Belgian armed forces. Canada did not want to be seen as acting in concert with its NATO ally in the Congo, and therefore it did not want to be associated with the movement of Belgian forces anywhere in the Congo, especially near the secessionist province of Katanga. Diefenbaker decided on 22 July that the planes could not be used for this purpose and notified Howard Green of his decision. Charles Ritchie was told to make this policy clear to the Secretariat. The dilemma was compounded by the discovery that the planes already had been used to transport UN forces to numerous locations within the Congo so that Belgian paratroopers could be withdrawn. Evidently, the senior RCAF officer in the Congo contacted Air Transport Command HQ in Trenton at the suggestion of Ralph Bunche and somehow obtained permission to use the RCAF aircraft for deploying Moroccan and Tunisian troops.[76] Ritchie spoke to the executive assistant to the secretary-general, Andrew Cordier, who assured the Canadian representative that the whole incident had been a "crash operation." Nevertheless, Ritchie emphasized that the planes could not be used for purposes other than those identified by the Canadian government and insisted that all future requests of a political nature be forwarded through the Permanent Mission.[77]

The Canadian position was made crystal clear following consultations between Green and Pearkes. Officials at External Affairs and National Defence were told, "From now on use of the R.C.A.F. North Stars is to be restricted to the transport of supplies and equipment for the UN force from Pisa to Leopoldville ... The use of these aircraft for the transportation of troops is not authorized by cabinet and is to cease forthwith." Pearkes understood this policy to prohibit the transport of any passengers aside from Canadian military personnel, the transport of supplies or equipment originating outside Pisa, carrying anything back to Pisa from Leopoldville, and the delivery of anything to any point inside or outside the Congo aside from Leopoldville. Concerned this would seem unduly restrictive to the UN, especially given that it fully expected to reimburse Canada for the cost of the airlift, External Affairs subsequently lobbied to ease these conditions once other nations came forward to provide internal airlift. The government was clearly determined to participate in ONUC only in a non-combat capacity; any use of the North Stars that appeared to compromise this principle was quickly curtailed.[78]

In New York, the Security Council resumed consideration of the Congo situation from 20 to 22 July. Thomas Kanza, the newly appointed Congolese minister at the UN, addressed the council and downplayed the earlier Kasavubu-Lumumba ultimatum to turn to the Soviets for assistance. He called on the council to end the Belgian aggression, evacuate Belgian forces, refuse recognition of an independent Katanga, and facilitate the return of technicians to the Congo. Pierre Wigny, the Belgian secretary of state for foreign affairs, argued that Belgium had intervened only for humanitarian reasons and recognized Congolese independence as an accomplished fact. A second Security Council resolution on the Congo situation passed unanimously, calling upon the Belgian government to speedily withdraw its forces, as it was already required to do by the first resolution.[79] During these meetings, Hammarskjöld raised two issues that would subsequently prove to be contentious. In reference to the first Security Council resolution, he argued that it applied to the entire Congo, as it existed when it was recommended for admission to the UN on 7 July. This meant ONUC was entitled to freedom of movement throughout the country, including Katanga, but it could not be party to any internal conflicts. No one on the council questioned this interpretation. Resolution 145 (1960) was, in many ways, a vote of confidence in Hammarskjöld's handling of the crisis.[80] Worryingly, however, the debate preceding the adoption of the resolution foreshadowed the Cold War tensions soon to erupt. The Soviet and American representatives exchanged barbs, Vasily Kuznetsov warning, "If the United States representative thinks that by speaking in this way he can influence the Soviet Union's attitude, or possibly intimidate the Soviet Union, he is very gravely mistaken."[81] The Soviets again raised the issue of ONUC's composition, protesting the use of American forces, if only in a logistics and transport role. The United States had in fact played a key role in airlifting ONUC personnel and equipment to the Congo. By comparison, the Soviets did not object to Sweden's role in the peace force but did reiterate their view that ONUC should comprise principally Afro-Asian independent states.[82]

In Canada, the military continued to plan for further Canadian participation in ONUC. "Mallard" was adopted as the operational codeword to cover the preparation and dispatch of a Canadian contingent for ONUC. By 26 July, the government had permitted nine officers (five from UNTSO and four from UNEF) to be transferred to service in the Congo. In accordance with the cabinet's earlier decision, the army began to select and immunize personnel, in advance of an actual decision to send peacekeepers. Headquarters, signals, and logistics establishments were expected to require 53 officers and 434 other ranks, drawn from various locations across the country. The CGS was anxious to concentrate personnel and equipment in Barriefield, Ontario, as soon as possible. He warned Pearkes that there could be complications relating to personnel and logistics if the concentration of peacekeepers and their equipment, drawn as they would be from across Canada, happened at the last moment. Yet, the minister remained cautious and refused permission to concentrate the force until the government had given its approval. Plans to transport certain equipment to the Congo also proved troublesome because it was too heavy for the RCAF to airlift. The chief of the naval staff,

H.G. DeWolf, explored the possibility of using the aircraft carrier HMCS *Bonaventure* to transport 494 personnel and 199 vehicles but concluded it would not be feasible to disembark vehicles or troops in the Congo River or estuary. This particular difficulty would eventually be resolved with the assistance of the United States Air Force.[83]

## Patrice Lumumba Visits Canada

As the end of July approached, Prime Minister Lumumba visited North America. The United States gave Lumumba and his party a fine reception but did not agree to a program of bilateral assistance, the principal goal of the Congolese mission. Instead, the Americans insisted the Congo receive its aid through the United Nations. Although this was not at all what Lumumba wanted, Canadian officials initially believed the Congolese "cheerfully accepted" this condition. Secretary of State Herter discussed Lumumba's efforts to secure bilateral aid with Howard Green in a telephone conversation on 28 July. Green agreed that Canada would take the same position with Lumumba: all aid would need to be channelled through the UN. While in Washington, Lumumba met with Canadian diplomats to make plans for a visit to Ottawa. The prime minister had earlier told a press conference in New York that he would travel to Canada because "this country has always drawn me to it and because I have special sympathies for it and I hope to be able to meet friends there and to see whether I might not find some French-speaking technicians and specialists who might be willing to come and work in the Congo."[84]

Anticipating Lumumba's arrival, the Belgian chargé d'affaires in Ottawa visited Green to express concerns about the Congolese prime minister and his impending visit. He emphatically labelled Lumumba a Communist, educated in both Prague and Moscow and elected to office using money provided by the Eastern bloc. Green replied that there was little he could do about the visit, as it had already been announced in the press. The Belgian diplomat tried to rally support for Belgium's efforts to retain its military bases in the Congo and hoped the Canadian government would take a sympathetic view toward the Belgian position in the UN. For his part, Green avoided any commitment, his comments reflecting the government's attempt to remain friendly with both Belgium and the Congo. He concluded by saying that the Canadian government "would do all they could to avoid making the situation more difficult." Out of respect for Belgium, Canadian officials did try to limit the fanfare associated with the visit. Belgian authorities were incensed by the reception accorded the Congolese prime minister by the Americans, particularly because Lumumba had gone on to use press conferences there to "Belgium bash" – much to the chagrin of career diplomats who looked upon the prime minister with scorn for not observing diplomatic niceties.[85] As difficult as Lumumba had been in Washington,

Canadian officials simply were not convinced by the Belgian assertion that he was an avowed Communist. Rather, he was seen as an inexperienced and untrained leader, eager to grasp at anything that might consolidate his political position. In Leopoldville, he had demonstrated a willingness to accept advice from every political vantage. They believed he played East and West against each other, politically and economically, and seemed to concur with Hammarskjöld's view that Lumumba was "very responsive to friendship and to frankness, impressionable but apt to be swayed by changing influences ... ignorant, very suspicious, shrewd but immature in his ideas – the smallest in scope of any of the African leaders."[86]

Lumumba's visit to Canada began in Montreal where, during a "whirlwind" visit of the city, he paid a formal visit to City Hall and met with University of Montreal officials to discuss the recruitment of French-Canadian experts to assist with the Congo's development. His public statements alternated between harsh accusations against Belgium for the role he maintained that country played in fostering the conditions that led to the political crisis and optimistic overtures clearly meant to convey a willingness on the part of his government to work with the Belgians, at least after their troops had been withdrawn. The prime minister described his visit to the United States as "completely successful," having received assurances that aid would be forthcoming. He was clearly hoping that Canada would prove equally generous. Quoted in the *Montreal Gazette*, Lumumba said, "We have come to Canada ... because Canada is not a colonial nation. We need technicians of all types, engineers, lawyers and teachers, and we hope to recruit them in Canada."[87]

Finished in Quebec, Lumumba moved on to Ottawa later in the day. His visit to the capital proved more awkward and a little disappointing. In preliminary conversations, and in his meeting with Diefenbaker, Lumumba was curt in his replies to questions. Geoffrey Murray, head of the UN Division at External Affairs at the time, recalls that discussions with Lumumba during his visit were simply not very coherent. Diefenbaker, in an attempt to understand the requirements of a newly independent African nation, asked his counterpart a series of questions designed to discover the specific needs of the Congolese, in spite of an earlier warning from the Washington embassy that discussions with the Congolese would likely be "rather general and not backed up with very much technical detail." Lumumba was either unable or refused to answer. The temperature began to rise, until Diefenbaker frankly asked Lumumba whether he expected Canada to pay for French-speaking technical experts the Congolese delegation hoped to recruit in Canada. By the time Lumumba met with the prime minister, he had already learned that Canada was not willing to provide bilateral assistance. He swiftly answered that he "did not expect another Government to pay for the services of Congolese civil servants." This seemed to mark a turning point in his meeting with Diefenbaker, because from then on the conversation became cordial. Diefenbaker did offer administrative assistance to the Congolese to facilitate their recruitment of bilingual experts in various fields. Canadian diplomats were vexed by Lumumba's approach. In his earlier discussions with them, he had expressed the hope that Canada would provide financial assistance and had became somewhat annoyed when he discovered that Canada was unable to give such assistance, except through already established UN channels. He changed his story for the afternoon meeting with Diefenbaker and blamed Canadian officials for any misunderstanding that may have led to the perception that he was hoping to have Canada pay a share of the planned technical assistance program. This left a bad taste in the mouths of Ottawa diplomats. Following his departure, Robertson summed Lumumba up as "vain, petty, boorish, suspicious and perhaps unscrupulous."[88]

There was also the curious matter of the Congolese prime minister's secret visit with the Soviet ambassador to Canada. Robertson later wrote that Lumumba greeted Aroutunian in a "very friendly and warm fashion" when he first arrived at the Ottawa airport. There was also at least one man from the Soviet embassy constantly on duty at the Château Laurier, where the Congolese party was staying. While speaking with Bernard Salumu, Lumumba's private secretary, one Canadian official was interrupted by someone from the Soviet embassy, who only reluctantly revealed his identity after asking for Salumu's room number in French with a Slavic accent. At the time, few details were known about the meeting between Aroutunian and Lumumba. An RCMP guard reported seeing the Soviet ambassador with the Congolese prime minister on Saturday morning and that during the visit a phone call had been placed to Washington. Later, it was discovered that Aroutunian promised Lumumba a gift of transport vehicles.[89]

The rather farcical cloak-and-dagger activities in the Château Laurier lobby and the blunt Canadian assessments of Lumumba and his entourage obscure the underlying importance of the prime minister's visit: it was significant because his experiences in North America coloured his subsequent actions and decisions. Lumumba's call on Ottawa did little to aid Diefenbaker's understanding of the Congo situation. By contrast, it was a formative experience for the Congolese leader. His mood changed during the visit, and his opinion of the UN was diminished. Both American and Canadian officials had couched their decisions not to give any bilateral assistance by reiterating commitments to provide aid through the UN. Lumumba, therefore, came to perceive the UN as an obstacle.[90] He realized he was not going to get the bilateral help he desired from either the United States or Canada and so turned to the Soviets, even before he had left Ottawa. In subsequent months, reports of Lumumba's view of Canada filtered in to External Affairs. He clearly thought Ottawa had rebuffed him. In October, at a dinner to celebrate the second anniversary of Guinea's independence, Lumumba delivered a speech in which he said that he had gone to Canada "to seek bilateral aid in belief that it was a truly democratic land but had been disappointed to find that although honest Canada was just another imperialist country."[91] Diefenbaker later added another reason for Lumumba's poor opinion of Canada: the failure of Howard Green and External Affairs to provide female companionship during the visit.[92]

## Canadian Peacekeepers for ONUC

The day before Lumumba arrived in Ottawa, the Canadian cabinet decided to provide the logistics and signal personnel the UN had requested. From discussions with the Secretariat, the precise needs of ONUC finally emerged. The minister of defence noted the crisis was moving swiftly and changing constantly; this had made it difficult to determine ONUC requirements. He recommended that Canada provide a signal detachment for ONUC HQ, including signal office, message centre, a hundred-line switchboard, linemen and dispatch riders; five ground-to-air communication links, and possibly two more at a later date; twelve mobile wireless detachments; eight cipher detachments; and four composite logistic depots. To meet these needs, cabinet agreed to the dispatch and maintenance of up to five hundred officers and men, two hundred of which were to be provided as soon as possible for signals and communications. None of the Canadian peacekeepers was to be attached to units below brigade headquarters level. That same day, External Affairs contacted the Permanent Mission in New York to request that it inform the Secretariat of Canada's willingness to provide signallers and a small Canadian headquarters detachment. This was to be kept in confidence until after Parliament was notified. The UN gratefully welcomed the news.[93]

In support of Canadian participation, Howard Green argued, "Much had been made of Canada's support of the United Nations. Not to do what the Minister of National Defence had suggested would be a mistake." The importance of public opinion and Canada's self-image did enter into the decision, but other considerations were also taken into account. At the time when the government made its decision, the situation in the Congo had improved somewhat. General Alexander had reported that he "foresaw no danger to white personnel serving the United Nations, so that noncombatant Canadian support troops need to be supplied with personal weapons only." In a memorandum to cabinet, Pearkes and Green further argued that initial political objections to the addition of white personnel to the force, even if these forces were drawn from NATO countries, were no longer valid because ONUC contained both African and non-African combat contingents. That Canadian peacekeepers would provide technical support and avoid a combat role, unlike some of their non-African and most of their African counterparts, certainly made the proposition more palatable; the government was consistently concerned to limit the risk to Canadian lives. Because some peacekeepers were bilingual, the cabinet also recognized that they were uniquely suited to UN service in the Congo. An overriding concern for the success of ONUC, and indeed the United Nations itself, was expressed by Norman Robertson:

> The significance of the United Nations role in the Congo cannot be fully measured at this time but there is no doubt that it has far-reaching implications for the Congo, for Africa and for the United Nations itself. Success in the Congo may lay the groundwork for many other operations of the United Nations in Africa, especially as regards the peaceful parts of the programme. Success for the United Nations in the Congo and in Africa might establish the Organization firmly as the strongest influence for peace in the world. Undoubtedly, success in the Congo will rally public support but with that public support must come the material support, as distinct from lip service from member states. Failure, on the other hand, in the Congo might mean the final failure of the United Nations.

The success of the United Nations in Africa also meant the failure of Communist penetration. The Cold War implications of the crisis were taken into consideration. Clearly, the government supported ONUC, not simply from a single-minded fear of public reaction to a limited Canadian response, but for a number of reasons.[94]

There remained the question of how best to involve Parliament in the decision to send peacekeepers. Following a review of precedents set in the dispatch of Canadian forces to Korea and for service in NATO and UNEF, the judge advocate general suggested an order-in-council be passed, then tabled, in the House of Commons. The prime minister or minister of national defence could then table a motion asking the House to approve the action taken by the government. On 28 July, cabinet seems to have rejected this approach in favour of placing a $1 supplementary estimate before Parliament for its approval. Two days later, it reconsidered and decided to introduce a resolution in the House of Commons to permit all parties to indicate a stand by means of a vote. Only after a resolution had been passed would the cabinet issue the appropriate order-in-council. The Diefenbaker government was keen to have the positions of all parties on the record before it took the final, legal step toward sending peacekeepers overseas.[95]

The decision to provide personnel and equipment was announced in the House of Commons on 30 July. The resolution in support of participation in ONUC was debated on 1 August. In his address to the House, Diefenbaker recalled the history of Canadian participation and support of United Nations forces. He paid particular tribute to the Canadian officers currently serving in the Congo, organizing the airlift, and serving at force headquarters. He noted that a meeting with Canadian missionaries recently returned from the Congo had confirmed for him "that wherever there is anarchy, chaos or economic dislocation there is a field for communist operations." The actions of the Soviet Union during the crisis were seen to be "a continuance of the belligerent and even blatant attitude now being taken in many parts of the world by that country." The prime minister even drew attention to the Soviet ambassador's recent meeting with Lumumba in Ottawa. He concluded on a higher note, suggesting that his government's decision to contribute to ONUC represented "a major step forward to that day when, wherever difficulties may arise anywhere in the world, as I stated in March, 1945, the nations comprising the United Nations will all make available to an international force whatever is requisite to assure peace." Both opposition parties supported the resolution. Perhaps fearing the Canadian public might not share their enthusiasm, Cooperative Commonwealth Federation MP Herbert Herridge went so far as to suggest Parliament "arouse public interest and pride in our participation in this very important work which I am quite sure many people do not fully appreciate at the present time." The resolution was approved unanimously, and cabinet subsequently approved an order-in-council on 5 August that authorized up to five hundred officers and men to serve in support of UN operations in the Congo.[96]

Evidence presented in this chapter paints a complex picture that raises questions of historical interpretations that rely too heavily on a single, predominant determinant to account for the Diefenbaker government's decision to dispatch Canadian peacekeepers to the Congo. Central to explanations that have stressed public opinion is the notion that the government made a decision not to send peacekeepers to the Congo but soon after reversed that decision in response to public outcry, criticism in the media, and calls for action in the House of Commons. This flip-flop is certainly consistent with the widely held view that Diefenbaker was generally indecisive, incoherent, and not especially successful in his approach to foreign policy. Undoubtedly, Diefenbaker's infamous debacle over nuclear weapons has contributed mightily to this critical assessment. In the case of the Congo crisis, however, careful reconstructions of the sequence of events and of views at the UN reveal more consistency than inconsistency in his government's actions. External Affairs and the prime minister both expressed grave concerns about sending Canadians to the Congo in a combat role, though such concerns were unwarranted because Hammarskjöld's need to take into account political considerations when deciding force composition ruled out any infantry or combat personnel from a NATO country, including Canada. From the outset of the crisis, the Diefenbaker government carefully considered and consistently agreed to specific UN requests for assistance that incrementally increased Canada's contributions to ONUC – again, always short of sending front-line forces. In the case of the Congo crisis, there was no flip-flop. Public opinion was undoubtedly an underlying and at times recognized factor in decisions to provide aid, air support, and signal personnel; there is, however, no evidence to suggest it was the most important of the many determinants weighed, as policy was formulated.

Although Sean Maloney argues that "Canadian actions during the Congo crisis were in line with Canadian NATO interests at several levels," Canada's actions were at times at odds with NATO, or at least with a number of its NATO allies.[97] The Cold War was an inescapable reality during the Congo crisis, but sometimes Canada tempered its ideological allegiances. At External Affairs, officials were less strident than their Belgian counterparts. Conflicting views of Patrice Lumumba and the earliest meetings between Belgian and Canadian diplomats reveal a degree of circumspection toward Belgian claims of Communist threats. These differences may be subtle at first, but in the months and years ahead this divergence widened as the Canadian government actively resisted coordination of NATO policy on the Congo. Indeed, before long, Belgium began to complain that Canada was insufficiently supportive of its ally. This is not to suggest that Canada was neutral in its response to the crisis. Both at the time and in retrospect, Prime Minister Diefenbaker was keenly aware of the dangers posed by opportunities the crisis would afford for Communist infiltration in central Africa. That said, Canada's Western interests were balanced against many other, at times conflicting, considerations. As with public opinion, overemphasizing the significance of Canada's NATO relationship at this early stage is problematic and becomes even more so as time and the crisis marched on.

# 3
# Deployment: Trials and Tribulations in ONUC's Early Days

Within hours of the Security Council's decision to create ONUC, the first international contingents arrived in the Congo. The acting Canadian trade commissioner, Roger Bull, was disappointed in the United Nations' initial response to the crisis. He found Ralph Bunche, the secretary-general's special representative, to be a "quiet self-effacing man" who did not want to "expose himself to criticism" by doing too much before it was clear that the UN was willing to assume a role in resolving the crisis. Then, on 14 July, Maj. Gen. Henry Alexander, commander of the Ghanaian contingent, arrived with his troops. Bull suggested this "immediately stiffened the U.N.'s backbone." Because Gen. Carl von Horn, ONUC's commander, was unable to get to the Congo until 18 July, Alexander assumed a prominent role in directing the early activities of UN peacekeepers. During this initial period of deployment, Alexander ordered peacekeepers to disarm the Force Publique. This may have seemed a reasonable course of action to him at the time, but it was clearly outside ONUC's mandate, and Bunche disagreed with this decision. Nonetheless, the Ghanaian troops did start to disarm the force, much to Prime Minister Patrice Lumumba's dismay. Although Alexander's attempts at disarmament met with initial success, Congolese troops took up arms once again by 23 July. The whole affair did much to colour Lumumba's early perceptions of ONUC.[1] The arrival of von Horn and his "triumvirate of Canadian staff officers" infused the mission with an "an air of decision and activity," yet the sheer size of the Congo operation meant that the initial chaos and confusion inherent in any multinational military operation was multiplied. Within days, five to six thousand peacekeepers were deployed over a vast area, without adequate transportation. Some had only four days' worth of hard rations. In addition, von Horn had insufficient notice of when reinforcements were expected to arrive. He knew little about the equipment they intended to bring or how their units were organized. The Irish, for example, arrived in winter uniforms.[2]

The European exodus continued, but by 18 July Roger Bull believed conditions were sufficiently safe to recall the families and office staff evacuated to Brazzaville in the early days of the crisis. The appearance of UN peacekeepers in Leopoldville provided an initial sense of safety and comfort. Bull wrote, "We have Swedes practically next door to us in the office building, Ghanaians across the street from the Residence and blue armbands lurking behind every bush to protect us. Miss Morel, in fact, has found the excitement so invigorating that her health is almost restored to normal."[3] Regular office work at the Trade Commission, much like the rest of Leopoldville, came to a standstill, but the staff was kept busy. The first of the Canadian North Stars arrived in Leopoldville with their cargo of food aid on 21 July. The Trade Commission staff fed and housed the twenty-four crew members and then arranged for them to stay in the guesthouse of a local company. By 24 July, another thirty-nine RCAF personnel had arrived and the seven available beds in the official residence, as well as the entire guesthouse, were filled.

Once cabinet decided to send signallers, the army moved quickly to complete the necessary arrangements for their departure. Two units were formed: Canadian HQ, ONUC, and No. 57 Canadian Signal Squadron.[4] The UN withdrew its request for logistics assistance "presumably because it could not wait the time necessary to immunize, equip and despatch these forces." Sudan and the United Arab Republic agreed to provide logistics, but the army continued to immunize those earmarked for service in case staff from either country was unable to carry out these duties.[5] As equipment and personnel arrived in Barriefield, pressure mounted in New York; the Canadian liaison officer, Lieutenant Colonel Johnson, reported that the UN was "extremely anxious to know when the first load of operating personnel will leave Canada. The urgency of getting 'working personnel' on the ground as soon as possible cannot be over-emphasized." Full immunization and the acquisition of the necessary equipment were taking time. The Treasury Board approved the purchase of thirteen tropicalized AN/GRC-26D heavy wireless sets from the United States, on the understanding that the UN would eventually reimburse this cost.[6] Johnson noted the UN was eager to have the personnel, with or without their equipment, and believed "it was going to be extremely difficult to explain our delays in terms of the need to immunize personnel when so many other nations had 'taken a chance' on this."[7]

Col. Albert Mendelsohn, an officer with a military engineering background and experience in the United Nations Military Observer Group in India and Pakistan, led a reconnaissance party of six officers to the Congo on 30 July. He was instructed to determine personnel and equipment requirements, assess organizational requirements of the Canadian HQ unit and justify its necessity, and resolve a conflict between the UN's request to deploy Canadians below brigade headquarters and Minister of National Defence George

Pearkes's directive against this.[8] Mendelsohn's initial reports were generally favourable. He found that Leopoldville was gradually returning to normal. Some of the basic utilities were restored and the "white area" of the city appeared to be quite modern, with buildings "equal to the best in Ottawa." He noted that ONUC HQ personnel did not carry personal weapons and were able to move about freely without any trouble. The local Congolese seemed "quite unconcerned and happy." He acknowledged that his observations were based principally on Leopoldville but expected the accommodation and utilities in other major cities where Canadian personnel might be deployed to be comparable.[9]

The presence of the reconnaissance party in the Congo permitted further clarification of UN requirements. Consultations with von Horn revealed ONUC required the signal squadron to provide communications between ten mostly stationary positions throughout the Congo, instead of the eight cipher detachments and twelve mobile wireless detachments initially approved by cabinet.[10] It appeared that ground-to-air communication links were also no longer required, as the Canadians could not discover who had made the initial request; those concerned disclaimed any knowledge of it. This pointed to the level of disorganization at ONUC HQ. The Canadians reported, "We are working in a vacuum here. Info very difficult to obtain and when obtained is almost invariably conflicting. No coordination anywhere. In summary can only say that pers should be sent over ASP as they can certainly be used in many capacities."[11]

During the first two weeks of August, the concentration and preparation of personnel and equipment continued apace in Barriefield. Lt. Col. B.J. Guimond was appointed acting commander of the Canadian HQ unit, and Maj. R.C. Bindoff commanded No. 57 Signal Squadron. With personnel arriving from across Canada, measures were taken to ensure swift processing and immunization, especially since the latter would determine dates for departure to the Congo. Peacekeepers were given training in small arms, attended lectures on tropical disease, and were briefed on conditions in the Congo by Air Commodore F.S. Carpenter, recently returned from assisting the UN with its initial airlift. Depending on rank, the troops were issued with either Browning automatic pistols or C1 submachine guns, weapons the non-combatant peacekeepers carried for personal defence only. By 8 August, the headquarters unit had reached its authorized strength of 52 all ranks and the 57th had actually exceeded its establishment of 193 by 11. Army headquarters agreed to increase the establishment accordingly, presumably working within the minister's limit of 200 personnel from the Royal Canadian Corps of Signals. At noon the next day, the first group of ten peacekeepers left for Trenton, where they embarked on a forty-hour, 10,170-kilometre trip to the Congo, with stops in Gander, Lajes, Dakar, and Accra.[12] Throughout the next weeks, the RCAF reassigned the North Stars

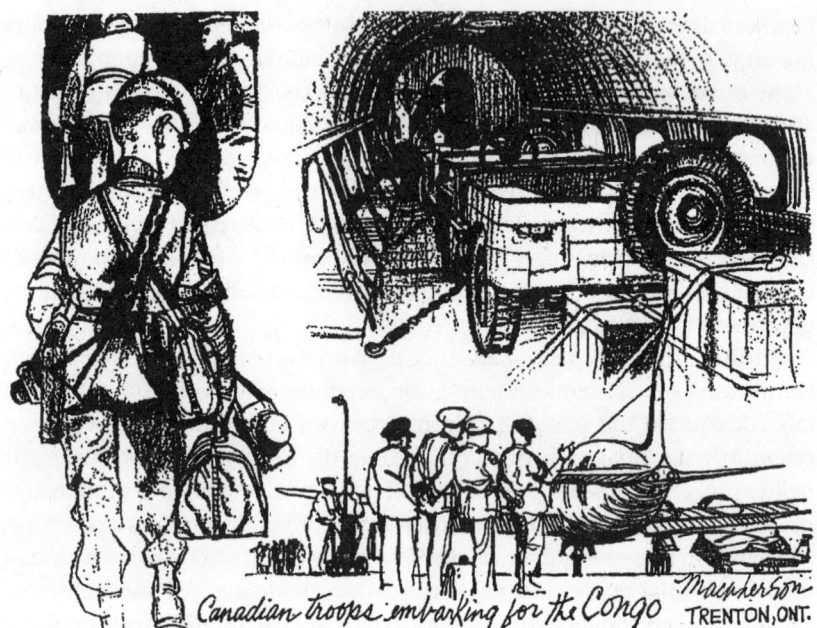

"Canadian troops embarking for the Congo," by Duncan Macpherson.
Reprinted from *Toronto Daily Star*, 10 August 1960, with the permission of Torstar Syndication Services. © Estate of Duncan Macpherson.

used in the original UN airlift to transport the remaining men and equipment. They were assisted by the United States Air Force, which used C-124 Globemasters to transport vehicles and equipment too heavy for RCAF aircraft; in addition, the USAF flew 117 peacekeepers to the Congo. As J.L. Granatstein has observed, the Canadian military's reliance on US planes, in this instance, serves as a stark reminder that peacekeeping is not as independent as it is often assumed to be.[13]

As the first peacekeepers arrived in the Congo, the government sent its formal reply to Secretary-General Dag Hammarskjöld's request for peacekeepers and, in so doing, outlined conditions and understandings. The army asked for it to be made clear that the UN withdrew its request for logistics personnel not at Canada's suggestion but because this support had been sought from other nations. Although the army faced a limit of two hundred signallers, references to this were deleted in the final text of the reply, on the assumption that the ministers of national defence and external affairs could work within the framework of the original cabinet decision to meet additional requests, from either the Canadian commander or the UN, for extra personnel. Because the reconnaissance party had reported that ONUC was being organized through territorial commands and not traditional field brigade headquarters, Pearkes agreed to amend the original restriction against the deployment of peacekeepers below the level of brigade headquarters. The UN was advised that the Canadians should be "concentrated as much as possible" and not "deployed below 'subordinate territorial commands' which it is understood are being set up in established centres." Canada agreed to provide pay and allowances to its peacekeepers on a basis similar to UNEF and assumed that other financial arrangements with the UN, especially regarding foreign allowances and the depreciation costs of equipment, would also be the same as in UNEF. Officials at National Defence and External Affairs did not interpret Pearkes's earlier warning to his cabinet colleagues that equipment might have to be purchased as implying that the UN would need to acquire the equipment in question; yet, aside from depreciation costs, the Canadian reply made no mention of the UN reimbursing Canada for the acquisition of equipment. This directly contradicts the basis on which the Treasury Board approved the purchase of signal equipment from the United States. Finally, the reply asserted the right of the Canadian commander to communicate directly with the CGS on purely administrative matters; later, this provision would prove important when ONUC was forced to confront the problem of inappropriate communications between its contingents and their home governments.[14]

## Political Developments in the Congo: Katanga and Resolution 146

In the initial weeks following ONUC's deployment, the political situation in the Congo was tense. Bull described three political demonstrations in Leopoldville as relatively orderly; he noted that a Canadian reporter who got too close to one of the demonstrations had his foot stepped on and received an immediate apology. Prime Minister Patrice Lumumba was not so lucky. When he appeared at one of the demonstrations, he was stoned and a hostile crowd smashed his car. The acting Canadian trade commissioner was equally unimpressed, not only by Lumumba but by most ministers in the Congolese government. He wrote, "If the ministers as a group were considerably more intelligent, they would rise to the spectacularly incompetent. The majority appear to be too stupid to make mistakes." Many UN officials came to share this harsh assessment. Only the minister of foreign affairs, Justin Bomboko, was singled out as "intelligent, energetic and courageous." To many, the Congolese seemed naive and ignorant. Bunche would later write, "There was not at this time very much understanding on the part of any Congolese official about the nature of the United Nations, or about what it could or could not do, its functioning and structure, and particularly about the meaning and status of the United Nations Secretariat."[15]

Conflicting views as to the purpose of ONUC contributed to a deterioration in relations between the UN and the Congolese, and between Hammarskjöld and Lumumba in particular. Legum suggests, "Lumumba's loss of faith in the United Nations started the moment he discovered he would not be allowed to determine how its forces should be used" and that the prime minister "had little or no idea of how the United Nations worked, or of the conventions that applied to the U.N. Emergency Forces."[16] Although Belgian forces withdrew as ONUC deployed throughout most of the Congo, they remained at military bases in Kitona and Kamina, and in the province of Katanga. Lumumba believed that ONUC was empowered by the Security Council to assist the central government in its attempts to end Katangan secession by force. The secretary-general, however, disagreed with Lumumba's interpretation of Security Council Resolutions 143 (1960) and 145 (1960). He argued that ONUC could not use force, except in self-defence, and was clearly prohibited from intervention in any internal Congolese conflict.[17]

Hammarskjöld also disagreed with the Katangese and Belgian authorities' views on the implementation of the UN resolutions. Belgium gave essential support to Katangan premier Moïse Tshombé's separatist regime, and the Belgian mining conglomerate Union Minière du Haut Katanga provided 80 percent of the regime's revenue.[18] Thus, it is not surprising that the Belgians perceived little need for the UN to enter Katanga. They argued the Belgian military, together with forces loyal to the secessionist government, had already restored law and order. However, the secretary-general believed that ONUC's mandate required the force to be deployed throughout the Congo, including Katanga. The Canadian Mission learned Hammarskjöld had privately persuaded the Belgians to withdraw their troops and was encouraging them to declare their intention to do so publicly. His negotiations were complicated "by the erratic attitude of members of the Congolese Government," who not only pressed for the complete withdrawal of the Belgians but also expected to travel to the Katangan capital of Elisabethville with the secretary-general. Instead, Hammarskjöld sent Bunche to Katanga on 4 August to negotiate the entry of UN forces. Tshombé had warned Hammarskjöld that the arrival of peacekeepers would be resisted and would trigger civil unrest in the province. In turn, through Bunche, the secretary-general explained that, under Articles 25 and 49 of the UN Charter, the Security Council had the authority to implement its decisions throughout the *entire* Congo; any resistance would have legal consequences. Hammarskjöld reassured Tshombé that the arrival of UN forces would not "represent interference in the internal affairs of the Congo or influence in favour of any particular constitutional solution."[19] When the Katangese interior minister, Godefroid Munongo, later threatened to shoot down the plane dispatched to return Bunche to Leopoldville, the secretary-general's representative decided it was unlikely that ONUC could enter Katanga peacefully. He believed the "political realities of the United Nations ... would not long permit a peace force to be in the posture of an army of occupation."[20] Hammarskjöld resolved to consult with the Security Council before pressing forward. He recognized an important distinction in the council's mandate: Belgian forces had to leave the Congo, but the UN could not forcefully subdue an uncooperative Katanga. Nations contributing contingents did so on the basis that the troops would be used in a peacekeeping mission, not an enforcement action. Hammarskjöld believed any significant change in the legal basis of ONUC would require renegotiation with the nations contributing contingents.[21]

Canada generally observed a policy of not publicly taking sides on the Katanga issue, and Belgium's role in particular. The Belgian ambassador to Canada was concerned that remarks by Prime Minister John Diefenbaker delivered in the House of Commons on 1 August had given the impression that Belgians had fled the Congo immediately after independence and during the mutiny in a calculated way. Officials at External Affairs considered the ambassador "unduly worried," noting that the prime minister had clearly stated that "he implied 'no criticism whatever of the action taken by the Belgian Government or by Belgian nationalists.'" The ambassador was anxious to know Canadian views on the withdrawal of Belgian forces from Katanga and its military bases in the Congo. Undersecretary of State for External Affairs Norman Robertson thought it was reasonable for Belgian troops to leave Katanga only after UN forces were in a position there to maintain law, and he suggested this point might be raised with Hammarskjöld in the Elisabethville negotiations. The undersecretary was less supportive of the Belgians' ambitions to retain their presence at Kamina and Kitona, even if this was of significance to NATO. He argued, "The strategic advantage of maintaining Belgian troops in the Congo has to be balanced against the very serious political difficulties which will result both in the Congo and in neighbouring territories if the Belgian government will not withdraw their forces." In this respect, Robertson's view was comparable to that of the American secretary of state, Christian Herter. In earlier discussions with Henry Cabot Lodge, the American representative at the UN, Herter had noted that Kamina had a good airfield but that it was not a "NATO base as such." Herter was willing to accept language in Security Council Resolution 143 (1960) that called for the withdrawal of Belgian forces in the greater interest of getting a peacekeeping force into the Congo as soon as possible. In the end, the Canadian secretary of state for external affairs thought it best not to give any advice to the Belgians. He believed they were looking "for a scapegoat in Nato itself."[22] Publicly, Howard Green simply advised the House of Commons of Hammarskjöld's decision to consult with the Security Council and added, "The secretary general has made clear that the difficulty which the council faces in Katanga does not have its root in the attitude of the Belgian government, which acquiesced in the security council decisions." He was critical of countries who demanded "direct action," and "whose interest in the Congo may not coincide with the aims of the United Nations."[23]

On 9 August, the Security Council passed Resolution 146 (1960), with nine votes in favour, none against, and two abstentions.[24] It confirmed the authority vested by the council in the secretary-general and called upon Belgium to immediately withdraw its forces from Katanga. It also asserted the necessity of ONUC's entry into the breakaway province but required that ONUC not become a party to, or influence the outcome of, any internal conflict. Because the UN force was now clearly obliged to prevent civil war in the Congo, Hammarskjöld could condone neither the Lumumba government's subjugation of Katanga by force nor the province's use of force to secede.[25] Jane Boulden suggests that Resolution 146 did not really change ONUC's mandate; it did make "explicit aspects of the mandate previously thought to be implicit, ... stopping short of any authorization to use force."[26] Mona Gagnon concurs. She notes that the council declared it necessary for UN forces to enter Katanga, without yet authorizing the peacekeepers to use force to achieve this objective.[27] The Security Council's latest pronouncement on the Congo situation was the first to explicitly cite Articles 25 and 49; in doing so, all member states were reminded of their charter obligation to "accept and carry out Security Council decisions and to afford mutual assistance for such measures."[28] Once the Security Council endorsed his actions, the secretary-general was in a much stronger position to return to Katanga to press for the *peaceful* entry of UN forces. On his return trip to the Congo, Hammarskjöld drafted a memorandum outlining his interpretation of ONUC's role and emphasizing the UN force's obligation not to intervene in the conflict.[29] This memorandum, along with Hammarskjöld's decision to fly directly to Elisabethville for negotiations with Tshombé, infuriated Lumumba. The prime minister wanted the secretary-general to consult the central government before taking any action to resolve the Katanga issue and expected to accompany him on this trip to Elisabethville. Hammarskjöld's decision to take along Swedish peacekeepers, as the first of the ONUC forces to be deployed in Katanga, further annoyed Lumumba. The Congolese prime minister suspected Hammarskjöld was conspiring with the Belgians and perceived the secretary-general's decision to be accompanied by Swedes as proof of such a conspiracy.[30]

These differences of opinion over ONUC's role in Katanga resulted in a marked shift in Lumumba's views. Bunche later wrote, "From that time on Mr. Lumumba rejected all normal relations with the United Nations."[31] He became increasingly hostile to Hammarskjöld, the West, and white UN forces. His press attaché, Serge Michel, recounted Lumumba's belief that "all Westerners in the Congo were racists." He said of white UN forces: "'They're afraid. How can you imagine that, just like that, a hat painted blue is enough to eliminate the complexes of conservative officers from Sweden or Canada or Great Britain?' Their vision of Africa ... was one of lion hunts, slave markets, and colonial conquests, and they sympathized with the Belgians because they had 'the same past, the same history, the same taste for our riches.'"[32] Lumumba began to call for the withdrawal of white peacekeepers, but Hammarskjöld strenuously rejected this on the grounds that the UN alone had the authority to determine the composition of its peacekeeping forces. To Lumumba, it must have seemed as though the UN increasingly dictated the means by which the standoff with Katanga would be settled. As one expert has noted, the very presence of peacekeeping forces "is an indication that the host state has in some important way been unable to cope on its own."[33] For Lumumba, steeped as he was in the ideology of anti-colonialism, these developments must have been bitter pills to swallow. The Canadian trade commissioner reported that, as a result of the disagreement between Hammarskjöld and Lumumba, the prime minister attempted to reassert the government's authority by announcing over the radio that "Belgian spys [sic] and saboteurs were masquerading in UN uniform." A "witch hunt" ensued.[34]

Hammarskjöld arrived in Elisabethville on 12 August after a brief stop in Leopoldville. Bunche remained in the capital to explain the secretary-general's interpretation of Resolution 146 to the central government, but Hammarskjöld deliberately avoided meeting with Lumumba. There were a few tense moments when Katangese authorities threatened to refuse landing to the four aircraft carrying troops that accompanied Hammarskjöld's plane. Tshombé, however, intervened directly and suggested there had been a "misunderstanding" once Hammarskjöld made it clear that, unless all five planes landed, he would return to Leopoldville. While Hammarskjöld met with Tshombé, his representatives met with Belgian military representatives to discuss arrangements for the withdrawal of Belgian troops. A press communiqué announced the successful conclusion of negotiations, with United Nations peacekeepers set to begin relieving Belgian troops on Saturday, 13 August 1960, at 5 p.m. At the designated hour, the Swedish peacekeepers who accompanied the secretary-general took over guard duties at the Elisabethville airport. More Swedish and Moroccan troops arrived in the following days. Ultimately, ONUC HQ planned to deploy four thousand peacekeepers throughout the province.[35] The Katanga deployment resulted in the urgent need for a signal team in Elisabethville, but instructions for the Canadian reconnaissance team dispatched to the Congo in July included a restriction against the presence of any Canadian personnel in Katanga. The chairman, chiefs of staff, Air Chief Marshal Frank Miller, brought this to the attention of External Affairs and the minister of national defence, George Pearkes, who finally lifted this restriction to allow Canadian peacekeepers to be deployed to Katanga, on 19 August.[36]

Even as the UN established a presence in Katanga, it became increasingly clear that Lumumba was simply not prepared to accept the status quo implied by the UN's policy of non-intervention there. He turned to the Soviets for assistance to end the secession. During the Congo crisis, the Soviet Union publicly supported the principle of non-intervention in the internal affairs of a state; however, it was prepared to assist Lumumba because it interpreted the conflict between the central government and the Katangan authorities as not exclusively internal but, rather, inspired and sustained by Belgium. In the final two weeks of August, Lumumba used Soviet aircraft and trucks to transport Armée Nationale Congolaise (ANC) forces into Luluabourg, the provincial capital of Kasai, in preparation for an attack on Katanga. Earlier in the month, hostilities between the Lulua and Baluba peoples in this city resulted in the latter retreating south to Bakwanga. Once there, the Baluba leader, Albert Kalonji, declared the secession of South Kasai. Faced with yet another separatist movement, Lumumba ordered the ANC into South Kasai en route to Katanga. Inadequate supplies and planning left the Congolese army to live off the land. When the Baluba resisted, the army massacred many.[37] The events in South Kasai, and Lumumba's reliance on Soviet assistance in particular, hardened the views of many in the West against the Congolese prime minister. From Washington, External Affairs learned that the deputy assistant secretary for African Affairs viewed Lumumba as unpredictable and questioned "whether the position of the UN in the Congo and the internal stability of the country could be maintained so long as Lumumba continues on his present course." American documents reveal frustration over Lumumba's continuing prominence and, by August, a clear desire to see him eclipsed by any other political figure who could be counted on to be less inclined to turn to the Soviet Union for assistance. This sentiment is probably best captured in a conversation between President Eisenhower and the British foreign secretary, during which the president is reported to have expressed his desire that "Lumumba ... fall into a river full of crocodiles."[38] David Gibbs argues that the United States was definitely and actively opposed to Lumumba and his policies. He writes, "US officials detested Lumumba" and maintains that overthrowing the Congolese leader was the principal objective of early American policy in the Congo. He suggests that the US embassy in Leopoldville supported the Katanga secession and that the CIA delivered French-built jet fighters to the Katangese military.[39]

These recent events caused the Belgians to become even more convinced that Communists were infiltrating the Congo, and they shared various reports in support of this view with Canadian diplomats. From Brazzaville, they learned Lumumba wanted to accept a Russian offer of one hundred doctors in spite of his health minister's objections. Belgian officials in Elisabethville suggested the Soviet plane given to Lumumba for his personal use had broadcasting equipment that operated from N'Djili airport. Equally ominous was a warning that "28 Russians including three women carrying with them very heavy material of an unknown nature landed in Luluabourg."

Lumumba was said to be considering the dispatch of cadet officers to Moscow for military training and the acceptance of Soviet technical and financial aid for the construction of the Inga dam. And the Belgian secret police had identified Serge Michel, Lumumba's information officer, as a "staunch communist." By comparison, the Canadian trade commissioner reported on similar offers of Russian assistance and questionable Lumumba colleagues but concluded, "I do not think many Congolese have the foggiest idea of what communism is." He did warn, "Communist methods and psychology may serve as a stick to beat the Belgians or belabour unkind fate. They will not hesitate to use it."[40]

### Canadian Peacekeepers Arrive in the Congo

In the midst of this political turmoil, Canadian peacekeepers continued to arrive on regular flights from Trenton. There was initially some concern at National Defence over the quartering of Canadians serving in the Congo. Air Commodore Carpenter warned that outside Leopoldville Canadians might face living with "the native troops serving under United Nations." The army was keen to avoid being "accused of refusing to quarter Canadian soldiers with coloured soldiers." It argued that "it would not be a matter of a colour bar so much as not wishing to quarter our troops with foreign troops who speak a different language whose customs may be widely different from our own." Colonel Mendelsohn was asked to make "cautious" inquiries about separate accommodations for the Canadians. "This matter," he was warned, "would have to be handled delicately because Mr. Ralph Bunche, the senior UN official in the Congo, is coloured." The entire issue was recognized as so sensitive that Mendelsohn was asked to wait to report his findings until he had returned to Canada himself so that no United Nations officials would "know about this subject."[41] The colonel was successful with this delicate mission. After the Canadians' short stay in the Otraco company guesthouse, arranged by Roger Bull, the earliest arrivals of the 57th Signal Squadron and the Canadian HQ took up residence in the Athenee Royal, a two-storey cement structure that previously was the main boarding and day school for white children. Peacekeepers stationed at territorial detachments in the Congolese interior also appeared to have been quartered separately, usually in private residences. Messing often proved particularly difficult for these personnel. One commanding officer (CO) observed: "Differences between the Canadian diet and that of the contingent with which a detachment may be serving makes it impossible to mess with the contingent with which they work; a meal of hot curried rice is very enjoyable once in a while, but having it served twice a day does not appeal to all Canadians."[42]

On 23 August, army headquarters recalled all but two members of the original reconnaissance party. Colonel Mendelsohn and Maj. R.C. Daigle remained, as contingent commander and medical officer respectively. By the end of August, the 57th had dispatched detachments to the outlying provincial capital cities of Luluabourg (Kasai), Stanleyville (Orientale), Coquilhatville (Equateur), and Elisabethville (Katanga). Each detachment consisted of one officer and nine men and provided radio-teletype communications twenty-four hours a day. Commanding officers were usually drawn from outside the signal service but "proved to be invaluable, particularly in times of trouble" and acquired sufficient knowledge of signals to administer their detachments. Often, the officers were drawn from the Royal 22e Regiment and became important links between district Congolese commanders, UN troops, and ONUC HQ.[43]

The 57th used the AN/GRC-26D radio sets purchased especially for use in the Congo. While these sets were supposed to have a range of only 400 kilometres when used for radio-teletype, the shortest circuit serviced was actually a distance of 800 kilometres (Leopoldville to Luluabourg). The sets were even used to communicate with Nairobi, Kenya at a distance of 2,650 kilometres. In order to exceed their normal range, the transmitters were used at maximum power at all times. This led to frequent breakdowns, as did the heat. In Leopoldville, the average temperature in the transmitter room at the Athenee Royal was 35 degrees Celsius, while the tape relay centre averaged 32 degrees, even with three air conditioners running. Repairs at outlying detachments were often complicated by a lack of spare parts and because aircraft schedules delayed the arrival of replacement parts or senior technicians from Leopoldville. Until such repairs could be made, detachments sometimes reverted to the use of Morse code. At ONUC HQ, the Canadian signallers provided several important services. They operated a tape relay centre, a message centre, a crypto centre, a transmitter station, and the UN headquarters automatic phone system, and provided dispatch rider services between all units in Leopoldville. The message centre typically processed four to five hundred messages a day, in various languages. Although most radio circuits were within the Congo, the link to Nairobi connected with the Commonwealth Communication System so that messages could be sent to and from Canada and the home countries of other Commonwealth contingents. The signallers both maintained and operated the phone system. Some bilingual personnel operated the switchboard twenty-four hours a day, while others worked and cooperated with the local phone company to ensure that services the UN needed would be efficiently installed. The 57th also established a repair shop in ONUC HQ and was often called upon to repair equipment belonging to the UN civilian communication system, other contingents, the Nigerian police, UN military police, the UN Field Security section, and the International Telecommunication and International Civil Aviation Organisation.[44]

In addition to the signal personnel, Canadians served within most branches of ONUC HQ. At various times, Canadians served as chief operations officer, chief signal officer, and chief air officer. David Wainhouse has determined that, for the duration of ONUC, there were almost always more Canadians serving as officers at headquarters than there were of any other nationality. He attributes this disproportionate presence to "their language capability, peacekeeping experience, generally good political acceptability, professionalism, and familiarity with both Commonwealth and U.S. military procedures." By mid-August 1960, twelve Canadian officers served at ONUC HQ. Most had been transferred either from UNTSO or UNEF.[45] In addition, Canada provided a Food Services section and a Canadian Provost Corps (C Pro C) detachment. The latter, under the command of the force deputy provost marshal, worked and lived with Danish military police. Because many were bilingual, the Canadians were chiefly responsible for investigations that involved the local Congolese.[46] Indar Jit Rikhye, the secretary-general's military adviser during the Congo crisis, notes English was used as the common working language at ONUC HQ because it was easier to find peacekeepers who had English as their second language.[47] Yet, the C Pro C detachment is just one example of how Canadians were able to play an important role at ONUC HQ because of their ability to communicate with the Congolese in French.

Although the Canadian peacekeepers did not serve in a combat role in the Congo, they still regularly came into contact with both the Congolese and Lumumba's Armée Nationale Congolaise (ANC). Soon after their arrival, an incident occurred that foreshadowed the serious difficulties Canadian peacekeepers would encounter in the coming weeks. On 15 August, a crowd of two hundred Congolese surrounded a Jeep carrying two Canadian members of ONUC. The crowd shouted "Flamand, Belgium," believing the peacekeepers to be Belgian. One of the peacekeepers tried to calm the crowd; as this was accomplished on one side of the Jeep, three or four agitators rallied people on the other side. The incident was defused when a Congolese police patrol arrived on the scene, confirmed the identity of the peacekeepers, and dispersed the crowd.[48]

Three days later, the first incident of serious violence between the Congolese and Canadians occurred at N'Djili airport, just outside Leopoldville, and demonstrated how vulnerable the Canadians could be. Two groups of peacekeepers were waiting to depart on reconnaissance missions to Coquilhatville and Luluabourg, to plan and prepare for the arrival of signal detachments. Those destined for Luluabourg were delayed on the tarmac. A patrol of about ten to twelve Congolese soldiers suddenly rushed toward them. The peacekeepers presented their UN identity cards and tried to identify themselves as Canadian. The Congolese were unimpressed and forced them face down onto the tarmac, arms extended. They then kicked the peacekeepers, focusing their efforts particularly on the commanding officer, Capt. J.C.A.A. Taschereau. The peacekeepers destined for Coquilhatville, along with the Indian aircrew and some Moroccan passengers, were removed from their aircraft and, together with the first group of Canadians, herded into an awaiting truck. Their wallets and valuables were stolen and blue UN berets removed. Taschereau was then hit in the face with the butt of a rifle and knocked unconscious, while another Canadian was struck in the back with such force that the rifle butt broke. Others suffered cuts and bruises. After about ten minutes, a Danish officer accompanied by Ghanaian troops rescued the Canadians.[49]

Hammarskjöld, once informed of the incident, promptly drafted a letter to the Congolese ambassador to the UN. He stressed the "extreme gravity" of the incident, drawing attention to the unacceptable conditions peacekeepers faced in ONUC. The secretary-general threatened the Lumumba government with the withdrawal of UN support and assistance with a warning that "further activities may be rendered impossible" if the peacekeepers' working conditions did not improve. This letter was followed by an official note of protest to the Congolese government, which repeated his threat by suggesting that all UN activities in the Congo might have to be submitted to the Security Council for reconsideration. The secretary-general made it clear that he expected the government to immediately take "all measures necessary to forestall the recurrence of any such incidents."[50]

Howard Green, who happened to be in New York on the day of the incident, met with Hammarskjöld and discussed the secretary-general's protest to the Congolese authorities. Meeting with reporters later, Green noted there had been no suggestion that Canada would withdraw its peacekeepers. Rather, he said, "I presume they'll go right ahead." On his return to Ottawa, the minister met with Diefenbaker for an hour. The prime minister then summoned Norman Robertson to his office and set to work drafting a Canadian letter of protest. In a note described as being "as strong as any employed by a Canadian head of government to a foreign leader," he stated: "Such totally unwarranted and unjustified attacks on Canadian Service personnel are of a most serious character. I expect an immediate assurance that effective measures will be taken to ensure that the forces under your control will refrain from threatening the security of Canadian personnel who proceed to your country on friendly and peaceful missions in the performance of tasks determined by the United Nations." Reporters were called to the Prime Minister's Office and shown the contents of the letter sent to Lumumba. With "rumpled" hair and in a harsh tone, Diefenbaker warned that the Canadian government took a "serious view of the totally unwarranted and unjustifiable conduct of the Congolese soldiers."[51] He had considered the implications of possible Canadian casualties weeks before cabinet finally decided to participate in ONUC. Once injuries actually occurred, he dealt with them forcefully and quickly.

Doubtless Diefenbaker anticipated that Canadians would be indignant over the treatment of their peacekeepers. Newspapers featured blazing headlines: "Canadian Troops Attacked" stretched atop the front page of the *Chronicle-Herald*; "Sauvage attaque des Congolais contre des soldats canadiens" stridently appeared on the front page of *Le Devoir*. Given such coverage, the editorial that appeared in the *Globe and Mail* the following day must have been something of a surprise to the prime minister. It seriously questioned the wisdom of Diefenbaker's letter of protest and argued that only the UN had a right to condemn the Congolese government because Canadian soldiers were serving as peacekeepers, under the auspices of the international organization. The editorial concluded by exhorting the Canadian government to display the same "conspicuous self-control and patience in the face of all provocations and dangers" displayed by the UN personnel involved in the incident. Interestingly, the *Chronicle-Herald* made a similar distinction, noting in a later editorial that the insults suffered by the peacekeepers "were offered, not to Canadian troops as such, but to forces under the command of the UN." The *Toronto Daily Star* considered Diefenbaker's protest to be a good expression of the Canadian public's concern over the incident, but also concluded its editorial entitled "Let's Not 'Bring the Boys Home'" with a clear commitment to ONUC: "Canadian and other U.N. detachments should stay on the job, whatever the difficulties and dangers."[52] The first Canadian casualties in ONUC certainly did not lead to any resounding, urgent calls to withdraw the soldiers; in fact, many newspapers took a relatively calm, tempered approach to the whole affair.

The principal UN officials paid tribute to the conduct of the Canadian peacekeepers at N'Djili. Brigadier Rikhye told External Affairs that Taschereau and his men "behaved admirably throughout the incident under the most severe provocation." They would have been justified in using their arms in self-defence; instead, they demonstrated extreme restraint in their attempts to reason with their attackers. Von Horn sent a message to the Canadian chief of the general staff, S.F. Clark, expressing his "admiration for the very high standard of discipline and for the courage and forbearance shown by your troops." He added, "I thank them, congratulate them on their splendid conduct in the face of needless and senseless provocation and I am proud and honoured at having them under my command." In his memoirs, von Horn recalled that the N'Djili incident profoundly impacted everyone in ONUC. From this point on, according to von Horn, very few members of the force disguised their hostility towards the Congolese. He remembered strapping on his own pistol before heading to the airport to oversee the arrival of the remaining Canadians. In a radio broadcast to all the military and civilian staff of ONUC, Bunche paid "high tribute" to the Canadians. He noted, "They might, so easily and effectively, have dealt with the situation

"Is It Our Fault That Everybody Looks Like A Belgian?" by Robert Chambers.
The author is grateful to the estate of the late Dr. Chambers for permission to reproduce the
Robert Chambers political cartoon originally appearing in the *Chronicle-Herald* [Halifax] of
30 August 1960.

in their own way. Instead, in the interest of the UN, they exercised patience
and restraint of the most commendable nature."[53]

On 19 August, Lumumba held a press conference in Leopoldville to address Hammarskjöld's note of protest. The Congolese prime minister considered the N'Djili incident "commonplace" and suggested it had been blown
out of proportion by the secretary-general as a diplomatic manoeuvre. He

made reference to an identity control system recently implemented by the government as a means to discover the "many persons of foreign national-ity" infiltrating the Congo. He maintained the Congolese soldiers at N'Djili airport on 18 August were simply trying to verify the identity of the Can-adian soldiers, who had in turn "categorically refused to show their papers and behaved rudely." To counter Hammarskjöld's charges, he argued the Congolese army was subjected daily to "uncalled-for affronts and humilia-tion by the UN European troops." He concluded his press conference with a demand for the withdrawal of the white UN troops who had "provoked the latest incidents." Howard Green declined to comment on Lumumba's allegations against the Canadian peacekeepers before the Security Council could meet to consider the situation, but a UN spokesman "curtly" denied the charges, asserting that identification badges were shown and that the peacekeepers had not "behaved badly."[54] Notably, the Congolese army's chief of staff also contradicted Lumumba's version of the events at N'Djili. Even as the prime minister was holding his press conference, Col. Joseph Mobutu delivered an official apology to Ralph Bunche stating, "We are extremely sorry that precise instructions had not been given in time to the company on duty at the airport, as that might have prevented the shameful occurrence at Ndjili." Bunche was assured that strong measures had been taken against the soldiers responsible for the incident. In the days that followed, Lumumba himself somewhat softened his stand by apologizing for the "minor" N'Djili incident and for his soldiers' excessive zeal in carrying out their orders to check all identification. He ordered the army to act "with tact and dignity in future."[55]

In conversation with the secretary of state at the Congolese Ministry of Foreign Affairs, the Canadian trade commissioner learned that Lumumba's call for withdrawal of non-African forces was directed primarily at Swedish peacekeepers. William Mackenzie Wood attributed Lumumba's particular hostility toward the Swedes to the prime minister's disagreements with the secretary-general and to the fact that Swedish peacekeepers had recently intervened to prevent the arrest of Belgians by the Force Publique. To Wood, it seemed as though the difficulties between the UN and the Congolese forces were increasingly of a racial character. He worried particularly for the position of the Canadian peacekeepers in Leopoldville, especially if the Swedes were withdrawn and the Canadians were left as the only remaining white troops. This may have been a moot point. Hammarskjöld is said to have confided in the Americans that he would recommend the full withdrawal of ONUC if Lumumba pressed his demand for the withdrawal of white contingents. In his view, the UN could not "adopt a policy of 'inverted racism.'"[56]

Within two weeks there was another serious and violent incident between Congolese forces and Canadian peacekeepers. Six members of the signal squadron left Trenton on 27 August aboard two United States Air Force

Globemaster aircraft. The United States had agreed to transport heavy equipment required by the signallers that could not otherwise be transported by RCAF planes. The Canadian officer in charge, Capt. J.J.B.L. Marois, was accompanied by three other peacekeepers in the first plane. He assigned two others, Corporal Gavel and Signaller Bone, to accompany the remainder of the squadron's equipment in the second plane. Marois and his group left first, an hour and fifteen minutes before the others, so that they could organize equipment and arrange to meet the second plane when it landed.

The first plane reached Stanleyville at 8:30 a.m. The four Canadians noticed what looked like three companies of the Congolese army, as well as a company of Ethiopian peacekeepers, on the tarmac. They disembarked, unloaded the aircraft, and assisted in the departure of the airplane. A UN officer then escorted them to the UN headquarters at the Hotel Wagenia. Moments later, Congolese soldiers looking for Belgian paratroops rushed into the Stanleyville headquarters and demanded to see the recently arrived Canadians, to establish their identity. The Canadians were loaded into Jeeps at gunpoint, along with three UN civilian employees and three other Canadian peacekeepers, including Capt. J.J.B. Pariseau, who had already been detained the previous week for the same reason. The Congolese commander assured Pariseau that no one would be killed and explained that the whole affair was only for "political appeasement." Still, they were beaten, searched, stripped, and placed in cells where they were kept for forty-five minutes until an Ethiopian brigade commander arrived to rescue them.

In the meantime, Corporal Gavel and Signaller Bone arrived in the second American plane. A crowd formed on the airfield and was stirred into a frenzy by reports that the plane contained Belgian paratroopers. Patrice Lumumba was expected to arrive shortly in another airplane and rumours quickly spread that the supposed paratroopers had been sent to assassinate the Congolese leader. Congolese soldiers pulled Gavel, Bone, and the American aircrew from the plane and beat them severely. The two Canadians were then flown to Leopoldville to be hospitalized, for a week. General von Horn deployed three hundred peacekeepers around the plane bearing the wounded soldiers when it landed at N'Djili airport, threatening to fire the first shot if there was any interference. Speaking to a reporter from his hospital bed, Bone simply said, "You can't hold it against them – they don't know what it's all about." He also praised Gavel as a hero; the corporal had covered Bone with his own body to protect the signaller after Bone fell to the ground semiconscious. Others held less forgiving views of the incident. In a statement to a senior officer, one Canadian peacekeeper declared, "I couldn't help thinking that our Canadian responsible heads, political or otherwise[,] had not thought too much when they sent us in such an area without adequate protection. In fact as soon as I can, I'll ask for my release from the army, that is how much I feel about it."[57]

Canadian reaction to the Stanleyville attack was swift. Wood, now the acting consul general in Leopoldville, made a verbal protest to Congolese foreign minister Bomboko. In Ottawa, Diefenbaker once again spoke out against the latest assault on Canadians. In a press release, more subdued in tone than that which followed the N'Djili incident, he said he was "naturally gravely concerned that Canadian personnel are again encountering difficulties." He expressed the hope that the Congolese authorities would cooperate with the UN to ensure that there would be no further incidents. When stopped by reporters on his way into a cabinet meeting, the prime minister could not help but take a swipe at those who had criticized his reaction to the earlier incident involving Canadian peacekeepers. He chastised, "Some who thought there should not have been any message from me to Premier Lumumba when Canadians were first attacked in Leopoldville now find that the United States was prompt, when its nationals were affected, to send a message requesting assurances." Privately, Canadian officials were stern. External Affairs suggested an urgent meeting of the secretary-general's advisory committee to consider the situation. It warned, "If it should transpire that UN forces cannot be allowed to operate by the Congolese authorities in such a way that minimum security is provided to UN personnel the whole problem of continued UN operations in the Congo will have to be considered by the Security Council." The Canadians sought assurances from the UN that, in future, adequate security would be in place at Congolese airports. The Canadian commander in Stanleyville took a more direct approach. Captain Pariseau invited the local ANC commandant to dinner and assured him there were no hard feelings, but he warned that Canadian peacekeepers would respond with force in the future.[58]

## Diplomacy at the United Nations

Ireland closely watched reactions to the N'Djili and Stanleyville incidents. There were two Irish battalions, totalling almost 1,400 officers and men, stationed in the Congo and, unlike the Canadians, Irish peacekeepers were there in a combat capacity. Sweden, Denmark, and Norway also had white forces serving in ONUC. After N'Djili, the UN representatives of Canada and these other countries began to meet informally to share confidential personal views of Congolese developments. They recognized that the reaction of any one government to incidents in the Congo could affect the position of the others, especially if withdrawal of an entire national contingent was contemplated. They each assured the other that their governments were not considering this option and noted Hammarskjöld's decision to stand firm against Lumumba's demand for the withdrawal of white forces. Charles Ritchie, Canada's permanent representative to the UN, explained that Canadian opinion was in "complete support" of participation in ONUC but that the recent ill-treatment of Canadian peacekeepers "had caused indignation."

From the earliest days of ONUC, common concerns and a sense that the fates of "white" contributing nations were linked brought this group of representatives together. Yet, these countries remained willing to criticize one another privately. The UN desk officer in Dublin, for instance, expressed "apprehension" to a Canadian diplomat about "Swedish antipathy to blacks," and suggested the "attitude of Swedish forces might eventually create serious friction with Congolese."[59]

Members of this group were anxious to understand the causes and implications of the violent actions of the soldiers in Lumumba's ANC. The Congolese government suggested the attacks were simply a case of mistaken identity: white peacekeepers were confused with Belgian paratroopers. Publicly, Ralph Bunche issued statements supporting this interpretation of events. He characterized the Congo as a society "in which suspicion leads to fear and fear easily leads to panic." He pointed to the mob that had mauled the Canadians in Stanleyville as an example of how the mere mention of paratroopers could set off a crowd that would not otherwise be concerned with white peacekeepers. The Congolese were not generally anti-white; they were anti-Belgian. However, there was always the danger that any white person could be mistaken for a Belgian. Similarly, Consul General Wood acknowledged that it was difficult to know to what degree mistaken identity had contributed to the earlier N'Djili incident. He recalled at least one account that placed a suspicious man near the Congolese troops just prior to their attack on the Canadians who seemed to be "either directing or inciting them, presumably by saying that the Canadians were Belgians in disguise." Brigadier Rikhye cited additional factors that contributed to an atmosphere of paranoia among the Congolese. In conversation with Bunche, and in the presence of Congolese General Victor Lundula, a Belgian paratroop major mischievously implied that twelve Belgian soldiers were unaccounted for and left behind after their final withdrawal. Lundula initiated a search for the soldiers, which was inflamed by Belgian nationals wearing Sabena airline caps similar in colour to UN berets and rumours that UN armbands were for sale on the Congolese black market for a thousand Congolese francs.[60]

In private, Bunche considered another plausible explanation. In a confidential report to New York, he said the incidents directed against white peacekeepers were "not accidental but were part of a pattern which might possibly be inspired deliberately by the Congolese government." The secretary-general concurred with this view. While unwilling to say so publicly, Hammarskjöld was convinced that Lumumba was behind the Stanleyville incident. Given the deteriorating relationship between the secretary-general and the prime minister, this interpretation is plausible. By early September, Consul General Wood was less convinced "the attacks on Canadians have all been made in the genuine belief that they were Belgian paratroops, and without the knowledge of the Prime Minister." He surmised, "Mr. Lumumba has on several occasions shown that he would prefer to see the United Nations operation in the Congo Africanized as much as possible. He may therefore, at the suggestion of some of his advisers, have felt that by creating difficulties for the Canadians, he would be furthering this end."[61]

The Soviet Union was quick to make good use of the N'Djili and Stanleyville incidents. Soon after the Canadian parliament approved participation in ONUC, Soviet officials delivered a *démarche* to the secretary-general. They objected to the use of Canadian peacekeepers because Canada was one of Belgium's NATO allies. The Soviets argued Canadian participation in ONUC was contrary to the Security Council's decision to "take all necessary resolution toward the speediest cessation of aggression, the immediate withdrawal of troops from the territory of the Republic of the Congo and respect for its territorial integrity and political independence." They called upon the Canadian government to "display due objectivity" by not sending forces to the Congo. The secretary-general decided not to take the memorandum too seriously. He noted that Vasily Kuznetsov, the deputy foreign minister of the USSR, seemed to "make light of it." In his formal response to the Soviets, Hammarskjöld outlined the serious communications difficulties ONUC faced, particularly given the many languages used by the various contingents. He maintained that Canada was uniquely qualified and equipped to provide communications in English and French.[62]

As relations between Lumumba and Hammarskjöld deteriorated during the remainder of August, the Soviets began to attack the secretary-general's actions. Canadian officials in New York noticed that "at times Soviet public criticism of Hammarskjold appears to follow closely the pattern of alternating praise and blame that Lumumba gives him." As countries in the West became increasingly suspicious of Lumumba, the Soviets provided him with bilateral assistance and moral support. On the basis of numerous articles in the Soviet press, which vigorously criticized Hammarskjöld's handling of the Congo crisis, the Canadian ambassador in Moscow, David Johnson, concluded, "The Soviet Government is encouraging Mr. Lumumba to bypass the United Nations and take direct action against Katanga with the military forces of Guinea and Ghana." The Canadian representative in Yugoslavia, Robert Ford, who reported a conversation in which the acting head of the Yugoslav Foreign Ministry deplored the withdrawal of Lumumba's confidence from Hammarskjöld and placed blame for the crisis on past Belgian policies and the Russians "in equal measure," confirmed this view.[63]

Following the N'Djili incident, the Soviets returned to the issue of Canadian participation in ONUC with a vengeance. On 21 August, the leading Soviet newspaper, *Pravda,* reported that "a detachment of the armed forces of Canada – Belgium's ally in NATO – landed in Leopoldville a few days ago, which aroused the fully justified indignation of the Congolese people and led to further aggravation of the tension in the country." Just the day before,

Kuznetsov had held a press conference in New York and demanded the withdrawal of "armed groups from Canada." The Soviet official no longer made light of Moscow's protests over Canadian participation. Instead, the inclusion of Canadians in ONUC turned into ammunition in what became, as the month wore on, a concerted Soviet attempt to discredit and undermine Hammarskjöld. The secretary-general told Charles Ritchie that Kuznetsov "had taken the line that 'now you realize how unwise it was to send Canadian troops to the Congo'"[64] During the Security Council session on 21 August, Kuznetsov once again vigorously attacked Canadian participation in ONUC and demanded they be withdrawn. He did not take issue with Swedish participation, or the inclusion of troops from Denmark and Norway, even though the latter two countries were also members of NATO. Hammarskjöld defended his decision to enlist the help of Canada and showed "no sign of regretting or changing his position." He argued that of the 127 civilian experts in the Congo, 87 were from countries that "by no stretch of the imagination" were connected with NATO, and only 500 of the 18,000 ONUC peacekeepers were from NATO countries. Half of these would not have been required if Poland had been able to contribute the forces the UN had requested. The secretary-general believed that membership in either NATO or the Warsaw Pact did not necessarily preclude participation in ONUC. Hammarskjöld argued the N'Djili incident should not be seen as directed against Canadians in particular because both Indian and Moroccan personnel were also involved.[65] In his address to the council, the Congolese representative raised neither the issue of white forces generally nor Canadian participation in particular. Many countries came to Canada's defence. Argentina, for example, considered the Soviet allegations against Canadian peacekeepers an insult to a country "whose international conduct had been universally recognized as serious, responsible and worthy of respect."[66]

Less than a week later, Kuznetsov criticized Hammarskjöld again for continuing to use Canadian troops. In addition to their opposition to the presence of Canadian signallers, the Soviets were upset that so many officials at ONUC HQ had been drawn from NATO members. This, combined with Soviet opposition to the decision to temporarily replace Ralph Bunche with another American, Andrew Cordier, raised tensions to yet a higher pitch. These criticisms persisted well into September, when the Soviets continued their campaign against Hammarskjöld in the General Assembly. Charles Ritchie reported widespread concern at the UN for the secretary-general's future with the organization, given the strength and severity of the Russian criticism. Diplomats wondered if the Soviets were "out for his scalp." Ritchie thought it premature to conclude that the Soviet Union was aiming for Hammarskjöld's resignation but was concerned the Congo crisis had become an issue in the Cold War. This made the potential for intervention by one of the Great Powers in the internal affairs of the Congo seem all the more likely, a far greater threat to the international community than the initial mutiny by the Force Publique and the subsequent Belgian intervention. In this context, Lumumba's threats to expel UN forces, if he carried through on them, would have presented a new dilemma. Because the departure of ONUC would have constituted a potential threat to international peace and security, the decision to withdraw UN forces could no longer be made by the Congolese government alone. Such a decision would have to be deliberated in the Security Council. As early as 17 August, the Canadian cabinet was aware that a day might come when a decision on the withdrawal of the Canadian ONUC contingent could mean choosing between either the Congo government's demands or the UN's wishes.[67]

## Canada's Contribution to ONUC

By the middle of August and on into September, the Diefenbaker government found itself in a difficult position because of a commitment it had made to send four Caribou aircraft to support Canadian peacekeepers serving with ONUC. On 1 August, the government announced in the House of Commons its intention to purchase these planes from the de Havilland Aircraft Company. Because of their ability to take off and land within short distances, they were considered ideally suited to conditions in the Congo. Arrangements to purchase the aircraft were quickly completed, with delivery of the first operational aircraft by 15 August. Air and ground crews would be trained by the time the aircraft arrived. Initially, the RCAF used North Stars to transport the gift of Canadian food aid. The cabinet subsequently approved a plan to use these aircraft in an airlift of UN supplies and equipment from Pisa, Italy, to Leopoldville, for a period of thirty days. But after cabinet discovered that the North Stars were being used for internal transport of UN forces, the North Stars were recalled to Canada, with the agreement of UN officials, to transport the Canadian signallers to the Congo. Once all Canadian forces were airlifted, the North Stars were expected to return to duties on the Pisa-Leopoldville external airlift, leaving the new Caribou to primarily provide internal air support for Canadian forces in ONUC. When the needs of Canadian forces were met, the planes were then to be available for other UN duties. However, officials at External Affairs expected it to be difficult to persuade the UN to accept the Caribous if they were to be used in direct support of Canadian peacekeepers but not placed under the operational control of ONUC's commander. Such an interpretation of the Caribous' role would have required the Canadian government to negotiate a direct bilateral agreement with the Congo government, something considered politically impractical. Still, Pearkes, the minister of national defence, believed it was best to adhere to the cabinet's position. He noted that restrictions had been placed on the UN's use of the Canadian signallers (i.e., they were not to be used in advance of brigade headquarters, subsequently modified to sub-territorial commands) and felt that the best policy would be to suggest a compromise: the RCAF Caribou unit would be under the operational control of the United Nations commander but priority would be given to Canadian force requirements.[68]

By mid-September, the Caribou problem was still not resolved; it actually became more complicated. When Canadian officials offered the Caribou to the UN, the secretary-general was neither in New York nor Leopoldville. Bunche initially reacted favourably, given the UN's very real need for air transport in the Congo. Subsequently, Hammarskjöld made it clear that he considered it politically inadvisable to increase the number of Canadians serving in ONUC. In Leopoldville, Bunche was contacted by the Secretariat to clarify this difference in opinion. He confirmed the practical advantages of the Canadian offer but added that von Horn rejected the Canadian proposal that the Caribou be used primarily to support the Canadian signal unit or that priority should be given to their requirements. The force commander wanted the Caribou to be assigned to the ONUC air transport unit, under his command. In the end, Bunche said he understood Hammarskjöld's view of the political implications of accepting the Caribou. In effect, the UN had decided not to accept Canada's offer, and the Permanent Mission concluded that only a direct approach to the secretary-general might reverse this position. Stories of a mix-up began to appear in the Canadian press. One report, while noting that no one was willing to make an official comment on the situation, surmised that the government had ordered the aircraft before finding out if the United Nations wanted them. Moreover, it correctly traced the root of the problem to the government's decision to limit the use of the aircraft to supplying only Canadian forces.[69]

Even though the confusion over the Caribou had the potential to become a public embarrassment, External Affairs decided not to press the Canadian position in New York after it learned that Hammarskjöld "responded negatively in very firm terms" to the compromise proposal the government suggested. Given the criticism he had faced from the Soviets over his decision to include Canadian signallers in ONUC, Hammarskjöld believed a proposal to send a Canadian air unit would leave him in an "untenable position." He suggested that the Caribou might still be used if Canada was prepared to make them available on a lend-lease basis, so that aircrews from other UN units could staff them. When Colonel Mendelsohn returned to Ottawa in September to give a preliminary report to National Defence, he argued that, in spite of the secretary-general's concerns, there was an urgent need for the Caribou and that von Horn fully recognized this need. The only thing standing in the way was Hammarskjöld's desire not to "upset the Russians."[70]

Political difficulties aside, the RCAF was of considerable assistance to the UN, especially in the early days of ONUC. The UN was impressed with the services of Air Commodore F.S. Carpenter, who was in the Congo when the first ONUC peacekeepers arrived. After Carpenter's return to Canada, the secretary-general asked if the Canadian officer could be sent back to Leopoldville, accompanied by five RCAF staff officers, to form an air staff at von Horn's headquarters. Group Captain W.K. Carr was dispatched in Carpenter's place, along with ten other personnel, to serve at force headquarters and as RCAF communications technicians and operators. The RCAF initially envisaged its contribution to ONUC as an air transport unit consisting of two key elements: four Caribou aircraft to be employed in support of Canadian forces and the routine North Star airlift between Pisa and Leopoldville. The latter was considered a temporary commitment, initially undertaken for thirty days, while the Caribou were seen as the key long-term commitment. Ironically, as we have seen, the Caribou portion of the air transport unit never materialized for political reasons, but arrangements governing the "temporary" North Star airlift were repeatedly renewed every ninety days.[71]

In late August, von Horn advised New York of his proposed establishment of the United Nations Air Transport Force. He expected Canadians to fill many key roles. He argued that the position of air commander should be filled by a Canadian because "of the familiarity of Canadians with air transportation principles, ICAO standards, and requirements." He warned, "If for some unforeseen reason it would not be desirable to have a Canadian as the air commander, then it is absolutely essential that an appropriate RCAF officer fill the SASO [senior air staff officer] establishment." He maintained that, because of their experience and familiarity with procedures to be followed and equipment to be used, the chief operations officer, engineering officer, and supply officer should all be Canadians; but, perhaps anticipating Hammarskjöld's concerns that he might be seen as relying too heavily on Canadians, von Horn planned to reduce the number of Canadians at UN Air Transport Force HQ by a third, over a period of three months. Overall, RCAF strength fell from fifty-eight personnel in August to fifteen by December.[72]

On 2 August, a special request for technical assistance arrived from an unexpected quarter. Ghana was planning a bilateral training program with the Congo to train Congolese cadets as Force Publique officers at the Ghana Military Academy. The Ghanaian president, Kwame Nkrumah, hoped Canada would cooperate in this venture by providing approximately twenty French-speaking members of the Armed Forces to assist in the training. The Canadian high commissioner in Ghana, Bruce Williams, confirmed that General Alexander supported the Ghanaian proposal and was especially keen for Canadians to assist. Canadian officials considered the request with caution and questioned Ghanaian motives for the proposal. Ghana and Guinea had recently made known their interest in establishing a federation with the Congo. One member of the prime minister's office observed, "In free Africa, as in free Asia, power politics are regarded as the monopoly of the West – or, at least, of East and West," but added, "can it be, nevertheless, that a game of African power-politics, with strictly African goals and within African regional confines, is also emerging?" Officials at External Affairs preferred to coordinate Congolese assistance through the UN. They suggested Britain, the United States, and the UN all be consulted to ascertain their views on such a proposal. The minister of national defence was even more reluctant. He wrote to Prime Minister Diefenbaker to encourage him to reply negatively to the request, citing a shortage of highly trained French-speaking personnel. Yet, Pearkes added that a UN-sponsored initiative would be preferable to a bilateral agreement, implying he actually opposed the Ghanaian plan less because of the stated shortage of personnel and more on the grounds of the bilateral nature of the arrangement. The cabinet considered the request on 12 August, and its deliberations were greatly simplified when Hammarskjöld cabled Canadian authorities to request a similar training program under UN auspices. The timely arrival of the UN request provided the government with a diplomatic reason to reject participation in Ghana's training scheme. A later suggestion by Nkrumah to channel Congolese aid through independent African states was also rebuffed. Although Diefenbaker appeared to adopt a position that was sympathetic to the Ghanaian view that all aid need not necessarily be delivered through the UN, he ultimately asserted that there was not "a real alternative at the present time to the United Nations presence in and assistance to the Congo."[73]

The government was clearly of the view that the Congo crisis would be best addressed through multilateral, not bilateral, solutions. On 26 August, the government officially declined involvement in Ghana's plans. Canada's involvement in helping to re-establish order in the Congo, Nkrumah was told, was being carried out through the United Nations. Two weeks earlier, External Affairs had advised the Permanent Mission in New York that the government was willing to consider Hammarskjöld's training scheme and might supply between fifty and one hundred personnel; by the time the secretary-general was informed of Canada's willingness to contribute to such retraining, however, Hammarskjöld decided it was best to temporarily shelve these plans pending developments in the Congo. Throughout August, External Affairs and National Defence continued their joint efforts to respond to the UN's increasing number of requests to second and transfer Canadian personnel from UNTSO to ONUC HQ, although the CGS, Lieutenant General S.F. Clark, continued to express concern that the UN not transfer officers without first consulting Canadian authorities. By month's end, the first Canadian casualties in ONUC justified Clark's cautious approach, and cabinet halted plans to send any more Canadians to the Congo, including those earlier considered for the UN's training scheme.[74]

## Political Developments in the Congo and Hammarskjöld's Advisory Committee on the Congo

The isolated incidents of violence suffered by Canadian peacekeepers shortly after their arrival were soon followed by a significant deterioration in the internal Congolese political situation. Two events were crucial: Lumumba's abortive attack on Katanga through South Kasai in late August and the subsequent coup by President Kasavubu. While Lumumba's reliance on Soviet transport planes to move his troops into Kasai further alienated him from the West, Hammarskjöld believed that the ANC massacre of Baluba in South Kasai not only was a "flagrant violation of elementary human rights" but also "had characteristics of the crime of genocide."[75] The barbarity prompted the UN to act, in spite of legal stipulations in its charter against intervention within a state. A neutral, demilitarized zone was established between tribal groups.[76] President Kasavubu used the Kasai events as a pretext to dismiss Lumumba, a decision he announced in a radio broadcast from Leopoldville on the evening of 5 September. Lumumba, in turn, took to the airwaves, denounced Kasavubu's actions as inspired by imperialists, and dismissed the president.

Andrew Cordier, who had recently replaced Ralph Bunche as the secretary-general's special representative, feared the situation would deteriorate into a state of civil war and ordered UN forces to take control of airports throughout the Congo to prevent the movement of troops. The next day, after several pro-Lumumba radio broadcasts that Cordier feared would incite civil war, he ordered ONUC to take control of the Leopoldville radio station. These actions proved controversial because, although they stabilized the conflict, they worked to Kasavubu's advantage. Without access to airports, Lumumba was unable to transport the ANC forces that remained loyal to him from their positions in Kasai to Leopoldville, and Kasavubu's allies across the river in Brazzaville were willing to continue broadcasting his political announcements.[77] Carole Collins offers the most damning interpretation of Cordier's actions, suggesting that his decisions "effectively threw U.N. support behind Kasavubu and reinforced US and Belgian efforts to oust Lumumba – seriously compromising the United Nations' impartiality."[78] Other scholars are more forgiving. Marion McVitty, for example, succinctly identifies the difficult position Cordier faced: "At times inaction was as capable of affecting the volatile internal situation as action would have been."[79] Nonetheless, the Cold War implications of Cordier's decision were not lost on at least one Canadian diplomat. Within a week of the coup, Escott Reid, then the ambassador to Germany, noted, "Already the United Nations has demonstrated in the Congo that it can in Africa act as the executive agent of the free world."[80]

Ironically, just two weeks earlier, Hammarskjöld had responded to criticism that ONUC's administration was too Western, and American in particular, by announcing that an Indian diplomat, Rajeshwar Dayal, would replace Ralph Bunche as head of ONUC. His choice of Cordier, another American, to serve temporarily between Bunche and Dayal was, with the benefit of hindsight, unfortunate.

The establishment of an advisory committee was one step Hammarskjöld took to insulate himself against criticism of his direction of ONUC. During the 1 August debate in the House of Commons on Canadian participation in ONUC, Liberal leader of the Opposition Lester Pearson raised the question of whether the secretary-general intended to strike an advisory committee, following the precedent set by UNEF. Initially, External Affairs did not perceive the need or desirability for such an advisory committee. Norman Robertson observed that ONUC, unlike UNEF, was established by the Security Council, and Hammarskjöld could simply turn to it for advice instead of a separate advisory committee. Robertson believed the question of composition would be so controversial that Hammarskjöld would be best to rely on established channels for obtaining advice. It would appear that Hammarskjöld initially shared Robertson's views because the secretary-general's initial plans for ONUC did not include an advisory committee. Once the Soviets raised the possibility of an Afro-Asian commission to assist the secretary-general in his activities in the Congo, and pressed their proposals for a troika to replace Hammarskjöld, the secretary-general seriously considered the establishment of an advisory committee as an acceptable alternative to these suggestions. On 23 August, the Canadian government received an invitation to join fifteen other countries in membership on the committee. The turbulent events of August had clearly influenced Canadian policy; in a complete reversal of its earlier position, External Affairs now argued, "While the secretary-general has received and will no doubt continue to receive, broad policy direction from the Security Council, he would find it useful to share some of the day to day problems with representatives of governments directly involved in the United Nations operations." The secretary-general was informed the next day that Canada was willing to serve as a member of the advisory committee.[81]

Ottawa was quick to provide the Permanent Mission in New York with advice on how best to participate in these meetings. The politics of race were an immediate concern. External Affairs anticipated that the meetings would inform all members and provide "a common basis for consultation" but considered it quite likely that representatives of governments "providing white troops will be consulting more closely with one another than with some of the other reps on the [committee]." This assumption was based on previous experience with UNEF. External Affairs further cautioned,

In the proceedings of the newly established advisory [committee] it will be very desirable to avoid any impression that opinions are divided on racial lines about the operation of the force in Congo. You will readily appreciate why, in a UN context, the [governments] providing white troops should not [repeat] not appear to be banded together either in favour or against suggestions made by the [secretary-general]. As a general approach to the [committee] we would suggest that African members be allowed to make the running on most questions raised. Certainly, it would appear wise for the reps of non-African [governments] to withhold their advice to the [secretary-general] until after Africans have had an opportunity to express theirs.

Canadian representatives were, evidently, successful at carrying out these instructions. One British diplomat remarked, "The Canadians on the Committee 'make a practice of not throwing their weight about among all these black faces.'" Although the United Kingdom was not permitted to attend the committee's confidential meetings, Canada followed the precedent of the UNEF Advisory Committee, where it was common practice for members to filter information to other member states on a confidential basis, and regularly advised Britain on the discussions that had taken place.[82]

## Reaction in Canada to Congo Developments

Some Canadians were so disturbed by events in the Congo they wrote to either Diefenbaker or Green to express their views on the developing crisis, as concerned individuals or as members of organizations. On the issue of Katanga and Belgian intervention, for example, the Delta Committee of the Communist Party of Canada urged Diefenbaker "to use [his] good office to the end that all Belgian troops be immediately removed from that country, including the Province of Katanga," whereas the Canadian Council of Churches was sympathetic to the position of the Belgians and suggested that their post-independence military intervention could not be "fairly regarded as 'aggression.'" V. McFaul wrote, "We are very sorry for Belgium, who *gave* Congo it's [sic] freedom, now under U.N. pressure must also vacate Katanga. U.N. will go into Katanga against the will of that government. Rather points up and makes a *FARCE* of U.N. democratic objectives doesn't it." The Victoria branch of the Communist Party of Canada urged the prime minister to "press for the speedy removal of Belgian troops from every foot of Congo territory." Finally, Bronson McNair questioned, "Should Dag H. and Bunche be given the awesome power to bludgeon Katanga and deny it the Self Determination of Nations right?"[83]

One common trend in the correspondence was discernible following the two incidents in August when Canadian peacekeepers were beaten by Congolese forces: the number of letters expressing extreme views increased.

Many were blatantly racist and viewed Diefenbaker's protests against the ill-treatment as inadequate. Robert Blair wired, "What good protests to apes who cannot read or comrehend [sic] if they could stop Suggest only recourse to show minimum dignity is recall Canadians immediately stop Let blacks stew in own mess." "Citizen Jones" scolded Diefenbaker: "As a Canadian tax payer I demand that you cease forwarding these 'stern letters of protest' to the Congolese Govt. I say let this chap Lumumba buy his own toilet paper." Yet another wire arrived from John Madden in Newfoundland: "I am ashamed to belong to the Canadian federation when the citizens of a country can be beaten up by savages in a country to which we have to help with taxes either get all people out of there immediately and let them eat one another or do not send any more help to Lamumba [sic]." Mrs. C. Critchell, first vice-president of the Sechelt Conservative Association, wrote to Howard Green, "I used to feel very sorry for those poor natives, for there is no doubt they have been abused, but it is no doubt now they are more animal than man. From now on I shall only think of them as smelly dirty *niggers* ... Tell them to shoot and not to wait until they 'see the whites of their eyes.'" And, perhaps most direct, "Who was the Big Dumb Nut, who sent French-speaking Canadians to the Congo?"[84]

Yet, even after these incidents, some letters were much less strident and did remain supportive of Canadian participation in ONUC. Someone from Edmonton wrote, "This was to be a protest on your handling of the treatment of our soldiers in the Congo. But I must say I am pleased with your handling of the situation ... Please keep in mind you have the Canadian people behind you." Maxwell Cohen, a McGill University professor with considerable experience in the civil service and a Canadian delegate to the United Nations, often corresponded with Diefenbaker on issues of foreign policy. On the difficulties Canadians faced in the Congo he advised the prime minister: "It is imperative that despite all the embarrassment and provocation Canada remains part of the United Nations force in the Congo ... A withdrawal by Canada now would encourage a future pattern of discrimination in any future United Nations force." In spite of the harsh criticism the government received from some citizens, Howard Green, in a response to Mrs. Critchell's letter, echoed Professor Cohen's views: "I continue to believe, and I am sure that the majority of my fellow citizens must share my view, that the best hope for re-establishment of law and order in the Congo is through the efforts of the United Nations and that Canada is right to back up that endeavour to the utmost."[85]

Howard Green's expression of faith in the United Nations came at a time when that institution's ability to cope with the increasing complexity of the Congo crisis was beginning to be tested, and would in the months and years ahead be tested even more sorely. In ONUC's initial weeks, as Canadians began to deploy throughout the Congo, the seeds for future discord were being sown. Tshombé's separatist regime in Katanga was taking root, but the Belgians failed to find an overly sympathetic ear in Ottawa to listen to their complaints about the required withdrawal of their forces from the breakaway province or to their pleas to retain their military bases in the Congo. Publicly, Green was not unsupportive of Canada's NATO ally, but privately, both he and Norman Robertson expressed the view that Belgium's desires had to be weighed against the political difficulties that would be created if the former colonial power failed to cooperate with the United Nations. Canada's Cold War allegiances had to be balanced against desires not to alienate newly independent countries or to undermine their decolonization. This is not to suggest that Canadian policy during the Congo crisis was not also being influenced by Cold War politics. The Soviet attacks against Hammarskjöld over his decision to employ Canadians in ONUC are clear evidence of this, as is the secretary-general's subsequent decision to decline the Canadian government's offer of Caribou aircraft and aircrew in the wake of his difficulties with the Russians. Further evidence of the Cold War's impact can be seen in the hardening of views toward Patrice Lumumba following his decision to rely on Soviet assistance to carry out his offensive in Kasai and as a result of his response to the attacks on Canadian peacekeepers as they began to deploy throughout the Congo. Particularly in the case of the latter, though, the issue of race and ONUC's composition intersected with ideology. In any case, Lumumba's position and the Congolese political situation were about to take a turn for the worse.

# 4
# Constitutional Crisis: Peacekeeping in a Political Vacuum

Rajeshwar Dayal, a noted career Indian diplomat who had served as India's permanent representative to the UN in the early 1950s and Secretary-General Dag Hammarskjöld's representative in Lebanon, arrived in the Congo on 8 September to replace Andrew Cordier as head of the Opération des Nations Unies au Congo. Political confusion reigned. President Joseph Kasavubu and Prime Minister Patrice Lumumba had each dismissed the other, and attempts within the Congolese parliament to legitimize either leader's actions, or reach a compromise solution, proved futile. Dayal was faced with increasing accusations that the UN, because it closed the Leopoldville radio station and all airports, was biased in favour of Kasavubu. ONUC was in a difficult position. It was assumed that the UN mission would work in co-operation with the Congolese government, but, as one scholar notes, such a government ceased to exist on 5 September and the UN was then faced with a "governmental interregnum."[1] Perhaps in an attempt to improve the UN's relations with the Congolese, Dayal took action soon after his arrival to reopen the radio station and the airports to civilian traffic. These efforts were soon overtaken, however, by a coup orchestrated by the chief of staff of the Armée Nationale Congolaise (ANC), Colonel Joseph Mobutu.

Mobutu, still not quite thirty at the time of these events, was born in Equateur province. A smart but difficult student, he was educated for some time in a Catholic boarding school. He served in the Force Publique in the early 1950s, until he left to pursue a career as a journalist. After making his way to Belgium, he was soon running in the circles of the budding Congolese political elite then agitating for independence. While in Brussels, he befriended Patrice Lumumba; it was the Congolese prime minister who appointed Mobutu chief of staff after the mutiny of the Force Publique. Nonetheless, on the evening of 14 September, Mobutu announced by radio that the army was temporarily taking power. The rival Lumumba and Kasavubu governments, and Parliament, were effectively neutralized and replaced by a college of commissioners, consisting mostly of students and recent graduates appointed by Mobutu.

In reports of these events, William Wood, the Canadian consul general, said Dayal dealt firmly with Mobutu. In the days following the coup, the army harassed many of Lumumba's supporters in the African quarter of Leopoldville, until Dayal was said to have strongly protested, telling Mobutu "to control the Army or else." In addition, Dayal intervened to prevent Lumumba's arrest and resisted Mobutu's attempts to cloak his coup with the College of Commissioners. The colonel reportedly asked if the UN would recognize a government established and led by him. Dayal refused, unwilling "to let the UN act as midwife at the birth of a military dictatorship," but was left with little choice but to deal with the College of Commissioners on a de facto basis; it was made clear that this was not tantamount to official recognition.[2] Dayal's position strained relations between the UN and the United States and with the American ambassador to the Congo, Clare Timberlake, in particular. Although some in the State Department had misgivings about contradicting the UN position, US policy generally supported the Mobutu regime from the outset; the Central Intelligence Agency certainly played a significant role in prompting Mobutu to launch his coup.[3] This divergence in US and UN policy toward Mobutu was significant. In the months ahead, it seriously affected Dayal in his position as head of ONUC.

During the first week of September, the secretary-general's advisory committee considered an important question of principle facing ONUC, arising out of the Baluba massacres in South Kasai and Hammarskjöld's response. The secretary-general planned to send a letter to the Congolese authorities suggesting that he was sure the government would support the UN in any efforts to prevent such arbitrary acts of violence against civilians. Unless he heard otherwise from the Congolese, he would issue instructions to UN forces to take action to prevent such atrocities in future. While the white members of the committee remained silent, Guinea, Liberia, and Morocco were vocal in their opposition to Hammarskjöld's plans. They suggested the unfortunate events in Kasai were a result of the civil war. They expected that the secretary-general's proposed instructions to ONUC would be "extremely unpalatable" to the Congolese government. Instead, it was decided that Cordier would approach the Congolese authorities and discuss the matter informally. If their response was "not helpful," the issue was to be raised again in the Advisory Committee.

Although he remained silent at the meeting, it is clear the Canadian representative, Charles Ritchie, also had serious reservations about Hammarskjöld's plan to revise ONUC's instructions. He highlighted the terrible burden of judgment that would confront mission commanders as they contemplated how to implement such orders. Pointedly, he asked, "What criteria should be used to differentiate between action taken in pursuit of the civil war and those which are merely abhorrent on grounds of human rights and civilized conduct? What are the specific grounds on which a UN commander would be entitled to take such action which would involve the shooting of Congolese troops, from either side?" Ritchie was anxious for advice from Ottawa. Along with the other white representatives, he had remained silent during this meeting but speculated, "Continued abstention on our part, particularly in the type of debate which is expected at the next meeting, might well be questioned." He added, "Issues of principle and of wide implications for the future of UN operations in the Congo and elsewhere are now coming to the center of the debate." The Legal Division at External Affairs shared Ritchie's concerns. After reviewing the relevant UN resolutions, it maintained ONUC could not take "any forceful action which is in direct contravention of the express instructions of the recognized Congolese Government, nor [could it] take any steps to interfere in conflicts, armed or otherwise, between organized bodies." And, although the Legal Division acknowledged the Balubas' human rights had been violated, it did not believe this alone was grounds to alter ONUC's mandate without seeking further authority from the Security Council. Canada may not have shared the political objections of the African members of the committee, but clearly Hammarskjöld's views raised legal and practical concerns in both Ottawa and New York.[4]

### Canada's Contribution to ONUC
Initially, the Canadian government did not enthusiastically respond to the possibility of involvement in UN efforts to address the Congo crisis. However, once UN requirements were clarified and the government decided to participate in ONUC, National Defence and External Affairs recognized the significance of the peacekeeping mission and worked together to meet the UN's requests for assistance. Then, in mid-September, it seemed that National Defence began to have second thoughts. The deteriorating political conditions in the Congo raised concerns, but negative reports from Colonel Albert Mendelsohn's early reconnaissance mission and the trying experience with the Caribou aircraft also may have curtailed National Defence's willingness to either increase or maintain the Canadian presence in ONUC. Geoffrey Murray, of the UN Division at External Affairs, attended one of Mendelsohn's briefings and cautioned, "If Col. Mendelsohn has reported to his superiors in the same pessimistic and critical vein, we can expect the Canadian Army to be rather cool to additional requests from the United Nations for military assistance in the Congo." Mendelsohn warned that the Communist bloc nations were poised to assist Lumumba in seizing control of the Congo and cited the presence of Soviet aircraft in particular as evidence of this. His most venomous criticism was saved for the UN and ONUC itself. While he

complained about von Horn's "lack of firmness," this was scathingly attributed to political interference by authorities in New York. The commander's staff was deemed "woefully inefficient," and the colonel questioned their ability to conduct ONUC "even in the best of conditions." He complained "bitterly about the preference which was given to African members of the Force," even suggesting that Hammarskjöld "was not really happy about the inclusion of Canadians." Consequently, the Canadians, according to Mendelsohn, "had no part in the planning of operations in the Congo even those concerning the use of the signals detachment."[5]

Murray noted there were tensions over the role of the Canadian HQ unit in the Congo; its anomalous position meant that ONUC HQ often overlooked it, and this, Murray speculated, may have prejudiced Mendelsohn's views. Concerned this report would prompt National Defence to expect External Affairs to protest at the UN, Murray wrote to Charles Ritchie. He described Mendelsohn as a "highly emotional type who would make a better back room planner than a field commander" but warned, "The Canadian Army may be disposed to pay heed to Col. Mendelsohn's pessimistic report, because there seems to be considerable disappointment at [National Defence HQ] that Canada has not been given a more prominent part in the Congo operation." This latter statement is difficult to reconcile with the army's initial reluctance to part with Canadian service personnel but may also explain why Murray added, "This is not altogether the fault of the United Nations."[6]

Evidently, National Defence chose to raise its concerns in cabinet rather than at the UN. When cabinet considered the question of Canadians serving in ONUC on 14 September, George Pearkes, the minister of national defence said, "The condition of the Canadian troops in the Congo was far from satisfactory because they were apparently unwelcome both to the Congolese and to the personnel of the United Nations military organization there." Pearkes went so far as to suggest that Secretary of State for External Affairs Howard Green, while in New York at the upcoming session of the General Assembly, should raise with Hammarskjöld the possibility that the Canadians be "relieved by Asian or African signallers." Then, as the issue was discussed, Pearkes's concerns were set aside. Cabinet recalled the secretary-general's intent to assemble ONUC from a variety of nations to reflect the organization's universal character, and there was concern Canada could seem unwilling to meet the commitments made to the UN. In spite of the minister's misgivings, they were unwilling to pre-emptively end Canada's contribution to ONUC. Pearkes was offered some consolation: Green was instructed to raise once again the issue of the Caribou aircraft with Hammarskjöld.[7]

## Diplomacy in New York
The Security Council resumed consideration of the Congo crisis on 9 September, to review the fourth report of the secretary-general and to consider

how best to respond to the latest Congolese political turmoil. Hammar-skjöld's report urged the council to issue a request for funds, and in statements to the council he defended Cordier's decision to close both the radio station and airports. As telegrams arrived from the competing Congolese political factions, each announcing the dispatch of rival delegations to the UN, the council decided to adjourn until 14 September, but not before seating the Soviet deputy foreign minister, Valerian Zorin, who had arrived to replace Vasily Kuznetsov. When the council met on the 14th, Ritchie reported that Zorin delivered a "harsh, vituperative" attack on Hammarskjöld's conduct of ONUC. Zorin suggested, "UN command and the [secretary-general] personally from the very beginning had pursued a policy of interference" and was especially critical of Hammarskjöld's decision to recruit "so-called experts" from countries in the "western camp," including Canadian signals. The Soviets had already raised this issue with Hammarskjöld in August but had done so only half-heartedly. Now their tone changed. When Ritchie spoke with Zorin after the meeting to point out "the absurdity of stating that this small group of non-combatant troops could be described as a 'colonialist plot' of NATO," the Soviet representative bluntly criticized Canada's decision to send any troops to the Congo. The next day the American representative came to Canada's defence, ridiculing Soviet efforts to portray Canadian and Norwegian contributions to ONUC as NATO-inspired imperialist designs on Africa. He countered, "I believe rather that when African states recall the honourable and consistent attitude of [Canada] and Norway towards African problems they will prefer to draw other conclusions." Cold War politics were clearly at play. Both the Soviet and American delegations introduced draft resolutions. Ceylon and Tunisia responded with an Afro-Asian resolution that generally supported Hammarskjöld, his conduct of ONUC, and the recommendations contained within his fourth report. It did, however, encourage closer coordination between ONUC and the Congolese authorities. The resolution obtained eight affirmative votes but was vetoed by the Soviet Union.[8] The United States then proposed, and the Security Council concurred over Soviet objections, to convene an emergency session of the General Assembly using the Uniting for Peace Resolution.[9]

On 17 September the General Assembly was convened. The Soviet Union introduced a draft resolution embodying much of its criticism of ONUC and the secretary-general. Seventeen of the Afro-Asian nations also introduced a resolution based primarily on the vetoed version Ceylon and Tunisia had co-sponsored in the Security Council, effectively undermining the Soviet resolution. As a result, the Soviets did not press for a vote on their resolution, and the Afro-Asian resolution was adopted by a vote of seventy in favour, none against, and eleven abstentions.[10] Most agree this was a victory for Hammarskjöld and a vote of confidence in his handling of ONUC.[11] Ottawa's instructions to vote in favour of the seventeen-power resolution contained the first clear and succinct statement of Canadian policy on the Congo crisis: "The [Canadian government] has throughout the Congo crisis taken the view that the UN's presence represents the best hope of preserving stability and of preventing the Congo from becoming a cold war arena. We think the internal constitutional difficulties are a matter for the Congolese people to work out for themselves but they may need the help of the UN in doing so. Interference outside the framework of the UN is clearly to be deplored. In the prevailing confusion moreover there is every justification for the UN taking the measures necessary to keep the peace." These principles governed Canadian policy in the years ahead, but the government was reluctant to advocate its views vigorously. Ottawa thought it best if the Afro-Asian nations were the most vocal in the debate and saw no reason why Canada would intervene, unless it proved necessary to demonstrate full support for Hammarskjöld or to not seem conspicuously silent. External Affairs believed that Canada's contentious participation in ONUC was further reason to remain silent. Others could speak in defence of the secretary-general's inclusion of Canadians. The presence of Canadian forces in ONUC came to be a frequently cited justification for not overtly and openly advocating Canadian policy objectives. During this emergency session, however, Charles Ritchie felt compelled to speak. Aside from a veiled reference to the Soviets, whom he suggested had dangerously and selfishly interfered in the Congo, the statement was positive in tone and supported the seventeen-power resolution.[12]

The emergency session of the General Assembly was immediately followed by the fifteenth regular session. Cabinet issued instructions for the Canadian delegation, urging its members to be "alert to seize every opportunity that may be presented to encourage an improvement in the conduct of relations between Eastern and Western countries and to promote understanding between the latter and the countries of Asia and Africa."[13] Although the Congo situation was not originally on the agenda of this session, cabinet suggested the issues of financing ONUC and material support for the Congo should be raised, if the opportunity presented itself. These instructions demonstrate an inconsistency or contradiction in the Canadian position. On the one hand, Canada was clearly a member of NATO and a developed nation; yet the government perceived a role for Canada as a bridge between East and West, North and South. Through quiet diplomacy, it seems, Canada hoped to rise above its geopolitical position to facilitate communication between blocs of nations.

Unfortunately for Canada, the fifteenth session proved an unlikely stage on which to play the role of conciliator. Attended by thirty-two heads of government, including President Dwight Eisenhower, Premier Nikita Khrushchev, and Prime Minister John Diefenbaker, it quickly degenerated into a bitter exchange of Cold War accusations. Khrushchev was particularly vitriolic in his denunciations of Hammarskjöld and his conduct of ONUC, but the secretary-general's spirited defence of his actions and his office brought most delegations to their feet in a standing ovation. Diefenbaker's speech demonstrated the contradiction of presenting Canada as moderate and detached but also aligned with the West. By calling upon the Soviets to abandon their "colonies" in Eastern Europe, the prime minister left little doubt in the minds of delegates as to Canada's position in the Cold War.[14] In a subsequent meeting with Eisenhower and State Department officials who expressed "in very warm terms their appreciation of the Prime Minister's speech," Diefenbaker noted that Krishna Menon, the Indian representative, was said to have called the speech "a continuation of the cold war."[15] For the moment, Canada's position as ally took precedence over its aspiration to be a mediator.

## Developments in the Congo

In the Congo, a diplomatic episode of a different sort was taking place. Canadian ONUC officers and the consul general were anxious to explain to Ottawa their presence, and the events they witnessed, at a reception in honour of the second anniversary of the independence of Guinea, hosted by the commander of ONUC's Guinean contingent. Lieutenant Colonel Berthiaume and Group Captain Carr were seated at the head table and were surprised when, partway through lunch, Patrice Lumumba arrived. Following their host's speech, the two officers left, fearing Lumumba might make a speech and that their presence might prove embarrassing to the UN. Lumumba did address those at the luncheon and, according to the Canadian journalist Peter Worthington, said that his recent trip to Ottawa in search of bilateral aid left him disappointed to discover that Canada, while honest, "was just another imperialist country." The Canadian consul general, who was dining with the UK consul just outside the restaurant where the reception was held, denied Worthington's suggestion that he had gatecrashed the reception. Wood first speculated that Lumumba's critical remarks about Canada might have been prompted by the departure of the two Canadian officers but later reported that the walkout failed to evoke any comment.[16] Although relatively minor, this incident does suggest that Lumumba, by October, had come to view Canada as simply another Western nation.

The Canadian contingent was busy throughout September and October establishing new detachments, consolidating the signal squadron and headquarters unit, and addressing questions related to their command instructions, as originally issued by National Defence. In addition to continued support in the capital, Leopoldville, and the four outlying detachments already established, signal personnel were now sent to Kamina in Katanga, Gemena in Equateur, and Matadi in Leopoldville province. Because of the continued tense political situation facing the Stanleyville detachment in Orientale, and especially after the ill-treatment accorded the peacekeepers upon their arrival, the signal commanding officer considered their withdrawal. In the end, Capt. J.J.B. Pariseau, the detachment commander, convinced Major Bindoff that conditions had completely changed, mostly because of the departure of the ANC, the "stabilizing influence of Mobutu," and "the enforced departure of the Russians and the consequential cessation of rumour-mongering."[17] For the time being, the detachment stayed in the field.

On Colonel Mendelsohn's recommendation, National Defence decided to amalgamate Canadian HQ, ONUC with No. 57 Canadian Signal Squadron. The existing arrangement had two weaknesses: the headquarters unit had not been requested by the UN and, in Mendelsohn's view, was "not the best organization to look after Canadian interests"; the commanding officer of the headquarters unit was isolated from ONUC HQ, with "little or no access to staff planning likely to affect [Canadian] troops."[18] The new unit was redesignated 57th Canadian Signal Unit and was commanded by a lieutenant colonel in the Royal Canadian Corps of Signals. Col. P.D. Smith arrived in the Congo on 24 October to assume command from Colonel Mendelsohn, and the two units were officially amalgamated three days later.

Confusion soon arose over the Canadian command instructions related to their provisions for communication between the 57th Signal Unit and Canadian army headquarters. In mid-October, the Permanent Mission in New York received a letter Hammarskjöld wrote to each nation contributing forces to ONUC. He was concerned senior officers of military contingents in ONUC were communicating with their national governments prior to carrying out instructions from ONUC HQ. Cordier assured Ritchie that the letter was directed toward the African governments that had "taken a very forward position in relation to the activities of their contingents." Nevertheless, the Canadian command instructions clearly stipulated that "no limitation is placed on your [CO's] direct channel of communication on any matter with the Chief of the General Staff." External Affairs recognized this contradiction. After consultations with National Defence, it was decided to respond to Hammarskjöld by reminding the secretary-general that, following the precedent of UNEF, command instructions for Canadian commanders in ONUC were made available to him and to ONUC's supreme commander, Gen. Carl von Horn, and that the appropriate chain of command between Canadian forces in the Congo and the Canadian government would continue to be observed. In light of the secretary-general's concerns, instructions to Colonel Smith were clarified. He was explicitly told, "Provided an order is within the general conditions under which the force was assigned, and even though you may have appealed the order to the Supreme Commander, you should obey the order but you have the right of appealing direct and immediately to me for corrective action."[19] The army was determined to retain the right of its commanders to communicate with Canadian HQ about

ONUC orders but acknowledged the need first to obey the orders. Yet, the question of communication between the 57th HQ and army headquarters on matters other than questionable orders or routine administration remained ambiguous. ONUC operation directive No. 5, for instance, prohibited the transmission to national governments of any ONUC documents (such as situation reports) or information acquired in the course of peacekeepers' duties. Yet, the Canadian command instructions continued to state that there were no limitations on communication between the commanding officer and the chief of the general staff. The presence of detailed and abundant military intelligence on ONUC and the political situation in the Congo, within the files of National Defence and External Affairs, suggests that Canadian commanders, when communicating with army headquarters, more often followed their command instructions than ONUC directives.[20]

The possibility of Canadian involvement in the training of ANC officers arose again in early October. Mobutu approached a number of Western embassies to see if they would provide officer training, and Consul General Wood received phone calls seeking advice about military studies in Canada. The United Kingdom planned to take sixty candidates, but the UN prevented the first group of thirty-six from leaving because New York had not waived General Assembly Resolution 1474's prohibition against the provision of military assistance by parties other than the UN. The officers concerned were "bitterly disappointed," and Mobutu reacted "vigorously" to reports that the UN was considering the establishment of an officers' training school at Kamina in Katanga because he favoured sending the Congolese to foreign countries for training. Ottawa decided against bilateral involvement in Mobutu's ANC training scheme but remained open to the prospect of providing assistance if requested by the UN. Mobutu eventually circumvented UN opposition and sent this particular group of officers to Belgium.[21]

Relations between Mobutu and Dayal continued to deteriorate throughout the month. Wood's reports to Ottawa portray the secretary-general's new special representative as generally critical of the Congolese and biased in favour of Lumumba. According to Wood, Dayal "deplored criticism of UN by all factions and said he had never found it necessary to speak so bluntly as to Congo politicians." In addition, he was annoyed with the Congolese habit of describing people "as black or white." Orders were issued to all ONUC contingents to "identify people according to the continent or country of their origin," rather than their colour. Dayal was said to have also antagonized the Western embassies with his "pro-Lumumba" and "anti-Mobutu" attitudes. In Wood's view, both Dayal and the secretary-general's military adviser, Indar Jit Rikhye, had not been "very neutral in their dealings with Mobutu." This, it seemed to Wood, was attributable to the position of the Indian government, which favoured Lumumba. Wood reported, "From here looks as though Nkrumah and Nehru may have made a deal in [New York]."

The impact of the Cold War was clearly felt in Leopoldville; the East increasingly supported Lumumba, while those in the West supported Kasavubu and Mobutu. Perhaps it was not a coincidence that, aside from Wood, no NATO ambassadors and very few Congolese attended Dayal's UN day parade that October.[22]

## Diplomacy in New York

On 21 September, the Permanent Mission in New York received an urgent request from the secretary-general for contributions to a UN fund for the Congo, established in accordance with the General Assembly's recent resolution. Hammarskjöld was hopeful Canada would make a substantial contribution. While in New York for the fifteenth regular session of the General Assembly, Green and Diefenbaker discussed aid for the Congo. The prime minister later indicated, in his address to the assembly, that Canada would provide financial assistance but did not specify an amount. In Ottawa, Norman Robertson, undersecretary of state for external affairs, prepared a submission to cabinet proposing a contribution of $4 million, arguing, "Unless those countries with relatively strong economies are prepared to contribute an amount more than the equivalent of their share of the regular budget of the Organization, there is no hope of attaining the targets fixed for the programmes in question." Nevertheless, Green reduced the request to $1 million and raised the possibility of further contributions at a later date. This revision addressed the concerns of Donald Fleming, the minister of finance. Fleming was anxious for the contribution to be seen as equitable by the Commonwealth African states, which shared $3.5 million in Canadian aid. He was also concerned that Hammarskjöld's objectives for the fund went "well beyond the purview of normal responsibilities assumed in U.N. programmes." Cabinet approved a $1 million contribution in time to make an announcement at the General Assembly and agreed to keep "under active review" the option of an additional contribution, depending on "the manner in which the Fund was applied in the Congo, and the response of other states to the Secretary-General's appeal."[23]

In New York, Canada's awkward diplomatic position became increasingly apparent during the meetings of the secretary-general's advisory committee. Resolution 1474, approved by the emergency session of the General Assembly, appealed to the Congolese to settle their political differences with the assistance of a conciliation commission consisting of Afro-Asian nations on the Advisory Committee. External Affairs acknowledged the dire implications of continued turmoil in the Congo but wondered if UN intervention was wise given the "sharp criticism in recent weeks of the UN role in the Congo and of the Secretary-General." In keeping with its earlier position, Ottawa suggested, "There is much to be said for as far as possible leaving the Congolese to sort out their own difficulties." Canadian authorities favoured less formal mechanisms of intervention, such as fact-finding missions and roundtables. Ritchie was cautioned, "You no doubt agree that Canada should not take a very active part in the discussion of these delicate questions."[24]

It was early November before the Advisory Committee decided to proceed with the appointment of a formal conciliation commission and reached agreement on its composition: the African states contributing forces to ONUC, as well as four Asian nations that contributed sizeable infantry or administrative contingents. Canada's reluctance to encourage UN intervention in Congolese affairs soon seemed justified. When Dayal advised Kasavubu of the commission's appointment, the president refused to recognize it on the grounds that he had not been previously consulted as to its composition or terms of reference. In reality, Kasavubu disagreed with the primary purpose of the commission: to create conditions that would permit Parliament to be reconvened. Kasavubu's negative reaction divided the Advisory Committee. Some members – India, for instance – argued for the immediate dispatch of the commission regardless of Kasavubu's objections. Others, including Nigeria, favoured delay pending clarification of Kasavubu's position. Canada agreed with this more moderate position, but Ritchie thought it inadvisable "to enter into the discussion on these issues because support from the only NATO country on the [committee] might only embarrass the moderates." The Canadian representative worried that Hammarskjöld's insistence that this decision rested entirely with the Advisory Committee would ultimately require Canada to put its views on record. He warned, "To impose a body of this sort on the only legally-constituted authority with the right to speak for the Congo would create a questionable precedent." This view, subsequently endorsed by Ottawa, is revealing because it acknowledges Kasavubu as the legitimate authority in the Congo. This interpretation was shared by many Western nations and, without doubt, set Canada apart from the Eastern bloc and Afro-Asian nations that favoured Lumumba.[25]

### Canada and ONUC

In October, Douglas Harkness replaced George Pearkes as minister of national defence, after Diefenbaker appointed the latter to the position of lieutenant-governor of British Columbia. The new minister was keen to review the RCAF commitment to the UN. In the early days of ONUC, the government approved RCAF participation in the Pisa-Leopoldville airlift and in the transport of Canadian forces to the Congo. Following the initial deployment of ONUC and the signal personnel, the government agreed to an additional request from the secretary-general to continue RCAF participation in the airlift for ninety days. Flights specifically in support of the Canadian contingent were simply integrated into this airlift. The agreement with the UN was scheduled to expire on 9 December. Howard Green, who favoured continued involvement, wrote to Harkness: "This external airlift represents one way in which we can contribute to the United Nations activities in the Congo without an additional commitment of Canadian personnel and equipment in the Congo itself." Harkness was not entirely convinced. He advised Green that he had instructed the chief of the air staff to make inquiries at the UN to determine if it was possible to reduce the airlift by transporting more ONUC supplies by sea. National Defence's inquiries in New York simply resulted in an urgent request from the Secretariat to continue the airlift on its "present basis," with the added assurance "that a constant check will be maintained on the cargo carried and the continuing need, and you will be immediately notified if it is possible to reduce or discontinue these flights." In October, ONUC supplies were arriving in equal measure by air and sea, approximately forty tons a day. Air support was considered especially critical, given the limited transportation infrastructure throughout the Congo. In late November, Green reminded Harkness that a decision was required, and the airlift agreement was extended for another ninety days.[26]

Meanwhile, incidents in the Congo continued to demonstrate the dangerous and precarious position of the Canadians serving there. On 8 November, a patrol of Irish peacekeepers was inspecting a damaged bridge in northern Katanga when two hundred Baluba tribesmen ambushed it. Only two peacekeepers survived the hail of arrows. In his apology to the UN, the Baluba leader explained that his followers mistook the Irish for Belgians. Such an explanation was little comfort to Canadian authorities. In cabinet, Gordon Churchill, the minister for veterans' affairs, questioned the terms and conditions under which Canadian peacekeepers served in the Congo. He was sure the public would hold the government responsible if Canadian soldiers met a similar fate. With the Irish peacekeepers in mind, Diefenbaker assured his colleagues that the government had taken steps to ensure Canadians serving in ONUC could not be dispatched to isolated areas.[27]

Two weeks later, an incident in Leopoldville demonstrated that a posting to a headquarters location was not a guarantee of safety. In October, Kasavubu and Foreign Minister Justin Bomboko declared Nathaniel Welbeck, a Ghanaian diplomat in Leopoldville, *persona non grata*. In part, this was done to retaliate against Ghana's support at the United Nations of policies that favoured Lumumba. When Welbeck refused to leave, the Congolese decided to forcibly remove him. On 21 November, anticipating trouble, General Rikhye deployed 215 Tunisian peacekeepers to protect the Ghanaian embassy, and a Canadian, Major Bouffard, was sent by the ONUC Operations Section to investigate. Bouffard met with the Congolese outside the embassy and returned to ONUC HQ to report he was convinced the Congolese would resort to force if Welbeck did not leave on his own accord. Within hours of

Bouffard's visit, an ANC battalion surrounded the embassy, but ONUC HQ failed to take any additional action. That evening, violence erupted when the ANC confronted the Tunisians, who refused to hand over Welbeck. There was an exchange of fire between ONUC and ANC troops; a Tunisian lieutenant was injured and an ANC colonel was killed. The ANC, using armoured cars with 37mm guns, opened fire and hit the neighbouring Canadian officers' mess. The ANC were eventually persuaded to permit the Canadian officers to leave their mess for the Athenee Royal, where the other Canadian peacekeepers were quartered. In the confusion of night, it seemed to the Canadian consul as though even his residence was under fire. He reported that one ANC soldier not far from the residence garden "kept letting off a few rounds every five minutes for no apparent reason." In addition to the ANC colonel, one Tunisian peacekeeper was killed and six were wounded. Although there were no Canadian casualties, Lieutenant Colonel Berthiaume was detained by the ANC as he made his way to the embassy to investigate. He later said he entertained his captors, who at first threatened to shoot him, with stories of winter and snow in Canada until Mobutu arrived and ordered his release. The 57th Unit was not the direct target of these attacks, but this incident illustrated the volatility of conditions, even in urban centres, and the danger this posed to the Canadians. One group of concerned citizens was prompted to write to Diefenbaker to "*insist* that our loved ones be returned to us before they needlessly forfeit their lives in the Congo."[28]

In spite of these concerns and incidents, the government agreed to increase the size of the Canadian contingent by 50 peacekeepers. At 13 December, there were 239 army officers and other ranks and 22 RCAF personnel stationed in the Congo. Amalgamation of the headquarters unit with the signal squadron resulted in the need for an additional 34 personnel. Then, in mid-November, the UN requested 16 additional signal personnel. Despite the political difficulties Hammarskjöld had earlier faced by including Canadians in ONUC, Secretariat officials justified turning to Canada again because the personnel had to be bilingual and Canada already provided the established signal unit. The CGS consulted with Colonel Smith and decided that the alternatives to Canada providing additional peacekeepers were undesirable. Green, although in agreement with Harkness' recommendation, recalled that cabinet had rejected the last request for additional personnel and was of the view that this new request should be put to cabinet for a decision. Because Green left Ottawa without attending cabinet, this was left for Harkness to do. The minister of defence, however, appears to have approved this request on his own, as there is no record of cabinet discussing the matter.[29]

Canadian authorities were united in their opposition to the use of Canadian peacekeepers for espionage. In December, Brigadier Rikhye asked Colonel Smith for permission to send a Canadian provost NCO (non-commissioned officer) to Brazzaville to undertake an intelligence operation. ONUC was keen to investigate questionable shipments entering the Congo from Brazzaville. It planned to assign the peacekeeper to work with the World Health Organization "ostensibly as the UN movement control representative." The officer would be in a position to report on all movement of arms and ammunition through the airport. Smith, suggesting the assignment "amounted to espionage," raised numerous concerns with the plan and told Rikhye it would require government approval. Notably, when asked by Smith, Rikhye admitted the operation had not been discussed with Gen. Ben Hammou Kettani, the acting supreme commander. At National Defence, Lieutenant General Clark was against Canadian involvement. He argued, "This is a form of espionage which could make Canadian relations with the de facto [government] of the Congo Republic difficult ... Canadians could be accused of spying for NATO, USA." External Affairs took the matter one step further. Ritchie was instructed to bring Rikhye's plan to the attention of either Hammarskjöld or Bunche and to confirm that Canadian peacekeepers could not be used for spying. Moreover, the "propriety" of Brigadier Rikhye's approach was called into question. It is quite difficult to reconcile the proposed Brazzaville mission with Hammarskjöld's early pronouncements, in the Advisory Committee, against the "secretive practices habitually associated with intelligence services." In any event, once Canada refused to cooperate, the mission was cancelled for lack of suitable personnel.[30]

The command and leadership of ONUC was proving difficult. Von Horn was ill and on leave in Sweden. Colonel Smith reported that the supreme commander had been "at odds with the UN civilian heads and is not anxious to return to the Congo." New York was searching for a replacement, likely from Ireland or Ethiopia. Von Horn's departure, according to Smith, raised questions about Lieutenant Colonel Berthiaume's future at ONUC HQ. Berthiaume first served as the supreme commander's chief of staff, and later as his military assistant. Smith observed, "[Berthiaume] is one of the few people in the UN whom the Congolese trust and he exerts an influence out of proportion to his appointment. It is unlikely that Berthiaume will be able to continue to function in the same manner under a new commander." It is clear that Berthiaume found it difficult to work with Rikhye and many of the other Indian officers who served at ONUC HQ. As early as September, Rikhye suggested to Colonel Speedie, National Defence's liaison officer in New York, that it might be necessary to replace Berthiaume. When asked why, Rikhye said Berthiaume was not bilingual. Rikhye "professed surprise and had no further comments" once Speedie pointed out Berthiaume was French Canadian and completely bilingual.[31]

As Colonel Smith predicted, tensions surrounding the Canadian peacekeeper resurfaced in December and January as the UN prepared to replace von Horn with Gen. Sean MacEoin, the new commander of ONUC. National

Defence agreed to second Berthiaume to UNTSO for two weeks so he could assist von Horn with the preparation of the commander's final report. They then expected Berthiaume to return to the Congo to complete his tour and perhaps take up a position on the new commander's staff. At first, MacEoin seems to have favoured retaining Berthiaume. In a cable to Bunche, albeit written by Berthiaume, the commander stated, "Would appreciate your reconsideration decision so as to allow me to benefit from services Berthiaume can render due to his considerable experience and intimate knowledge of Congo operations." Perhaps sensing the UN might be unwilling to retain Berthiaume, External Affairs advised the Canadian Permanent Mission in New York to make representations in the Secretariat to at least replace the officer with another Canadian. Ottawa wanted a Canadian and Western presence in ONUC HQ. Cordier was approached and reassured Ritchie that ONUC HQ had been contacted about this; he was awaiting a reply. By February, the situation was not resolved. It was worse: Ritchie advised, "The Secretariat was taking it for granted that Col. Berthiaume would not return to ONUC." Colonel Smith reported that MacEoin had decided to use an Irish officer as his military assistant. He no longer intended to ask for a replacement for Berthiaume. Smith warned that this would seriously weaken the Canadian position at ONUC HQ, as there would no longer be an officer present who could influence policy.[32]

It is difficult to know with certainty why the UN appeared so keen to get Berthiaume out of the Congo. Tension with his fellow officers may have been one significant factor. An official at External Affairs noted, "It is quite possible that Berthiaume is not popular with the Indians, who hold most of the positions on the staff of the Supreme Commander, and with a number of the African-Asian participants in ONUC." In recognition of this, Canadian diplomats in New York were directed not to discuss the matter with Rikhye. In a memo, Berthiaume was very critical of the conduct of his Indian colleagues, Rikhye in particular:

> From shortly after the arrival of Brigadier Rikhye to the Congo in August 1960, there was a systematic policy on the part of ONUC officials to ignore the military and not to seek the advice of the Supreme Commander and his Senior Staff Officers. Military matters were being run by Brigadier Rikhye who dealt only with Indian officers and in many occasions usurped the authority of the Supreme Commander. From that time on, the undersigned had to devise his own ways and means of finding out ONUC civilian policy ...
>
> In the same manner, Brigadier Rikhye would take it upon himself to issue direct orders to the troops without previous reference to the Supreme Commander, his Deputy or the Chief of Staff. The feelings amongst ONUC personnel, military and civilians alike, were that the Indian coterie were

running the whole show and had no intention of allowing other nationals to interfere.

Berthiaume was convinced that Dayal and Rikhye were behind the decision to deny his reappointment at ONUC HQ. Dayal, in classified messages to New York, was said to have expressed a "firm desire" to get "rid of someone who was but too familiar with unethical activities on the part of certain UN officials, including himself and Brigadier Rikhye." Although he did not cite specific incidents, Berthiaume accused Dayal and Rikhye of attempting to discredit Kasavubu, Mobutu, and any other Congolese leader who leaned toward the West, while favouring Patrice Lumumba, Antoine Gizenga, and others who opposed Kasavubu.[33]

Berthiaume's close relationship with Mobutu may have been a factor in New York's decision not to reappoint him as MacEoin's military assistant. While working at ONUC HQ, Berthiaume fostered relationships with many Congolese. He later wrote, "Through meetings and discussions, contacts and relations were established with Congolese leaders, civilians and military alike. As time went on, these relations changed from a business to a friendly and personal basis." Indeed, even a story appearing in the *Montreal Gazette* announcing the end of Berthiaume's tour of duty in the Congo noted the many "friends and acquaintances" the Canadian peacekeeper had made there. "To the Congolese," the newspaper reported, "he was 'Papa' Berthiaume." In the end, though, the particularly strong relationship Berthiaume cultivated with Mobutu left him open to charges of being biased, akin to those he directed toward Rikhye and Dayal. External Affairs was aware that Berthiaume was "sympathetic to the aims, if not always the methods, of the Kasavubu-Mobutu elements in the Congo." At times, the relationship proved useful. Following the Welbeck incident, for example, Berthiaume was able to use his influence with Mobutu to smooth the very strained relations between ONUC and the ANC. There is evidence, however, that Berthiaume gravely crossed the line of impartiality and neutrality expected of all peacekeepers. In an interview with Pauline Dumont-Bayliss, of the Directorate of History and Heritage at National Defence, Berthiaume admitted to playing a role in Mobutu's capture of Patrice Lumumba. Berthiaume tracked the prime minister as he fled Leopoldville for Orientale province and then informed Mobutu of Lumumba's whereabouts. If Rikhye or Dayal were aware of Berthiaume's participation in this plot, they seem not to have said anything to the Canadian authorities, but it would help to explain their reticence to agree to the reappointment. In March 1961, reports questioning Berthiaume's role in ONUC arrived in Ottawa from Ghana. Officials at External Affairs considered it very difficult to know the extent to which Berthiaume had given advice to Mobutu and whether or not this would have been beyond his UN mandate.

They concluded, "In the absence of any adverse reports from either the former or the present U.N. Commander, we can only assume that he acted in accordance with his instructions ... I would suggest that we let the matter rest." Even if Berthiaume cooperated with Mobutu out of frustration, to counter the political bias of Dayal and Rikhye, the implications of Lumumba's arrest hardly justified his actions but might explain the controversy over a continued position at ONUC HQ.[34]

### Political Developments in the Congo

As 1960 drew to a close, it was increasingly apparent that the Congo was a divided country. Apart from the obvious separation caused by the Katangan secession, there were significant political divisions within and between the remaining provinces. Three figures continued to be central to the national political crisis: Lumumba, Kasavubu, and Mobutu. Although Mobutu, by establishing the College of Commissioners, professed to neutralize both politicians, in reality he maintained a working relationship with Kasavubu. The president, for instance, was willing to recognize the college as the provisional government of the Congo. Kasavubu had the geographic advantage of Leopoldville province as his political stronghold. As president, and consequently head of state, Kasavubu also had the advantage of title. He could, with some credibility, justify his decision to attend the upcoming session of the General Assembly as the Congo's rightful representative. His colleague, Justin Bomboko, argued, "[the] President has as much right to attend assembly as Nkrumah, Sekou Toure, Nasser and other African heads of state." Wood, the Canadian consul general in Leopoldville, provided External Affairs with the following assessment: "Kasavubu's position has improved, thanks to the prestige attached to the chief of state and he probably now has more following outside [Leopoldville] than at independence. But he is still far from being a traditional 'strong man' (and he does not seem to have the personality or inclination to become one)."[35] By the time the General Assembly met for its regular session, Kasavubu was clearly the political candidate favoured by the West.

Wood had the opportunity to meet with Mobutu in November. Presumably for his safety, the ANC commander had moved to the outskirts of Leopoldville. Wood had to pass two barbed-wire roadblocks and armoured cars, and was then subjected to a search before being escorted to Mobutu's house. Once inside, Mobutu greeted Wood as he concluded negotiations with a "well-nourished European woman" for newer, larger accommodations. Mobutu denied widespread accusations that he was pro-Belgian, but Wood deduced from the presence of several Belgian publications in the room where he awaited his meeting that he was not anti-Belgian. The colonel maintained that "foreign interference should stop and that the Congolese should be left alone to settle their own problems." The Canadian consul was "generally impressed" by Mobutu. He perceived him to be a "man of intelligence and some sophistication." As with Kasavubu, he concluded that Mobutu was not a "strong man," nor a "military man," and he speculated the colonel might have "difficulty in maintaining the support of the army against stronger rivals, either military or political." Mobutu also faced a significant obstacle: the United Nations, although prepared to work with him because he exercised de facto control, was unwilling to recognize either the colonel or his appointees as a legitimate government.[36]

For both Kasavubu and Mobutu, Patrice Lumumba remained a political force to be reckoned with. Wood noted that only Lumumba could lay claim to being a "national leader." Favoured by the East and a number of the Afro-Asian nations (notably Ghana and Guinea), Lumumba retained Orientale province as a political stronghold. As earlier noted, his actions soon after ONUC's arrival, particularly his acceptance of bilateral Soviet aid, alienated him from both UN officials and the West. Wood acknowledged that Lumumba had been labelled "a Communist, a mad man, a dope addict and a drunkard," but stated, "I do not believe he is any of these things (although there may be a grain of truth in each of them)." The Canadian consul general captured, quite succinctly and in a balanced, realistic manner atypical of many Western diplomats, the fundamental problem the Congo faced: "Lumumba, in my view, is still a major force despite the humiliations he has suffered ... therefore, the dilemma facing the Congo is that the one man most qualified to be Prime Minister is unacceptable to the two most important areas of the country, Léopoldville and the mining region of Katanga." The political instability, compounded by Mobutu's ensuing coup, ultimately hurt Lumumba the most. It also led Rikhye to conclude that "despite efforts to avoid it[,] cold war was actually operating in Congo."[37]

## Diplomacy in New York

The Cold War was operating in New York, too, as the United Nations considered which Congolese delegation, Lumumba's or Kasavubu's, should be seated as the legitimate representatives of that country. The United States led efforts to seat Kasavubu. In Ottawa, the American embassy lobbied External Affairs to support its position in the General Assembly. In New York, Ritchie met with representatives of Australia, Belgium, France, the Netherlands, Norway, the United Kingdom, and the United States to discuss "tactics for dealing with the Kasavubu credentials." The Americans had every reason to believe Canada would support their view. In his meeting with Eisenhower, just one month earlier, Diefenbaker had expressed his view that Kasavubu had the stronger claim for recognition. Although Canada willingly revealed its preference for Kasavubu in private, Howard Green instructed Ritchie not to engage with efforts to seat Kasavubu's delegation. The UN Division outlined the Canadian position: "Especially if the African-Asians, as a group, should be ranged against the West in this matter, Canada should abstain. Our position on the United Nations force in the Congo made this desirable and also our general position in relation to the African and Asian countries. If it turned out that the Africans were divided on the issue, there might be some reason for altering the Canadian stand but for the time being the Canadian delegation should not be drawn into partisan discussions about tactics and should be prepared to abstain in any voting on the credentials." As was the case with the Advisory Committee, Canada considered that its presence in ONUC made it desirable to refrain from active participation in the debate. The rationale was, in this instance, expanded further to include the preservation of good relations with the Afro-Asian nations. Canada intended to maintain a public image as a more moderate state, while others fought to seat the Kasavubu delegation, an outcome it privately preferred.[38]

The United States began its efforts to accredit the Kasavubu delegation in the Credentials Committee, but procedural wrangling kept the committee from considering the issue. Then, in the General Assembly, the Afro-Asian nations moved to adjourn the debate, fearing an eventual decision in the Credentials Committee might require the assembly to approve the recognition of Kasavubu's delegation. Many did not support Kasavubu, but they were equally reluctant to vote against him openly. Over American objections, and in spite of their attempts to forestall it, the assembly was adjourned. Publicly, Canada did not support the United States; the delegation abstained in the vote to adjourn so that it would not appear as though Canada was taking sides. The matter then returned to the Credentials Committee, which finally decided to accredit Kasavubu's delegation. Bolstered by French and British attempts to lobby their former colonies, the Americans became convinced they could obtain a majority in favour of accepting the committee's report if only there were no further attempts to adjourn debate in the assembly. In Washington, State Department officials called on the Canadian embassy and asked for support of their efforts to continue the Congo debate. In Ottawa, Green was given a US *aide-mémoire* that expressed the hope that "the Government of Canada shares [the American] view of the gravity and urgency of the issue and will see its way clear to instruct its delegation to vote against any postponement of consideration of the matter and to support the seating of the Kasavubu delegation." Similar representations were made by the United Kingdom, but pressure from allies had to be balanced against Canada's role in ONUC and the Advisory Committee. The UN Division presumed that Canada would not want to vote against the Kasavubu delegation but worried that a vote for the Congolese president would be construed as taking sides in an internal dispute. Canada would look particularly bad if it was the only member of the Advisory Committee to vote in favour of the Credentials Committee's report. Surely this would be seen as support for a NATO ally and the West more generally. It would not be wise, it was suggested, to line up "with pro-Western elements only, and especially if they are in danger of being defeated." The delegation in New York favoured accepting Kasavubu's credentials but only if it appeared as though the recommendation would be adopted anyway. Canadian policy attempted to strike a balance: there was a need to appear neutral or detached and, at the same time, not jeopardize Western interests in the Congo.[39]

On the evening of 17 November, Green instructed Ritchie to abstain on the adjournment issue. The minister continued to weigh the option of abstaining on the vote to accept Kasavubu's credentials. On the latter issue, he planned to consider the positions adopted by Ireland and Sweden, the other two nations with white contingents in the Congo. The next day, both issues came to a vote in the General Assembly and, after last-minute consultations with Ritchie, Green instructed the delegation to abstain on the motions to adjourn the debate and to seat Kasavubu. Ross Campbell, special assistant to the minister, in explaining Green's decision to Robertson, acknowledged that Canada wanted the Kasavubu delegation seated; because a Canadian vote was not needed for the motion to pass, however, it was considered illogical not to abstain. The key factors leading to this decision were the need to avoid taking sides to protect the welfare of Canadian personnel in the Congo, a desire to avoid isolation in the Advisory Committee, and concern over the appearance of participating in a manoeuvre orchestrated by Belgium and the United States. All members of the Advisory Committee were expected to vote for adjournment, with the exception of Pakistan, which planned to abstain. Had Canada voted against adjournment, it would have been the only member of the Advisory Committee to do so. Sweden and Ireland both abstained on the question of Kasavubu's credentials. In the end, the Congolese president's delegation was seated by a vote of fifty-three in favour, to twenty-four against, and nineteen abstentions.[40] Without doubt, Canada preferred this outcome; it was simply not prepared to sacrifice the appearance of neutrality to achieve it. Persistent pressure by the West swayed a sufficient number of countries to vote for Kasavubu so that Canada's vote was not critical. Still, the Canadian consul general in Leopoldville was left in the awkward position of explaining the Canadian vote to the Congolese Foreign Office. Officials there seemed satisfied with Wood's explanation and assurances that "we were well aware in any case that [Kasavubu's delegation] would be seated without our vote." He later reported being seated ahead of other members of the consular corps at a dinner hosted by the president. This was interpreted to mean Canada was not yet in the doghouse.[41]

From the earliest days of ONUC, Canadian officials were determined to see the mission's financing established on a sound footing. They did not want the UN to resort to a "succession of *ad hoc* measures," as had been the case with UNEF financing. Peter Bishop identifies three principles that guided Canadian financial policy on peacekeeping: frugality, fair share, and universal/compulsory payment for all operations. Because several nations, notably those from the Soviet bloc and France, subsequently refused, for political reasons, to pay their share of UNEF's expenses, Canada considered it vital for the General Assembly to "put itself on record as affirming the collective responsibility of the membership for the Congo operation." The Canadian principle of frugality, Bishop notes, was more "elastic" than that of compulsory payment; even when they threatened to dwarf the entire UN regular budget, peacekeeping costs were seen as a necessary, reasonable price to pay for the preservation of peace. And ONUC was expected to be expensive: the Secretariat estimated the total costs for the first six months of ONUC could reach $66,625,000, and this sum was distinct from the $100,000,000 voluntary fund established by Hammarskjöld to restore the economic life of the Congo.[42]

In contrast with its timid manner on the Advisory Committee, Canada was quite vocal on the issue of financing, using its presence on the General Assembly's Fifth (Budgetary) Committee to stress not only the financial but also the political significance of peacekeeping activities. In a statement to the committee, the Canadian delegation argued adequate financial support for ONUC was a political question that transcended "differences of national interest" and struck at "the heart of the reason for the existence of the UN." Highlighting the inability of the Great Powers to fulfill their peace and security responsibilities as originally envisaged in the UN Charter, the Canadians suggested these responsibilities had shifted to the middle and small powers that largely shouldered the burden of providing personnel, equipment, and facilities. The delegation was critical of those who refused to pay their share of peacekeeping costs but, in an effort to meet the concerns of poorer nations, acknowledged the need to reduce expected contributions from states that simply could not afford to pay. "A sharp distinction," delegation members said, "must be drawn between those who can support these peace-keeping operations fully but who will not; and those who wish to support them fully but cannot." Canada recognized the need to compromise with the lesser-developed UN members in order to gain support for efforts to normalize the procurement of funds to cover peacekeeping expenses.[43]

Canada's arguments became all the more credible when the government backed its pronouncements with additional funds. The initial transport of contingents and equipment to the Congo cost US$14 million. The vast majority of this, $12 million, was initially borne by the United States. In response to a request from the secretary-general, the Americans subsequently agreed to waive these costs. The airlift of Canadian forces cost Cdn$600,000. Diefenbaker, Green, and Harkness recommended to cabinet that Canada do likewise and absorb these costs instead of passing them on to the UN. "This year," it was argued, "when the Organization is facing its severest test since the Korean War, it is particularly necessary that those countries [that] are in a position to do so ... assist the United Nations in every way possible so that lack of the means does not become an impediment to the discharge of the essential peace-keeping functions of the Organization." Although the minister of finance had reservations, Diefenbaker was "now satisfied with the fairness and necessity of this operation." Cabinet agreed to absorb the costs of the initial airlift and the delegation in New York was so informed. The United Kingdom also agreed to absorb US$500,000 in transportation costs but awaited Canada's decision so as not to be the only country, apart from the United States, to make such a gesture.[44]

## Patrice Lumumba's Arrest

Events in the Congo took a serious turn for the worse just as President Kasavubu returned triumphant from New York. Patrice Lumumba remained in Leopoldville, his residence surrounded by two concentric circles: the first a guard of UN peacekeepers who prevented his arrest by ANC forces, the second a ring of ANC soldiers who surrounded the peacekeepers. On the evening of 27 November, Lumumba and some of his supporters left his residence and managed to sneak past the ANC. They headed for Stanleyville, the capital of Orientale province, Lumumba's political stronghold. When the Leopoldville authorities discovered he was missing, they began to search for him with the help of a low-flying airplane, thought to have come from Brazzaville.

Catherine Hoskyns reports ONUC peacekeepers "all over the Congo were given orders 'to refrain from any interference in regard to Mr Lumumba's movements or those of his official pursuers.'"[45] As revealed earlier, however, von Horn's military assistant, Canadian lieutenant colonel J. Berthiaume, has said he assisted Mobutu in the efforts to locate Lumumba. In a September 1990 interview, Berthiaume stated,

> Alors, de toute façon là j'ai le choix. Qu'est-ce que je fais. Puis là j'ai appelé Mobutu. J'ai dit: "Mon colonel, vous avez un problème quoi, vous cherchez à récupérer votre prisonnier, Monsieur Lumumba. Je sais où il est et je sais où il sera demain. Mais il dit qu'est-ce que je peux faire. Mais c'est bien simple, mon colonel, vous venez avec l'aide des Nations-Unies de créer l'embryon de vos para-commandos on venait de qualifier une trentaine de ces gars, triés sur le volet des marocains entraînés comme parachutiste là puis qui ont sauté puis il n'y en a pas un qui a refusé. Puis pour être bien sûr de mon affaire j'avais même mis notre capitaine Mario Côté dans l'avion, pour être bien sûr qu'il n'y avait pas de tripotage. En tout cas, mais c'est bien simple vous prenez un Dakota vous envoyez vos parachutistes puis vous allez cueillir Monsieur Lumumba dans le petit village là, il ya une piste

puis tout le bazar. C'est tout ce que vous avez à faire mon colonel." Il l'a récupéré comme cela puis je l'ai jamais regretté moi.

[So, I have a choice. What do I do? Then, I called Mobutu. I said, "Colonel, you have a problem, you are trying to retrieve your prisoner, Mr. Lumumba. I know where he is, and I know where he will be tomorrow. He said, what do I do? It's simple, Colonel, with the help of the UN you have just created the core of your para-commandos – we have just trained thirty of these guys – highly selected Moroccans trained as paratroopers. They all jumped – no one refused. To be on the safe side, I put our captain, Mario Côté, in the plane, to make sure there was no underhandedness. In any case, it's simple, you take a Dakota, send your paratroopers and arrest Lumumba in that small village – there is a runway and all that is needed. That's all you need to do, Colonel." He arrested him, like that, and I never regretted it.][46]

Berthiaume considered this intervention justified, believing it prevented Lumumba from rallying political and military support in Orientale and a full-scale civil war. The immediate results of Lumumba's arrest were, however, a dangerous deterioration in the political conditions in Orientale and a new round of diplomatic hostilities in New York.

Ghanaian peacekeepers, stationed in Kasai close to where Lumumba was arrested, requested permission to intervene and to place the prime minister under UN protection. The Secretariat denied this request.[47] Hammarskjöld subsequently argued against similar Soviet and Afro-Asian demands for UN action to obtain Lumumba's release on the grounds that this would "constitute a measure of internal intervention unauthorized by the existing U.N. resolutions." In the secretary-general's view, ONUC's enabling resolutions did not authorize enforcement action under Chapter 7 of the charter, so the UN had no legal authority to intervene in the domestic affairs of the Congo.[48]

In Stanleyville, Lumumba's supporters threatened to arrest and kill all Belgians if Lumumba was not released within forty-eight hours. Officials at External Affairs feared Lumumba's forces would not distinguish between Belgians and other Europeans. In addition to the nine Canadian peacekeepers stationed in Stanleyville, some twenty Canadian missionaries were thought to be living throughout Orientale. The Canadian detachment in Stanleyville warned that the provincial authorities intended to force all white personnel, including the Canadians, to leave the Congo. ONUC personnel were also told not to interfere with any arrests of Europeans. Together, this was sufficient cause for concern in Ottawa. Howard Green instructed Charles Ritchie to speak with the Secretariat to seek assurances that adequate transportation would be available to evacuate those UN units that found themselves heavily outnumbered by opposing forces. Green added a notable caution: he asked Ritchie to ensure that this *"demarche"* would not "leave any impression that [Canada] is contemplating withdrawal of [Canadian] units or would advocate any general withdrawal of UN forces."[49]

Although Canada was not in favour of a general withdrawal of ONUC, Cordier secretly told Ritchie the UN was in fact contemplating the evacuation of its peacekeepers in the Congo. Cordier was deeply pessimistic. Antoine Gizenga, Lumumba's deputy prime minister, had just declared the provisional installation of the central government in Stanleyville, in opposition to the College of Commissioners in Leopoldville.[50] It seemed possible that ONUC contingents from nations aligned with Lumumba might rally to the side of Stanleyville, and this could prompt the Indonesians and Ethiopians to withdraw their troops altogether. Cordier was concerned for the impact this would have on the UN as a whole. The Secretariat planned to tentatively approach the United States to ask for planes to be placed on standby in case it became necessary to evacuate UN peacekeepers. Ritchie was warned that Canada might also be approached with a similar request.[51]

Lumumba's arrest prompted some Canadians to write to Diefenbaker, and to the UN, expressing their concern. One resident of North Bay was less concerned for Lumumba's personal safety than for the potential repercussions if the Congolese prime minister died: "Lumumba's death in prison will make him a martyr of African nationalism and rallying point of all anti Western feelings on that continent please try to intervene and save his life. Alive Lumumba might be difficult, but a dead Lumumba will be impossible." Others, including the Congress of Canadian Women, supported the imprisoned leader, arguing, "The only way to bring peace to the Congo is to give support to the elected representatives of the people." Finally, Alicia Humphries was very critical of Diefenbaker for not doing more to help Lumumba. She wrote, "This time the U.S.A. has gone just too far. She has placed upon herself a stain of blood that Time can never erase and Lumumba will be remembered in history, a hero and a martyr, as great as any of our Canadian martyrs. And YOU did not say one word in protest. Coward, sneak, slave of corruption, stooge of the U.S.A." The Congolese prime minister's arrest did not go unnoticed by Canadian media, either. Both the *Montreal Gazette* and the *Toronto Daily Star* ran editorials encouraging the Congolese authorities to treat Lumumba with caution and sympathy. Although the *Gazette* labelled Lumumba a troublemaker, its editorial expressed concern that divergent and conflicting international reactions to any trial might further escalate tensions. The *Star* went further, suggesting Secretary-General Hammarskjöld should continue efforts to build a coalition government in the Congo, "in which Lumumba would sit at the same table with the men who oppose him, President Kasavubu and Col. Mobutu."[52]

Against the backdrop of the increased political tension resulting from Lumumba's arrest, discussion of the Congo crisis resumed in New York, first in the Security Council and then in the General Assembly. The seriousness of the situation, combined with the possibility Canada might need to declare its position during the forthcoming debate, prompted External Affairs to review its Congo policy. Despite recent events, Ottawa perceived, and welcomed, a general trend toward stability in the Congo "occasioned by the ascendancy of Kasavubu and Mobutu" but was concerned that the Congolese authorities had fallen out with the UN. The preference for Mobutu and Kasavubu was a not-so-subtle indication of Canada's political position; the Western bloc tended to favour both these leaders. However, conflict between the UN on the one hand and Mobutu and Kasavubu on the other was problematic for Canada because it became increasingly difficult to balance support for the United Nations with tacit support for the de facto Leopoldville government. Officials noted, "While we are concerned to maintain UN prestige, it is also recalled that we supported the UN action with the object of maintaining peace and security and, by the same token, forestalling communist intervention." Canada was committed to the United Nations and multilateral diplomacy but also hoped for an outcome to the crisis favourable to Western interests. Ottawa was even critical of Belgian policy when it was seen to threaten wider Western objectives. Robertson, for example, criticized Belgium's insistence on its right to provide unilateral assistance to whichever Congolese authority it chose, including the secessionist regime in Katanga. Such a policy, he believed, constituted "an open invitation to the Communist powers to intervene whenever they may wish to do so." Canadian policy became increasingly complex as it attempted to reconcile these varied, sometimes contradictory, objectives.[53]

One concern remained foremost in the minds of Canadian officials: the safety of Canadian peacekeepers serving in ONUC. As the Lumumbists became entrenched at Stanleyville, Charles Ritchie warned, "Unless relations can be improved between the Congolese [government] and the UN forces, there is a continuing danger that UN forces including the [Canadians] may be exposed to physical danger, and if control of the airports is lost, to the possibility of being trapped in different areas of the Congo." Ritchie was more explicit and pragmatic in his telephone conversations with department officials. The Canadian representative was anxious to do something "for the record," in case "everything went wrong in the Congo, and there was a massacre which included Canadians." He added, "The Government and the Department would be called upon to say what if anything they had done to ensure the safety of our troops." Ritchie suggested raising the matter either directly with the Secretariat or in the Advisory Committee so that Canadian concerns "would be on the record and could be cited if someone asked why Canada was not speaking up, or if it became necessary after a catastrophe to say what we had done." Within the week, Ritchie had an opportunity to speak with Hammarskjöld to express the government's concern for the security of UN forces and the Canadian contingent in particular. He found the secretary-general to be less pessimistic than his assistant, Cordier. Hammarskjöld did not consider it necessary to evacuate ONUC yet but was concerned for the long-term prospects of a political solution to the Congo crisis.[54]

From 7 to 13 December, the Security Council once again addressed the Congo situation. Two draft resolutions were introduced: a Soviet-sponsored resolution called for Lumumba's release, disarming Mobutu's forces, and the expulsion of all Belgians; the second, sponsored by the United States, the United Kingdom, Italy, and Argentina, called for the fair treatment of political prisoners but not the release of Lumumba. Ceylon and Tunisia attempted to draft a compromise resolution to bridge the differences between the East and West, but they were unsuccessful. When the Soviets vetoed the West's resolution and the Soviet resolution failed to receive the minimum number of votes, the debate was transferred to the General Assembly.[55]

Geoffrey Murray, head of the UN Division at External Affairs, hoped the West would take a constructive and conciliatory tone in the resumed debate in the General Assembly. He thought the best approach would be for the Western powers to reassure African-Asian members that the West's key interest was the stability of the Congo. Murray cautioned, "If the debate should be a confused combination of cold war propaganda and a sharp argument between the extreme African-Asian nationalists and the 'imperialists' of the West, the Western Powers are likely to suffer heavily." Conciliation was not meant to be. Eight Afro-Asian states took the initiative and introduced a draft resolution that called for the UN to be more forceful in its implementation of previous resolutions, the release of political prisoners, the reconvening of the Congolese parliament, disarmament of Congolese armed factions, and the immediate withdrawal of all Belgian military and civilian advisers. The Americans interpreted this resolution as an attempt to create conditions that would facilitate Lumumba's return to power. The United States lobbied Canada, both in Washington and Ottawa, to oppose the eight-power resolution. American diplomats suggested the proposal was "a very serious threat to Western interests not only in the Congo but in the whole of Africa." In their view, it was imperative to defeat the resolution. Canada was asked to oppose any propositions that would undermine Kasavubu and to support efforts to postpone the debate all together. The UN Division, Charles Ritchie, and Norman Robertson were agreed in their opposition to the American idea to delay the debate. "The present drift in the Congo situation," it was argued, "could hardly be allowed to continue for three months without some United Nations action, unless we were prepared to contemplate a complete erosion of the United Nations position there." At a minimum, they hoped for a resolution that would call upon all political and military forces in the Congo to cooperate with the UN; authorize steps to restore law, order, and constitutional authority, including the recall of

Parliament; and renew the injunction against bilateral intervention by the Soviets, Belgium, or any neighbouring African state. Canada continued to be less strident than its ally in advocating a wholly Western Congo policy. In fact, Charles Ritchie believed it would be very difficult for Canada, given its participation in the Advisory Committee and ONUC, to follow "the straight NATO line."[56]

The Western view came to be embodied in a resolution sponsored by the United States and the United Kingdom. External Affairs considered the text to be unexceptionable but did not expect it to receive the required two-thirds support from the assembly because it did not include a call to release Lumumba, a provision Canadian officials assumed was the main objective of the eight-power resolution. Diefenbaker instructed the Canadian delegation to vote in favour of the Western resolution, but in order to compromise with the Afro-Asians, the delegation was also advised not to oppose any "African-Asian move to have the text amended to call for the freeing of political prisoners." This was an important departure from American policy, which was clearly against any proposition to release Lumumba. Canada distanced itself from the firm Western position when it declined American and British requests to co-sponsor the Western resolution, ostensibly because of Canadian participation in ONUC. Further evidence of Canada's effort to distance itself from a perceived NATO line can be found in the weight Ottawa gave to Ireland and Sweden's positions, when it ultimately decided to vote in favour of the Western resolution and against the eight-power resolution.[57]

The Canadian statement in the Congo debate justified the votes in favour of the Western resolution and against the eight-power resolution on the grounds that the former was constructive and clarified the role of ONUC, while the latter was ambiguous and likely to result in further confusion. Although the speech conceded that Canada might have had political aspirations for the Congo, it stressed the neutrality and objectivity of Canadian actions, exclaiming, "We have considered that it was important to ... exercise a degree of restraint even when events were taking place, the immediate results of which were not to our liking." The Canadian intervention was also used to chastise the Soviet bloc and ridicule attempts to draw attention to Canada's membership in NATO. "Who, I wonder," asked the Canadian representative, "could honestly believe that [Canada] has imperialist or aggressive designs against the Congo? The real objectives of these propagandistic attacks by the Soviet bloc must surely be clear to four-score-and-ten states represented here." This speech revealed the twofold nature of Canadian policy: it professed Canadian neutrality and objectivity and, at the same time, attempted to score political points by criticizing the Soviets. In the end, neither resolution received the required number of votes, and the debate closed with a procedural motion, by which the assembly unanimously decided to retain the Congo as an agenda item and simply noted that the previous General Assembly and Security Council resolutions remained in force.[58]

As 1960 drew to a close, political conditions in the Congo were fragile, and relations between Congolese and ONUC officials remained tense. Nonetheless, when the acting Canadian consul general, George Hampson, met with Kasavubu, he found the president to be optimistic about the prospect of holding a conference of Congolese leaders in order to resolve the governmental and political crisis. Kasavubu told the consul general that Joseph Ileo would be charged with forming a new government to represent different provincial interests in the Congo, early in the new year. Hampson found that Ileo spoke in the same general terms about the need for discussion and negotiation but was unsure of how much significance to attach to these comments. Ileo, he noted, "seemed to be having a quiet afternoon in a back office without many visitors." Dayal, according to Hampson, was much less optimistic about the ability of the Congolese to negotiate a solution to their difficulties. Hammarskjöld's special representative was of the view that the Congolese leaders should "first accept the idea of working under the 'constitution.'" Although Dayal was critical of the Congolese, Hampson noted the American and British ambassadors were critical of Dayal and his management of ONUC. He was said to have "poor personal relations with the Congolese leaders in Leopoldville whom he treats with reserve and disdain," and to have been "interpreting his instructions from the Security Council in a negative way." From his interviews, Hampson concluded, "one of the primary difficulties between the UN and the Congolese is lack of understanding of each other's positions compounded by [a] superior attitude on the part of Dayal."[59]

## Canadian-Belgian Relations

When Howard Green attended the regular ministerial session of the North Atlantic Council in Paris in December 1960, he availed himself of the opportunity to explain to his NATO colleagues his views on the alliance's image and its relationship to the United Nations. He expressed concern over what he considered was a "good deal of misunderstanding about NATO's aims and intentions" by many in the world. Green argued it was unwise for the allies to take a coordinated approach to voting at the UN. "Given the composition of the United Nations," he said, "we must recognize that we are a very small minority and must co-operate with like-minded countries. For the moment I merely point to the disadvantage of attempting to present a unanimous view on every issue before the United Nations." The *Toronto Daily Star* was far less diplomatic in an editorial account of the meeting entitled, "Howard Green Needles NATO." The Canadian minister was said to have "gotten under the skins of several of our allies by implying that some NATO members cut poor figures in the United Nations." Supportive of

Green's approach, the paper went even further in openly declaring, "The peoples lately freed from colonialism are still rampantly suspicious of it. We can hardly expect them to trust an alliance some of whose members still practise repressive colonialism."[60] Thus was the stage set when, in early January 1961, Belgium found itself embroiled in a diplomatic incident and looked to its NATO allies for support.

As 1960 drew to a close, the Stanleyville "government" moved to strengthen its hold in eastern Congo. ANC troops loyal to Lumumba were sent to neighbouring Kivu province, where they arrested local military and political leaders and reinforced a military garrison in the capital, Bukavu. Hundreds of Stanleyville soldiers then moved through Kasai into northern Katanga. In response to these attacks, Mobutu and a hundred soldiers flew to the nearest available airport to Bukavu, at Usumbura in the neighbouring Belgian trust territory of Ruanda-Urundi. They boarded trucks, drove to the Congolese border, and crossed into Kivu. The campaign quickly disintegrated when the Stanleyville ANC failed to rally to Mobutu's side, as the colonel had expected it to do. Belgium immediately came under fire for assisting Mobutu in his transit through Ruanda-Urundi. Explaining the events to their NATO partners, Belgium claimed not to have received Mobutu's request for transit until just before the planes landed at Usumbura. Given the circumstances, the Belgians decided to allow the troops to land and to transport them to the Congolese frontier by truck. They argued that "Belgium and the West have both an interest and a moral responsibility in the Congo," and that "it was necessary to face Communist-Afro-Asian unity with Western unity." The African and Middle Eastern Division was skeptical of the Belgian claims to have had little or no warning of Mobutu's arrival; it asserted, "It was no secret that some sort of expedition was planned." The division questioned whether the Belgian account was the full story but acknowledged it might be wise not to admit this publicly. It was best, in the view of the division, not to heed Belgium's call for NATO solidarity, especially given the differences between Hammarskjöld and Belgium on this issue. The European Division and the Defence Liaison Division, by comparison, were more sympathetic toward Belgium in their assessments of the Usumbura incident. In the end, Ottawa decided not to support their NATO ally openly. Canada had to maintain a "reputation for disinterestedness."[61]

Before long, the Belgians grew tired of Canada's "lukewarm" support. The Canadian ambassador, Sydney Pierce, came to believe he exercised very little influence in Brussels. Even though he pressed the point with Pierre Wigny, the Belgian foreign minister, and with others that Belgian co-operation with the UN seemed the wisest policy and best tactic, "I didn't make any impression," he reported. "I could hardly get a word in edgewise." In an effort to once again influence the views of its allies, Belgium dispatched an ambassador to the NATO Political Advisers Committee. Initially, Canada and Britain were both reluctant to discuss Congo policy within this committee. Ottawa told its NATO representative, "We fully share [the] U.K. assessment of the danger of possible leaks of the fact that NATO is discussing the Congo and the consequent interpretation that a 'NATO line' on Africa was being developed. Such an interpretation could not fail to arouse apprehension and resentment in a number of African and other countries." In spite of these misgivings, Canada agreed to a discussion of the Congo crisis in the hope that Belgium might be helped to see the advantages of more fully cooperating with the UN. The Belgians were unimpressed. In a later meeting with the Canadian ambassador, Pierre Wigny expressed concern that Canada was not more supportive of Belgium. The ambassador replied that although Belgium's ally and friend, Canada felt that, given the political balance in the world and at the UN and given Canada's membership on the UN Advisory Committee on the Congo and its participation in ONUC, the best approach for Canada was to avoid taking sides too openly. Wigny remained unconvinced; he hoped that Canada "would reexamine the position and reconsider her attitude, and would come to the conclusion that our common interests would best be served by supporting Belgium more openly and fully in [the] UN and elsewhere." In Belgium's view, the private assurances and subtle suggestions of Canadian quiet diplomacy amounted to poor support from one of its NATO allies.[62]

## Lumumba and the Advisory Committee on the Congo

The consolidation of Lumumbist support in Orientale and the military incursions into Kivu and northern Katanga by ANC forces loyal to Stanleyville caused concern in Leopoldville. When elements of the ANC then mutinied at Thysville, where Patrice Lumumba was being held, these events were seen together as resurgence in Lumumba's support. The Leopoldville authorities decided to counter this by transferring Lumumba from Thysville to Katanga. Hoskyns suggests that it was "by no means clear" who planned and carried out the transfer, but both Kasavubu and Bomboko, but not necessarily Mobutu, appear to have been involved. A more recent account of Lumumba's assassination, by Ludo De Witte, clearly implicates Mobutu in the decision to transfer Lumumba.[63] When the secretary-general's advisory committee met to consider this situation, Hammarskjöld explained that it had not been possible for ONUC to intervene in the transfer of Lumumba because the Congolese leader had been detained in an ANC camp not under UN control. When the plane carrying Lumumba arrived at the Elisabethville airport, Jeeps, armoured cars, and 130 gendarmerie met it. Six peacekeepers were able to view the scene from a distance and watched as the severely beaten Lumumba was thrown to the floor of a Jeep, which then drove through an opening specially cut in the fence so that the usual control centres could be bypassed. Hammarskjöld immediately sent a message to Tshombé "urging humane treatment and Lumumba's right to a fair and speedy trial" outside Katanga.[64]

Members of the committee generally approved of Hammarskjöld's actions, but many, led by India, were keen to see Lumumba released so that he could fully participate in any political negotiations or attempts at conciliation. Although Charles Ritchie expressed Canada's "shock and disgust at the brutal treatment" of Lumumba, he did not go so far as to suggest Lumumba be released. In his statement to the committee, he simply agreed, "Mr. Lumumba should be brought to a fair and speedy trial in accordance with the guarantees which are normally given to accused persons." Canada's awkward position in the committee was then highlighted when Morocco made "an oblique and rather caustic" remark concerning a statement made by Howard Green, which was seen to be insufficiently supportive of Lumumba. In response to a question in the House of Commons as to whether the government had protested the beating of Lumumba, Green had remarked, "No, Mr. Speaker, there has been no protest launched. It would keep us very busy if we were to protest all the beatings which take place in the Congo. I agree ... that it was an unfortunate incident." The Advisory Committee agreed that Hammarskjöld should send a further message to Kasavubu "pointing out that negotiations for a political settlement could not be effectively pursued if Lumumba continued to be incarcerated under conditions where he could not be regarded as a free agent."[65]

In his report to Ottawa, Ritchie was critical of the "rather peculiar way" the Advisory Committee functioned. He noted that during the discussion a number of representatives, including himself, had gone no further than to suggest Lumumba be brought to a speedy trial. Yet, when Hammarskjöld summed up the consensus reached by the committee, provision for Lumumba's release for the purpose of participating in negotiations had been incorporated. Short of expressing an explicit reservation, there was little Ritchie could do but go along with Hammarskjöld's interpretation. He noted, "In any case it would be difficult to oppose such a principle in the Advisory [Committee] given its strongly Afro-Asian complexion." Eyebrows were raised in Ottawa nonetheless. Norman Robertson noted, "This is the first time that the secretary-general has recommended that Lumumba be released from custody to engage in political negotiations and he has thus raised an issue of considerable importance." Previously, Canada had been willing to go along with UN resolutions that called for the release of Lumumba. Now, Ottawa seemed more concerned at the prospect of Lumumba's return. The following views, though subsequently edited from the final draft of instructions to Ritchie, are revealing: "For your own info and as background for any talks you may have with the [secretary-general] privately, we have some concern as to the effect which the return of Lumumba to active political life may have, both on the possibility of creating stable political institutions in the Congo and on the international posture the Congo might adopt." Ottawa hoped Lumumba's release, if it was to occur, would be at a time decided by the "Central Congolese Government rather than the Advisory Committee." Ottawa was safe in assuming the Leopoldville authorities would never release Lumumba at a time when he might easily return to power. Although there was a clear policy preference in Ottawa to limit the impact of any move to release Lumumba, Ritchie was told to maintain a "restrained and impartial" attitude in the Advisory Committee.[66] Private views were not for public consumption.

### ONUC, Chain of Command, and Canadian Concerns

When it raised concerns about ONUC's chain of command and leadership, Canada was somewhat more direct in its diplomatic interventions with the secretary-general. Canadian officers serving with ONUC reported serious shortcomings with the organization and operation of ONUC HQ. General von Horn, the supreme commander, was variously described as ill, ineffective, indecisive, and weak. The UN Division noted von Horn had no experience commanding a formation in the field and, in Sweden, he was derisively nicknamed "general transport," which suggested that his military abilities were limited to logistics. Group Captain Carr found that von Horn was contemptuous of civilians; this, he stated, spoiled relations with the civilian side of ONUC. It should be remembered that Rajeshwar Dayal, a civilian, was the highest-ranking UN official in the Congo and was ultimately responsible for both ONUC's military and civilian operations. For a short time in the fall, while Dayal was in New York, Gen. Indar Jit Rikhye, Hammarskjöld's military adviser, stood in as acting representative of the secretary-general. The majority of the officers on von Horn's staff were Indian. Group Captain Carr reported that frequently these officers followed instructions received directly from Rikhye or Dayal, without any reference to von Horn. The force commander's mounting frustration with this state of affairs was reflected in a December 1960 memo from von Horn to Dayal, in which the former accused the latter of taking action over and above his head, directly with the secretary-general. Asked to delay his impending departure from the Congo, von Horn retorted, "If [the] Secretary-General were unable to find anyone willing to take on this most thankless task and therefore, as indicated in his first signal to me, would ask me to return, I must emphasize the necessity of satisfactory terms of reference between Supreme Commander and the Civil Administration." Once it was clear to Ottawa that von Horn was leaving his post, External Affairs thought it an opportune time for Ritchie to raise Canadian views with Hammarskjöld, prior to the secretary-general's appointment of the next force commander.[67]

Ritchie was apprehensive about raising the topic with Hammarskjöld. The secretary-general completely relied on Dayal and Rikhye and was said to be in a "state of extreme tension and sensitivity." Ritchie planned first to meet with other Secretariat officials, while Ottawa considered how to present Canadian concerns so that they would not be interpreted as yet another complaint about Hammarskjöld's direction of the UN's efforts in the Congo. Although a lengthy list of concerns was drafted following consultations with National Defence, External Affairs decided to concentrate particularly on issues related to ONUC's chain of command. By the end of December, Ottawa had learned from the Canadian contingent in the Congo that Rikhye had been asked to return to New York. Robertson wrote to Green suggesting that "our worries about Brigadier Rikhye may be approaching an end and that our approach to the Secretary-General need not be too pointed as regards Rikhye's activities in the Congo." Dayal, however, remained problematic. There was increasing pressure in the press and from the Leopoldville authorities to recall Dayal. The UN Division cautioned, "If our intention is to support the United Nations position rather than to press for a Western position, which may be divided in any case, I can see little advantage in adding to the Secretary-General's worries by joining the chorus of demand for withdrawal of Mr. Dayal." The African and Middle Eastern Division departed from this view somewhat. It agreed that Canada should not publicly press for Dayal's withdrawal, but because it believed he was an impediment to the eventual resolution of the crisis, it argued against "joining any counter-chorus in defence of Mr. Dayal." More significantly, it took the opportunity for intradepartmental discussion to elaborate on the more general political course Canada should pursue. The very idea that there were two alternatives, the Western position and the United Nations position, was challenged. Such a view was premised "entirely on the analysis of the Congo situation as part of the East-West struggle." The African and Middle Eastern Division was keen not to be confined by a "solid NATO front on the Congo," preferring instead "to help elaborate a general Western position which is consonant with or at least not irreconcilable with the Hammarskjold approach." This argument is indicative of the tactics Canadian diplomats often used during the Congo crisis. They avoided hard and fast political positions, sought out room for constructive compromise, and quietly convinced others to see the sensibility of Canadian views.[68]

In this instance, it fell upon Charles Ritchie to employ his powers of quiet, tactful persuasion with Hammarskjöld. Ottawa instructed its representative in New York to raise numerous issues with the secretary-general: reconciling the factions within the United Nations which favoured the various Congolese leaders, the lack of co-operation between the Congolese and ONUC, the threatened withdrawal of certain ONUC contingents, and chain of command. The last point was considered the most important. The Canadian government was of the view that the force commander should be entirely responsible for ONUC's military operations and for advising Hammarskjöld's respresentative in the Congo. Put bluntly, Ottawa wanted Rikhye to return to, and remain in, New York. Ritchie was advised, "It is the firm opinion of the [Canadian] military authorities that the confusion in the directives given to the force will not be removed unless and until the role and function of the Commander is clarified in this way." External Affairs hoped Ritchie could discuss the matter "in a friendly and frank way," without reference to specific personalities. Ritchie found Hammarskjöld in a "relaxed and almost buoyant mood." The secretary-general acknowledged there had been difficulties at ONUC HQ and that the chain of command needed to be clarified. Hammarskjöld justified Rikhye's presence in the Congo on the grounds that he needed "a senior military officer who was capable of conducting delicate and difficult negotiations with various Congolese military and para-military elements." It was implied that von Horn was "too poor in health or lacking in sufficient vigour to undertake this function." The situation was expected to improve with Irish lieutenant general MacEoin's appointment as ONUC commander, permitting Rikhye's return to New York. Hammarskjöld still anticipated the need for a senior officer who could be dispatched throughout the Congo when emergencies arose and expected one might be found from among the commander-in-chief's staff. It may be recalled that MacEoin had initially urged the Secretariat to retain Colonel Berthiaume for this purpose, but Hammarskjöld now told Ritchie that von Horn "had attempted to use Col Berthiaume in this way on one or two occasions but that Berthiaume had not shown the qualities needed for political appreciation." This issue appears not to have been pursued, and one is left to speculate on what was meant by "the qualities needed for political appreciation." Although it appeared as though Ritchie was persuasive on the issue of Rikhye's role at ONUC HQ, the secretary-general was "immediate and categorical" in his defence of Dayal. At this point, there was little prospect of Hammarskjöld replacing his special representative.[69]

### Canada, ONUC, and Air Operations

In mid-January, Canada refused to provide the UN with twenty-seven RCAF technical personnel, some three months after the UN asked. This was the first significant ONUC request the government chose to decline. Initially, details from the UN were unclear, and when National Defence prompted External Affairs for clarification of the UN's precise needs, the chairman, chiefs of staff advised the undersecretary, "The organization of the RCAF is such that they are much more able to contribute a complete unit such as a squadron, rather than to weaken several units by supplying a piecemeal group as requested by the United Nations." By mid-November, details had been obtained, planning was undertaken, and the RCAF approved a plan to provide the necessary personnel to operate a telecommunications network for ONUC's three main air transport bases in Leopoldville, Stanleyville, and

Kamina. The chief of the air staff abandoned his earlier reservations because Canada had since been asked to fill the position of air commander in ONUC, and he did not want either the flexibility or safety of the air operations to be compromised because of inadequate communications. Cabinet, however, postponed a decision on the request because of the "disturbed" political situation in the Congo. Following discussions with Group Captain Carr, the chief of the air staff asked Harkness to raise the matter in cabinet again. The minister suggested a further delay of two weeks. When that interval passed, and political conditions in the Congo had still not improved, National Defence finally asked External Affairs to advise the secretary-general that it would not be possible to meet his request.[70]

## The South Kasai Famine

The continued deterioration of political conditions in the Congo eventually led to a famine in South Kasai. An earlier group of 80,000 Baluba who had fled to the region were joined by an additional 150,000 refugees as conflicts worsened. Mortality was said to be high, estimated at two hundred famine-related deaths daily, due primarily to diseases caused by protein deficiency. From time to time, Canadians had written Diefenbaker and Green to offer their views on events in the Congo, but nothing compared with the out-pouring of letters the government received urging it to act to relieve suffering in Kasai. The words and sentiments of Florence Waterworth were typical of dozens of letters sent to the prime minister: "You are our Prime Minister and your influence and power are great. You and your government must act immediately and be assured you are expressing the will of the hearts of the Canadian people." Many were dismayed by the government's lack of im-mediate action: "Make [a] national call for substantial aid (cash and food) plus government help for starving Congo and China. Have we no conscience? Why are we always lagging in humanitarian effort?" An entire elementary school class from Richmond Hill, Ontario, wrote letters – according to one student, "All the class at school were talking it over and we thought that we wanted to send some food to the people in the Congo, and we want to ask you to. We have to [sic] much food here and we don't need it all. We want very much to send some." While two letters retained in the Diefenbaker papers did urge the government to assist the Canadian unemployed as well as the starving Congolese, all others exclusively addressed the urgent need to send aid to the Congo.[71]

Many Canadians probably learned of the Kasai famine from the coverage it received in newspapers. The front page of the 29 December issue of the *Globe and Mail* featured a story entitled "Famine Sweeps Kasai." Some 1,200 Congolese were reported to be crowded into a hospital capable of caring for 120 patients. The *Toronto Daily Star* called upon the government to "do more than ponder the terrible famine in the Congo. It should take the lead in sending food, and with the utmost speed." In response to that particular editorial, one reader subsequently wrote, "How dog-in-the-manger can we get, when we won't even give away the food we can't eat ourselves and can't sell?" Finally, the national director of the United Nations Association in Canada, Willson Woodside, wrote to several newspapers to say that his office had been "flooded with calls from people wanting to know what they can do to help relieve the dreadful famine." He encouraged Canadians not only to send contributions directly to the UN Association but also to write the Canadian government, urging it to offer the Congolese food.[72]

Despite this public outcry, the government prevaricated. Canada was asked particularly for dried fish. Aid agencies required 3,250 tons, and although the government did not maintain stocks of this commodity, Canadian industry did. Moreover, the Department of Fisheries welcomed a government purchase of the commodity. Howard Green, in a submission to cabinet supported by the ministers of agriculture and fisheries, suggested a gift of one hundred tons of dried fish and one hundred tons of dried skim milk, at a cost of $50,000. Consideration was also given to covering the cost of transporting the food, if this could not be borne by aid agencies. Green noted, "The FAO appeal has evoked considerable sympathy in Canada, as evidenced by letters urging a Canadian contribution." Cabinet considered the matter on 26 January 1961 and seems to have been persuaded by Diefenbaker to delay any decision on aid until the minister of agriculture could study and propose "a possible programme of distribution of surplus foodstuffs to needy persons within Canada." Diefenbaker said he had received a number of letters objecting to plans to provide aid to the Congo when there were needy unemployed in Canada. If this was the case, many of these letters appear not to have been retained in his personal files. The vast majority of the letters present in the Diefenbaker papers are united in their call for immediate aid for the Baluba. Howard Green seems to have been aware of this discrepancy. The very next day he wrote to the prime minister requesting that cabinet immediately reconsider the issue, "particularly in the light of the mounting public interest in this question." Green argued that dried fish and skim-milk powder were not suitable for relief distribution in Canada. He added, "I am aware of numerous letters from the general public asking what the Government will be doing to help," and drew the prime minister's attention to a letter just published in the *Montreal Gazette*. The matter was raised in cabinet again on 31 January, but Diefenbaker stood his ground. He said representatives of several groups of unemployed persons had approached him and that "surplus foodstuffs should be distributed to unemployed persons in Canada before any announcement was made about donations to other countries." Cabinet reaffirmed its earlier decision to delay a decision. In the end, Canada appears to have given little if any aid. There was some effort at External Affairs to locate funds within existing budgets to circumvent the need for a supplementary estimate, but it is not clear whether any aid was eventually provided this way.[73]

## ONUC Composition

A number of nations with ONUC contingents became increasingly bitter as Kasavubu continued to consolidate power and undermine Lumumba. In protest, Guinea, the United Arab Republic (UAR), Morocco, and Indonesia formally asked the secretary-general to withdraw their forces from the operation, a total of approximately 6,150 peacekeepers. Hammarskjöld turned to Ethiopia, Iraq, Sudan, India, Mexico, and Senegal for replacements. Concerned about the public's perception of this withdrawal, Norman Robertson suggested that Howard Green take advantage of any questions raised in the House of Commons to point out that the situation was not as bad as had been, for instance, reported in the *Globe and Mail*. Indeed, Ottawa seemed to take this news in stride. Hammarskjöld was seen to be "acting energetically to counteract the situation," and the withdrawal of troops from Guinea and the UAR was seen as a positive development for ONUC that could "result in improvement in the operations of the Force." When the United Kingdom suggested the Security Council be apprised of the UAR's "mischievous activity" in the Congo, Canada thought it best to let sleeping dogs lie, even though Ottawa was keen to ensure the UAR contingent did not remain in the Congo once its status with ONUC was terminated. Unlike the United Kingdom, Canada favoured raising concerns about the conduct of UAR peacekeepers in private with the secretary-general. Once again, quiet diplomacy was the order of the day.[74]

While some nations withdrew their contingents from ONUC, Canada was increasing its representation at ONUC HQ. On 5 January, the UN asked Canada to provide 4 bilingual army staff officers: a major for movement control duties, a major for information duties, a major for operations staff duties, and a captain for logistics staff duties. At the time, there were 280 army officers and men serving with ONUC, including 9 officers and 2 other ranks with ONUC HQ. In addition, the RCAF had a total of 12 officers and men in the Congo. This was well within the ceiling of five hundred personnel set by cabinet when Canadian participation was originally approved. Both Harkness and Green agreed to the UN's request, but Green wanted the role of the information officer to be clarified before the matter was brought to cabinet. Recalling Rikhye's earlier attempt to use a Canadian peacekeeper as a spy in Brazzaville, External Affairs sought assurances that this officer would not be used to gather intelligence. After consulting with the commanding officer of the 57th, Colonel Smith, it became clear that the primary responsibility of this officer would be the preparation of situation reports and other documents on developments in the Congo. Smith was very much in favour of accepting the additional commitment. He wired army headquarters, "Need for bilinguàl [officers] is urgent and need for [officers] who know something about what they are doing is even more so. Errors have been made in [movement control] for example that cost millions." The UN's decision to request Canadians for ONUC HQ appeared to be a turning point, perhaps prompted by the sudden withdrawals of the contingents from nations that staunchly supported Lumumba. According to Colonel Smith, up to this point in time, Hammarskjöld had resisted the appointment of any additional Canadians. Cabinet agreed to the request on 31 January. The minister of national defence argued that the provision of these officers "would enable the Canadian government to obtain more complete information on developments in the Congo, and would enable Canada to exert a greater influence upon U.N. affairs in that area."[75] It is difficult to reconcile the minister's expectation that provision of these officers would provide Canada with information on Congo developments with National Defence's earlier assurances to the UN that Canadian forces would respect UN expectations that peacekeepers not communicate such information to their governments. In meeting this request, a degree of self-interestedness was evidently a factor in the cabinet's decision.

### Canadian Views of Kennedy's Congo Policy
In the United States, the transition in presidential administrations from Eisenhower to John F. Kennedy invigorated attempts to address the Congo crisis. Madeleine Kalb notes, "The mood in Washington shifted significantly."[76] Kennedy was committed to supporting the UN and Hammarskjöld. He recognized that Lumumba might have to be included in any Congolese government that hoped to enjoy broad-based public support. Early in February, the American embassy in Ottawa delivered an *aide-mémoire* identifying three policy objectives: the establishment of a broadly based government; a new mandate for ONUC that would allow it to "establish control over all principal military elements in the Congo, thus neutralizing the role of the Congolese forces in the country's political affairs"; and an increased, improved effort by the civilian side of ONUC to provide aid so as to eliminate the likelihood of outside assistance. The Canadian government was pleased with the new American approach, which was deemed "reasonable and constructive." Although it had usually shared the objectives of the Eisenhower administration, Ottawa was not always willing to openly cooperate with some of its divisive tactics in the UN: the manoeuvring to seat Kasavubu's delegation, for example. Kennedy's productive approach was more compatible with Canada's key policy objective of helping the UN succeed in its efforts in the Congo. Robertson wrote to Green: "The views of Canada and the United States coincide exactly on the need to stop further outside interventions in the Congo, to reorganize the Congolese forces, to effect political conciliation and to revive the economic life of the Congo." Canadian diplomats were

instructed to give support to the US initiative, but External Affairs recognized that some American aims would be difficult to achieve. While Ottawa appeared to be supportive of suggestions to neutralize and control armed elements in the Congo, it did not underestimate the difficulties in doing so. The proposed timing of Lumumba's release was also questioned. US policy favoured his release only after armed elements had been neutralized and conciliation toward a new government was well under way. Ottawa noted, "It may have to be faced that the immediate release of Lumumba may be a condition set by some of the Asian and African powers for their cooperation in achieving any of the general objectives now set forth." By accepting the necessity of Lumumba's release and by considering the need for a strengthened ONUC mandate that would require the neutralization of the ANC, Canadian policy appeared to be emboldened by the American initiative to shift slightly toward a more activist, moderate, stance.[77]

The American initiative caused an open rift within NATO, and with the exception of the United Kingdom, Canada found itself increasingly at odds with its European allies. At a NATO council meeting on 9 February, Belgium was especially virulent in its criticism of the United States for its failure to consult with NATO allies before acting on a new policy it considered "could only give comfort to the Russians." In the face of opposition from virtually all other members, Norway, Canada, and to a degree Britain tried to support the United States. According to Alan James, at about this time, Britain recognized the "changing context" ushered in by a more "pro-African" Kennedy administration; the Foreign Office came to believe the United Kingdom would "do well to give the Belgians a nudge." Canada, it was said, "generally welcomed the line taken" in Washington. In a statement clearly directed more toward Belgium than the United States, Jules Léger, the Canadian representative, remarked, "It would be in the interests of those who are involved more than we, that they should consult their allies early in the game and not after matters are raised at the UN. The proper time for discussion of a number of these matters was not two weeks or two months ago, but two or three years ago." Belgium, and others on the council, reiterated the view that NATO should concert its policy on the Congo and present a united front. In his instructions to Léger, Howard Green strongly disagreed with this proposition, echoing the views he had expressed at the earlier NATO ministerial meeting: "Even if general agreement were possible, to attempt to adopt a NATO front in the UN would be counter-productive ... Apart from diminishing the possibility of gaining wider support in the UN for any positive move, it would probably serve to discredit NATO's own reputation in the UN."[78] The minister clearly preferred that individual NATO members worked separately in New York, each seeking support for their own respective policies. Canada was convinced of the need to look somewhat independent of its NATO allies at the UN. The appearance of involvement in a united Western front would serve only to undermine its efforts to play a constructive role in the resolution of the Congo crisis – a role that required it to support, first and foremost, the secretary-general and the institution of the United Nations itself.

The constitutional crisis precipitated by Lumumba and Kasavubu's dismissals of each other began a period of intense instability, creating a situation ripe for Cold War rivalries to surface in the Congo and in New York. The East and many Afro-Asian nations supported Lumumba, and the West increasingly backed the Kasavubu/Mobutu alliance. This state of affairs made Canada's diplomatic balancing act all the more precarious. Participation in ONUC and membership on Hammarskjöld's advisory committee came to be used as convenient excuses for not pursuing a united NATO front on the Congo crisis. Although the Canadian government preferred Kasavubu to Lumumba, as became clear in the Advisory Committee's discussion on the dispatch of the Conciliation Commission to Leopoldville, the government also was unwilling to take a hard line against the Congolese prime minister. Voting at the United Nations demonstrated Canadian cautiousness: an abstention on the question of Kasavubu's credentials and a willingness to go along with a General Assembly resolution that would have called for the release of Lumumba – an outcome inimical to Western interests. The activities of Lieutenant Colonel Berthiaume ultimately may have helped seal the fate of Patrice Lumumba, but there is no evidence to suggest either the Canadian government or ONUC prompted his actions. Finally, the Diefenbaker government supported the Kennedy administration's efforts to take a more constructive approach to the Congo crisis, even after this initiative landed the new president in hot water with his NATO allies. In fact, rifts within NATO were widening, and Canada and Belgium appeared to be further apart than ever before. Canada's unwillingness to support Belgium during the Usumbura incident and Foreign Minister Wigny's protestations over Canada's Congo policy leave little doubt that the Belgians considered Canada to be inadequately wedded to what they considered were the West's best interests.

# 5
# Continued Chaos: Balancing Peacekeeping and Politics

In late January 1961, President Joseph Kasavubu followed through with plans to deal with the ongoing political instability in the Congo. Working with Joseph Ileo, who was briefly prime minister before Col. Joseph Mobutu's coup, Kasavubu called for a roundtable conference of all the Congolese political leaders to take immediate steps to replace the College of Commissioners with a more representative interim authority, prior to the reconvening of Parliament. Kasavubu is said to have persuaded Mobutu to give up the College of Commissioners in favour of a government led by Ileo, a move intended to create a more "legal" government. Without the concurrence of Parliament, the legality of Ileo's government was dubious, and it never managed to exercise effective control over more than half of the Congolese provinces. Key leaders from Kivu, Orientale, and Katanga did not attend the roundtable conference. In part, the Congolese central authorities took this step to forestall any further intervention by either neighbouring African states or the United Nations. Kasavubu warned the Congolese would "not tolerate any attempt whatever to put them under trusteeship." "The Congo," he said, "is an independent country and has the sovereign right to decide its own future."[1]

As the Ileo government assumed power in Leopoldville, Canada prepared to send a new consul general, Michel Gauvin, to the Congolese capital. In advance of his departure, representatives from External Affairs and National Defence briefed Gauvin on Canadian policy and the situation in the Congo. The Canadian position on the Congo, Gauvin was told, was one of impartiality. The primary objective of Canadian policy was to support Secretary-General Dag Hammarskjöld and the United Nations. The impact of the Cold War still was acknowledged, however; one official said, "It is a fair assumption that all Western countries feel we should prevent Soviet domination of or infiltration into the area." Significantly, it was suggested that Canada was "prepared to accept a neutralist Congolese state." In this respect, Canadian policy continued to differ from its European counterparts. For example, through its staunch support of Kasavubu and Mobutu, Belgium clearly favoured the establishment of a solid, Western-oriented government in the Congo. And the United Kingdom, which had earlier half-heartedly defended the United States in NATO meetings, became openly critical of provisions within the new American plans for the disarmament and reorganization of the Armée Nationale Congolaise. Ottawa learned that the British government had instructed its delegation in New York to discourage Hammarskjöld from pursuing a policy of disarmament. If these attempts failed and the matter was brought before the Security Council, Britain planned to oppose such a policy there.[2] Although the Canadian government had expressed practical concerns about how the ANC and other armed elements in the Congo could be disarmed, it did not oppose the policy in principle.

Since December, when both the Security Council and the General Assembly failed to adopt a positive policy for UN action in the Congo, ONUC was adrift. Guinea and Mali withdrew their contingents, and other contributing nations keen to see a more forceful implementation of existing resolutions reiterated their threats to leave as well. Hammarskjöld visited the Congo early in 1961 and came away convinced that a more active approach was needed. Support from the new American administration for a more interventionist policy strengthened the secretary-general's hand. In a statement to the Security Council when it reconvened on 1 February, Hammarskjöld called for more far-reaching measures, including "the reorganization of the national army, preventing it, or units thereof, from intervening in the present political conflicts in the Congo."[3] Hammarskjöld was clearly advocating disarmament of the ANC, a controversial step that both Britain and the Congolese government opposed. As was often the case during the Congo crisis, events in the Congo soon overtook debate in the Security Council.

On 13 February, Katangese authorities announced that Patrice Lumumba, the deposed Congolese prime minister, and two of his colleagues had been killed following their "escape" from prison. In the House of Commons, the opposition asked if the government had any information on Lumumba's demise. The secretary of state for external affairs, Howard Green, deplored "this act of violence." He said, "While Mr. Lumumba has been a controversial figure, the fact remains that he was a duly elected Member of Parliament and formed the first government of the newly independent republic of the Congo. His death, if it has taken place, is unlikely to settle anything." In New York, Canada's permanent representative to the UN, Charles Ritchie, met with his colleagues from Ireland, Denmark, Sweden, and Norway. It was said that their collective assessment of the situation "could scarcely have been darker." Lumumba's death was recognized as a blow to recent American diplomacy, some elements of which were now seen as hollow or impractical. The Americans themselves recognized that Lumumba's demise could result in a major crisis and encouraged their ambassador in Leopoldville to warn the Congolese government not to allow itself to be placed in a position of condoning or supporting political assassination. Upon learning of Lumumba's death, the Soviet Union was vehement in its condemnation of Hammarskjöld. It called for his removal, the withdrawal of ONUC within a month, and the immediate recognition of Antoine Gizenga, Lumumba loyalist and provincial leader of Orientale, as the head of the Congolese government. In spite of this dramatic development, Charles Ritchie held out hope something could still be done to prevent external intervention in the Congo or to achieve the neutralization of Congolese armed forces. He perceived an additional reason to be guardedly optimistic: most Afro-Asian nations appeared to favour a moderate, compromise position instead of this extreme Soviet stance.[4]

The Canadian press, in numerous news stories and editorials, addressed the political significance of Lumumba's murder. The *Chronicle-Herald,* not unlike Charles Ritchie, took a more optimistic view of the possible outcome of the assassination. It was said to have "generated a new spirit of urgency among the African and Asian peoples for a settlement of the Congo problem in the shortest and most efficient manner." The *Montreal Gazette* clearly blamed Tshombé, Kasavubu, and Mobutu for Lumumba's death but recognized, in the crisis it had sparked, that there was a renewed opportunity to address the Congo's problems more effectively. In a front-page story, the *Gazette* also reported on a demonstration by African students living in Montreal. Positioned at the front gate of McGill University, the students delivered a statement that deplored "the external forces that have contributed to this savagery and the attitude of foreign nations who ... made possible the assassination of a great African nationalist leader." The *Toronto Daily Star* was pessimistic. Its editorial on the subject, "Lament for Lumumba," seemed critical of the Congolese leader yet sorry and fearful for the implications of his death: "Young, ill-tutored and mercurial, he was something unique in the Congo – a politician who argued, intrigued and fought for a unitary and modern government in a land still ruled by primitive fear and custom."[5]

News of Lumumba's death prompted another series of letters from concerned Canadian citizens. Various branches of the Communist Party of Canada sent half of them. Regardless of author, the letters were almost unanimous in the outrage they expressed at Lumumba's fate. One Canadian living in the Congo wrote to Prime Minister John Diefenbaker, "Lumumba is dead. We are all guilty ... I long for the day when Canada stands up and denounces America for what it is. I am not Communist." From Alberta, one woman wrote, "Its [sic] shameful! To me and I'm sure to people all over the world Lumumba's murder could have been prevented if United Nations forces were doing their duties." The B.C. Young Communist League was more blunt: "Patrice Lamumba [sic] was elected and supported by the majority of Congolese people. His murder by Belgian running dogs makes it imperative that the Canadian government presses in the United Nations for the immediate convening of the rightfully elected Congolese parliament."[6] Although the government did publicly deplore Lumumba's fate, it did not follow through on the many, often repeated, suggestions raised by the authors of these letters: to recognize the Gizenga government, to call for Hammarskjöld's resignation, to denounce the Belgians and Americans, and to withdraw UN peacekeepers. As was the case with the letters addressing the Kasai famine, the Lumumba letters did not influence government policy.

Not surprisingly, Canada never recognized Gizenga's regime in Orientale as the legitimate government in the Congo, though the matter was discussed in cabinet. In Howard Green's absence, Prime Minister Diefenbaker noted the USSR, Ghana, Guinea, and the United Arab Republic had all recognized Gizenga as Lumumba's successor and his government as the rightful authority in the Congo. The prime minister was concerned that Gizenga would attempt to establish control over other parts of the Congo; two thousand soldiers loyal to Gizenga were thought ready to attack Stanleyville, in Orientale province. The Soviets threatened to intervene on behalf of Gizenga, and a report by Charles Ritchie in New York would have served only to confirm the view that this threat was not an idle one. In a conversation with Ambassador Platon Dmitrievich Morozov, deputy permanent representative of the Soviet Union at the UN, Ritchie attempted to seek out areas of compromise and middle ground. Morozov rejected all of Ritchie's arguments. The Soviet ambassador simply countered, "There is no middle ground." Ritchie ominously concluded, "Morozov's attitude revealed complete lack of interest in any attempt to reach a peaceable solution in Congo and moreover lack of any recognition that such a solution was even remotely attainable or indeed desirable."[7] The Canadian cabinet was certainly aware of the continuing and escalating Cold War implications of events in the Congo, even as Ritchie attempted, in vain, to seek out room for compromise.

When news of Lumumba's death arrived in New York, the Security Council was adjourned. Still, this did not curtail the Soviet Union's angry public pronouncements against Hammarskjöld and ONUC, to which were added calls for the arrest of both Mobutu and Katangan premier Moïse Tshombé. Howard Green, in answer to a question posed by Leader of the Opposition Lester Pearson, dismissed the Soviet attitude and fulminations as a "culmination of the bitter but unfounded attack launched by the Soviet union [sic] against the secretary general late last summer and all during the autumn session of the general assembly." Green was effusive in his praise for the secretary-general: "For its part the Canadian government will continue its firm support for the United Nations effort in the Congo and for Mr. Hammarskjold, who in the face of the greatest difficulty has served the high principles and purposes of the charter with courage, determination and endless patience." The severity of the Russian response prompted the government to vigorously defend not only Hammarskjöld but also the United Nations as an institution. One Canadian official bemoaned, "The Soviet Union seems determined to wreck the contribution to stability which the United Nations is making in the Congo." Concerned that the neutral and independent countries seemed either to be siding with the Soviet Union or passively allowing the situation to deteriorate, Marcel Cadieux identified a particular question for Canada: What could be done "to induce these uncommitted states to do anything to prevent what would in fact be a major Soviet victory"?[8] Once again a Canadian diplomat patently cast the Congo crisis in Cold War terms but also sought out a constructive role for Canada as interpreter of Western views to the neutral states.

## Resolution 161 (1961)

When the Security Council resumed consideration of the Congo situation on 15 February, the Soviet Union introduced a draft resolution calling for both the dismissal of Hammarskjöld and the withdrawal of ONUC. It was defeated by a vote of one in favour, eight against, and two abstentions.[9] A second resolution, Resolution 161 (1961), sponsored by Ceylon, Liberia, and the United Arab Republic, passed with nine affirmative votes, none against, and two abstentions, on 21 February.[10] Presented in two parts, this resolution brought about a significant shift in the role of ONUC. The UN was urged to take measures to prevent civil war in the Congo, even by the use of force "if necessary, in the last resort." All foreign military personnel, mercenaries, and even political advisers were required to leave the Congo. All states were asked to take measures to prevent the departure of such personnel for the Congo. An investigation into Lumumba's death was ordered, and the perpetrators of the murder were to be punished. Adequate protection was to be provided to facilitate the recall of the Congolese parliament. Finally, armed units in the Congo were to be brought under control, reorganized, and removed from any involvement in the political affairs of the country. Charles Ritchie cited key factors that accounted for the council's success in passing this resolution: firm American support of UN involvement in the Congo; a united effort by the Afro-Asian states to "preserve the United Nations approach" once they realized both the United States and USSR "meant business" in the Congo; a significant shift in Indian policy away from staunch support of the Lumumbists and an immediate recall of Parliament and toward the prevention of civil war and strengthened military support for the UN; and the United Arab Republic's loosening of the "Soviet embrace" because it was not prepared to risk an open conflict between Gizenga and Kasavubu, in which each side would be supported by rival superpowers. External Affairs was guardedly optimistic in its assessment of the resolution. It expected that Belgian and French reactions would be critical and that Belgian policy would depend on the degree of pressure applied by its allies, especially the United

States and United Kingdom. Perceptively, Canadian officials recognized that the 21 February resolution would refocus attention on Tshombé and Katanga. They noted, "If the United Nations presence in Katanga can be reinforced and if the external props are removed, his [Tshombé's] position will be less tenable and he will be better disposed to reach accommodation with the other political leaders in the Congo." The implications of the Security Council's decision to use force in the last resort to prevent civil war were not lost on the undersecretary of state for external affairs, Norman Robertson, who concluded, "While there is cause for mild optimism about the fact that the Security Council has been able to reach a decision in favour of further action by the United Nations in the Congo, it would be a mistake not to be cautious about the difficulties. In trying to prevent civil war, for example, the United Nations could become involved in heavy fighting."[11]

The 21 February resolution had far-reaching, though uncertain, implications for the question of ONUC's use of force. The legal basis for the resolution's authorization of the use of force to prevent civil war was not explicit. This subsequently led to conflicting interpretations by diplomats and scholars alike.[12] Uncertainty surrounding the meaning of this operative clause was immediately evident at External Affairs, where it was vaguely noted, "The Security Council resolution apparently gives the force somewhat broader scope for action than previously, when its military function has been largely limited to self-defence." Publicly, in the House of Commons, Howard Green appeared to acknowledge that the repercussions of the resolution were not yet fully understood, though he expressed confidence in the ability of the UN to exercise its mandate responsibly: "The resolution states clearly that force would be used only if necessary and in the last resort. I am sure that we can rely on the good judgment of the Irish commander of the U.N. forces in the Congo, General McKeown [sic], to act responsibly." In contrast, days before this most recent resolution, the British were explicit in their views on the question of the UN using force in the Congo. In a message to Green, Duncan Sandys, the British Commonwealth secretary, stated, "It is no good looking to the United Nations force to do more than it is physically capable of doing. Nor is it possible or desirable for the United Nations to take over the job of governing the country and to assume a colonial function there. These two considerations seem to rule out imposing any political solution on the Congolese by force." Alan James is clear in his assessment of British views of the 21 February resolution; though having voted for it, the United Kingdom dearly hoped the secretary-general would not interpret it as empowering the UN to use force to achieve a political settlement. These early views on ONUC and its use of force are significant because by the end of 1961 the peacekeeping mission would find itself actively involved in hostilities with the Katangese gendarmerie.[13]

Responsibility for the implementation of the 21 February resolution fell once again to the secretary-general. In a clever move, Hammarskjöld began to use the Advisory Committee to shield himself from future criticism. Charles Ritchie noticed the change in tactics at once. Previously, communications were simply shared with the committee before being issued by the Secretariat. Now, Hammarskjöld involved the committee in the actual drafting of these communications. In a conversation with Ritchie, the secretary-general revealed that he was "following a deliberate policy of facing the sponsors of the resolution ... and other Afro-Asian members with their responsibilities." All members of the committee came to be associated with his decisions, including Canada. This entailed certain risks, especially because it was not always possible for Ritchie to obtain advance instructions from Ottawa on proposals raised by the committee. Overall, Ritchie favoured continued participation because Canadian membership provided an important link with the Afro-Asians, helped the UN operation as a whole, and safeguarded the interests of Canadian peacekeepers serving with ONUC.[14]

In a break with its usual cautious and quiet approach, External Affairs advised Ritchie to "exercise a restraining influence whenever it should appear that the African-Asians might be pushing the UN into extreme positions." Ottawa suggested it was "desirable from time to time in the [Advisory Committee] to remind the African-Asians, especially the extremists, about the financial requirements and the need for collective responsibility in meeting them." This rather pointed remark was meant to draw attention to the fact that the West paid the vast majority of ONUC's expenses. Despite these instructions, Ritchie was not "too vocal," fearing any attempt to mitigate the more extreme interpretations of the 21 February resolution would lead to accusations that he was "furthering 'unafrican'designs." Yet, Ottawa worried that "extreme" Afro-Asian opinion might pressure the secretary-general into using ONUC to force a political solution in the Congo. The UN Division was in favour of intensifying efforts to establish neutral zones and ceasefires but was against any suggestion that the 21 February resolution authorized enforcement action. Geoffrey Murray, head of the UN Division, argued in favour of blocking any efforts by committee members to have ONUC use force to impose a political solution, for example, by attacking Katanga to coerce Tshombé. The Advisory Committee did take up the question of how best to interpret the reference to the use of force in the resolution's first operative paragraph. Hammarskjöld was of the view that the new resolution entitled ONUC to "occupy territory to prevent civil war and take defensive action for all positions held." This, the secretary-general felt, "gave the UN command in the Congo new and significant military strength." Not satisfied with this interpretation, the Indian ambassador, C.S. Jha, was reported to have launched into a "series of almost metaphysical statements on 'defensive-offensive' force coupled with suggestions that the

UN forces in the Congo should be more 'pushful' but at the same time apparently should keep out of trouble." The Canadian view coincided with Hammarskjöld's: ONUC "should be used 'in the protection of agreed peaceful solutions.'" Ottawa favoured negotiation and conciliation, thinking it doubtful that the UN could force solutions on any Congolese faction and that the organization would find itself in great difficulty "if it succumbed to the pressure from some member [governments] for the use of force as a sanction against unco-operative elements in the Congo."[15]

### Canadians in ONUC

By mid-February 1961, there were 28 officers and 186 other ranks serving in the 57th Signal Unit. Twenty-one of the officers and 132 of the other ranks were stationed in Leopoldville. The remaining personnel were assigned to seven detachments of 1 officer and 7 to 9 men, throughout the Congo. In addition, 7 officers and 2 men served with ONUC HQ, along with a provost detachment of 11 men and a food services section of 1 officer and 4 men. Twelve RCAF personnel were located in Leopoldville, either on staff with ONUC or in connection with the RCAF external airlift (see Table 1 for a breakdown of ONUC personnel). The arrangement with the UN for the airlift had been extended in December for another ninety days and was set to expire on 9 March. External Affairs and National Defence agreed that the airlift should be continued for a further ninety-day period. Norman Robertson noted, "It would seem more than ever essential that the U.N. presence there be maintained and adequately supported logistically, and that Canada should not take any action which might suggest a declining interest in the ONUC, or which might imply that we intend to scale down Canadian participation in the Force." National Defence did plan to replace the North Stars with CC-106s and asked External Affairs to consult with the United Nations on changes in the flight schedule that would result from use of the larger planes and a switch in the European stopover to Marville, France. By maintaining the 57th at strength and extending the airlift, the government demonstrated its willingness to support its commitment to the UN even at a time when Congolese political conditions continued to be unsettled.[16]

Canadian authorities expected any outbreak of violence to occur in eastern Congo, in either Kivu or Orientale provinces. In truth, Leopoldville proved to be as dangerous. On 26 February, in the northwest part of the city, four Canadian peacekeepers were stopped by ANC para-commandos at a roadblock. They were disarmed, marched barefoot almost a kilometre to an ANC camp, and beaten with rifle butts along the way. Personal weapons and possessions were stolen. Questioned in the House of Commons on the right of the Canadian peacekeepers to defend themselves, the minister of defence answered, "If there is a concerted attack on a body of Canadian or other troops, they fire to defend themselves. However, if it is a matter of two or

*Table 1*

## Opération des Nations Unies au Congo force composition

| Nation | 21 April 1961 Combat troops | 21 April 1961 Support forces* | 21 February 1962 Combat troops | 21 February 1962 Support forces | 26 December 1962 Combat troops | 26 December 1962 Support forces | 27 December 1963 Combat troops | 27 December 1963 Support forces |
|---|---|---|---|---|---|---|---|---|
| Argentina | | 24 | | 16 | | 52 | | |
| Austria | | 48 | | 48 | | 44 | | |
| Brazil | | 29 | | 55 | | 2 | | 51 |
| Canada | | 284 | | 318 | | 310 | | 250 |
| Ceylon | | 8 | | 13 | | | | |
| Congo: Leopoldville | | | | | 615 | 2 | 781 | 2 |
| Denmark | | 70 | | 89 | | 100 | | 83 |
| Ethiopia | 2,470 | 15 | 2,998 | 53 | 2,973 | 19 | 1,699 | 19 |
| Federation of Malaya | 980 | 1 | 1,505 | 9 | 774 | 8 | | |
| Ghana | 1,642 | 2 | 648 | 2 | 702 | 4 | | |
| Greece | | 21 | | | | | | |
| India | 3,252 | 764 | 4,701 | 1,071 | 4,608 | 1,018 | | 271 |
| Indonesia | 1,135 | 4 | | | 1,626 | 1 | 3 | 2 |
| Iran | | | | | | | | 8 |
| Ireland | 646 | 25 | 695 | 34 | 820 | 47 | 333 | 22 |
| Italy | | 128 | | 132 | | 52 | | 57 |
| Liberia | 226 | 10 | 235 | 3 | 233 | 9 | | |
| Morocco | 7 | 1 | | | | | | |
| Netherlands | | 6 | | 6 | | 6 | | 1 |
| Nigeria | 1,671 | 7 | 1,696 | 7 | 1,835 | 17 | 613 | 11 |
| Norway | | 111 | | 132 | | 146 | | 88 |
| Pakistan | | 551 | | 671 | | 687 | | 782 |
| Sierra Leone | | | 111 | | 122 | | | |
| Sudan | | 1 | | | | | | |
| Sweden | 518 | 124 | 672 | 204 | 692 | 352 | 302 | 96 |
| Tunisia | 3,149 | 11 | 546 | 2 | 1,040 | 2 | | |
| Totals | 15,696 | 2,245 | 13,807 | 2,865 | 16,040 | 2,878 | 3,731 | 1,743 |
| | 17,941 | | 16,672 | | 18,918 | | 5,474 | |

* Support forces consist of all other personnel (including those in air operations and force administration) not serving as combat troops.
*Source: Yearbook of the United Nations*, 1960, 1961, 1962, 1963 (New York: Office of Public Information).

four soldiers, something like that, going along the street and being stopped by a patrol of Congolese soldiers, they do not start a fight." The force commander, General Sean MacEoin, vigorously protested to the ANC command, warning that in future ONUC would "oppose such acts with the maximum of force, and that responsibility for the consequences will fall squarely on the ANC and on the authorities concerned." The Canadian consul general protested at the Congolese Ministry of Foreign Affairs. He stressed the "damaging effect such incidents had for Congo not only in [Canada] but all over the world." In reports to Ottawa, Gauvin attributed this incident to ANC nervousness arising from poor relations between ONUC and the Congolese and the implicit threat of the 21 February resolution to disarm the ANC.[17]

The extent to which relations between ONUC and the ANC had deteriorated became patently clear within a week, in a far more serious incident at Matadi. Some 125 kilometres upriver from the mouth of the Congo, Matadi was a key port at which ONUC supplies arrived by sea and were stored. Since the previous September, Canadian peacekeepers had been stationed there, providing communications for ONUC forces. On 3 March, Capt. G.E. Belanger, commanding officer of the 57th's Matadi detachment, dined with the ONUC Sudanese contingent and discovered they were wearing pistols as though "fully equipped for battle." When asked why, the Sudanese commander was not entirely forthcoming, but Belanger suspected it had something to do with fighting in nearby Kitona and Banana, so he asked the Sudanese to send some guards to the Canadian detachment in case of hostilities between ONUC and the ANC. The next day, while Belanger was away from the detachment, a fully armed and equipped Sudanese section took up defensive positions at the Canadian detachment, including a light machine gun pointed directly at a nearby ANC guardhouse. Belanger had expected his request to be met with one or two guards and was surprised, on his return, to find so many Sudanese. He discovered that the ANC had countered the deployment of the Sudanese with a light machine gun of its own, not far from the detachment's front door. Belanger tried to speak with the ANC sergeant commanding the machine gun but found him to be "very excited"; the sergeant simply screamed at him to get the Sudanese out of the building. At that point Belanger returned inside and moments later firing started, continuing for about two hours. It is not clear who fired first, but Colonel Smith, the commanding officer of the 57th, later reported that the Canadians and Sudanese were outranged and outgunned. The ANC fired at the building with 37mm anti-tank rounds. According to two Canadian peacekeepers, the defence of the building was largely left to the Canadians after the initial exchange of fire. One said of the Sudanese: "They were not very effective. They hid under a table or stood in corners." Following numerous failed attempts to arrange and sustain a ceasefire, and after one attempt resulted in Belanger's separation from the detachment, the decision was made to surrender to the ANC. Before doing so, the cryptographer burned the codes and sabotaged the communication equipment. By all accounts, the ANC officers ensured the captured Canadians were well treated and intervened when other ranks of the ANC were threatening. While awaiting their evacuation to Leopoldville, they were provided with food, drink, and even beer. Some Canadians suffered minor injuries, primarily from shell fragments and masonry chips. The Sudanese casualties included one dead and four wounded. Belanger was evacuated to Leopoldville a day after others in the detachment, escorted by an ANC officer and a Congolese government official.[18]

In the meantime, Colonel Smith had left Leopoldville for Matadi to search for Belanger. The Canadian peacekeeper was in fact safe, but Smith used his time in Matadi to assess the situation first-hand. He was unable to determine who fired first and in the end concluded, "In any case I don't see it matters much when 2 groups excited and jittery Africans facing each other at short range with weapons loaded and cocked someone is certain to open fire." He found the ANC officers to be quite amicable. Several said they regretted the involvement of the Canadians, as they considered the peacekeepers friends. The ANC commander was said to have asked Smith, "Why do you send us soldiers the same colour as we are (pointing to his skin). They are no better than we are. What can we learn from them." The officer asked Smith to send the Canadians back and noted he had guards at the Canadian detachment to ensure no one could damage the signal equipment. All other UN equipment and vehicles, aside from that belonging to the Canadian detachment, were seized by the ANC. Although the ANC officers were generally kind, Smith found the rank and file surly and the civilian police and population hostile. He considered it unlikely that armed peacekeepers could return to Matadi or that the port could be retaken by force. The UN, he said, "has clearly suffered major defeat and it will take a lot of talking our way out."[19]

In the days following the Matadi confrontation, both Consul General Gauvin and Colonel Smith met separately with Foreign Minister Justin Bomboko and ONUC commander General MacEoin. Gauvin also met with Rajeshwar Dayal, the secretary-general's special representative. In his conversation with Colonel Smith, Bomboko apologized for the Matadi and Leopoldville incidents. He said he had great respect for Canadians and was assured by his people that everywhere Canadians were located they were liked and respected. He was anxious for the Canadians to return to Matadi and had issued orders to protect Canadian equipment and allow the return of the 57th detachment whenever it wished. Bomboko was highly critical of Dayal. He assured Smith that he wanted to cooperate with the UN but said that Dayal made this impossible. In this context, Bomboko mentioned Colonel Berthiaume, whom he held in high regard, and implied that Dayal had dismissed him. Smith was generally impressed with Bomboko. He thought the foreign minister was genuine and keen to restore relations with the UN. Bomboko's criticism of Dayal was given credence when, in a subsequent conversation with General MacEoin, Smith learned even the force commander was considering submitting his resignation if Dayal continued in the role of Hammarskjöld's special representative. Gauvin visited Bomboko to express "serious concern and indignation" at the treatment of the Canadian peacekeepers in Matadi, as instructed by Ottawa. Again, Bomboko apologized, cited the previously good relations between the Canadian peacekeepers and the ANC in Matadi, and assured Gauvin that any involvement of Canadians was purely accidental. He also repeated his criticism of Dayal. Then, in a subsequent conversation with the secretary-general's special representative, Dayal suggested to Gauvin that the Matadi incident was part of a scheme to force ONUC out of the port. The consul general reported, "Both sides act as if there existed a cold war with threats and counter threats without any attempt at conciliation." Dayal was said to have no contact with the Congolese, as he did not invite them to his home and was openly contemptuous and disdainful of Congolese soldiers. In contrast to Dayal, Gauvin perceived MacEoin to be quite balanced. MacEoin was not convinced that the ANC should be blamed entirely for Matadi. The force commander questioned the conduct of the Sudanese officer in charge, describing him as "well intentioned but inexperienced." Canadian diplomats and military officers generally found the central Congolese authorities to be reasonable but identified the growing rift between Leopoldville and the civilian leadership in ONUC as a cause for concern.[20]

The events in Leopoldville and Matadi once again raised questions about the level of force ONUC was entitled to use to fulfill its mandate. Previously, in the House of Commons, Defence Minister Douglas Harkness suggested Canadian peacekeepers were authorized to use force only in self-defence against a concerted attack. The judge advocate general, in a letter to the chairman, chiefs of staff, questioned this interpretation: "This appears to me to put a very severe restriction on the right of Canadian soldiers to defend themselves." He noted UNEF peacekeepers were given greater latitude in their use of force. Nonetheless, Harkness was correct in his characterization of the way in which peacekeepers had so far responded to ANC harassment. Although soldiers in ONUC may have been legally entitled to resist being disarmed, in practice peacekeepers normally complied with the demands of the ANC in order to de-escalate tense situations. On numerous occasions, the military and civilian leadership of ONUC commended peacekeepers for their demonstration of restraint in response to such direct provocation. This changed on 1 March, when General MacEoin ordered all ONUC troops not to surrender their arms under any circumstances and authorized them to open fire to prevent being disarmed. The 57th Signal Unit's war diarist described the Canadian peacekeepers' reaction upon hearing this order from

Colonel Smith: "He told them that a new order had been issued to UN forces whereby it was now compulsory for them to fire in protection of their weapons. It stated, he said, that UN troops would not in future be disarmed. The unit's reaction to this announcement was an immediate outburst of clapping and shouting which lasted a full ninety seconds." The Permanent Mission in New York took note of this significant change in policy. It confirmed that MacEoin had indeed issued the order and that he had notified the secretary-general. Ottawa was advised, "It would appear that the order was issued under authority already existing within UN policy."[21]

A parallel discussion took place within the Advisory Committee on the question of when it was appropriate for ONUC to employ force to achieve its mandate. As Hammarskjöld prepared to approach twenty-one African governments for additional troops, he consulted with the committee in order to "spell out the circumstances in which UN troops might use force." He resisted an Indian suggestion to be vague, arguing, "We have been living on obscure mandates for seven months. This has harmed UN prestige, and must not be repeated." The secretary-general drafted the following passage on the use of force, all members of the committee reviewed it, and no objections were raised:

> The latest resolution adopted by the Security Council does not seem to derogate from the position that UN troops should not become parties to armed conflict in the Congo. The basic intention of the resolution is, in my opinion, the taking of all appropriate measures for the purposes mentioned, resort being had to force only when all other efforts such as negotiation, persuasion or conciliation were to fail. If following such efforts, or measures taken in support of their result, UN troops engage in defensive action when attacked while holding positions occupied in prevention of a civil war risk, this would not, in my opinion, mean that they become a party to a conflict, while the possibility of becoming such a party would be open were the troops to take the initiative in an armed attack on an organized army group in the Congo.

Ottawa did not want Ritchie to take a "leading part" in Advisory Committee discussions on this issue but largely shared Hammarskjöld's interpretation. External Affairs stressed the need for the UN to "rely mainly on processes of consultation[,] persuasion and conciliation" yet acknowledged additional circumstances when the use of force could be justified. For instance, use of force was acceptable to defend ONUC-held positions that were critical either for the prevention of civil war or for the establishment of stability. With Matadi clearly in mind, ONUC was also seen to have a "right and obligation to reoccupy positions important to UN operations from which UN troops had been ejected by force." Ottawa was unequivocal, however, in its insistence that ONUC not use force on behalf of any of the political factions in the Congo.[22]

## Canadian-Belgian Relations

Following the 21 February resolution, Canada continued its attempts to strike a balance between supporting the United Nations and its NATO ally, Belgium. Because the resolution required all foreign advisers, both political and military, to leave the Congo, Canadian officials considered Belgium's "immediate acquiescence" to be "a good deal to expect." External Affairs acknowledged that relations between Canada and Belgium were already strained and was concerned about the wider implications of further Belgian disillusionment with, and resentment of, its NATO allies. "Continued efforts," it was thought, "may be required to convince Belgium of our sympathy with its distress and our sincerity in wishing to help it find a reasonably satisfactory way out of the present situation." Nonetheless, Norman Robertson maintained that in taking an attitude of "sympathetic encouragement" toward Belgium, Canada should not deviate from its "insistence on the paramount importance of implementing the Security Council resolution." Guilt and obligation were factors to consider, but the success of the United Nations in the Congo remained the paramount objective.[23]

Canada's awkward position was made all the more obvious when the Belgian chargé d'affaires approached External Affairs with an "embarrassing request." The Belgian government was hopeful that Canada would provide them with information about the secretary-general's advisory committee. The chargé was told the question was of "considerable delicacy," as Canada could do nothing that would jeopardize its position on the Advisory Committee or its relations with Hammarskjöld. The African and Middle Eastern Division succinctly identified the difficulty posed by this request: leaked information of any real value to the Belgians would likely influence its dealings with the UN, in turn suggesting it had been made aware of the Advisory Committee's confidential proceedings. Given the NATO connection, Canada would quickly be identified as the leak. Nonetheless, the Belgians were keen for Canadian co-operation. The Canadian ambassador in Belgium, Sydney Pierce, was lobbied and asked to emphasize "the importance Belgians attached to a favourable response." Robert Rothschild, the director of the Congo section in the Belgian Foreign Office, "in good humour" observed "that it was possible at times to be 'too objective.'" Although Charles Ritchie was worried that leaks might be traced back to him, he went along with, and Howard Green approved, a plan to provide the Belgians with broad, general information on the proceedings of the Advisory Committee, provided the passing of information was used as an opportunity to influence the

Belgian government to cooperate with UN objectives in the Congo. Canadian officials had particular confidence and trust in Rothschild, and this also appears to have been an important factor in their decision. After agreeing to share information, Ottawa wasted no time dipping into its reserve of diplomatic credit with Belgium. External Affairs instructed the Canadian ambassador to use his influence with Belgian officials to convince them of the need to persuade Mobutu and Kasavubu to adopt a conciliatory attitude on the UN's plans to return to Matadi. The ambassador was assured that Belgium was already working on Kasavubu and that the UN sooner or later would be able to return to Matadi in a satisfactory manner.[24]

## Canada's Congo Diplomacy

In mid-March, Diefenbaker attended the Commonwealth Prime Ministers' Conference in London. This was an opportunity to discuss the Congo situation with other heads of government. Early versions of the notes for Diefenbaker's statement on the Congo stressed Canada's detachment: "[Canada] has no territories in Africa and no territorial ambitions. It has no financial or commercial interests in the Congo sufficient to influence its judgment. Canada – as anyone may verify by examining our record on this issue in the United Nations – has been and remains, relatively speaking, impartial." Given the direct and partial involvement in the Congo of many other members of the Commonwealth, it is perhaps not surprising that this passage did not survive successive drafts of the speech. Yet, these views provide a revealing glimpse into the thinking of officials at External Affairs – or at least the ideas they hoped to impart to others. Diefenbaker maintained that Canada held "no brief for any of the contenders for power in the Congo" but also said that Canada considered the regime in Leopoldville to have the "greatest claim to constitutional legitimacy." Although Kasavubu had been recognized by the General Assembly, Diefenbaker's statement would have been unpopular with those present who supported the Orientale regime. In addition, the prime minister argued against the notion that ONUC should consist entirely of non-white troops, a proposition favoured by Ghana at the time. On the whole, the conference was not an important event in the shaping or implementation of Canada's Congo policy for several reasons: the South African issue dominated the agenda, in one session on the Congo Diefenbaker did not participate because he could not "get a word in edgewise," and the issue was barely discussed when he privately met with British prime minister Harold Macmillan. Diefenbaker found it stimulating to hear the views of other leaders who had more direct experience with the Congo and was pleased that the final communiqué stressed the importance of ONUC. And, in something of a fluke in circumstance, the prime minister met with Rajeshwar Dayal, who also happened to be in London, though the majority of the meeting appears to have been used by Dayal to present a spirited defence of his role in ONUC and a critique of both the Belgians and the American diplomats in Leopoldville.[25]

In New York, Charles Ritchie went to speak with Hammarskjöld on 13 March and found the secretary-general in a "somewhat tense state." Hammarskjöld was indignant with the Congolese authorities over the Matadi hostilities and a recent incident in which Swedish personnel captured by the ANC were made to walk naked in the street. He was especially critical of Kasavubu's participation in the Tananarive conference, held from 6 to 12 March and attended by a number of Congolese leaders, though not Gizenga. Those present at Tananarive agreed to a confederation of separate Congolese states. In Hammarskjöld's view, Kasavubu had abandoned the *loi fondamentale* and the "validity of his position as head of the Congolese state." Instead of working with Kasavubu, as Ottawa hoped, Ritchie learned that Hammarskjöld planned to raise the question of the legitimacy of Kasavubu's presidency at the next meeting of the Advisory Committee. Ritchie unsuccessfully tried to talk the secretary-general out of doing this. Hammarskjöld's intervention, Ritchie surmised, would only worsen relations with the Congolese authorities. Above all, the Canadian representative wanted the UN to "improve working relations with the existing Congolese authorities by a mixture of firmness and active conciliation." Continuing instability in the Congo was expected to lead to grave difficulties, especially for those states with peacekeepers in ONUC. Ritchie went so far as to suggest that Canada assimilate its position to certain members of the Afro-Asian bloc, including Tunisia, Sudan, Nigeria, Liberia, and Pakistan. Even India, Ghana, Indonesia, and the United Arab Republic were cited as having points of common interest. Ritchie observed, "We are certainly not the only ones to wish to avoid an impossible dilemma in Congo."[26]

Canada's effort to further develop its relationship with the Afro-Asian bloc was evident when the General Assembly considered three new resolutions on the Congo in mid-April. India was the driving force behind two of the resolutions, Pakistan behind the third. During the debate, Canada delivered a lengthy speech in which the violent incidents against Canadian and other members of ONUC were condemned. The Canadian representative said, "[Canada's] contribution to UN forces in Congo is small in terms of total numbers, but this fact does not make the life or the welfare of any one of these men a matter of any less concern." In what was to become a common Canadian refrain, the delegation warned that if the UN failed in the Congo, the organization's continued ability to take effective action in cases of threats to peace and security would be jeopardized. The first Indian resolution was directed entirely at Belgium; initially, it contained a definite deadline for the withdrawal of Belgian personnel and an implied threat of sanctions if this was not met. Canada planned to abstain on this resolution if these particular provisions were not removed. External Affairs was hopeful that reasoning and influence could be brought to bear on Ireland, Sweden, and the moderate Afro-Asians to secure a "constructive amendment of the more unrealistic portions of [the] Indian draft." When the offending elements were dropped, Canada voted in favour of the resolution, along with Ireland and Sweden, even though both the United Kingdom and the United States abstained, and Belgium voted against it.[27] In addition, Canada voted in favour of the second Indian resolution that established a commission of investigation into Lumumba's death. Again, Canada voted with Ireland and Sweden but this time against the Congo. Once more, the United Kingdom and the United States abstained.[28] In this round of assembly diplomacy, Canada openly supported resolutions sponsored by the Afro-Asians, even though this contradicted its NATO allies.[29]

Relations with Belgium continued to be something of a balancing act throughout the spring of 1961, as the Belgian government faced increased pressure from the UN to comply with the 21 February resolution. At External Affairs, the European Division prepared a memorandum presenting a spirited defence of Belgium; it suggested Belgium's sixty-year record in the Congo had "much on the credit side of the balance sheet which the judgment of history is likely to confirm." In contrast, Patrice Lumumba and UN officials were blamed for the poor state of relations between the Congo and Belgium. The European Division concluded, "There are indications that Belgium considers that Canada has not been as helpful as it could have been over the Congo issue and our silence in PAC and elsewhere seems to have been misinterpreted." It suggested Canada intervene in the Advisory Committee to urge its members not to interpret the 21 February resolution too restrictively and to be more empathetic toward the Belgians.[30] These suggestions appear to have been rejected outright because the memo was filed without ever being circulated to other divisions.

Abstract discussions on how best to preserve relations with Belgium were superseded by yet another request from Rothschild for additional information on the proceedings of the Advisory Committee. When the UN sent a representative to Brussels to discuss arrangements for the withdrawal of Belgian nationals in the Congo, in accordance with the 21 February resolution, the Belgian government insisted on tripartite discussions with the Congolese. An official of the UN told Brussels that the Advisory Committee opposed such talks, so Rothschild turned to Canada for confirmation that this was the case. Ritchie could not recall any recent discussion in the Advisory Committee of tripartite consultations, though the general issue of Belgian withdrawal had been addressed often. Ritchie did recall that Canada's principal objective in passing information to the Belgians was to "facilitate or induce more forthcoming and active Belgian cooperation with UN on implementation of [the] withdrawal provision," so he suggested the Belgians be told that "the crux of the issue is not so much whether discussions should be three-sided as [it is] what these discussions are about." He added, "The principle of speedy and complete withdrawal is not considered by the Advisory Committee members as being negotiable, but they recognize that the means for achieving this are open for discussion, both with the Belgians and with the Congolese." Ritchie cautioned against providing Belgium with any information that could be used by Brussels to undermine the UN and rejected as entirely inappropriate any disclosure to the Belgians of views attributed to specific nations. Following this recommended course of action, the Canadian ambassador in Brussels was told to advise Rothschild on the overall tone in the Advisory Committee, without divulging specific details of its deliberations, in hopes this would dispel the Belgian inclination "to underestimate the intensity of Afro-Asian suspicion of and impatience with what is regarded as Belgian procrastination." Once again, Canada prioritized its position with the United Nations above its relations with Belgium, but the decision to provide some information can be seen as an attempt to reach out to Brussels, albeit on Canadian terms.[31]

Officials from the departments of Finance, External Affairs, and National Defence met in early April 1961 to discuss Canadian policy on the financing of ONUC. To this point, Hammarskjöld and the General Assembly met ONUC's substantial financial commitments through a series of interim resolutions and *ad hoc* measures that, at times, resorted to loans from other UN accounts. The need for a more systematic and positive approach to ONUC financing was underlined when the UN's Advisory Committee on Administrative and Budgetary Questions estimated Congo costs in 1961 would reach $120 million. Several measures were considered: Canada could decline any rebates offered on its 1961 Congo assessment; costs already incurred for airlifts, allowances, and equipment could be waived; and the Canadian delegation in New York could make a concerted effort to "bring home to potential defaulters the inevitable consequences not only for the peacekeeping operations but for all United Nations programmes of large-scale defaulting." Howard Green rejected these suggestions. He thought it best not to raise proposals regarding ONUC financing with cabinet until a payment or pledge was required in New York and believed it should be left to the Americans "to make the running in rounding up support for payment by others of their assessed shares of the $120 million Congo cost." Instead, Canada continued its behind-the-scenes efforts to regularize ONUC financing. The previous December, the delegation worked to ensure that General Assembly Resolution 1583 (XV) on ONUC financing contained a perambulatory paragraph that deemed ONUC expenses to be binding, mandatory costs of the UN. Now, the delegation took the lead in the Fifth Committee (i.e., the Administrative and Budgetary Committee) by tabling a draft proposal that eventually became the basis for General Assembly Resolution 1620 (XV), calling for the sixteenth session of the General Assembly to reconsider urgently the administrative and budgetary procedures related to the costs of peacekeeping operations. It also established a working group to consider principles applicable to the development of a special scale of assessments, a provision designed to appeal to Afro-Asian and Latin American states concerned about the additional financial burden peacekeeping might impose on them.[32]

From the Congo, Gauvin sent External Affairs reports praising the efforts of the secretary-general's acting special representative, Mekki Abbas, to normalize relations with the Congolese authorities and warning of the potential consequences if Dayal returned from New York to resume his position in ONUC. Dayal was at the UN headquarters consulting with Hammarskjöld. Gauvin wrote, "Dayal's return would provoke Congolese to [the] point where open conflict between Congolese and ONUC might well be expected and all opportunity for cooperation and understanding lost." He urged External Affairs to make representations to Hammarskjöld to ensure the secretary-general appreciated the great risks involved in returning Dayal to the Congo. Ottawa advised Ritchie to speak with Hammarskjöld and proposed "face-saving" scenarios that might be employed to avoid Dayal's return; Ottawa considered it "desirable to find some satisfactory formula for averting the return of Dayal to Leopoldville ... or at least for mitigating the adverse impact of his return." Murray, in the UN Division, believed Hammarskjöld's steadfast support of Dayal could not be dismissed simply as blind loyalty or worries about the loss of prestige. In his view, Hammarskjöld and Dayal's shared ideological objective of establishing the Congo as a neutralist state and the secretary-general's increased dependence on India for political support were important factors. By the end of April, it still seemed possible that Dayal would return to Leopoldville, perhaps for a brief period or with additional deputies. In a conversation with Murray, Dayal suggested the key was removing "the unhelpful Belgian influence." Hammarskjöld concurred. The secretary-general was reported to have said, "The Belgians have acted 'like the Israelis at their very worst' but with the difference that, while the Israelis were clever, the Belgians were 'stupid' in their dealings with the United Nations." For the time being, Dayal's future remained unclear.[33]

### Canadians in ONUC

Conditions throughout the various Congolese provinces remained tense, and on 2 April the 57th Signal Unit received orders to restrict movement to safe areas within Leopoldville. The next day, still unaware of the new orders, a group of five Canadian peacekeepers left Leopoldville on a recreational trip to Zongo Falls. All were unarmed and wearing civilian clothes. Twenty-five kilometres from Leopoldville they were stopped by an ANC roadblock, ordered out of their Jeep, and forced to kneel in a ditch at gunpoint. One ANC soldier, thought to be intoxicated, kicked and slapped the Canadians, all the time shouting, "Indians." The peacekeepers were then taken to Thysville but released after the local ANC commandant contacted Mobutu. ANC soldiers escorted the Canadians back to Leopoldville, to protect them from a hostile crowd gathered at the camp. Both Colonel Smith and Gauvin contacted Ottawa to suggest the incident be minimized. They noted the Canadians should not have been in the area where they had been, and Smith acknowledged that, aside from the behaviour of the one ANC soldier, the Congolese soldiers "went out of their way" to protect the Canadians, buy them food, and point out places of interest. Initially, Colonel Smith ordered a Canadian Press correspondent accredited to the 57th to postpone filing his story on the incident. The next day, after ONUC HQ released information to other reporters, the correspondent was allowed to submit his story. According to the war diarist, this was much to "his relief, and [the] relief of others who watched him fret for fourteen hours."[34]

The 57th's commanding officer took measures to reduce the likelihood of such incidents between Canadian peacekeepers and the local Congolese. In addition to the areas in Leopoldville ONUC HQ declared unsafe or dangerous, Smith identified other locations as "out of bounds" to members of the 57th in particular. As well, an order was posted on a recurring basis in an attempt to discourage the "habit," acquired by some personnel, of calling the Congolese "Blacks, Black Bastards, Jigaboos, and Coloured." In spite of Smith's efforts, "a long expected event" happened on 15 April. While AWOL, one of the Canadians "got into trouble with local Congolese civilians in the red-light district," and when found by the ONUC provost claimed he had been captured and manhandled by the ANC. The next evening, the ANC arrested two peacekeepers when they attempted to cut their vehicle through an ANC barbed-wire roadblock. Because the peacekeepers had been in Leopoldville for eight months and the Afro-Negro nightclub was "in line with their travel at the time they were taken prisoner," their account of the events was met with skepticism. Later, when this same nightclub was placed out of bounds because senior Canadian NCOs were involved in several riots and incidents there, the decision prompted much discontent. The war diarist noted, "For some reason it was the proverbial straw on the camel's back. Despite the fact that several other night clubs in town are similar, if not more typical, the exclusion of this particular one was the cause of much grumbling." These restrictions did have a cumulative impact on morale; limited recreation opportunities were recognized as a factor to be taken into account in any decision to post peacekeepers for longer than six months. In spite of these many restrictions, however, the senior medical officer still observed, "Our troops apparently have quite an active sexual life." Indeed, the limited number of cases of venereal disease among the peacekeepers led him to question rumours that 90 percent of Congolese women were infected with sexually transmitted diseases.[35]

A far more serious incident occurred in Stanleyville on 8 April. Captain Stubbs, the commanding officer of the detachment, thought the peacekeepers "clung to the security of the UN building far too much," and so he set out to establish contacts with civilians who could help relieve the peacekeepers' boredom. Unfortunately, ANC soldiers interrupted a supper party and film night arranged with local European civilians. Except for two signallers Stubbs quietly dispatched to find UN assistance, the Congolese soldiers arrested everyone, peacekeepers and civilians alike. The detainees were beaten, threatened, and generally maltreated. Members of the Ethiopian battalion arrived three hours later and secured the release of ONUC personnel but "implied that it was hard luck on the civilians." When he arrived back at the Stanleyville headquarters, Stubbs unsuccessfully tried to convince ONUC officials of the need to rescue the civilians. He then took matters into his own hands. After a failed attempt to bribe the guards where the prisoners were being held, he went to see General Lundula, head of the Stanleyville faction of the ANC. "Very tired and irritable," Stubbs roused Lundula and "ordered him to the phone at gun point." Lundula immediately arranged for the release of the civilians. Colonel Smith noted that UN reports of the incident made no mention of Stubbs threatening Lundula, and he proposed to suppress this information. In his report to Mekki Abbas, the local head of ONUC in Stanleyville briefly noted, "Captain Stubbs of the Canadian Signals made an attempt to get the other men released at 0600 hours by going alone to the camp." And in a later official statement by Stubbs, the captain simply said, "The General spoke to me, he was cool but formerly correct. I asked him for the release of the prisoners, he phoned the Etheopians [sic], who arrived at the house and neogations [sic] then commenced to effect the release of all civilians." In what was clearly a very serious incident, the record has almost erased the remarkable exchange between Lundula and Stubbs.[36]

Between April and June 1961, the UN made five additional requests of Canada. The first was for assistance in airlifting Indian troops from Dar es Salaam to Kamina. The United States transported twenty-three hundred Indian peacekeepers by sea to Tanganyika but backed out of an earlier commitment to airlift half these troops onward to Katanga. Rikhye then turned to Canada with an informal enquiry for assistance, as he did not want to place the Canadian government in the awkward position of having to turn down an official request. External Affairs identified several political difficulties posed by the request, so National Defence was asked only to give it sympathetic consideration. In Leopoldville, Gauvin urged Ottawa to decline the request in light of Congolese opposition to the arrival of additional Indian peacekeepers. The United States, he noted, was criticized for airlifting the first thousand Indians. He advised, "If without letting down [the] UN too badly and if it is possible to discourage their request I would think it wise to do so especially since [the] nature of [Canadian] contribution to ONUC has been such up to now that we have been able to avoid being involved in controversial issues between Congolese and ONUC." The UN made other arrangements to transport the troops before a final decision could be reached, and the enquiry was suspended. The UN also withdrew an additional request for four bilingual staff officers to serve on ceasefire teams when General MacEoin decided the risk of immediate hostilities between Gizenga and Mobutu forces had diminished to the point where there were sufficient officers available from other countries.[37]

The RCAF received two requests from the UN. Air Commodore Chapman's tour in the Congo was set to finish on 14 July, and at the end of May the UN asked Canada to name a replacement. The RCAF chose Air Commodore H.A. Morrison, considered to be one of the air force's most experienced officers in air transport. The second request for three teams of one officer and one non-commissioned officer each to assist in air transport work at various airfields throughout the Congo was rejected. The acting chief of the air staff acknowledged that ONUC's need was very real but argued that the safety of RCAF personnel was paramount. Complete units had been provided in the past, but it was considered too dangerous to provide individuals for service in isolated areas of the Congo. The RCAF was willing to consider providing replacements for staff at ONUC HQ if this would enable peacekeepers from other nations to take up positions in the field.[38]

The army also turned down a UN request for three officers to oversee a transit camp ONUC planned to establish in Leopoldville to care for troops as they were rotated in and out of service. The UN envisioned a Canadian captain or lieutenant quartermaster in charge of the camp, with one warrant officer and one sergeant to assist in the running of the camp and perform clerical duties. The chairman, chiefs of staff advised Robertson that the camp would be under an Indian headquarters and would have to provide for "various nationalities with diverse habits and diets unfamiliar to Canadians." Canadians would not use the camp, and the 57th Signal Unit could not spare any personnel for this employment. For all these reasons, National Defence asked External Affairs to tell the UN that Canada was unable to provide the personnel requested.[39] National Defence continued to be judicious in its consideration of each UN request. Of the five requests during this period, only one was approved, while two were rejected outright. The other requests were withdrawn – though it seems unlikely that National Defence would have agreed to these had the UN persisted.

In early May, questions arose in the House of Commons about the safety and defence of Canadian peacekeepers in the Congo. These were prompted by an incident in Port-Francqui, Kasai, where ANC troops overpowered and massacred a detachment of forty-four Ghanaian peacekeepers. One Member of Parliament asked, "What are the orders to our Canadian forces, who are there on the authority of the government and the House of Commons, as to what they should do under such circumstances, and what equipment do they have for their own defence?" In his response, Diefenbaker noted the Canadians were "still under basically the same orders as those issued by the first United Nations commander," but these orders had been "reinforced and given more detailed interpretation by the current commander." The prime minister said, "In essence the orders to Canadian troops provide that they may use their weapons for defence in certain clearly defined circumstances. Resort to force is, of course, to be used only if normal discussion or negotiation has proved impossible or unavailing." Pressed to clarify what was meant by "clearly defined circumstances," Diefenbaker responded, "They have the right to resist attempts to disarm them; to resist attempts to arrest or abduct any United Nations personnel, military or civilian; to resist attempts to prevent them by force from carrying out their responsibilities as ordered by their commanders; and, in addition, to use weapons in defence of positions they have been ordered to hold." He added that as well as the pistols and submachine guns originally sent with the Canadian contingent, the peacekeepers now had a quantity of semi-automatic rifles, six light machine guns, and two 3.5-inch rocket launchers. Diefenbaker's explanation was a sound interpretation of the 21 February resolution, and his confirmation that peacekeepers had been provided with additional weaponry suggests the government recognized that ONUC could become more forceful in the implementation of its mandate.[40]

Within a week of this statement in the House, the commanding officer of the 57th found himself in a difficult position. Abbas wanted a Canadian signal detachment to return to Matadi with two ANC officers, in advance of a party of one hundred unarmed Nigerian police who were expected to reoccupy UN positions. The commanding officer spoke with MacEoin and expressed concerns about the temper of the civilian population in Matadi and the discipline and capability of the ANC to protect the signal personnel. MacEoin agreed with the commanding officer's assessment and delayed the order pending consultation with Abbas and New York. In the meantime, the Canadian commander wired army headquarters: "If ordered to proceed to Matadi without arms or in advance of Nigerian police propose to comply and to info you by immediate message particularly in view of recent statement in [Canadian] parliament on protection as I do not consider risk justifiable in view [of the] temper [of the local] populace and lack of control by ANC." Ottawa contacted the Permanent Mission in New York at once and instructed Ritchie to tell Hammarskjöld that Canadian peacekeepers were not to be sent to Matadi unless they were armed and dispatched with an armed Nigerian provost detachment. Having in mind the Secretariat's earlier objections to direct communications between contingents and their governments, Robertson acknowledged "there may be some delicacy in raising this matter with the Secretary General because of the channel through which we have received our information" but maintained that the commander of the 57th was clearly within his rights and acting in accordance with his command instructions when he reported his concerns to the chief of the general staff. Ritchie spoke with both Bunche and Rikhye and found that each had a different understanding of what the UN was planning to do in Matadi. Nonetheless, he pressed Bunche for an explicit assurance that Canadians would be sent back to Matadi only if they were armed and accompanied by the Nigerians.[41]

The entire operation was called into question when the Nigerian government also expressed concerns, but these were resolved when it was agreed the Nigerians would return unarmed, a solution thought to be safer because the peacekeepers would pose less of a threat. This was not acceptable to the Canadian government. When the United Nations announced that Canadian signal personnel would accompany the Nigerians, Ottawa once again reiterated to the Secretariat its unwillingness to send unarmed Canadians to Matadi, even if they were accompanied by unarmed Nigerian troops. To ease a difficult situation for Hammarskjöld, Ottawa agreed not to announce publicly that the Canadian Government had been inadequately consulted before ONUC reached this agreement with the Congolese authorities. External Affairs even advised Diefenbaker: "It might be preferable not to indicate that a final decision has been taken not to despatch Canadian signalmen to Matadi." The commander of the 57th was pleased with the decision not to send Canadians. He believed the UN was "merely providing hostages free of charge" and added, "if a scrap develops anywhere in Lower Congo [the] police will probably reap any revenge that is taken." In his view, it was gambling to put anything less than one battalion there. ONUC HQ announced that Canadian signal personnel were not sent to Matadi for technical reasons, and UN civilian field personnel provided communications for the Nigerians.[42]

On 13 May, Col. H.W.C. Stetham replaced Colonel Smith as commanding officer of the 57th Signal Unit, as Smith had been promoted to director of signals. Smith returned to Ottawa and met with officials at External Affairs to share his impressions of ONUC and peacekeeping in the Congo. Smith saw the Welbeck incident as the beginning of the deterioration in relations between the Kasavubu government and ONUC. The fracas over Welbeck was then compounded by the removal of Berthiaume, which caused a further "loss of confidence." Smith said that Berthiaume "had been friendly with Congolese leaders, particularly Bomboko and Mobutu, and when he was removed, the Congolese had come to the conclusion that he had been fired because he was their friend." It seemed to Smith as though ONUC relations with Kasavubu were improving, but at the same time they were worsening with Tshombé. Smith provided a frank assessment of ONUC contingents.

The reputation of the Canadians was said to be excellent because officers at ONUC HQ were bilingual and the Canadian army, relative to other contingents, was highly professional. He praised the Malayans and Indonesians. Troops from the United Arab Republic were dismissed as "rabble," though their officers were considered good. Tunisians and Moroccan peacekeepers were rated as fair, and the Liberians were seen as the worst. Indian peacekeepers were said to be the most disliked, but Smith attributed this to a "general African attitude towards Indians" and Dayal's bad reputation. Although Smith did express some concerns during his debriefing, his overall impressions were much less pessimistic than Colonel Mendelsohn's had been upon the latter's return to Ottawa, after serving as the first Canadian commander in the Congo.[43]

### Political Developments in the Congo
In fact, there was evidence that relations between ONUC and Kasavubu were improving. Hammarskjöld sent Robert Gardiner of Ghana and Francis Nwokedi of Nigeria to negotiate with the Congolese authorities on the implementation of the 21 February resolution, and by mid-April they had reached an agreement. This was a significant step forward, as both Tshombé and Ileo were reported to have regarded the resolution as a "declaration of war by the United Nations." Ottawa welcomed this development as a positive sign of real co-operation between the Congolese authorities and the UN. Ritchie was instructed to intervene in the Advisory Committee, though not to take a leading role in the discussions, in order to express Canada's satisfaction with the agreement. Ottawa believed that although the terms fell short in some respects, they were at least not in conflict with the spirit and intention of the UN resolution.[44]

In addition to the amelioration of ONUC-Congolese relations, positive movement toward a settlement of the constitutional crisis was discernible. Following a conference of political leaders in Coquilhatville at the end of April, where Kasavubu announced his intention to reconvene Parliament, there was a limited rapprochement between the Stanleyville and Leopoldville authorities. ONUC was not involved in the discussions between the leaders, but it facilitated meetings through the provision of transportation and security. Acting Consul General Gauvin's account of his first meeting with President Kasavubu revealed a definite shift in hostility toward Katanga, as opposed to Orientale. There was no love lost between Kasavubu and Gizenga (the president referred to the leader of the Stanleyville faction as *un homme fini, un homme mort*), but his invective was saved primarily for the Katangese leader. Kasavubu said, "Tshombe can yell as much as he likes I will never agree to anything that would amount to recognition of [a] separate Katanga state." Ottawa studiously avoided wading into the waters of Congolese internal politics. In May, Ottawa received telegrams from various Katangese political and tribal elements, but these were deliberately left unanswered so as not to imply that Canada ascribed any legitimacy or recognition to the separatist regime. Likewise, External Affairs never approached the Leopoldville government to request exequatur for Gauvin, in fear this could alienate one, or all, of the other various provincial factions. The implications for ONUC of the shift against Tshombé were not lost on External Affairs. Undersecretary Norman Robertson noted, "It is difficult to see how, under existing UN directives, the UN operation could be directed to active support of military action against Katanga. On the other hand, ... it would evidently be very awkward politically for the United Nations Command to attempt to obstruct action against Katanga by a central Congolese government invested by Parliament." The undersecretary hit the nail on the head. Once the constitutional crisis was settled, this was the precise challenge ONUC was required to face.[45]

Just as relations between ONUC and Leopoldville appeared to be on the mend, news of Dayal's return to Leopoldville threatened to undo the improved state of affairs. From his perspective in Leopoldville, Gauvin first said it was difficult to anticipate how the Congolese would react to Dayal's return. The central government appeared preoccupied with Katanga, and he thought Dayal might be accepted without too much fuss. Abbas informed Kasavubu and Mobutu that Dayal was expected to return on 16 June. Dayal later wrote that Kasavubu's reaction was very negative, while Mobutu's was actually violent. Rikhye was dispatched to the Congo to calm the situation, and he subsequently downplayed the Congolese reaction in reports to New York. As a result, Dayal continued to plan for his return. But Rikhye was mistaken. The Congolese Foreign Ministry called together all heads of embassies and legations. The diplomats were told their respective governments should speak to Hammarskjöld and advise him against sending back Dayal. Gauvin, though not present at this meeting, advised Ottawa: "Probabilities are that they are not bluffing and therefore it might be advisable to consult with UK and USA to add our weight to any representation they may make to [the secretary-general]." When Abbas visited Kasavubu and Mobutu to confirm Dayal's expected date of arrival, both leaders remained vehemently opposed to Dayal. In his memoirs, Dayal stated, "Kasavubu said he would abrogate every single agreement with the United Nations and would turn his soldiers on all United Nations personnel and there would be a state of war with the Organization. Both uttered threats and imprecations and said they would stop at nothing to prevent my setting foot in the Congo, Mobutu even threatening assassination." Under these circumstances, Dayal submitted his resignation, and Hammarskjöld reluctantly accepted it. The Congolese had won, but Gauvin told Ottawa the UK chargé d'affaires was instructed to see the Congolese authorities to ask them to avoid any statements presenting the secretary-general's decision as a Congolese victory. Dayal's resignation would have been a relief to Canadian diplomats and peacekeepers in ONUC. They saw the special representative as a hindrance to relations with the Congolese and had made this clear to Hammarskjöld.[46]

## ANC Retraining

One provision of the 21 February resolution required the reorganization of the ANC, and in the new spirit of co-operation between the UN and Leopoldville, Mobutu and Abbas reached an agreement that would see ONUC organize the training of ANC officers. Mobutu stipulated that the instructors would have to speak French and be either French or Canadian. Gauvin learned of the agreement from a reliable source at ONUC and without delay contacted Ottawa. He presumed that Canada would be forced to seriously consider the request if Hammarskjöld raised it in the Advisory Committee and if the "more extreme Afro-Asian members" agreed to the plan. France, he assumed, would be unacceptable to the Advisory Committee. Neither Kasavubu nor Mobutu had approached Gauvin directly about this, so the consul general said he would take no immediate action. At External Affairs, Howard Green was "prepared to give full backing" to the use of Canadian officers as instructors for the ANC. And National Defence engaged in preliminary planning for a retraining scheme after Lieutenant Colonel Speedie, in New York, warned National Defence that "the Military Advisory staff [at the UN] ... is quite incapable of producing a coordinated plan for the retraining of the ANC and that decisions are being made now on a haphazard basis which may well involve Canada in a badly planned operation." External Affairs and National Defence were both agreeable to Canadian participation, but the UN did not immediately follow through with any plan to retrain the ANC. Almost two months later, Gauvin met with Mobutu. The colonel said he was still awaiting a response to his request of the UN to arrange for Canadian or French instructors. Canada, he said, was welcome in the Congo. He wondered why Ottawa was so careful not to offend the Afro-Asians. Gauvin reassured Mobutu that there could be any number of reasons why Canada had not provided officers. External Affairs later told Gauvin the government was still waiting for an official request from the UN because all military assistance had to be channelled through the organization, in compliance with existing UN resolutions. The matter was dropped and not raised again until September.[47]

As the internal Congolese political situation and ONUC were about to enter a new stage in the Congo crisis, Canadian officials paused to reflect on both the nature of the peacekeeping operation and the major considerations that shaped Canadian policy. The UN Division, for instance, was critical of a report that assessed the peacekeeping operation from a strictly military perspective. Murray viewed peacekeeping as both a military and political instrument. It was necessary, he argued, to measure ONUC operations also by "their political impacts and in an international context of great complexity." He added, "While national soldiers may have seen ready solutions on the basis of their national training and experience, those solutions may well have been impracticable because of their international implications and particularly because of the United Nations role and interest in such situations." One document described Canadian policy, particularly as a result of membership in the Congo Advisory Committee, as governed by a need to "preserve an entirely impartial attitude on controversial Congolese issues." While this may have been a guiding principle for policy development and implementation, there were many additional, pragmatic factors to take into account. Another, more complete, assessment identified no less than ten major considerations that shaped Canadian decisions on Congo questions: (1) preventing the Soviet Union from gaining a foothold in Africa; (2) preventing a Soviet-American conflict over the Congo situation; (3) supporting UN intervention as both appropriate and necessary; (4) respecting Congolese sovereignty by scrupulously observing the limitations of the UN Charter in relation to action that could be taken on the territory of a member state; (5) ensuring the UN's success in the Congo so as not to impair the institution's peacekeeping activities elsewhere in the world; (6) avoiding the alienation of Afro-Asian countries, and so not compromising Canada's influence with these states, by not associating Canada with Western positions the Afro-Asians considered colonial in character; (7) avoiding the alienation of Belgium, sympathizing with Belgium, and mitigating friction between Belgium and the UN; (8) adhering to the principle of self-determination, leading to the view that the Congolese people themselves should settle the Congo's political problems; (9) recognizing the Congo's need for economic and technical aid, though channelled through the UN; and (10) safeguarding the welfare of Canadian personnel in the UN force.[48] This lengthy list underscores the complexity the Canadian government faced as it formulated Congo policy. Factors relating to the Cold War, multilateralism, and colonialism all had to be weighed, at times against one another. In the months ahead, this would get only more difficult.

# 6

# The Challenge of Katanga: Peacekeeping and the Use of Force

On 2 August 1961 the Congolese parliament reconvened at Lovanium University near Leopoldville and almost unanimously voted confidence in a new government of national unity, headed by Cyrille Adoula, bringing to an end the months-long constitutional crisis. Adoula, a founding supporter of Lumumba's Mouvement National Congolais, would struggle for the next three years to maintain some semblance of unity in the face of the divisive and conflicting agendas advocated by provincial premiers. For instance, Antoine Gizenga nervously remained in Stanleyville, but parliamentarians loyal to the Orientale faction did participate in the reconvened parliament and assumed at least nine posts in the new cabinet. Members of the Leopoldville faction retained eleven posts, including Justin Bomboko, who continued in his position as foreign minister, and Joseph Ileo who became minister of information. Moïse Tshombé's Katanga group did not attend. Adoula faced two immediate obstacles: persuading Gizenga to fully participate in the new government and resolving differences with the regime in Katanga. External Affairs predicted the stability and effectiveness of the new government would be "determined largely by the ability of a small number of key personalities to achieve a workable relationship." And on this point, Undersecretary Norman Robertson pessimistically observed, "The record of their past performances is by no means entirely reassuring as to the degree of compromise and accommodation which may be expected of these personalities." Nevertheless, Prime Minister John Diefenbaker sent Prime Minister Adoula congratulations on the formation of the new government.[1]

In the weeks immediately following the formation of the new government, Gizenga's position was unclear. He remained in Stanleyville instead of taking up his position as first deputy prime minister in Leopoldville. Colonel Stetham, the commanding officer of the 57th Signal Unit, reported that Gizenga refused to allow a provincial minister to travel to Leopoldville on the grounds that the central government remained in Stanleyville. When Consul General Michel Gauvin met with Adoula for the first time, on

22 August, and inquired about the situation in Orientale, the Congolese prime minister assured him that Gizenga did intend to come to the capital and that the diplomatic missions in Stanleyville had been advised to recognize Leopoldville as the one and only government in the Congo. In Gauvin's words, "Although Mr. Adoula did not give [the] impression that difficulties with Stanleyville were over he appeared determined and confident to overcome conditions one way or another." Adoula's confidence seems to have been derived from a meeting with Gizenga in mid-August; External Affairs, however, noted that there were conflicting reports as to the agreement reached between the two leaders at this meeting. Hoskyns suggests Gizenga demanded Adoula take action against Katanga as quid pro quo for participation in the central government. Ottawa considered it unlikely that Adoula would be able to consolidate his control over the rebellious Congolese provinces until the difficulties with Gizenga were resolved. In reality, the opposite was true: for Adoula, action against Katanga was the key to integrating the Gizengist faction.[2]

## Operations Rumpunch and Morthor

On 24 August the Adoula government issued an ordinance requiring the expulsion of all separatist foreign officers and mercenaries in Katanga, and ONUC was asked to assist in their detention and repatriation. In a move that caught the Katangese authorities by surprise, ONUC initiated Operation Rumpunch on 28 August; 338 of the 442 European officers in the gendarmerie were rounded up and detained for repatriation.[3] Considerable tension in Elisabethville was the result. A Canadian peacekeeper serving at ONUC HQ, Captain Mario Côté, was sent to the Katangan capital to serve as a liaison officer between ONUC and the Katangan armed forces. Soon after his arrival, he was surrounded by demonstrators and "briefly menaced but subjected to no violence." The group was content with shouting and booing at the Canadian officer.[4] Tension eased somewhat when ONUC agreed that the Katangan authorities, in co-operation with the consulates of Western nations in the provincial capital of Elisabethville, could take the lead in arranging the repatriation of the captured officers.

Not only did Côté have difficulty with the Katangese, he also found ONUC's actions problematic. Conor Cruise O'Brien, an experienced Irish diplomat who had served as a member of the Irish delegation to the UN in the late 1950s, was appointed by Dag Hammarskjöld to be the secretary-general's representative in Elisabethville. Côté discreetly complained to Colonel Stetham about an incident in which he was required to have a Belgian woman who was eight months pregnant submit to a medical examination against her wishes, after O'Brien was said to have insisted on documentation from a non-Belgian doctor in order to permit the husband, a Belgian officer, to remain in the Congo until after the baby was born. Stetham complained to ONUC Commander General MacEoin and insisted that Côté's employment would have to be changed if the Canadian officer was being asked to "perform tasks in a manner liable to reflect badly on the Canadian Army." The chief of the general staff concurred with Stetham. The colonel was told, "Feel sure if you explain [the] situation to General MacEoin he will understand that we expect all ranks to carry out their duties in an effective manner and that we know he would not wish any of our soldiers to be given tasks which would reflect adversely on Canada." When informed of the "harsh and almost ruthless character" of ONUC's actions against the Belgian advisers, Secretary of State for External Affairs Howard Green went one step further, instructing Undersecretary Norman Robertson to protest any further actions of this sort directly to the secretary-general.[5]

In New York, Hammarskjöld was in fact consulting with Canada's permanent representative, Charles Ritchie, as well as the permanent representatives of the United Arab Republic, Nigeria, and Sweden, on developments in Katanga. Given the delicate nature of the situation in the breakaway province, Hammarskjöld was reluctant to discuss matters with the entire Advisory Committee. He called together this select group of diplomats to explain the situation and hear their comments. Hammarskjöld was pleased with the UN's new relationship with the Adoula government, which he described as "an enormous improvement on anything they had ever experienced in dealing with Congolese authorities in the past." "It was," he continued, "a prime objective of UN policy that [Adoula's government] should survive and that the new and better prospects in Congo should not be wrecked." Hammarskjöld considered it was time for Katanga to "take its rightful place in a unified Congo." Although Tshombé was seen as obstinate on this point, the secretary-general was more concerned with the Katangan minister of the interior, Godefroid Munongo, who was reported to be inciting intertribal hatred. When Hammarskjöld raised the possibility of ONUC arresting Munongo, Ritchie expressed concern for the precedent this would set. Howard Green later confirmed Ritchie's view. The minister advised New York: "The possible future implications of establishing such a precedent are sufficiently disturbing that I consider every effort should be made to avoid having to resort to this move." The Canadian government was pleased with the prospects for new-found political stability in the Congo, made possible by the Adoula government, but believed there were limits to the measures that should be taken to support it. Nevertheless, according to Brian Urquhart, a senior member of the UN Secretariat at the time and subsequent biographer of Hammarskjöld, the secretary-general came away from this meeting, and others with Belgium, Tunisia, the United States, and Britain, with the impression that "most of the governments concerned would now be prepared to assist in putting all possible pressure on Tshombe to negotiate and that they now also realized that more drastic measures could be expected if these efforts did not produce the desired effect."[6]

Operation Morthor (Hindi for "smash"), initiated by UN peacekeepers in Katanga on 13 September, was undoubtedly a muscular response to Tshombé's dithering on the removal of the last of the European volunteers and mercenaries. One hundred and four were known to be in Katanga "re-infiltrating into the gendarmerie, distributing arms to groups of soldiers over whom they could assert control, and getting ready for violent resistance." In addition to rounding up these remaining foreigners, Colonel Stetham advised army headquarters that Morthor was intended to establish UN control of the Elisabethville airport, radio station, and post and telegraph offices, and capture key political agitators, including Munongo. Hammarskjöld's cautious consultations in New York, especially on the question of arresting Munongo, raise the possibility Morthor was initiated on orders from the Secretariat, but most accounts of ONUC are unequivocal in interpreting the operation as a strictly local initiative. Resistance by the Katangese gendarmerie was unexpectedly strong and resulted in eight days of pitched battles, not only in Elisabethville but also in Kamina, Jadotville, and Albertville. There were fifty Katangese and eleven ONUC deaths. The UN Secretariat maintained that "Belgian and white-led forces," and not the Congolese in Katanga, were responsible for the extended hostilities.[7]

The commanding officer of the 57th's Elisabethville detachment reported that he was disgusted by the lack of co-operation from ONUC brigade headquarters, as the Canadian peacekeepers were neither briefed or consulted about the operation and found out about it only by chance from the Indian signals. The eleven peacekeepers barely had time to evacuate their equipment to the new brigade headquarters outside the centre of the city. The logistics officer at brigade headquarters refused to provide soldiers to assist with the move, so the Canadians dismantled a generator, lifted it into a truck, and departed with a stockpile of water and rations. Their belated preparations paid off: in the days ahead there were shortages of both food and water at the new headquarters and the electricity was severed. A mercenary, flying in a Fouga Magister jet trainer, bombed ONUC positions in Elisabethville three times.[8] Captain Rich, the officer in charge of this 57th detachment, reported that one signaller continued to operate the teletype "in total blackout with amazing calm and dexterity," even though bombs landed within twenty-five feet of the transmitter room, causing shrapnel to break the windows. Two other signallers volunteered to retrieve wounded under fire.[9]

Two of the ten Canadian peacekeepers in the Albertville detachment had an especially harrowing experience when hostilities broke out there on 17 September. They remained at the mess after the evening meal and came under attack when three Katangese fired into the building. By phone, Captain Bussieres, the officer in charge at Albertville, ordered both to take cover, not to return fire unless the building was invaded or their lives were threatened, and not to do anything that would draw attention to themselves. Cut off from other ONUC forces, they could do little but wait. Firing continued late into the night but eventually trailed away, and the Katangese simply left at daybreak. At that time, the Indian troops retook the airports and railway, and secured the ONUC brigade area, "systematically" wiping out all opposition. The Canadians never had to fire a single shot, none was wounded, and their equipment was undamaged. At Kamina, the seven Canadian peacekeepers were protected by an ONUC battalion and suffered no casualties despite a series of attacks by the Katangese. Shelling did destroy their wireless set.[10]

From Leopoldville, Gauvin told External Affairs that ONUC authorities were unprepared for the strength of the reaction in Katanga. Morthor was expected to proceed as "smoothly" as the round of arrests in late August. At Adoula's invitation, Hammarskjöld arrived in Leopoldville expecting to negotiate a settlement of the differences between Tshombé and the Congolese government. Confronted by the outbreak of serious hostilities, he thought it best first to discuss ceasefire arrangements with Tshombé. Political extremists opposed any such negotiations with Tshombé, but the secretary-general convinced the Congolese parliament of the necessity for a ceasefire. Hammarskjöld also met with British officials, the ambassador in Leopoldville, Derek Riches, and the marquess of Lansdowne, the latter having been purposely dispatched from London to question Hammarskjöld. They expressed concern that the UN was using force to achieve a political settlement. The secretary-general rejected this view and held firm to the position that ONUC had acted within the terms of the 21 February resolution. After British prime minister Macmillan telephoned US president Kennedy to discuss the situation, the American ambassador in Leopoldville, Edmund Gullion, was also advised to meet with Hammarskjöld to express the US government's dismay that the UN had taken the actions it did without adequate, prior consultation. The Americans were particularly upset about the timing of the renewed hostilities because they had hoped to convince Tshombé to meet the secretary-general in Leopoldville.[11] Late on 17 September, Hammarskjöld flew out of Leopoldville to meet Tshombé at Ndola, in Northern Rhodesia. His plane never arrived. Its wreckage was found the next day west of the Ndola airport. All sixteen persons on board died, including Hammarskjöld.

External Affairs viewed the hostilities in Katanga, compounded by the death of the secretary-general, as a serious threat to Congolese stability. Both Adoula's government and Tshombé's regime were fragile coalitions dependent upon the support of extremists who threatened to pull the two leaders further apart and, therefore, lessened the likelihood of a negotiated settlement. In meeting Adoula's request to assist the central government with the expulsion of foreign officers and mercenaries, Ottawa believed the UN could "claim to have acted within a legal framework and have probably stayed within the letter of their mandate" but that the organization left itself "open to criticism by appearing to use force to bring about a political settlement in favour of the Central Government." External Affairs questioned the prudence, not the legality, of UN actions in Katanga, yet viewed with concern the growing divide between the majority of Afro-Asians and the Europeans, especially Britain and France. The press in both India and Ghana implicated the United Kingdom in Hammarskjöld's death. A dispatch from Gauvin, based on reports from the French consul in Elisabethville, confirmed that the successful defence of Katanga was "due to the mercenaries, backed by a European population acting out of fear of reprisals by the Baluba should the UN operation succeed." In a message to Howard Green, the British Commonwealth secretary, Duncan Sandys, rejected the "malicious" charges levelled against Britain concerning Hammarskjöld's death but admitted Britain was "distressed that some of the most virulent comment has come from our African and Asian Commonwealth partners." Sandys maintained that Britain never supported Tshombé in his "secessionist ambitions" and implied the UN, or at least its local Congo officials, had made errors that contributed to the events in Katanga. Sture Linner, ONUC's officer-in-charge, and most especially Conor Cruise O'Brien were singled out and particularly blamed by the British government for exacerbating hostilities. In the following weeks, the United Kingdom pressed the UN to remove O'Brien, who eventually agreed to be recalled to the Irish Foreign Service, only then to resign and to very publicly air his account of events in Katanga.[12]

Half-hearted apologetics did not play well in Leopoldville, where anti-Western demonstrations were on the rise. Outside the American and Canadian consulates, Congolese carried banners declaring, "Western imperialists have killed Hammerskjold [sic]," "Western imperialists are killing our brothers in Katanga," and "Death to Western imperialists." In the midst of this anti-colonial tension, Ottawa hoped cool heads would prevail and urged a return to constructive, impartial diplomacy. External Affairs viewed the facilitation of negotiations between Tshombé and Adoula as the most urgent task facing the UN but was also keen to see the organization "return to its impartial role of preventing civil war." In preparation for a meeting of the Congo Advisory Committee, Green advised Ritchie: "It would be our hope that the UN would not contemplate any new hostilities in Katanga likely to lead to a renewal of hostilities. We would certainly expect to be consulted before any new decisions are taken which might have serious consequences."[13] Canadian authorities were not critical of the UN in its first round of hostilities with Katanga, but they were certainly uncomfortable with the direction of events.

## Canada and ONUC

Unease with the events in Katanga curbed Canada's enthusiasm for UN requests, though the government usually remained willing to meet UN needs. On 20 September, the Secretariat urgently requested transport aircraft, aircrews, maintenance personnel, and spare parts for airlifts within the Congo for three to five weeks. ONUC relied, to a considerable extent, on charter airlines for internal transport of supplies and personnel. During Operation Morthor, Katangese jet fighters damaged or destroyed a number of these charter planes, so most airlines withdrew their services, reducing available charter aircraft from thirty to three. The aircraft requested were to resupply forces stationed throughout the Congo. Sweden and Ethiopia had already offered jet fighters to escort the transport aircraft. By the end of five weeks, ONUC expected the threat from the Katangese jets to be resolved and planned to revert to chartered transport. Officials warned Howard Green that there could be armed resistance and renewed hostilities if the UN tried again to arrest mercenaries in Katanga. Cabinet considered the request, and Green acknowledged it was a difficult decision. Although the aircraft would be at risk of attack, especially if the ceasefire ended, cabinet agreed on 23 September to send two C119s for one month, together with the necessary crews to permit their operation twenty-four hours a day. The planes and personnel left the next day.[14]

In acceding to the request, cabinet identified three important factors: the need to support Canadian and other peacekeepers deployed throughout the Congo, the significance of UN success in Katanga for the organization's future effectiveness, and public opinion. Harkness thought the Canadian public would criticize the government if it refused the request. This was one instance when public opinion was explicitly acknowledged to be a factor in the government's decision making. Editorial opinion in the Canadian newspapers was by and large supportive of the UN's action in Katanga. The *Chronicle-Herald* was perhaps the least enthusiastic, worrying about what the future implications might be of an international organization intervening with force in the domestic affairs of a country. Even then, however, its editorial argued, "It had ... become increasingly obvious that this rebellion – for it was not less – must be brought to an end if the Congo was to survive." The *Toronto Daily Star* worried over the potential consequences if the UN failed in Katanga but clearly supported the actions of peacekeepers there, calling for the world to "hope for the success of the Swedes, the Irish and the Indian Gurkhas now fighting in the streets of Elisabethville under the U.N. banner." Finally, the *Montreal Gazette* not only believed UN military action was necessary but questioned whether "such action should not have been taken sooner." Some letters to the editors of these newspapers were far less supportive. Typical of these was one from an anonymous correspondent to the *Chronicle-Herald,* who concluded, "There is quite obviously a perverse, evil influence at work behind the scenes of the United Nations, and unless it is uncovered and unless President Moise Tshombe is re-instated, we will have allowed the Communists another major victory in the cold war." While it is difficult to know how representative any of these views were of public opinion more generally, a poll conducted in September 1961 does provide a rare glimpse into wider public sentiment. When asked if they thought the UN was doing "a good job or a poor job in trying to solve the problems it has to face," 68.1 percent of respondents said the organization was doing a good job, and another 18.4 percent said it was doing a fair job. Although the question is framed rather vaguely, the overwhelming favourable response certainly suggests that hostilities in Katanga had not negatively impacted the UN's image.[15]

Two weeks later, a second request arrived from the Secretariat. ONUC required eight control tower officers and two maintenance ground communication technicians to aid in the operation of the Swedish and Ethiopian jet fighters and Indian light bombers now assigned to ONUC. Because of the policy implications of this request, further information was sought from New York. Ottawa learned that ONUC intended to use the fighters and bombers in the event hostilities were resumed, both to defend its transport aircraft and to "render unuseable" the runway available to Katanga's jets. Should the ceasefire be breached, MacEoin planned to move all jets to Kamina to operate from within Katanga. External Affairs was very concerned about the implications of Canadian involvement in this aspect of ONUC's operations. Robertson wrote to Green, "There is, of course, a possibility that if we agree to the present U.N. request, we could be placed later on in an awkward position if the U.N. engages in warlike operations in the Congo, and particularly in Katanga." The undersecretary was especially worried that such action might be taken in circumstances that would prove troubling to Canada, but Howard Green did ultimately ask the minister of national defence, Douglas Harkness, to give "sympathetic consideration" to the request. The personnel involved, it was argued, would still be considered "non-combatant" and the aircraft would provide protection for both members of the RCAF and the 57th Signal Unit already in the Congo. Harkness advised Green on 25 October that there was "an acute shortage" of suitable personnel required to meet the UN's request, so it could be met only by sacrificing the operational efficiency of RCAF units in Canada. He asked External Affairs to inform the Secretariat that "Canada would prefer not to accept this commitment." Disappointed and deeply concerned by the negative reply, UN undersecretary for special political affairs Ralph Bunche personally approached Canada's permanent representative, Charles Ritchie, and asked if Canada would reconsider its decision. The American and Ethiopian missions also expressed concern. The United States was unwilling to provide the necessary communications equipment unless Canadians agreed to operate it. The Americans had previously expressed disappointment over the outbreak of the latest round of hostilities in Katanga, but they were more gravely concerned, especially after the death of Hammarskjöld, by the prospect that Congolese leftists would be strengthened if ONUC's military operations collapsed. The need for this equipment became acute when Katangese planes carried out bombing raids in Kasai. In an Advisory Committee meeting, Bunche revealed that ONUC had warned the Katangan authorities that any further offensive action would be countered with the destruction of "all planes involved either in air or on ground." But the UN would not be able to carry out this threat without the American equipment and Canadian personnel. Green wrote Harkness asking him to reconsider his decision. The minister observed, "It would appear that Canada would be the object of widespread criticisms by Afro-Asian countries, particularly those who are members of the Congo Advisory Committee, if it is felt during the forthcoming developments that the capacity of the U.N. to resist aggression is seriously impaired because of our inability to provide the communications personnel needed for the servicing of the U.N. aircraft." Before Harkness received Green's appeal, the minister of defence raised the matter in cabinet on his own initiative and the earlier decision was reversed. Yet again, Canada set aside political reservations and competing operational requirements to meet the UN's needs. Cabinet also granted a thirty-day extension on the loan of the two C119s but cautioned there was "no intention of continuing this arrangement indefinitely."[16]

Both cabinet and National Defence were displeased when, on 20 November, Congolese forces seized a Yukon turbo-prop when it landed in Leopoldville. The plane was released only after Air Commodore Morrison appealed directly to Adoula and Mobutu. Worried additional aircraft might be detained, National Defence suspended all Yukon flights to the Congo, a decision that was subsequently endorsed by cabinet. It was late December before the matter was reviewed. At that time, the chairman, chiefs of staff asked Norman Robertson to seek assurances from the UN that any RCAF aircraft flying within or into the Congo in support of ONUC would not "be subject to seizure or impoundment." External Affairs learned from Leopoldville and New York that the Yukon incident was an isolated case of mistaken identity. The Congolese were confused by the unfamiliar design of the plane and because it bore only RCAF insignia, not UN markings. To reassure Ottawa, the UN put in place measures to prevent a recurrence of this incident: Congolese authorities were to be given adequate notice prior to the arrival of each flight. UN officials were, in fact, keen to use the Yukons because one flight with this larger aircraft could replace two troop rotation flights on North Stars.[17]

It has been suggested that incidents such as that with the Yukon happened frequently enough to cause Ottawa to become "less eager" to provide ONUC with assistance generally and to meet a particular request in November 1961 for help in establishing a security service. While the threat of violence toward Canadian peacekeepers was always a concern and a factor the government weighed when it assessed UN requests, political and even administrative concerns were often the more significant factors when it was decided to turn down or scale back Canadian involvement in ONUC. A security and intelligence service request, cited by historians J.L. Granatstein and David Bercuson, is one such example. This request was turned down for two reasons: Canada could not spare forty bilingual officers qualified to do intelligence and security work and, as was the case with the earlier request from Indar Jit Rikhye, the secretary-general's military adviser, for a peacekeeper to gather intelligence in Brazzaville, both External Affairs and National Defence questioned the wisdom of Canadian involvement in a service that had "the greatest possibility of embarrassment to any nation involved." Similarly, in late October, the chief of the air staff issued instructions to develop a case to get the RCAF out of providing an officer to serve as ONUC air commander. The timing of this decision, coinciding as it does with the addition of jet fighters and light bombers to ONUC's air services, suggests National Defence was uncomfortable having a Canadian oversee operations that went beyond transportation of supplies and personnel. Political considerations, and not just concern for casualties, were always evaluated and weighed heavily in the decision to either approve or reject any given UN request for assistance.[18]

Following Operation Morthor, External Affairs considered whether it should continue to obtain situation reports from Colonel Stetham. ONUC directives strictly prohibited the communication to home governments of any information peacekeepers learned during the course of their duties. This, it will be recalled, was the subject of an earlier exchange between the UN headquarters and troop-contributing states, Canada included. Command instructions permitted direct communication with Ottawa on purely administrative matters and questionable orders, but the commanding officers of the 57th also sent detailed situation reports. In the wake of the first round of Katangan hostilities, Canadian officials became concerned that other countries, particularly the Afro-Asians, would learn that Ottawa received regular situation reports from Canadians serving in the Congo, yet the benefits of continuing to receive the reports were seen to outweigh the risks. One official noted, "It is clear that our Consulate General alone could not provide all the information that we need. Neither could the U.N. nor our friends from other countries." The reports, he said, "provided invaluable background information on Congo crises, such as the Matadi affair and the U.N. action in Katanga." To minimize the chance of a leak revealing the transmission of these reports to Ottawa, it was suggested that only a small number of peacekeepers in the Canadian contingent be made aware of the existence of the reports and that they not be circulated outside Ottawa unless warranted in an urgent situation. Perhaps to ease guilty consciences or to offer further justification, an official noted, "We know that the Indians themselves are reporting to their Government the information made available to them through their participation in the U.N. contingent."[19]

The question of providing Canadian officers for training and advising duties was raised again on 12 September, when the UN asked if Canada could provide qualified French-speaking personnel to fill some of the eighteen officer and eleven NCO positions required as part of its plans to reorganize the ANC. On instructions from Washington, the American embassy in Ottawa asked External Affairs to give this request "most sympathetic consideration." But when National Defence studied the availability of bilingual officers, it concluded it was inadvisable to draw any officers from headquarters or units in Quebec command or from corps schools. A limited number of the personnel requested could be provided "but only at the expense of reduced efficiency elsewhere." Seven officers already serving in the Congo at ONUC HQ were considered the only viable candidates, and their release from current duties for employment with the ANC would be required. But before these conclusions were shared with External Affairs, the hostilities in Katanga and Hammarskjöld's death pushed the training and reorganization plans into the background, particularly because the training school was to be located at Kamina, in Katanga. Then, in November, the senior military adviser to the Congolese government, General Iyassu, spoke with Gauvin and asked Canada to provide eleven officers: nine staff for the training school and two advisers for the ANC. Iyassu threatened to resign if the UN did not take action to establish the training school. He believed neither the situation in Katanga nor the need to integrate the Stanleyville ANC should further delay the school's opening. "If Canada replied affirmatively and quickly," Iyassu thought, "the U.N. would be willing to fill the most important positions by Canadian officers, leaving other appointments to other nationalities." Because of Gauvin's reported conversation with Iyassu, External Affairs contacted New York and asked the Permanent Mission to obtain the Secretariat's views and intentions. At the same time, the chief of the general staff advised the chairman, chiefs of staff and Harkness that he was "most reluctant to accept this commitment" because of the impact on efficiency within French-speaking units. When National Defence advised External Affairs on 21 November that it was doubtful it could meet any requests for further French-speaking officers for the Congo, the Mission in New York was immediately advised not to approach the Secretariat after all, or if it already had, to inform the Secretariat that it was unlikely Canada could provide the peacekeepers requested. With this, the question of ANC training and organization was once again set aside.[20]

## Financing ONUC

The sixteenth session of the General Assembly was expected to consider and resolve the question of ONUC's financial woes. At the time of Hammarskjöld's death, the United Nations was $100 million in debt.[21] By mid-October, it was clear that a solution would not be found by the end of the month, when the authority to incur ONUC expenses to a maximum of $10 million per month would expire. Eleven members of the Advisory Committee, including Canada, cosponsored a resolution in the Fifth Committee to extend this authority to the end of 1961, to permit ONUC to continue. The Department of Finance expressed reservations about this resolution because it failed to include a provision for the apportionment of expenses; in its view, "the Canadian Delegation should have pressed for some provision concerning the obligation of members to meet any expenditures incurred under this resolution." External Affairs disagreed, considering there would be ample opportunity later in the sixteenth session to discuss this "at length and without pressure," so long as this technical resolution was not jeopardized by a general debate on the principle of assessment, a subject open to exploitation by the Soviet bloc. The resolution passed by a vote of fifty-five in favour, nine against, and fifteen abstentions. The troubling state of ONUC's finances, temporarily allayed by this interim authorization to incur $10 million for each of the last two months of 1961, was resolved to mid-1962 with an additional Fifth Committee resolution approved by the General Assembly in December. Resolution 1732 (XVI) continued the ad hoc Congo account, authorized average monthly expenditures of $10 million each month from January to June, confirmed the October measures that had provided $20 million for November and December 1961, and called for the apportionment of these expenses in accordance with the scale of assessment for the regular budget. Provisions were made to reduce or rebate the assessment for members that could not afford to pay, while permanent members of the Security Council and Belgium were urged to make additional contributions to offset these rebates. In its final report on the Fifth Committee's activities during the sixteenth session, the Canadian delegation said it had played a significant role in the behind-the-scenes negotiations that led to the adoption of the resolution. William Barton, a diplomat posted to the Canadian Mission to the UN, had chaired the session and worked assiduously to achieve a formula acceptable to developing nations. Most impressed by Barton's negotiating skills, the Pakistani ambassador told him if he was ever out of work the ambassador would give him a rug merchant's concession in Karachi. Although there were reservations about the size of the rebate offered and the fact that financing was arranged for only the first six months of 1962, Canada supported it because of the UN's poor financial position and because a UN bond issue was expected to raise enough funds to meet the additional costs for the remainder of 1962. Above all, Canada hoped that continued political conciliation in the Congo might limit the scope of ONUC's operations, and consequently its expenses, throughout the coming year.[22]

## Resolution 169 (1961) and Renewed Hostilities

Despite a 13 October ceasefire negotiated with Tshombé by the civilian head of ONUC, Mahmoud Khiari, the situation in northern Katanga worsened. Katanga launched offensive air action along its border with Kasai, and ANC forces from Leopoldville and Stanleyville were only partly successful in their attempts to take control of towns just south of the Katanga/Kivu border because of stiff resistance from European mercenaries. Concerned by the situation in Katanga and the mercenaries' continued presence and actions, Ethiopia, Nigeria, and Sudan requested a meeting of the Security Council. In considering ONUC's mandate and the issue of foreign military personnel operating in Katanga, External Affairs identified three potential choices facing the UN: ONUC could actively assist Leopoldville in a conquest of Katanga, ONUC could stand aside while Leopoldville renewed military operations against Katanga, and ONUC could interpose itself between the two rival forces. Because the United Kingdom insisted on a peaceful, negotiated settlement with Katanga, chiefly to avoid disruption of mining operations there, the first option was considered a non-starter. So long as the ANC continued to lack air support and the mercenaries remained in Katanga, the second scenario also seemed out of the question. As for the third option, External Affairs was of the view that the UN was obliged, under the terms of the 21 February resolution, to intervene to prevent any further fighting between the ANC and Katanga's gendarmerie but recognized that this would require the Secretariat to abandon its position that ANC operations against Katanga were essentially a police action. The essential question underlying all of this was "whether, and to what extent, the UN should side with the Central Government in its quarrel with Katanga." Howard Green agreed with Robertson's proposition that Canada and the UN give moral and political support to the central government on the issue of secession but not cooperate militarily in any operation against Katangan forces. In his first meeting with the newly appointed acting secretary-general, Howard Green advised U Thant of the Canadian government's view: ONUC was in the Congo to preserve order, not to support an ANC attack on Katanga.[23]

U Thant, the permanent representative of Burma, was chosen to complete Hammarskjöld's term in office after the tragic plane crash near Ndola. Brian Urquhart has written that U Thant "was in almost every way the opposite of Hammarskjöld."[24] In comparison with Hammarskjöld, U Thant was calm, simple, direct, and more apt to listen and take advice from others. By early 1962, Canadian diplomats and officials had worked with and observed the acting secretary-general enough to form general impressions of his abilities and handling of the Congo crisis. Charles Ritchie found him to be "in good form[,] unruffled by his responsibilities[,] firm and clear in his opinions and frank in his discussion." U Thant trusted Ritchie enough to share quite critical views of Soviet policy toward the Congo. The Canadian ambassador observed, "U Thant who is a patient and sympathetic listener may let more ambitious and voluble members of his staff talk themselves out and then pursue his own course. I suspect that this technique which I have seen him employ in [the] Advisory [Committee] may be one which he will follow in dealing with senior advisors who surround him." The acting secretary-general was more likely to delegate, particularly to Bunche and Rikhye, than was his predecessor but still approved all major decisions. The way in which U Thant employed the Advisory Committee was notably different from Hammarskjöld's. Hammarskjöld consulted the committee often, as a forum for testing ideas and assuring adequate support for his policies. In addition, associating all members of the committee with his Congo decisions provided some protection from Soviet criticism. U Thant was less likely to consult with the committee before taking action and used it more as a forum for communicating information about the Congo and UN actions. In sum, the African and Middle Eastern Division concluded, "U Thant's handling of Congo affairs so far has been effective and not basically inimical to Western interests."[25]

The Security Council adopted its fifth and final ONUC resolution on 24 November 1961.[26] Sponsored by Ceylon, Liberia, and the United Arab Republic, Resolution 169 (1961) was silent on the question of whether ONUC should support the central government militarily in its efforts to reduce Katanga. To achieve the widest possible support for the resolution, this issue had to be avoided because, in addition to Canada, most other Western countries, India, and the acting secretary-general opposed any suggestion that ONUC undertake offensive operations against Katanga. Yet, the resolution can be seen as an incremental step in the application of force to the Congo situation. U Thant was authorized to take "vigorous action, including the requisite measure of force, if necessary, for the immediate apprehension, detention pending legal action and/or deportation" of all foreign officers and advisers not under UN command. This provision was cause for concern in Ottawa, where it was thought that U Thant's "ideas about settling the mercenary problem could lead to a renewal of fighting or at least a number of unsavory incidents." External Affairs hoped "that it could be recognized that the primary responsibility for getting rid of mercenaries should rest with the Katanga authorities." The government's reluctance to see ONUC employ military force did not apply to the mission's right to reply with force in self-defence. The rationale for this distinction was underscored after the massacre of thirteen Italians serving with ONUC, in Kindu on 11 November. Robertson noted, "There is little doubt that a Canadian aircrew in the same circumstances could well have met with a similar fate."[27]

A second round of fighting between ONUC and Katanga soon over-shadowed discussions on the principles governing the use of force. Tshombé condemned the Security Council's 24 November resolution and dramatically called upon the Katangese to defend their homeland. In the following weeks, a number of incidents were directed against the UN. Brian Urquhart, sent to Elisabethville by the secretary-general to replace Conor Cruise O'Brien, and his deputy were seized and beaten by the Katangese gendarmerie. They were released only after ONUC threatened to storm the presidential palace and Tshombé intervened. Urquhart is said to have told reporters, "Better beaten than eaten." In addition, one Indian peacekeeper was murdered, and an Indian officer and eleven Swedish peacekeepers were captured. Events culminated on 5 December, when the gendarmerie set up a roadblock between Elisabethville and the local airport, and local ONUC authorities decided to take military action to clear it. Once fighting between ONUC and the gendarmerie erupted, U Thant authorized ONUC to take "all necessary action to ensure freedom of movement including the occupation of key points," a sound decision justified by the Security Council's resolutions. Additional peacekeepers were flown from elsewhere in the Congo to Katanga, and ONUC jets destroyed four Katanga aircraft on the ground in Kolwezi. External Affairs recognized a key difference between this round of hostilities and those that occurred in September: this time, the UN was clearly acting to protect its personnel and positions and was doing so only as a last resort, after all attempts to work with the Katangese authorities had proved fruitless. Charles Ritchie was confident both the secretary-general and Brian Urquhart would act with restraint but firmness. Urquhart, in particular, was seen to be "far less emotional and prejudiced than his predecessor [O'Brien]." External Affairs appeared satisfied the UN was acting reasonably to safeguard ONUC peacekeepers.[28]

This resumption of hostilities in Katanga brought to the fore differences of opinion within the West on how best to resolve the Congo crisis. Both Britain and France abstained on the 24 November resolution, whereas the United States voted for it – as did the Soviet Union. The Americans quickly recognized a differentiation in the US and UK positions. In what one Canadian official observed was tantamount to a pro-Tshombé policy, Britain insisted that the UN role be confined to the conciliation and pacification of differences between Tshombé and Adoula. "In short," he concluded, "it would seem that the United Kingdom in the past few months has tended to adopt a more 'European' policy towards the Congo." Britain wanted a formal ceasefire and asked the United States to consider a joint appeal to U Thant. In discussion with his Danish counterpart in Leopoldville, Gauvin learned that Washington rejected this suggestion; for good measure, the Danish consul general also criticized British policy and suggested the United Kingdom "would meet another Suez." Stephen Weissman argues that the

United States did begin to take a stronger line at this juncture and partly attributes this shift to the influence of the US ambassador in Leopoldville, Edmund Gullion, who flew to Washington mid-November and urged President Kennedy to deal with Tshombé more firmly. The split between the United States and Britain placed Canada in the awkward position of having to choose between the two opposing policy options favoured by its most important allies. The United States considered a ceasefire unacceptable until after ONUC was in a position to ensure it could protect its personnel and assure their freedom of movement, yet the distinction between military and political objectives was also somewhat blurred. A memo prepared by the United Nations Division argued, "There is more than a suggestion ... that in the armed conflict the Katangese forces will be shattered and that Mr. Tshombe will be obliged to enter into negotiations with the United Nations and with the Central Government of the Congo." In other words, it was possible that in the forceful exercise of its right to freedom of movement throughout Katanga, ONUC could overpower the gendarmerie and the mercenaries, effectively ending the secession. Such a political settlement, achieved through force, was unacceptable to Britain. Prime Minister Harold Macmillan wrote to Diefenbaker, explaining the British position: "It is the duty of the United Nations to bring about at the earliest possible moment an end to hostilities and a return to the path of conciliation and negotiation."[29] Macmillan's appeal to Diefenbaker, and the British prime minister's views on the Congo situation more generally, were undoubtedly shaped by the dire straits he perceived his government to be in as a result of divisions within his own party over Britain's Congo policy.[30]

In Ottawa, there seems to have been a difference of opinion as to which side to support. Although Diefenbaker initially appears to have been less critical of the British view, officials at External Affairs preferred the American position. They argued against a premature ceasefire, suggesting it would embolden Tshombé and undermine negotiations among the Congolese. Moreover, Canada had supported ONUC from the outset; the appearance of withdrawing support at this point, when the UN had taken action only after severe provocation, would be disconcerting. During an inconclusive discussion in cabinet on 7 December, Howard Green was more blunt: "Canada had troops in Katanga and must either back the U.N. or let it down." Britain's attitude against the military action taken by ONUC was attributed to "her other African interests, particularly Rhodesia." Some ministers considered it time to withdraw Canadian peacekeepers from the Congo, while others argued this would leave ONUC without communications and in a hopeless state. Evidently, External Affairs' rationale ultimately prevailed because one week later the prime minister emerged from a cabinet meeting and, though not commenting on Britain's demand for a ceasefire in Katanga, justified the UN action there as "the result of a series of provocative acts."

That same week, Green returned to Ottawa from a meeting of NATO ministers in Paris and was more explicit. Clearly contradicting the British position, he told reporters there should be a ceasefire only after the UN had achieved "certain military objectives." During the Paris meeting, only Canada and Norway had supported the United States in opposing the British position. Green put it simply: "The Americans took the right stand." In New York, on 16 December, the Advisory Committee also addressed the question of a ceasefire and everyone, including Canada, praised the US position, while Britain and France were criticized. By way of compromise, it was suggested that Canadian influence within the Advisory Committee be used to urge restraint and a halt to the fighting as soon as ONUC positions were secure. Even this, though, would have to be done tactfully. The UN Division warned, "The Western powers will be closely watched by the African-Asians for any sign that they are weakening in their resolve to ensure that the Congo is reintegrated with United Nations assistance. Sharp criticism could be expected if Canada appeared to equivocate in the current situation."[31]

With an eye not only to Britain but also to public opinion, Canada advocated a "speedy and effective" end to hostilities as soon as practicable. The government was concerned that continued reports of civilian casualties and confusion as to the UN's objectives in Katanga would eventually undermine public support of ONUC. In the battle of public relations, the UN appeared "to be losing some ground ... as a result of the emphasis which is being placed on the anti-Communist and self-determination aspects of the Katanga case." These were common themes in about two dozen letters sent to the government protesting UN action in Katanga. W.J.W. Bullock wrote, "In order to be consistent I suggest it is your bounden duty to appeal to the United Nations to send an Army into the Prov. of Quebec to suppress the Secessionist Movement there before it attains greater proportions. If slaughter & terror, initiated by U.N. Forces, are in order in suppressing secession in a Prov. of the Congo it surely is equally applicable to Quebec." Another letter exclaimed, "How glad I am to see the British are not afraid to stand up for Katanga! Surely any red blooded government with the smallest sense of fair play would do so ... The United Nations couldn't intervene in Hungary, etc but they, the cowards they are, can pick on a little province like Katanga. This U Thant? Is he a communist? I wonder." Letters supporting the UN were uncommon, but not altogether absent. One Canadian wrote, "It is tragic that the British government should take this stand. It also adds to the suspicion that directly or indirectly Britain, Welensky & Co. were responsible for the death of the great secretary-general. If we have to choose between membership in the U.N. or in the British Commonwealth I would choose the former." From mid-December, there was an increase in the number of published newspaper letters to editors quite critical of the UN action in

Katanga. This correspondence, however, may very well have been an angry response prompted by editorials in the respective papers that criticized British Congo policy and praised Canada's decision to support the American position. The *Toronto Daily Star*, for example, left little doubt in the minds of its readers as to where it stood on this issue. It entitled one of its editorials "Dubious U.K. Policy in Congo," and a week later published another under the headline, "Canada Is on the Right Side."[32]

By 19 December, ONUC had consolidated positions in Katanga required for its security, and peacekeepers were ordered to hold fire unless fired upon. Writing in 1965, Ralph Bunche asserted that the UN did not take offensive action in this round of fighting, that ONUC's actions were entirely consistent with the Security Council's resolutions, and that hostilities stopped "the moment the security and freedom of movement of the United Nations Force had been restored." Nevertheless, the fighting resulted in the deaths of 206 Katangan soldiers and 6 non-Congolese soldiers, and a further 50 civilians were either wounded or killed. A report from Gauvin implied that it was just as well the fighting ended when it did. The consul general learned from Air Commodore Morrison that the UN had almost bombed a building where women and children were taking shelter; only poor aiming was said to have prevented the building's destruction. Morrison also revealed that he intervened at the last moment to prevent the bombing of Tshombé's residence by two Canberras. The fighting took a toll on ONUC's civilian leadership in Elisabethville. According to Morrison, Urquhart was shaken, not from being attacked personally or from the pressure of work but from the confusion of battle and "the fact that he never knew what the UN troops would do next." Gauvin, Morrison, and Urquhart were all critical of ONUC's military commander in Katanga, Brigadier Raja. Gauvin said he had a pleasant personality but not the "qualities necessary to lead a delicate and intricate military operation with political considerations." To illustrate this point, the consul general recalled a social occasion at Raja's home when the Brigadier pointed into the darkness and assured his guests, "I have organized an all-round defence and if these Congolese bastards ever try to come in, we will shoot them like flies." Morrison and Gauvin's observations suggest it was probably for the best that ONUC consolidated its position and halted hostilities as expeditiously as it did.[33]

## Canadian Contributions to ONUC

The latest round of hostilities in Katanga convinced National Defence to follow through with its plan to vacate the position of air commander at ONUC HQ. Harkness wrote to Green on 7 December to say that once Air Commodore Morrison completed his tour in the Congo at month's end he would not be replaced. Harkness justified his decision on the grounds that, to this point, the air commander principally coordinated transport. ONUC's military involvement in Katanga was expected to result in increased responsibilities, including both defensive and offensive military operations. Because the enlarged staff required to meet these new responsibilities was expected to come mostly from countries other than Canada, Harkness believed that the country supplying the largest elements of the force should also provide the commander. The UN Division at External Affairs expressed concern at this decision. Geoffrey Murray stressed the political reasons why Canada should continue to provide an officer to fill this role. Senior officials in the Secretariat were said to have high regard for the RCAF contribution in the Congo. In the past, Murray said, the military had complained they were not given an adequate role in ONUC, yet the position of air commander provided an opportunity to "continue a contribution which is recognized as effective and for which we are well qualified." The safety and welfare of Canadian peacekeepers located in detachments throughout the Congo could be protected if a Canadian continued in this role. Murray cited Gen. E.L.M. Burns's command of UNEF as a ready example of how the United Nations did not consistently follow the principle of appointing commanders from the largest troop-contributing states. Above all, the political implications of not replacing Morrison were noted: "We should not wish to expose ourselves to a charge of backing away from the United Nations operation at a time when our support was needed most. There is no doubt in my mind that if we do not replace Morrison the news about our refusal will spread." It was not until 18 December, when he returned from a NATO ministerial meeting in Paris that Green wrote Harkness asking that the decision be reconsidered.[34]

The minister of defence was unmoved and asked Green to inform the UN without delay of the department's desire to withdraw Morrison by the end of the year. Because of the lateness in responding to the UN request, Harkness was willing to provide an additional two weeks of service in order to give the UN time to find a replacement. Green decided not to press National Defence any further and issued instructions to inform New York. The Secretariat was disinclined to accept no for an answer, however. Rikhye contacted Murray by phone to emphasize that the UN command "had become accustomed to dealing with RCAF officers on air matters and that the smoothest co-operation had been possible because the RCAF officers 'understood the United Nations.'" They were disturbed by the negative reply to their request; U Thant, the acting secretary-general, was considering a direct appeal to Diefenbaker. The next day a telegram for Diefenbaker did arrive from the secretary-general, which read: "I most earnestly appeal to you, therefore, to find it possible to replace Air Commander Morrison, who has rendered outstanding service in that position, with an RCAF officer of similar qualities." After further consultations with External Affairs and Harkness, the decision was made to extend Morrison's term by an additional three months, after which time National Defence would neither renew Morrison's term nor provide a substitute.[35]

Another ongoing issue was revived on 23 December when U Thant directly asked Diefenbaker for fifteen French-speaking officers to assist in the training of the Congolese army. General Iyassu last raised this matter in a similar request made urgently through Gauvin in November. At that time, National Defence concluded there were too few suitable officers available. Events in Katanga had preoccupied the Secretariat, and Canada did not send a negative reply because it had never received a formal request. It was not clear to National Defence whether this request bore any relation to the earlier one from Iyassu, but the shortage of officers identified then still applied. The chairman, chiefs of staff advised the prime minister that thirty-eight, mostly French-speaking, officers were already provided for the Congo. Living conditions required frequent rotation, so four to five officers were required as backup for each officer assigned there, and National Defence expected any commitment to train the ANC would continue "for a very long time." The request was not rejected outright and further information was requested, but it was clear the military was not keen to stretch its French-speaking officer corps any further than it already was. External Affairs, on the other hand, drew attention to the advantages of the request: retraining the Congolese army would eventually permit the withdrawal of ONUC, which U Thant hoped to achieve by the end of 1962; a positive response would be consistent with Canada's support of ONUC and its policy of helping the Congolese help themselves; helping the Congo would demonstrate that Canadian assistance in Africa was not exclusively for English-speaking countries; and Canada was one of very few acceptable sources of French-speaking instructors who would still be a Western influence on the Congolese army. Cabinet reviewed these arguments on 28 December but postponed a final decision until Harkness, who was in western Canada, could be present.[36]

Pressure to arrive at a decision was applied early in January, when Rikhye contacted External Affairs to follow up on the request. Prime Minister Adoula had set a deadline of 15 January for the United Nations to establish the school or he intended to look elsewhere to provide the training. To facilitate a positive response, Rikhye was willing to employ recently retired officers and provided assurances that they would receive satisfactory compensation. The reason for Rikhye's persistence was made clear in the Advisory Committee. Bunche revealed that both Canada and Switzerland had been approached for officers, but Switzerland had already turned down the request. "Everything now depended on Canada," Bunche said. On 26 January, cabinet debated the merits of providing assistance. Howard Green argued in favour of providing officer instructors; Harkness opposed the plan. The position of the minister of national defence prevailed, primarily because the recent fighting in Katanga highlighted the Congo's political instability and raised doubts as to the wisdom of sending more Canadians there. Information obtained from Air Commodore Morrison that the training was not for officers but for NCOs and that "it would be at least ten years before the U.N. could divest itself of its military commitment in the Congo" were also decisive factors. The acting secretary-general was told his request was given careful consideration but that no French-speaking officers with the required qualifications were available.[37]

### Political Conditions in the Congo

The first few months of 1962 were relatively stable in the Congo, largely because of an agreement reached by Adoula and Tshombé in the days following the fighting in Katanga the previous December. The Kitona Declaration provided a basis for settling the constitutional impasse on terms that generally favoured Adoula's government. Tshombé accepted the *loi fondamentale*, recognized the authority of the central government over all Congolese provinces, agreed to end the secession, and said he would uphold the UN resolutions. In this spirit of conciliation, Tshombé also agreed to the deployment of peacekeepers in Jadotville, Kolwezi, and Kipushi – towns known for the presence of mercenaries. This plan to station ONUC forces in the outlying areas of Katanga concerned Charles Ritchie and prompted him to question U Thant on the wisdom of carrying out what could appear, to either the gendarmerie or local inhabitants, to be an ONUC occupation. Ottawa was less concerned. Howard Green agreed that the arrival of ONUC in these towns could lead to friction but believed the UN was correct in its decision to deploy these peacekeepers. Yet, in the minister's view, this would need to be carried out tactfully so as not to create the impression that military operations were being resumed. External Affairs was more concerned with reports from London that the arrival of ONUC in these towns might be followed with ANC troops; this, they thought, would be premature and could "upset the apple cart."[38]

In any event, Tshombé subsequently reneged on the agreement to station ONUC troops in southern Katanga, as part and parcel of his failure to implement the measures called for in the Kitona Declaration. The Katanga provincial assembly refused to ratify the declaration and suggested it be used simply as a basis for continued negotiation with Leopoldville. Norman Robertson surmised, "Tshombe may try to turn the clock back by again taking the attitude that he is negotiating with the Central Government as an equal and demanding a confederal solution." Adoula's position as prime minister was seen as tenuous; if he failed to resolve the Katanga issue, it was thought that his political support would shift to another leader prepared to take more extreme measures. The result of this impasse was yet another extended round of negotiations between the two leaders. While these negotiations were taking place, Ottawa learned the UN might occupy Kolwezi,

Jadotville, and Kipushi, without Tshombé's co-operation, if the talks broke down. Howard Green had previously supported this idea but only if it could be done "in such a way as not to appear as a resumption of military operations against the Katanga gendarmerie." This new plan, implying occupation without any co-operation or consent, was an entirely different matter. However, the African and Middle Eastern Division thought there was no need "for Canada to express alarm in New York." If the UN attempted to carry out the plan, Britain could be counted on to protest.[39]

Against this backdrop of Congolese political strife, February 1962 provided an unprecedented period of comic relief at the Canadian consulate. Gauvin received instructions from External Affairs to investigate and report on his Communist colleagues in Leopoldville. One can only imagine the reaction in Ottawa when they received the consul general's first report, entitled "Lunch with Soviet Colleagues," on a luncheon hosted by the French ambassador, which Gauvin attended with the Russian chargé d'affaires, a second Russian introduced as the first secretary but who remained nameless, and the chargé d'affaires of Dahomey. Aside from brief, innocuous comments about Robert Gardiner replacing Sture Linner as ONUC's officer-in-charge, political topics were studiously avoided during lunch and in Gauvin's report. Instead, Ottawa was treated to an account of Russian perspectives on European literature, albeit a colourful account no doubt inspired by the menu of Amer Picon, whiskey, white champagne, red wine, red champagne, Armagnac, and cognac. Consumption of this much alcohol left the Russian chargé quite "loquacious," though the first secretary was noted to have held "his liquor much better." Ottawa did eventually receive a more traditional and far less entertaining report on the presence of Communist missions in Leopoldville and their relations with the Adoula government. The Soviet Union, Poland, East Germany, and Yugoslavia maintained diplomatic posts in the capital, but their relations with Adoula were described as non-existent.[40]

This same month, Ottawa received an unusual account of a "diplomatic" incident between Justin Bomboko, the Congolese foreign minister, and a staff member from the Canadian consulate. Hearing the continuous honking of a car horn and the rattling of a tin, Mr. Weidman went out onto his balcony and asked a man in the street to stop honking the horn. This turned out to be Bomboko, who according to Weidman screamed, "You don't know who [you're] dealing with. I am going to take away your visa. I am coming up to take down the number of your apartment. What do you mean by throwing a tin at me!" Weidman denied throwing a tin and went back inside his apartment. Moments later, Bomboko and another man burst into his apartment. Bomboko yelled, "People do this sort of stupid thing and then they call the Congolese 'savages.'" Weidman managed to convince Bomboko he had not thrown the can, and the foreign minister left "muttering dire threats against the person who had thrown the tin." Weidman's account concluded, "I am informed that Mr. Bomboko's white secretary who is rumoured to double as his mistress, lives in the same building as I." The acting consul general said, "The only explanation I can find for such behaviour was that Mr. Bomboko had had too much to drink."[41] February was a very odd month for Canadian diplomats in the Congo.

### Canadian Contributions to ONUC

In February and March, the United Nations made three additional requests of Canada. The most remarkable was a direct appeal from Ralph Bunche to Gen. E.L.M. Burns, asking the general to succeed General MacEoin as the next ONUC force commander. At the time, Burns was serving as the chief adviser to the Canadian government on disarmament. Burns referred the request to Howard Green, who decided that Burns's services could not be offered. The minister noted that it would be impossible to replace Burns as Canada's chief delegate to the upcoming disarmament conference. The politics of colonialism and the Cold War also influenced his decision. Green questioned the wisdom of appointing a commander from a NATO country, fearing this could lead to friction with African and Asian states contributing troops and to hostility from the Soviet bloc, all of which could negatively impact the prospects for the UN's overall success in the Congo. Ritchie broke the news to Bunche, emphasizing the significance of Burns's role as disarmament adviser. Bunche was understanding, acknowledged the importance of Burns's duties with respect to disarmament, praised the general's outstanding qualifications, and agreed that he would not press the suggestion further.[42]

The 57th opened a new detachment at Kindu, in the province of Kivu, in February. This fully committed the signal unit, so ONUC HQ became concerned by the possibility it might need to deploy forces into additional areas on short notice and would need additional signal personnel. To meet this shortfall, U Thant asked if the signal unit could be increased by two additional detachments of one officer and ten men each. The Defence Liaison Division recalled that this was "the first request for additional signalers to be received for a long time." It hoped National Defence would agree to meet the request and argued that it should be possible to find the necessary personnel to fulfill a legitimate need. National Defence, however, cited a shortage of technical tradesmen and said it could not provide the additional detachments without jeopardizing other commitments. Following consultation with the Canadian contingent in the Congo, Harkness offered a compromise: Canada would maintain a standby detachment of one officer and nine men that could be quickly sent to the Congo and that would be replaced by a second standby detachment, if and when the first was dispatched. The secretary-general was informed of the arrangement, following its approval by cabinet on 3 April 1962.[43]

The third UN request resulted in a peculiar reversal of roles: External Affairs expressed caution and reservations, but National Defence readily agreed to it. The UN sought an additional three peacekeepers for ONUC HQ. External Affairs was fine with the provision of a major to serve as deputy chief of military personnel and a corporal for clerical duties in the provost section; it had doubts "about the desirability of providing a Canadian NCO for military information activity, especially since it is specified in the U.N. request that experience in intelligence activity would be useful in this case." Previously, Canada had advised the UN that it did not want its peacekeepers to be involved in intelligence activities in the Congo. This request occurred just as ONUC was strengthening its intelligence resources. According to Walter Dorn and David Bell, the first two rounds of hostilities in Katanga demonstrated the need to improve ONUC's intelligence gathering activities. Rikhye responded with the establishment of a radio-monitoring organization and other enhancements to the Military Information Branch. Another plan to send a Canadian peacekeeper to Brazzaville to confirm information on the arrival of six Fouga jets destined for Katanga was evidence of this reinvigorated attempt to gather intelligence. In this instance, Colonel Stetham would not permit the officer to be sent outside the Congo without first obtaining government approval, and this, he told the chief of military information, was unlikely to be given. Discounting External Affairs' misgivings, National Defence said it was prepared to supply a sergeant, whom it assumed would be employed "on minor staff duties, ... for example the marking and maintenance of operational maps." The officer would not be permitted to do field intelligence work. External Affairs advised New York that the required officers would be provided but also asked National Defence to confirm with Colonel Stetham "our understanding that no Canadian officers or men are involved in field intelligence activities in the Congo." External was keen to know more about the nature of the work done by officers assigned to military intelligence at ONUC HQ. It was not uncommon for National Defence to be guarded when asked to meet UN requirements from its stretched resources; yet, External Affairs could also be cautious in its attitude toward UN requests, especially when potential risks to Canada's reputation or policy interests were involved.[44]

The thorny issue of contingents communicating directly to their governments from the Congo was raised once again by the United Nations in April. General Rikhye, in a meeting with the various military advisers from troop-contributing states, asked that all direct links be eliminated. Use of unauthorized radio frequencies was said to be causing confusion and jamming the signal of the Leopoldville radio station. The need to communicate with home governments on administrative matters was acknowledged, and Rikhye offered to provide communication facilities through UN channels. RCAF single side band voice communication, direct between Trenton and Leopoldville, was excepted. This caused something of a stir in Ottawa as External Affairs and National Defence conferred on how best to respond to Rikhye's statement. As when this issue was previously addressed, the command instructions and conditions set by cabinet when it approved the dispatch of signal personnel were reviewed. These clearly stipulated that the senior officer of the Canadian contingent had the right to direct communication with army headquarters. Earlier, the UN was concerned mostly with contingents that sought confirmation of the force commander's orders before following them. This time, the UN was worried about security leaks. Coming so soon after External Affairs had reviewed the question of whether it should continue to receive situation reports from the 57th Unit's commanding officer, Rikhye's comments appear to have struck a nerve. National Defence maintained that the Canadian communications station in Leopoldville was set up on the "express instructions" of the chief of the general staff and was operated by experts who would have ensured that there was no interference with the Leopoldville radio station. For this reason, Rikhye's comments were assumed not to apply to Canada in particular. Because the secretary-general's military adviser had raised the issue only verbally, National Defence considered a formal, written response unwarranted. As there is no record of a response, External Affairs seems to have agreed.[45]

Although cabinet decided on 26 January not to provide instructors for a Congolese army officers' training school, a new round of discussions resumed throughout February and March after the Canadian permanent mission in New York wired an anxious appeal from U Thant to Diefenbaker to request Canada's participation. The acting secretary-general pleaded, "We are so desperately in need of French-speaking officers for this purpose that I feel that I must renew my appeal to you in a modified form as sole means of avoiding necessity of abandoning training project altogether and informing Congolese [government] of our inability to assist them in this training." While the UN had earlier requested fifteen officers to form a homogeneous group to take charge of the school, it was now willing to take any officers Canada could spare, even those who were retired, on the inactive list, or in the reserves. Considering the question of Canada's participation a matter of great urgency, Ralph Bunche approached Gen. E.L.M. Burns and asked him to speak directly with the chief of staff of the Canadian army on behalf of the UN. These discussions with Lieutenant General Walsh failed to achieve immediate results, but Burns thought his "little missionary effort may do some good later." Bunche further lobbied William Barton, a diplomat at Canada's Permanent Mission. Barton learned that Greece, Argentina, and Finland were willing to provide French-speaking officers, but Bunche stressed that he and the secretary-general were still hopeful that Canada would come through with the required officers to form the nucleus of the school. Bunche was certain the UN would agree to any reasonable conditions of service Canada stipulated and even to the recall of the Canadian officers on short notice if an emergency required their return to Canada. Of all the UN requests related to the Congo, this strong effort to convince Ottawa to reverse its decision was unprecedented, and pressure came not only from the UN but also increasingly from the Congolese directly. At the UN General Assembly, Prime Minister Adoula appealed publicly for assistance in training the ANC one week after Harkness admitted, in answer to a question raised in the House of Commons, that Canada did not have the required number of French-speaking officers needed to operate the school. Because the UN, in its revised request, was willing to use retired or reserve officers and was no longer expecting Canada to assume sole responsibility for the school, officials speculated the previous negative response was "more difficult to justify publicly." When Ross Campbell, special assistant to Howard Green, spoke with Diefenbaker about the UN's latest inquiry, he found the prime minister not unsympathetic but unwilling to press the issue with Harkness if the minister felt unable to make any officers available. During further discussion in cabinet, the original decision not to provide any officers from the active list was confirmed, but the secretary-general was informed that the government was looking into the possibility of making available six or seven officers from the retired list. Robertson subsequently advised Green, "The problem of recruiting suitably qualified French-speaking officers may be in the process of finding a solution." National Defence was mostly concerned with the administrative details of incorporating retired officers into the army establishment for service in the Congo.[46]

Both Mobutu and Adoula were growing impatient with the UN, and Mobutu in particular was opposed to the idea of a school operated by a mixed group of officers from various nations. Adoula wrote to ONUC HQ, "It appears to me that [Canada] which has never been a colonial power which has no political or economic interests in Africa and which possesses good military schools could furnish these few instructors who are needed." Mobutu spoke directly to Gauvin, asking that the consul general make one last appeal to the government. At this point, the African and Middle Eastern and Defence Liaison Divisions at External Affairs began to question the wisdom of providing only a few officers for a school operated by a number of nations, especially if Mobutu opposed such a plan. They argued that Canada should either provide the entire complement of officers or none at all. This view was rejected, and the Permanent Mission in New York was asked to find out the specific appointments, ranks, and qualifications for the six or seven officers Canada could provide.[47] It remained to be seen whether the Congolese government and Mobutu would agree to UN plans for a school operated by officers of various nationalities.

In addition to the help sought in establishing an officers' training school, the UN continued to make additional requests in direct support of ONUC throughout the summer of 1962. Generally, National Defence acceded to fewer of these requests, usually citing a shortage of qualified personnel or a need to reduce departmental expenses. Still, in a review of the requests that arrived during the summer months, Norman Robertson concluded, "There has been no indication that the army or the Air Force are less willing to be forthcoming in their responses to U.N. requests for assistance to ONUC since the commencement of the government's austerity programme. Each request is carefully examined on its merits and with regard to the availability of the services to meet them." External Affairs recognized that they sometimes were at a disadvantage in assessing the utility and significance of UN requests relative to National Defence. To correct this, the consul general in Leopoldville was directed to gather information so that the department could more independently evaluate National Defence's decisions, which were often based on consultations with the commanding officer of the 57th. Gauvin was told, "We have no reason to doubt the accuracy of the information received through that channel [CO 57th] but we are uncertain whether in the end the political factors are weighed as carefully as the military ones." In a response to External Affairs, the consul general confessed that he also relied on the views of senior Canadian officers to assess the necessity of UN requests; he found them to be always cooperative and "anxious to stop any unjustified request from UN for further personnel." Ottawa was assured that Canadian military and diplomatic personnel were keeping an eye especially on senior Indian officers, who were said to have a "propensity to create staff jobs."[48] Even as ONUC began its third year, requests for assistance that were seen to have merit, and especially those that could be met from within existing establishments, could still expect to receive a fair hearing by the government.

National Defence continued to provide replacements for all personnel in the Congo during this period, including a new commanding officer for the 57th; Col. W.S. Hamilton replaced Col. H.W.C. Stetham on 13 May. Requests for additional commitments to ONUC were approved and rejected in almost equal measure. When the UN asked for further flying control personnel to serve at UN posts in Katanga, External Affairs identified several political disadvantages and recalled the difficulties National Defence faced in its earlier effort to provide such personnel. Although it passed along the request with the mild observation that the request appeared reasonable in the circumstances, it did not press the matter with National Defence, and the request was turned down. Likewise, requests for eight additional military police at the rank of private and a mobile photo-developing unit, with personnel, were declined. Four other routine requests were granted: four French-speaking switchboard operators, two officers and one NCO for service at ONUC HQ, a military auditor, and a projector technician. National Defence and External Affairs also concurred in the appointment of Major Normandin, a Canadian serving as liaison officer to the ANC, to the Military Committee of the Joint Reconciliation Commission, which was working toward the peaceful re-establishment of Congolese unity. Finally, the government agreed to provide a military assistant to the ONUC chief of staff and the chief logistics officer for Katanga and appeared willing to meet an anticipated, future request to provide two officers for ONUC HQ: the deputy chief of staff and chief of logistics for all of ONUC. Gauvin expected the latter request because the force commander was intent on reducing the number of Indians in senior staff positions "to avoid criticism of predominant Indians in key jobs." According to the consul general, the Indians were not keen to see their presence at ONUC HQ diluted. Following a meeting with Indar Jit Rikhye, he reported, "I gained the impression that Indians seemed to be reluctant to abandon key positions and, to be frank, suspect they badly need [Canadians] but do not want them to fill positions where they could interfere with their own plans." Overall, the evidence suggests that the government's support of ONUC was relatively stable throughout this period, in spite of personnel shortages and increasing financial pressures at National Defence, with one notable exception: the Pisa-Leopoldville airlift.[49]

In June 1962, the government agreed to a further ninety-day extension of the RCAF Pisa-Leopoldville airlift, in operation almost from the outset of ONUC. As had become customary, the UN was warned that the commitment would be kept under active review, to ensure more economical modes of transportation were also used to supply the peacekeeping forces. The following month, National Defence informed External Affairs that it would not be possible to renew this agreement after 9 September. The Diefenbaker government was confronting serious economic difficulties that had already led to the devaluation of the dollar in May; when a second exchange crisis occurred the following month, cabinet approved emergency measures that included significant reductions in government spending. As the prime minister explained his government's austerity program to all Canadians in television and radio broadcasts, National Defence justified to External Affairs its decision to end the airlift on the grounds that the government's austerity measures required the review of "all extraneous commitments in order to effect every economy possible." The airlift would be replaced with bimonthly, nonstop Yukon flights in direct support of Canadian peacekeepers in the Congo. An important Canadian contribution to the UN operation was about to come to an end.[50]

The implications of this decision were not lost on External Affairs, where officials immediately took action to get the decision reversed. They questioned

National Defence's argument that cancelling the airlift would result in financial savings. The vast majority of the expenses involved were recoverable from the UN, although National Defence's budget was negatively impacted if expenses were recovered in a year subsequent to when they were incurred and, thus, credited only to the Receiver General. External Affairs countered, "There will be little saving for the Canadian Government as a whole," adding that "the announcement that Canada is curtailing its assistance to ONUC at such a critical juncture in the Congo would throw unfavourable light on the Canadian attitude toward the U.N. without bringing us any substantial advantage in terms of the austerity programme." Rather than raising the issue either in cabinet or at the ministerial level, Howard Green instructed Robertson first to discuss the matter with the chairman, chiefs of staff.[51]

The undersecretary wrote to the chairman presenting External Affairs' financial and political arguments. Robertson wondered if some change could be made in accounting practices in order to resolve National Defence's budgetary dilemma and not deprive the UN "of a support which they consider necessary and which the Organization is prepared to pay for in its entirety." To the dismay of National Defence, which expected to end the airlift as an administrative decision, External Affairs expressed its intention to raise the matter in cabinet if National Defence proceeded with its plans. The chairman, chiefs of staff wrote to the chief of the air staff, noting, "It is apparent that if we are to get approval on this we will be up against Ex. Affairs in Cabinet." He asked, "Have we got enough ammunition to win? Can we get credit in our estimates for the UN payments – if we do not now do so." National Defence attempted to resolve the matter at the administrative level. In mid-August, Air Commodore Birchall told the Defence Liaison Division that, because 426 Transport Squadron had been disbanded as part of the government's austerity program, the RCAF simply did not have the aircraft to continue the Congo airlift. In the interests of time – the deadline of 9 September was quickly approaching – he suggested the UN be notified of the decision so that it would have time to make alternate arrangements. Even if considered by cabinet, he said, "there would not now be time to arrange to resume the flights." In a subsequent discussion with Ross Campbell, the chairman, chiefs of staff suggested there could still be some flexibility with the 9 September date, but that it would be best to "notify the UN as requested and reconsider the matter when the inevitable 'protest' follows." Howard Green made one last appeal to Diefenbaker to see if the prime minister would ask Harkness to reconsider the matter. Diefenbaker said he would not object if Green asked Harkness to review the decision but he would not direct the minister of national defence to alter it. Green chose not to make any further representations to Harkness but was told that if the UN pressed strongly for reconsideration of the decision, National Defence would review its decision.[52]

## Political Developments in the Congo

Canada decided to establish formal, diplomatic relations with the Congo in June 1962. The Canadian consulate became an embassy, and Michel Gauvin, the consul general, became Canada's first chargé d'affaires. Letters of introduction were prepared for Gauvin and presented to Foreign Minister Bomboko on 13 July. Bomboko said he "was touched by the sign of confidence Canada showed towards the Republic of the Congo" and spoke warmly about Canada's contribution to ONUC and the other forms of assistance that had been provided. Canada, he said, was in a "special position to help the Congo because they shared a common language, ... there were other countries which were willing to help the Congo, but because of cultural difficulties, were not in the same position as Canada to do so."[53] Congolese political developments in the remaining months of 1962 would test Canada's commitment to ONUC, the UN, and Adoula's government.

This change in diplomatic status coincided with a reinvigorated attempt by U Thant to address the political impasse between Tshombé and the central government. The acting secretary-general faced both financial and political pressures to resolve the Congo crisis: the UN had enough funds to finance ONUC at its current level only until January 1963, and he was anxious to achieve progress before his interim term in office ended and he had to stand for election to the post. Supported by the United States, the secretary-general engaged in a round of diplomacy to persuade the British and Belgians to apply financial pressure on Tshombé's regime. He was less successful with the British than the Belgians, though Alan James notes some British officials later speculated that Belgium was rather duplicitously encouraging the United States and United Nations to see Britain as the "stumbling block." That said, Norman Robertson observed, "They [the British] are anxious at all costs to avoid 'a third round' in Katanga. It seems unlikely, therefore, that the British will agree to the use of major economic sanctions against Katanga or any move to use U.N. troops to protect the mines." In a message from Harold Macmillan to American president John F. Kennedy in May 1962, the British prime minister warned that the United Kingdom would not accept another UN military operation against Tshombé. This is entirely in line with how British policy evolved throughout 1962, according to Alan James. He suggests the British government came to the conclusion that the best approach it could take was to let it be known, quietly, that it would not stand in the way of the application of sanctions against Katanga but also to continue its efforts to prevent the UN from resorting to force. Meanwhile, in New York, Congolese officials attempted to rally Afro-Asian support for renewed UN action against the Katangese mercenaries, the very option Britain opposed. Howard Green was against renewed hostilities in Katanga, but Robertson concluded, "Unless the British, Belgian and French are prepared to threaten Tshombe with real sanctions it seems unlikely that he will make the necessary concessions."[54] Once again, ONUC approached a crossroads on the question of using force.

The Congo Advisory Committee met on 31 July to discuss options after U Thant failed to reach a consensus with the European states on how best to apply economic pressure on Katanga. The secretary-general was weighing the possibility of summoning the Security Council in order to revise or clarify ONUC's mandate, conceivably to authorize greater use of force. The Canadian government opposed this for several reasons: uncertainty as to the likely outcome of a third round of fighting; concern that fighting by ONUC peacekeepers would weaken public support and the UN's image, limiting effectiveness in future emergencies; and, it was believed not to be in the long-term interests of the Congo for Katanga to be subjugated using outside forces – a lasting solution, it was thought, required the Congolese to settle their own constitutional issues. On the surface, this policy appears to support Britain's position, but there was a difference. External Affairs accepted that Tshombé's delaying tactics had to be ended soon and supported the secretary-general's efforts to persuade Britain, France, and Belgium to apply financial pressure. The undersecretary observed, "Adoula's prestige has suffered to the point where unless progress is made soon his government may fall ... The U.N.'s prestige is also involved and so is the personal position of U Thant especially in relation to his chances of being elected Secretary-General." In the Advisory Committee, Canada's new ambassador to the United Nations, Paul Tremblay, cautioned against both the use of force to settle Katangan secession and public debate of the issue in the Security Council. Rather, he suggested a moderate, constructive approach: support for U Thant's efforts to reach a negotiated settlement.[55]

Within weeks, a new plan emerged to compel a negotiated settlement between Katanga and the central government. Although hatched largely in the US State Department, with subsequent consultation with Belgium, Britain, and France, this framework for national reconciliation in the Congo came to be known as the U Thant Plan (or at times, the Plan of National Reconciliation). It consisted of a set of concrete steps to be implemented by both Tshombé and Adoula and four phases of action to be followed if Katanga proved uncooperative, culminating in a voluntary ban on mineral imports from the secessionist province. Britain objected to this latter provision for an embargo out of fear it would lead to fighting or set a precedent for future UN sanctions against the Rhodesias and South West Africa. The United Kingdom was said to have expressed reservations about UN demands for ONUC's freedom of movement, fearing Tshombé would interpret this as a threat of UN military action. While not in support of sanctions, Britain did intend to warn Tshombé that it would be unable to oppose or prevent their application. External Affairs appears to have had little faith in the efficacy of such warnings. One assessment of British policy in the Congo noted,

"They have on several occasions used their influence to persuade Tshombe to negotiate with the Central Government but they do not seem to have exerted much pressure on him to make the concessions necessary for a solution. By advocating negotiations in which Tshombe would hold most of the cards they are in effect encouraging a Tshombe-dictated solution." Of course, the United States, having largely authored the plan, favoured it. American diplomats lobbied Canada to endorse it and to consult with the secretary-general to encourage him to present it without delay.[56]

The Canadian attitude toward the Plan of National Reconciliation fell somewhere between Britain's reluctant co-operation and America's ardent support. While most features of the plan were acceptable, there were concerns about sanctions. Ross Campbell said, "Our object should be to devise for use in New York a form of words which would support the purposes of the proposals and the positive features of the four-stage programme ... while avoiding any language which would appear to endorse as well the embargo clauses about which we have reservations." Ambassador Tremblay rose to the occasion and met this call for ambiguity in subsequent discussions with Ralph Bunche, who was simply told that Howard Green recognized the need to maintain a united front on both the reconciliation proposals and the various courses of action contemplated. This was hardly a ringing endorsement, but it achieved an important goal: Canada remained uncommitted on the question of sanctions. Although not nearly to the same degree as the British, the Canadian government was somewhat concerned about the precedent that might be set should sanctions be applied to Katanga. It was, however, more appreciative of the need to have "some effective pressure in reserve to avoid another endless round of negotiations." Ultimately, this accounts for Howard Green's expression of support for economic sanctions in discussions with Lord Home during the 1962 Commonwealth prime ministers' meeting. Green was reported to have "scolded the British for their unco-operative attitude towards ONUC," a stand that was probably "warmly appreciated ... by most of the delegations other than the British." Canadian concerns about sanctions were largely limited to the fear that the central government would not be able to enforce them and the UN might be asked for assistance, increasing the risk of renewed hostilities between Katanga and ONUC. Canada still opposed a military offensive against Katanga. Green said, "We're on a peace-keeping operation, not a war-making operation."[57] Overall, the Canadian position on the Plan of National Reconciliation managed to be similar to certain aspects of each of the contradictory policies of both the United States and Britain.[58]

When efforts to implement the plan once again stalled because of disagreements between Adoula and Tshombé, many had a sense that the crisis was coming to a head. Gauvin thought both leaders were equally obstructive, but the chargé d'affaires was cognizant of Adoula's tenuous position in

Parliament. Extremists accused the prime minister of "being used by the colonialist interests to balkanize the Congo." Gauvin ominously reported, "Though I have been one to preach patience in the past, I now feel that the brink may have been reached here; that Western interest and influence in this part of Africa does rest on the success of the present UN proposals." Gauvin was not alone in recognizing that a turning point had been reached. In an August report to the Security Council, the secretary-general warned that if a solution was not found to the Congo stalemate soon, the UN's financial position and further deterioration in the Congolese political situation would require, once and for all, a decision on whether ONUC should be withdrawn or authorized to "seek by all necessary measures" an end to Katangese secession.[59]

Canada was forced to re-examine its Congo policy in mid-October, when U Thant asked members of the Advisory Committee for guidance. Both the UN and the Congolese government were concerned that Tshombé was dithering in order to build up his military forces and in hopes that Adoula's government would eventually fall. Adoula, therefore, decided to cut off Tshombé's revenue: Union Minière was ordered to stop paying any taxes or fees to the Katangese authorities. The secretary-general believed this might lead to a request from the company that ONUC protect its mining installations and transport routes against Katangese retaliation. Because deployment of ONUC on such a task could lead to another round of fighting, U Thant sought assurances from troop-contributing states that they were "prepared to accept the possible consequences." Citing the UN's financial predicament and the serious implications for future peacekeeping if ONUC failed, External Affairs argued the government should indicate in the Advisory Committee its approval of the Adoula government's actions with respect to Union Minière and its acceptance of increased risk to Canadian peacekeepers should ONUC be asked to protect the company's installations. Given the political significance of these issues, a memorandum was prepared for Diefenbaker requesting his views. The prime minister considered the matter to be of sufficient importance to require discussion in cabinet before instructions could be issued to the Mission in New York. In a submission to cabinet, Green contended that Canadian peacekeepers were playing a key and specialized, technical role that would make it very difficult for them to be replaced; a decision to restrict their role in Katanga could jeopardize ONUC at a critical juncture. If Canada did lessen its support, it would be more difficult for the acting secretary-general to refuse offers of troops from countries ready and keen to use force against Katanga. Green concluded that Canada "could hardly refuse to support the U.N. attempt to control Tshombe," but cabinet was not convinced. Some ministers regretted ever having sent peacekeepers to the Congo and suggested that if they were used this way in Katanga it would be viewed "with horror in the United Kingdom." Others felt that

ONUC was simply not up to the task. In the end, cabinet agreed that the delegation "should not indicate in the Congo Advisory Committee that Canada in any way approves of the proposed new approach to the Union Miniere, or accepts any increased risks to Canadian personnel in the protection of Union Miniere's interests." Cabinet was also against any attempt by U Thant to obtain a new mandate for ONUC from the Security Council. Despite External Affairs' arguments, there were limits to Canada's support of the UN. External Affairs remained hopeful events in the Congo would outpace discussion in the Advisory Committee and advised the delegation to remain silent, unless doing so would be construed as tacit approval for a course of action not in line with the cabinet decision.[60]

The Secretariat did not immediately press the issue. The possibilities of sanctions, boycotts, and pressure on Katangan companies dragged on for another month. Some progress was made when the Americans, British, and Belgians agreed to press Union Minière to pay its taxes to the Monetary Council in Leopoldville. But the threat of sanctions and embargoes lingered. In mid-December, the Liberal leader of the Opposition, Lester Pearson, asked Diefenbaker in the House of Commons what Canada's policy was on the imposition of sanctions on Katanga. The prime minister evaded the question. He simply outlined the more innocuous provisions of the U Thant plan and then concluded, "So far as the particular question [of sanctions] is concerned, I think until further discussions have taken place with the secretary general and member nations it would be better that I do not go further than I have gone at this point." Canadian policy, it seemed, was to avoid the issue unless it became impossible not to take a stand. Semantics facilitated such a policy. When Adoula and U Thant wrote to seventeen governments asking them not to import Katangan ores, the secretary-general said this did not amount to sanctions because the Congolese government was asking other governments only to respect its laws and not import ores on which "legal taxes and duties" were not paid. Canada was not expected to receive such a letter because it did not import mineral ores from Katanga.[61]

As 1962 drew to a close, high-level talks, including a meeting of the NATO ministers and discussions held in the Bahamas between Diefenbaker and both Prime Minister Macmillan and President Kennedy, offered an opportunity to share views on the Congo situation just as events there were about to render discussion of sanctions moot. In contrast with Diefenbaker's evasive remarks in the House of Commons, notes External Affairs prepared for the NATO meeting revealed that Canada was ready to support "severe economic measures" against Katanga. The strength of this position was weakened by the rather implausible condition that such measures not lead to widespread fighting. In his talks with Diefenbaker, Macmillan justified the United Kingdom's opposition to sanctions on the grounds that this would involve an intervention in the domestic affairs of a country. The Foreign Office, though, had already said the United Kingdom would not prevent any UN effort to end the Katangan secession through the application of economic sanctions. During the Bahamas talks, the British Foreign Secretary, Lord Home, did tell Canadian diplomat Marcel Cadieux that Britain would veto any Security Council measure to end secession by force, a threat that was repeated by Home in a meeting between Prime Minister Macmillan and President Kennedy. U Thant had previously intimated he might return to the Security Council to obtain a revised mandate; as it stood, ONUC was permitted to use force only to retaliate in self-defence, to prevent civil war, and to expel mercenaries. But, in a rather prescient conversation with Ross Campbell, Howard Green acknowledged that the time for forestalling the use of force was nearing an end. The point had nearly arrived, he thought, when the UN would have no alternative but to end Katangan secession by force.[62]

### Canada's Contribution to ONUC

The United Nations continued to request various forms of assistance from Canada, but in November the tenor of these requests clearly showed the UN was taking measures to strengthen ONUC's strategic position in the Congo. ONUC HQ was intercepting a considerable volume of encoded, tactical operational messages in Katanga, dealing primarily with troop movements, but was having difficulty decoding the messages. Although the Secretariat was reluctant to make a formal request, it wondered if Canada could provide an officer able to advise ONUC HQ on how to break the code. Ottawa was also asked to place the two standby signal detachments, earlier agreed to by cabinet, at a state of readiness for dispatch to the Congo on short notice. A most unexpected enquiry arrived from New York: the UN asked if Canada could supply napalm bombs. External Affairs, surprised the UN was contemplating the use of napalm in the Congo, speculated as to the possible rationale for equipping ONUC with such weapons and ultimately expressed reservations about responding in positive terms. Although willing to reconsider the matter if it came to light that Katangese forces had napalm and intended to use it against Canadian personnel, External Affairs thought it best to forestall an official request with a reply from National Defence that the bombs were not available at the moment. Together, these requests indicate the UN was taking definite measures to consolidate and support its position in Katanga. Significantly, at about the same time as Canada received these requests, the United States thought it wise to investigate rumours suggesting the UN might resort to force to end the Congo stalemate. Following discussions with U Thant and Ralph Bunche, American officials concluded that it was unlikely the secretary-general would use force as the primary means to reintegrate Katanga, and they received reassurances that consultation would take place before any strong action was taken.[63]

Late in 1962, Canada agreed to a UN request for a Canadian to serve as liaison and training officer with an ANC battalion. With this latest addition, the number of Canadians serving (or expected to serve) at ONUC HQ increased from fourteen to fifteen. In its overall review of ONUC HQ, National Defence found the UN valued the Canadians because those who were bilingual were "almost the only staff capable of communicating with the Congolese effectively." ONUC's chief of staff, Brigadier Guha of the Indian army, acknowledged that the Canadians "shouldered far more than their fair share of the work." The Canadians were considered to be at a standard "at least equivalent to one rank higher in the best of the other contingents," and for this reason it was decided to gradually raise the rank structure during rotations so that it would be commensurate with overall Canadian representation at ONUC HQ. In spite of the large number of Canadians serving at headquarters, practically all served beneath the rank of lieutenant colonel. By comparison, almost half of the Indian officers at headquarters served at the rank of lieutenant colonel or higher. Thus, Canadians performed an amount of work out of proportion to their numbers but enjoyed few senior, prestige appointments.[64]

Partly for this reason, National Defence decided in December not to follow through with its earlier commitment to the UN to provide a military assistant to the chief of staff of ONUC. At first, National Defence suggested the offer be rescinded in view of the shortage of bilingual officers. When External Affairs pointed out that the position did not require someone who was bilingual, National Defence admitted that this was not a valid reason to revoke the earlier commitment. The real reason could hardly be used in a reply to the UN: the Indian chief of staff was believed to have little work to do himself, so National Defence expected the Canadian would be used only as an office boy. The chief of the general staff felt "Canadian officers, because of their training and experience, can and should be used to greater advantage in more responsible positions." External Affairs suggested more cogent reasons to decline the request be found and, if possible, another peacekeeper be provided for an alternative, more acceptable assignment. To placate New York, the chairman, chiefs of staff agreed to provide an officer at the rank of lieutenant colonel or major as chief instructor for movement control courses in the Congo.[65]

### Hostilities in Katanga

As Howard Green anticipated, events in the Congo finally came to a head during the last week of December 1962. The Katangese gendarmerie opened fire on ONUC positions, established roadblocks in and around Elisabethville, and shot down a United Nations helicopter. When Tshombé proved unwilling or unable to restrain his forces, and after waiting several days for the gendarmerie to cease fire on its own, on 28 December U Thant ordered ONUC to remove the soldiers and mercenaries from Elisabethville and to restore its freedom of movement throughout Katanga. In Leopoldville, American ambassador Gullion told Gauvin that the Katangese defences fell like "card castles." Gauvin dismissed suggestions that the attacks on ONUC were part of a well-prepared attack; he attributed the outbreak of this third round of hostilities to the increased tension in Elisabethville, brought about by ONUC's increased presence there. With a certain sense of inevitability, he observed, "It is also evident that with Indian contingent (which represents largest unit of 5,000 men) due to leave at the end of Feb, some action had to be taken soon if UN was ever going to make use of its strength to settle Katanga secession. What it found in firing of gendarmerie was desired occasion to get at Tshombe once and for all." By 30 December, this was practically achieved; ONUC secured Elisabethville and Kipushi and had neutralized a number of Katangese aircraft on the ground, and a column of peacekeepers had almost reached Jadotville.[66]

Tshombé, who fled first to Rhodesia and then to Kolwezi, made one last diplomatic effort to prevent ONUC's consolidation of its position throughout Katanga. He threatened a scorched-earth policy and, specifically, to destroy mining facilities in Jadotville and Kolwezi if the UN entered these towns. According to Brian Urquhart, Bunche and U Thant were sufficiently impressed with arguments made by the Belgian and British ambassadors, keen to protect their respective mining interests, that orders were issued to ONUC's officer-in-charge, Robert Gardiner, to stop ONUC from crossing the Lufira River into Jadotville. In an attempt to rally support for Britain's position, the British foreign secretary sent Howard Green a message asking the Canadian government to use its status and influence at the UN to encourage the Secretariat to be "magnanimous and imaginative." Green instructed Ambassador Tremblay to speak with U Thant to express the government's "hope that the U.N. would find a moderate solution to the current difficulties in the Congo." Tremblay met with the secretary-general on 2 January and found U Thant "relaxed and satisfied with the way things were going in Katanga." The secretary-general was reported to have agreed with Tremblay's suggestions that a moderate solution be found and restraint exercised. U Thant was said to be determined to reach a final solution through political negotiation, not military action. Despite U Thant's assurances, ONUC arrived in Jadotville on 3 January, causing considerable controversy as to whether the peacekeeping operation's military leadership had overstepped, or even disobeyed, the secretary-general's orders. Maj. Gen. Dewan Prem Chand and his deputy, Brig. Reggie Noronha, largely talked their way into Jadotville. The mayor, it seems, favoured ONUC over threats by the gendarmerie and mercenaries to destroy local industries. The local populace cheered the arrival of the peacekeepers, and the manager and staff at Union Minière were also said to have warmly welcomed the UN's arrival. From Leopoldville, Gauvin reported that U Thant's decision to halt ONUC's advance on Jadotville had caused a "real commotion." Robert Gardiner was said to have threatened to resign if the secretary-general did not rescind this order and permit ONUC to exercise complete freedom of movement throughout the Congo.[67] It is debatable whether local officials deliberately ignored U Thant's orders or simply did not receive them in time to prevent the unexpectedly swift advance. At times during the hostilities, coded messages from Leopoldville to Katanga were delayed by six to forty-eight hours, in spite of Canadian signallers working forty-eight and more hours at a stretch. Whatever the difficulties in communications, there is no doubt that this final thrust brought Katanga's secession to an end, a result that very much worked to the UN's advantage. Sent to the Congo to investigate the breakdown in communications, Ralph Bunche acknowledged the seriousness of the incident but also reported, "There is unabashed elation, which I share, at the entry, at long last, of the UN into Jadotville and relief that this was accomplished with a minimum of fighting and of damage to the installations."[68] There were sixty Canadian peacekeepers in Katanga at the time of the third round of hostilities, at detachments in Elisabethville, Kamina, Albertville, and Kongolo. They played an important role that brought praise from Lt. Gen. Kebbede Guebre, ONUC's commander at the time. Addressing members of the 57th Unit, he recalled with pride how magnificently the peacekeepers had handled the tremendous volume of communications during the fighting in Katanga. "You withstood the strain," he said, "achieved the impossible and completed a task which might have daunted lesser men than Canadians."[69]

At External Affairs, officials debated the implications and legitimacy of ONUC's actions in Katanga. The Defence Liaison Division was concerned with the precedent that might have been established when military conditions appeared to have been prioritized ahead of political considerations. "Such a move," one official wrote, "in our estimation, endangers the whole concept of peace-keeping operations as they have been supported consistently by Canada since 1956." But neither the United Nations Division nor the African and Middle Eastern Division were keen to investigate or press the issue. Geoffrey Murray wrote, "We shall not remedy the ills of this situation by holding inquests and assigning blame. We can only hope to improve peace-keeping operations in the future by learning the lessons of the past and by strengthening the machinery (our own included) available to the United Nations." This view appears to have prevailed in the department. The American ambassador in Leopoldville reported to the State Department that all the embassies in the Congo, including Canada's, believed the occupation of Jadotville and ONUC's exercise of its right to freedom of movement throughout Katanga were indispensable as steps to carrying out U Thant's objectives. Ross Campbell provided the definitive assessment. He thought it clear that the secretary-general had been saying one thing in New York, to the British, Belgians, and French, while at the same time tacitly condoning what ONUC's commanders were doing in the field. "U Thant," Campbell concluded, "has had no option but to allow events to run their course, including the present military offensive. I do not think we should inject ourselves into this very delicate situation by a premature inquisition."[70] Significantly, Campbell uses the word "offensive" to describe the UN's actions in pressing onward to Jadotville. Although concerns about the UN's use of force had been expressed previously at the highest political levels and in direct relation to the situation in Katanga, in the end Canada accepted this *fait accompli*. Katanga's secession was at an end.

In the months following the installation of the Adoula government, the fundamental issue facing the central government, its international supporters, and the United Nations was the question of how to reintegrate Katanga into a unified Congo. If Adoula's moderate government was not to fall victim to more extreme political elements in Leopoldville, Tshombé had to be brought to heel. This dilemma presented two particular problems for the Canadian government: first, the Diefenbaker government was most reluctant to see ONUC cooperate with the central government to end the Katangan secession by force; second, Britain and the United States disagreed in their approaches to resolving the difficulties with Tshombé and Katanga. The three rounds of hostilities between ONUC and the Katangese gendarmerie undoubtedly caused discomfort in Ottawa. The government's reluctance to see ONUC take offensive action can be seen most clearly in the decision not to continue providing a RCAF officer for the position of air commander after ONUC's air operations incorporated jet fighters and light bombers. Notably, in Tremblay's first official meeting with U Thant, the new Canadian representative at the UN used the occasion to press the acting secretary-general not to resort to force in dealing with Katanga. This reluctance to see ONUC engaged in direct conflict was tempered, however, by support for the principle that self-defence might compel peacekeepers to respond to attacks on the positions or restrictions on their freedom of movement. With the possible exception of the march onward to Jadotville, Canadian authorities recognized that the gendarmerie's threats and actions that particularly prompted the second and third rounds of fighting justified ONUC's actions. By the end of 1962, Howard Green also seemed resigned to the idea that a final showdown was imminent and that force would likely be used if Tshombé continued to prove intransigent on implementing the Plan for National Reconciliation. In this respect, the minister's views were significantly closer to those of his American than his British counterparts.

# 7
# Preparing for Withdrawal: ONUC's Final Months

Once the secession in Katanga was finally brought to an end and the territorial integrity of the Congo ensured, attention shifted toward preparations for the eventual withdrawal of ONUC. Training and reorganization of the ANC was seen as a necessary prerequisite. As has been seen, Canadian involvement in schemes to retrain or reorganize the ANC were proposed and considered at various times since ONUC arrived in the Congo, but no definite decisions or actions were ever taken. Then, in early 1963, the question of military assistance for the ANC was revived by a US initiative, the Greene Plan. Based on a proposal formulated by an American colonel sent to the Congo to assess the ANC's requirements, the plan called for a series of bilateral aid programs to train the various services within the Congolese military, coordinated under the aegis of the United Nations. Canada, Belgium, Italy, Norway, and Israel were asked to participate.[1] In the ensuing months, Canada was asked to provide training for both officers and communications units, and the senior officer to oversee the entire training mission. Washington, Brussels, and Leopoldville pressed Ottawa to agree to a Canadian contribution. Michel Gauvin, the Canadian chargé d'affaires in Leopoldville, reported that Joseph Mobutu, chief of staff of the ANC, appeared unwilling to take no for an answer: "Where there is a will there is a way," the Congolese general insisted. This, the consul general maintained, demonstrated the "esteem and confidence" with which Canada was regarded. Nevertheless, both External Affairs and National Defence were willing to consider Canadian involvement only if the military assistance was directed by and through the UN. In fact, National Defence was unwilling to take the tentative step of preliminary discussions between military officials in Washington until it knew more about the Greene Plan and, particularly, the role it envisaged for the UN.[2]

Secretary-General U Thant's view of the Greene Plan was not immediately clear to Canadian officials. Canada's permanent representative at the UN, Paul Tremblay, believed support for the plan in New York to be strongest among Gen. Indar Jit Rikhye, the secretary-general's military adviser, and his staff but doubted U Thant would back a training scheme carried out primarily by NATO countries. The NATO label, Tremblay expected, would prove embarrassing not only for the secretary-general but also for any participating NATO countries. The UN Division concurred with Tremblay and suggested the basis for participation be broadened to include non-NATO nations and assurances be sought from the secretary-general that he was "100% behind the scheme." Tremblay was instructed to speak to U Thant personally to express Canada's concerns and to suggest the participation in the training schemes of African countries such as Nigeria and Tunisia. Any request for assistance, U Thant was told, would receive official consideration only if it came from the secretary-general and was supported by the Congolese government.[3]

Canadian officials correctly anticipated the political difficulties the Greene Plan would face. On 20 March, the secretary-general asked the Congo Advisory Committee whether the United Nations should act as an umbrella for the bilateral assistance envisaged. To make the proposal more attractive, the Secretariat suggested the addition of a coordinating group of African states, including Nigeria, Ethiopia, and Tunisia. During the meeting, Tremblay welcomed this initiative, though he did raise logistical and organizational issues as to the role and function of the group. The plan, however, ran into serious opposition. The African and Middle Eastern states "found it psychologically and politically difficult" to approve the plan. Perhaps for this reason, the Canadian ambassador later went to great lengths to assure members of the committee that, despite the inclusion of Canada in circulated correspondence relating to the Greene Plan, no bilateral negotiations had taken place between Canada and the Congo. Tremblay stated, "We have always assumed that any contribution that we would make to the ANC training scheme would be under the aegis of the United Nations." The African states were clear: either they should be included in the actual training or the program should be arranged entirely on a bilateral basis without UN involvement. This cool response from the Afro-Asians left Belgium wondering if it would not be best for it and the United States to proceed with retraining the ANC without assistance from their NATO allies.[4]

When Tremblay met with U Thant on 28 March, it was evident the secretary-general was questioning the wisdom of the Greene Plan. The previous day, the Soviets had warned him they planned to request a meeting of the Security Council if the UN became involved in the training plan, and he expected to hear shortly from a group of Afro-Asian states that had decided to advise him strongly against any UN involvement in ANC retraining. U Thant told Tremblay the problem of military assistance for the Congo could no longer "be treated as a technical one; it had become primarily a political problem to be dealt with as such." The ambassador left the meeting with the impression the secretary-general would have to "wash his hands of the present training programme." A subsequent discussion with Ralph Bunche, the UN undersecretary for special political affairs, confirmed this impression. Tremblay asked if there was a position Canada could take at the next Advisory Committee meeting that would support the secretary-general but was told U Thant intended simply to listen to the African representatives without advancing any position of his own. According to Bunche, it was no longer a matter of the degree to which the UN should be involved but whether it should be involved at all. He revealed that the UN legal department was trying to find a way for the secretary-general to bypass Resolution 1474, which prohibited the provision of military assistance to the Congo except at the request of the secretary-general. The UN was faced with a significant dilemma: the ANC needed to be retrained and reorganized in order for ONUC to be able to complete its withdrawal, but political realities ruled out both direct, bilateral military aid and aid provided under the umbrella of the United Nations.[5]

Once it became clear the UN would not oversee the retraining scheme, debate in the Advisory Committee focused entirely on the question of the Congo's right to obtain bilateral assistance. African members of the committee were divided: some argued the Congolese government could not solicit bilateral assistance so long as ONUC was present in the Congo, while others shared the Canadian view that the Congolese should be allowed to make their own arrangements if the UN was unable or unwilling to meet their needs. In advance of the 23 April meeting of the Advisory Committee, Congolese prime minister Cyrille Adoula wrote to U Thant and argued that any attempt by the UN to invoke the provisions of Resolution 1474 to prevent the Congolese government from securing bilateral assistance would "constitute an unjustifiable and intolerable restriction on its freedom of action." Because Resolution 1474 was passed so early in the crisis and at a time when political conditions were vastly different, the Congolese prime minister reasoned that it was no longer valid. In a statement delivered to the Advisory Committee, Ambassador Tremblay concurred with Adoula's interpretation; he stressed the danger of the UN placing limits on the sovereignty of a nation it was assisting and considered it likely that restrictions on bilateral agreements would come to be resented by both the Congolese people and their government. While Tremblay's comments would have alienated the more radical African members of the committee, the emphasis on the implications for the general principle of sovereignty would have appealed to the interests of most. The statement was appreciated in Leopoldville, where Foreign Minister Justin Bomboko expressed his gratitude to Gauvin for the Canadian stand in the Advisory Committee. Noting the lack of unanimity in the committee, Canadian officials expected that U Thant would not object directly to a Congolese effort to obtain bilateral military training assistance.[6] Publicly, the secretary-general turned a blind eye to the training programs later established by the Congolese, with the notable assistance of Belgium. In a report to the Security Council, U Thant simply said, "I have no official knowledge of subsequent developments."[7] Although this diplomatic manoeuvre enabled the Congo to enlist the help it needed to retrain its army, it also closed the door to any possibility that Canada could provide assistance to the Congo on a multilateral basis through the United Nations.

Once the UN decided against associating itself with the Greene Plan, the Congolese government took immediate steps to secure bilateral military assistance. As expected, Canada received a request from Prime Minister Adoula. The Congolese were keen to secure Canadian participation because Canada was considered "a non-colonial country politically acceptable to most African opinion" and to prevent Belgium's complete domination of the training program. After an April election in Canada, the Liberal Party came to power led by Prime Minister Lester Pearson. The new secretary of state for external affairs, Paul Martin, concurred with Undersecretary Norman Robertson's recommendation against Canadian involvement in ANC training, citing practical considerations – the shortage of suitable personnel. Although he clearly harboured doubts as to the political advisability of Canadian participation, the door was not closed to this possibility entirely. Martin wrote to Paul Hellyer, the new minister of national defence, to see if personnel would in fact be available to serve either as signal instructors or as the senior officer coordinating the program if "impressive political arguments are advanced by the Americans and Belgians in favour of some Canadian participation." The shortage of bilingual signallers ruled out meeting this aspect of the request, but as for the position of a coordinating officer, the chief of the general staff did recommend "the nettle ... be grasped and the commitment accepted, as an indication of Canada's practical concern for the future of the Congo in particular and black Africa in general." Consequently, the merits of Canadian involvement continued to be discussed.[8]

International pressure on Canada to participate mounted. In Washington, the assistant secretary for African Affairs approached the Canadian ambassador, Charles Ritchie, and intimated that both Italy and Norway were awaiting a Canadian decision before making a final determination as to their own participation. Gary Harman, the Canadian diplomat at the embassy in Washington responsible for consultation with the State Department on issues related to Africa, recalls the United States was pushing the retraining proposal and counting on Canada to be more supportive. The Americans hoped personnel limitations would not prevent Canada from making a "most important and valuable contribution" to the training scheme. A recent meeting in Washington between President Kennedy and General Mobutu, during which the issue of ANC training was raised and the president had asked his officials what steps the United States had taken to secure the participation of other countries, undoubtedly prompted the American overtures. In Brussels, Canadian ambassador Sydney Pierce reported that Foreign Ministry officials "never failed to tackle us ... [and] continued to show the keenest interest in our possible participation." However, the implications of the lengthy Canadian delay in responding to the Congolese request were not lost on the Belgian foreign minister, Paul Henri Spaak, who eventually met with the Canadian ambassador and presented his case "quietly without insistence or pressure and, indeed, without marshalling the arguments at his disposal." The ambassador speculated, "It may be that Spaak has assessed the chances of our accepting as poor and put the request to me as a matter of form." Back in the Congo, Mobutu grew increasingly impatient. In an interview with the Congolese press, he stated, "Italy, Canada and Norway seem to be hesitating. And I have [the] impression that these countries will not do anything as long as UN does not confer its patronage on this organisation."[9]

Still, in the face of this pressure from various quarters, the government continued to weigh its options. The military was not keen to sacrifice its capability to meet other defence requirements in order to provide officers for the communications training. And although the chief of the general staff was willing to contribute a coordinating officer, External Affairs foresaw political difficulties in doing so: the Congo Advisory Committee, to which Canada belonged, had taken a strong stand against the Greene Plan, and any co-operation with Israel, a partner nation in the training scheme, could complicate Canada's participation with UN peacekeeping in the Middle East. A further urgent enquiry from American officials indicating that the point had been reached when knowledge of Canada's intentions was becoming necessary prompted yet another round of interdepartmental discussions. Officials at External Affairs attributed the delay in making a decision to National Defence: Paul Hellyer was said to be reluctant to consider the request until a budgetary review was concluded and prioritized National Defence commitments. The chairman, chiefs of staff did not concur with the chief of the general staff's offer to provide a coordinating officer. He was said to be "against the idea completely" and was quoted as saying the position would be "the graveyard for a Canadian Officer and his inevitable successors." To avoid a flat refusal of the Congolese request, officials in both departments contemplated the dispatch of a fact-finding mission to the Congo, but Paul Martin considered this a misleading course and thought it better to "frankly say that our difficulty is due to scarcity of personnel because of the review now taking place." The message appeared finally to be getting through in Washington. The acting department of state executive secretary reported to the president's special assistant for national security affairs that Canada had many commitments for its French-speaking officers and had given no indication that military personnel for the program would be forthcoming.[10]

A definite decision not to participate in the training of the ANC was finally taken in the fall of 1963. By this time, the UN had decided to extend ONUC's stay in the Congo through to mid-1964. Canadian peacekeepers, because of the tasks they performed within the peacekeeping mission, were expected to stay till the end. This extended commitment, in addition to an affirmative response to an ONUC request to provide an officer to serve as chief of staff, was cited as the reason why Canada could not commit further military resources for service in the Congo. In October, Prime Minister Adoula had met with President Kennedy in Washington, and the latter had given assurances that he would personally take care of pressing upon the Canadian government the importance of assisting with the ANC retraining. Nevertheless, Gauvin was instructed to express the Canadian government's regret at being unable to meet the Congolese request but, in doing so, also to make reference to the "considerable amount of time, manpower and money which [Canada] has expended in Congo to date as evidence of our continuing concern for future stability of country." The Belgians and Americans were disappointed but not surprised. They had already interpreted the lengthy delay in responding to the request as a bad sign. For Norway, on the other hand, this was good news. Officials from the Norwegian embassy in Ottawa had expressed their concern at possibly being the only country to refuse the Congolese request. In the end, both military and political factors proved decisive in determining the Canadian response to this request for bilateral military assistance.[11]

### Canada's Contribution to ONUC

By early 1963, UN requests for various additional personnel for ONUC itself were increasingly scrutinized, especially by National Defence. The Secretariat asked Canada to provide four training and administrative officers for service with two ANC battalions, helicopter pilots and ground crew, and movement control personnel. After consultation with the navy and air force, the chairman, chiefs of staff turned down the request for helicopter personnel because it would seriously prejudice other commitments. External Affairs was not surprised by this and decided it was best not to press this further; the department's own preferences prioritized other forms of assistance. The chief of the general staff was frustrated by these "piecemeal" requests, which were said to be making it "almost impossible to do any career planning for the officers concerned," and because they were having "an adverse effect on the proper general administration of the Army." As a result, National Defence not only rejected the most recent request for movement control personnel but also decided not to proceed with an earlier commitment to provide an officer to serve as chief instructor for movement control courses. One request was approved: for signal personnel to be assigned to serve at a message centre in Katanga. National Defence expressed concern that this positive response would result in further requests for communications assistance "at levels below that included in our present commitment." To prevent this, it was decided at an interdepartmental meeting of officials from National Defence and External Affairs to advise the UN that Canada was "reviewing its present commitments to the Congo operations and that we would not wish to provide additional personnel to ONUC for the time being," and that "only specific and well substantiated requests for reassignments of [Canadian] officers already serving at ONUC HQ can be considered."[12]

In mid-January, the Secretariat anticipated that ONUC might be brought to an end by August or September. When the Canadian military liaison officer in New York suggested to the military staff that it would soon be possible to do without the services of the 57th Unit, the UN officials were said to have reacted with horror. The chief of the field operations service was of the view that it was too early to consider the withdrawal of the 57th and that the unit would be required a considerable time yet. Brigadier Rikhye described the Canadian unit as the backbone of ONUC and further stated he "would rather see any unit other than the 57 Signals Squadron repatriated." Within weeks of these conversations, it was clear that ONUC was not likely to leave the Congo altogether until 1964. But, National Defence was keen to reduce its commitment of signal personnel in ONUC, as they were "acutely needed in Canada." The director of signals was sent to the Congo to report on the possibility of personnel reductions. Given their earlier panicked reaction in New York, UN officials were reassured the director's visit was not an indication that Canada was contemplating an immediate withdrawal of its peacekeepers. As the secretary-general planned to reduce ONUC to seventy-eight hundred peacekeepers by July 1963, detailed discussions with the force commander resulted in a decision to reduce the establishment of the 57th to approximately two hundred personnel. A reduction in the number of signal detachments, from eight to four, was expected. Consequently, the chairman, chiefs of staff suggested to Paul Hellyer that the standby signal detachment maintained in Canada be cancelled. The minister concurred and External Affairs was asked to advise the UN that the detachment would no longer be available. Some reductions in personnel were achieved throughout 1963, but it also became clear that it was unlikely a complete withdrawal could by achieved by the end of that year.[13]

When U Thant indicated his intention to recommend to the Security Council that ONUC be withdrawn at the end of 1963, the United States anxiously asked Canada to voice support in the General Assembly for an authorization of funds that would enable ONUC to continue until June 1964. External Affairs found it difficult to disagree with the American view that peacekeepers should remain in the Congo until the ANC was better able to assume complete responsibility for internal security but was concerned that any effort to extend ONUC's presence be supported by both U Thant and the African and Asian members of the Security Council. Ottawa did not want it to appear as though only the West favoured ONUC's continuation. Officials feared the Afro-Asian members would "be suspicious that Western countries wanted ONUC to stay on in the Congo in order to give the Belgians more time to establish their influence." If these states supported a continuation of ONUC, External Affairs saw no political difficulty in supporting a General Assembly resolution to extend ONUC's financing.[14]

Encouraged by the United States, Prime Minister Adoula appealed to the secretary-general to leave three thousand peacekeepers in the Congo until mid-1964. Adoula said, "Our concern ... derives from the concern which we feel that this work, which has cost so much effort and sacrifice, should bear fruit and achieve the objectives which UN and Congo set themselves." U Thant and senior members of the Secretariat remained unconvinced. The secretary-general had detected little support from members of the Advisory Committee or the Fifth Committee for maintaining ONUC beyond the end of 1963 and was skeptical of the chances of the General Assembly authorizing continued financial support. The UN's perilous financial position was a paramount consideration. Following a round of inconclusive consultations between U Thant and members of the Advisory Committee, the matter was finally addressed definitively in the General Assembly. Resolution 1885 (XVIII) noted the support given to Adoula's request by other independent African states and authorized the secretary-general to spend an additional US$18.2 million to cover ONUC expenses to June 1964. The resolution passed by a vote of seventy-six to eleven, with twenty abstentions.[15] Canada voted in favour of the resolution; the Communist bloc cast the negative votes. One month before the debate on Resolution 1885, Prime Minister Pearson had addressed the assembly and made public Canada's willingness to maintain the signal unit in the Congo. Both National Defence and External Affairs supported the continuation of ONUC, though the chairman, chiefs of staff doubted the ANC would be "very much better in six months' time," when it would need to take complete responsibility for the maintenance of law and order. Paul Hellyer echoed this concern but assured Martin that National Defence was "willing to co-operate in any course which you are convinced would be wise in the national interest." An establishment of 31 officers and 217 other ranks was approved for the first six months of 1964, and Hellyer even intimated he was prepared to maintain the 57th Signal

Unit beyond June if it was "inopportune, and perhaps even difficult, for the United Nations to disengage." Thus, continued support for the core Canadian contribution to ONUC survived both the transition in government from the Conservatives to the Liberals and three years of trials and tribulations in the Congo.[16]

With a more definite end in sight, National Defence appeared more willing to accept senior military positions within ONUC. Earlier, they had successfully resisted pressure from the UN to provide a replacement for the position of ONUC air commander. In November 1963, however, they responded favourably to a renewed effort by New York to once again appoint a Canadian to this position. A Canadian already serving in the Congo was promoted to the rank of group captain in order to serve as both air commander and coordinator of air transport operations. National Defence also agreed to the appointment of Brig. J.A. Dextraze to the position of chief of staff – the most senior appointment ever held by a Canadian within ONUC. External Affairs believed Dextraze's appointment would send an important political message: Canada was prepared to have senior Canadian officers serve under Africans. Dextraze assumed his position just as command of ONUC was transferred from Maj. Gen. Christian Kaldager to Maj. Gen. Thomas Aguiyu Ironsi, of Nigeria. Officials at External Affairs were impressed by a meeting with Dextraze, held in advance of his departure for the Congo, at which he assured those present that he would respect his position as chief of staff to Ironsi. With the appointment of Canadians to two senior posts in ONUC, it was clear that Canada supported the UN's efforts to bring the mission to a successful close.[17]

Despite Brigadier Dextraze's best intentions, relations with Ironsi ultimately proved tense at times. Shortly after the new force commander's arrival in Leopoldville, the Canadian chargé d'affaires noted Ironsi had "given the impression in Military and High UN civilian circles of being very much of a play-boy." "His professional competence," the chargé continued, "would also appear to be in doubt." First impressions were subsequently confirmed in a later report to External Affairs:

> The difference between the previous Force Commander and the present one is that the former, who was well trained, had every intention of doing nothing, and the latter, who has little military ability, insists on doing something ... In addition to his other duties, the Brigadier [Dextraze] often has to kick out the drunks from the Commander's house at 2, 3 or 4 o'clock in the morning, stick the Commander in bed, and make sure he is dragged out and at his desk the next morning. That next morning will start with abuses, and abuse, often of an arrogantly personal nature, often continues all day. These are trials which Dextraze is accepting, (1) because he is a good profes-

sional soldier, (2) because he is a Canadian, and, I suppose, there are other reasons but God knows what they are.

The difficulties with Ironsi came to a head in early June, when Dextraze reported directly to the chief of the general staff on an incident involving the force commander. The officer-in-charge of ONUC, Bibiano Osorio-Tafall, called a meeting at 9:45 p.m. on 1 June to discuss an urgent message received from U Thant. Dextraze was instructed to notify Ironsi, but the force commander was reported to have said, "If Tafall wants me at any meeting tell him that he can telephone me personally. That's all I've got to tell you." When Ironsi arrived at 11 p.m., Dextraze noted, "It was evident that he was under the influence of liquor"; the force commander was further described as "belligerent." The incident was defused the next day when the Nigerian ambassador suggested Ironsi apologize to Osario-Tafall, who in turn suggested that apologies be extended to Dextraze and others present at the meeting. Although Dextraze contemplated a request to be recalled to Canada, he reconsidered and decided to stay for the remaining four weeks in June.[18]

Once the Katangan secession was resolved, and for the remaining months the 57th Signal Unit was in the Congo, life was generally routine – with two exceptions. On 10 April 1963, command of the 57th Signal Unit changed hands for the final time. At a ceremony attended by the ONUC force commander, Gen. Kebbede Guebre at that time, Col. D.G. Green accepted the command from Colonel Hamilton. Addressing the unit, General Guebre said, "Your performance has been second to none. You are a credit to your Army and your country and you have more than upheld the long and splendid tradition of Canadian Signals in the Congo." Colonel Green was transferred to the Congo from Edmonton, where he had previously been the command signal officer at Headquarters Western Command.[19]

Then, in early 1964, ONUC engaged in a series of rescue operations that foreshadowed some of the political difficulties the Congo would face once the UN peacekeeping mission had departed. Canadian personnel played key roles in the rescue of missionaries from Kwilu district who were under attack by members of the Congolese Jeunesse movement, a group of rebels composed mostly of young men. For their participation and acts of gallantry, Colonel Green recommended military awards for Sgt. J.A. Lessard, Lt. Col. P.A. Mayer, and Brigadier Dextraze. Dextraze both planned the rescues and participated in their implementation; Mayer was principally charged with carrying them out and succeeded, in one instance, in rescuing several missionaries after he recovered from being knocked unconscious and threatened with death; and Lessard saved two nuns by single-handedly assisting both into an awaiting helicopter while fighting off four Jeunesse, under a "shower of arrows." The secretary-general commended the peacekeepers: "The success of the entire operation is attributable to splendid co-operation among troops under the fine leadership of General Ironsi and his Chief of Staff, Brigadier Dextraze. In completing this mercy mission ONUC has won not only the gratitude of Member States whose nationals were saved but of the world at large."[20]

By January 1964, it was increasingly apparent that ONUC would not be extended beyond the end of June. From Leopoldville, Colonel Green reported that senior controllers and auditors had arrived from New York to make arrangements for the final disposition of equipment and supplies. And the American ambassador in Leopoldville, Edmund Gullion, confirmed the United States was no longer willing to continue its financial support because requests for assistance were being received from other African nations. The Permanent Mission in New York subsequently confirmed Green's appreciation of the situation. For various reasons, they also did not expect ONUC to continue beyond June: U Thant was said to be adamant that the mission be withdrawn and was supported in this view by his principal advisers, there was no mandate for ONUC funding beyond June, continuation would require a special session of the General Assembly and this seemed unlikely for extraneous political reasons, they perceived little support among "the vital African membership" or the Western bloc, and logistical planning was already in place based on the assumption contingents would be withdrawn. External Affairs advised the chairman, chiefs of staff, "We see no objection, therefore, to the development of plans for the withdrawal of the Canadian contingent by the end of June ... There remains the possibility of some development which might lead to a decision to reconsider the matter, but we do not at present foresee any such development."[21]

In subsequent months, it became clear Canada would not permit its forces to remain in the Congo after ONUC was withdrawn. When Nigeria expressed concern for the safety of four hundred of their police officers expected to remain till the end of 1964, External Affairs noted it would not be possible for Canadian peacekeepers to remain under the terms of the government's original decision to send forces. Plans were finalized to transport the remaining Canadians from Leopoldville in four Yukon airlifts, approximately sixty personnel at a time, throughout June. UN requests for three NCO storekeepers to assist in the preparation of UN stores for shipment and the retention of Lieutenant Colonel Mayer to serve as a UN liaison officer with the ANC were turned down. The chief of the general staff considered it undesirable to leave Canadians in the Congo after the UN had withdrawn. On 30 June, the war diarist for the 57th Signal Unit wrote, "Reveille came early this morning but nobody seemed to mind." In the end, the Canadians were among the very last of the peacekeepers to leave the Congo; the final Yukon arrived back in Canada on Dominion Day (1 July), 1964. In four years, over eighteen hundred officers and men served in the Congo. By order of the vice-chief of the general staff, the 57th Canadian Signal Unit was reduced to nil strength, ceased to be allocated for duty with the United Nations in the Congo, and was made dormant. The secretary-general thanked Canada for its contribution to ONUC, expressing the hope that the Canadian peacekeepers' efforts, having helped to prevent "the worst results of anarchy[,] disorder and civil war," would ultimately enable the Congo to achieve future peace and prosperity.[22]

In ONUC's final months, the key issue faced by both the Diefenbaker and Pearson governments was the question of retraining the ANC. Almost from the outset of the crisis, it was recognized that the Force Publique would need to be reorganized and that Congolese would need to be retrained to assume positions in a reliable officer corps. At various times, from 1960 to 1963, the Belgians, the Americans, the Ghanaians, the United Nations, and the Congolese themselves repeatedly asked Canada to provide personnel to facilitate retraining through either bilateral or multilateral schemes. Consistently, Canada stated a preference to provide such military aid through multilateral channels, particularly via the United Nations. For political reasons, however, the Congolese wanted to rely on bilateral agreements with non-African nations to reorganize the ANC, plans opposed by many of the Afro-Asian members of the secretary-general's Congo Advisory Committee. This fundamental impasse of the Congo's preference for bilateral aid and Canada's insistence on using the United Nations was never overcome. Even National Defence, though never keen about participation in any of the retraining propositions, was most amenable to those that would have come under a UN umbrella.

While remarkably successful in achieving many of its objectives in the Congo, not least of which was keeping the nation united, ONUC's failure to use its presence to reform the Congolese military was lamentable. This particular fault certainly did not bode well for the secretary-general's hopes for a peaceful and prosperous Congo. By the summer of 1964, Howard Green had been out of office for months, having been defeated in an election the year before. He stayed current with world events, though, and was a regular contributor to the *Victoria Colonist*. As ONUC prepared to leave, Green wrote in his column: "If it turns out that the Congolese authorities cannot cope with the situation which arises upon the withdrawal of the United Nations force the result will be severe criticism of the United Nations and a verdict around the world that it has failed in the Congo. This despite some excellent achievements during the years the force was in the country."[23] Green could not have been more correct. For the most part, ONUC had managed to carry out its complex mandate, though at tremendous cost to the UN. But even this success was soon overshadowed and forgotten, just as Green predicted. Less than two years after the last ONUC peacekeepers left, Joseph Mobutu carried out his second coup and established a ruthless and corrupt dictatorship that would last for more than three decades and end in civil war.

# Conclusion

> In the foreign policies of democracies ... there is always an element of calculation as well as conscience, and neither the cynic nor the idealist is ever right in an absolute judgement on motives.
>
> – John Holmes, 1963

In 1993, reporting on the possibilities for renewed interest in peacekeeping in the post-Cold War era, the Standing Senate Committee on Foreign Affairs concluded, "Canada has had an exemplary record in peacekeeping. In fact, it is the sole military activity which Canadians fully support."[1] For many, as this Senate report found, peacekeeping has become a potent symbol of the Canadian national identity, a fact confirmed by one poll that asked Canadians to identify Canada's most positive contribution to the world; 26 percent of respondents said it was peacekeeping – a higher percentage than for any other contribution.[2] Yet, in 2008, almost all of Canada's soldiers serving overseas are not doing so as peacekeepers but as combatants in the "war on terror" waged in Afghanistan. Some historians have urged Canadians to confront this obvious discrepancy and to recognize that peacekeeping is not currently a priority for the Canadian Armed Forces, certainly not to the degree imagined by the public. More to the point, they have argued, peacekeeping should be seen in its proper historical perspective, as just one (and certainly not the most important) of many roles played by the Armed Forces.[3]

As early as the 1970s, historian J.L. Granatstein was challenging Canadians to question whether there was more image than reality to Canadian peacekeeping.[4] Undeniably, Canada did consistently contribute to United Nations peacekeeping missions for most of the second half of the twentieth century, but what was behind the remarkable consensus successively formed by generations of Canadians and their political representatives that led to this particular role on the world stage? According to Norman Hillmer and Granatstein, "Moralism is one unifying thread running through the history of Canadian foreign policy." Support of peacekeeping, then, simply could be interpreted as one manifestation of this moralistic streak. To the larger Canadian public, "Canada was the real inventor of peacekeeping and its practitioner *par excellence*. Even our armed forces, in other words, were not the traditional 'brutal licentious soldiery' but arbiters in blue helmets, umpires enforcing the world's rules on the unruly." Yet, the two historians challenge us to question this stereotype: "Canada has never been a choirboy in the concert of nations; it has fought wars and bargained for advantage like all the rest."[5] In other words, we would do well to remember that foreign policy is ultimately driven less by altruism and more by concrete, realistic objectives and considerations.

Much of what little has been published on Canada's participation in ONUC attempts to address the fundamental question of motivation: Why did John Diefenbaker's government agree to participate in this peacekeeping operation in the first instance? The answer to this question has clear implications for the larger issue of the value of peacekeeping in relation to Canadian foreign and defence policies. Granatstein has emphasized Canadian public opinion as the decisive factor in the Diefenbaker government's decision making. Diefenbaker is portrayed as adamantly opposed to contributing to ONUC initially, but then he appears to have changed his decision when faced with tremendous public pressure to participate. This interpretation readily fits the established view of Diefenbaker as an indecisive prime minister who had great difficulty formulating and executing foreign and defence policies, a legacy earned principally because of his infamous mishandling of issues of continental defence. The primacy of public opinion in this historical account also allows those critical of the Canadian preoccupation with peacekeeping to make the argument that this episode serves as a prime example of how Canadian governments, and the Canadian public more generally, place far too much emphasis on an altruistic sense of purpose when deciding whether Canada should engage in peacekeeping. I trust this study has raised considerable doubt as to the validity of any version of events that places too great an emphasis on public opinion in explaining Canadian participation in ONUC. Throughout the Congo crisis, those responsible for shaping Canadian policy were certainly aware of the public's penchant for Canada's image as a moral superpower, but their decisions were driven by more pragmatic factors. While the archetypal image of "Canada the peacekeeper" may have served the role of conscience, Canada's Congo policy was still quite calculated.

It is important to remember that the Congo crisis occurred at a time of heightened Cold War tensions. In the previous weeks and months the Soviet Union had shot down two American reconnaissance aircraft, a planned summit in Paris broke down even before it really began, and Cuba increasingly became a point of contention between the two superpowers. Canada's membership in NATO left little room to doubt where Canada stood in the battle between East and West. Nevertheless, Canadian diplomats studiously worked to maintain an image of a nation that was objective, if not neutral. Hammarskjöld's decision to include Canadians in ONUC, despite membership in NATO, suggests a degree of success in achieving this image. Even Soviet diplomats downplayed protests from Moscow over Canada's participation in the peacekeeping mission, until Russian policy hardened against the secretary-general. In addition, Canada's voting pattern in the General Assembly on Congo resolutions was more akin to that of Ireland and the Scandinavian countries than its NATO allies. Furthermore, Canada resisted frequent Belgian attempts to develop a concerted NATO policy on the Congo – so much so that Belgian officials eventually accused their Canadian counterparts of being too objective. Similarly, Ottawa refused to allow the RCAF to participate in the transport of Belgian forces within the Congo, though the UN requested them to do so, out of fear Canada would be associated with its NATO ally.

At other times, it was evident that Canada was solidly within the Western bloc. In statements delivered in both the House of Commons and the General Assembly, Prime Minister Diefenbaker was often strident in his criticism of the Soviet Union. In turn, the Soviet attack on Hammarskjöld left the secretary-general less willing to use Canadians, as was seen when he declined Ottawa's offer of Caribou aircraft and accompanying aircrews. Limited Canadian representation in the senior levels of ONUC HQ, with one or two notable exceptions, was further evidence of this. More often than not, Canada's allegiance to the West was more obvious in the exercise of behind-the-scenes, quiet diplomacy. For example, Ottawa agreed to Brussels' request to be kept informed of the confidential discussions of the secretary-general's Advisory Committee. Publicly, Ottawa never declared a preference for any particular Congolese political faction and consistently stressed the need for the Congolese to be allowed to sort out their political and constitutional difficulties for themselves. Privately, however, Canada favoured the more Western-oriented Kasavubu. Congolese officials were assured Canada had not voted to seat Kasavubu's delegation at the UN only because it was confident this outcome could be achieved without its affirmative vote. Although it was eventually decided not to participate in any of the retraining and reorganization schemes for the Armée Nationale Congolaise, the most consistent argument in favour of Canada's involvement, advanced by officials at both External Affairs and National Defence, was that it would be a good Western influence on the Congolese military. Finally, Colonel Berthiaume's involvement in Mobutu's arrest of Lumumba definitely contributed to the solidification of a Western-oriented government in the Congo – though there is no evidence to suggest that Ottawa approved of, or was aware of, the colonel's actions.

Thus, in a number of ways, Canada's allegiance to the West was clear; yet, officials still attempted to maintain an overall impression of objectivity. To be fair, this effort was not simply window dressing. Canadian policy and officials were more constructive than some of their Western counterparts. Although it hoped for a Western-oriented government in the Congo, Ottawa was genuinely willing to accept a neutral one; this is a significant departure from the policies of most NATO states. In addition, relative to NATO allies, Patrice Lumumba was more often perceived in less threatening terms by Canadian officials. While there was evidence to indicate senior Canadian officers in the Congo had a definite sense the Cold War was operating there, the dozen or so rank-and-file peacekeepers with whom I have corresponded rarely had anything more than a vague awareness of this, suggesting the politics of the Cold War were not a significant factor in how they carried out their routine duties. Taken all together, the evidence presented here demonstrates that any account that portrays Canadian peacekeeping in the Congo as simply carrying out "cold war by other means" fails to convey the true complexity of Canada's Congo policy.[6]

Decolonization was the other significant international aspect of the Congo crisis. Again, Canadian policy studiously avoided any positions that would alienate the growing number of Afro-Asian members of the United Nations. This was most evident with Canadian tactics in the Advisory Committee, where the majority of members were either Asian or African. The Canadian representative was often instructed to remain silent during discussions of controversial issues whenever it was thought the Canadian view might be different from that of the majority; divergent views were saved for private discussions with the secretary-general. Occasionally, members of Diefenbaker's Progressive Conservative cabinet would express sentimental concern for Britain as a colonial power, but officials at External Affairs rarely sympathized with Britain, and even less so with Belgium, when these states were perceived to be acting to defend their colonial positions in Africa. Canadian policy, at these times, was more likely to follow the lead of the United States. This was seen in votes on General Assembly resolutions that were critical of Belgium. Ottawa also refused to support Brussels in its attempts to preserve the right to occupy military bases in the Congo. Katanga's secession was a lightning rod for charges of neo-colonialism against both Belgium and Britain. Canadian officials recognized this and consistently expressed support for the Congo's territorial integrity, even in the face of a vocal segment of the Canadian public that favoured Katanga's right to secede.

Ottawa was clearly successful in portraying Canada as sympathetic to the concerns of the newly independent states: Congolese officials often made reference, in warm terms, to Canada's lack of a colonial past. In the case of Patrice Lumumba, Canada's image did suffer following his visit to Canada. Once the Congolese prime minister learned aid would be provided only through the United Nations, he viewed Canada as just another imperial power. For the most part, however, Canada was sympathetic to the Congo's position as a new state and was disinclined to support its European, NATO allies when they were perceived to be pursuing neo-colonial policies. If the significance of Canada's place in NATO has been overemphasized in previous interpretations of Canada's role in ONUC and the Congo crisis, it is largely because the politics of decolonization have not been adequately taken into account. It is perhaps also worth noting the importance of French. While Diefenbaker was reluctant to see too much emphasis placed on language, well steeped in his "one Canada" vision as he was, the bilingual capabilities of many Canadian peacekeepers who served in the Congo were in fact critical. Through ONUC, Canada was engaged with an important part of French-speaking Africa for more than three years, deepening relations with Africa outside the Commonwealth, a development of some significance in the years ahead, as Prime Minister Lester Pearson began to grapple with Quebec's Quiet Revolution and all that this movement meant for Canada's foreign policy.

To return to Katanga, there was one facet of this issue on which both Ottawa and London agreed: neither thought ONUC should be authorized to use force to achieve a political settlement. From the earliest days of Canadian participation in ONUC, it was clear Ottawa expected the UN's peacekeeping efforts in the Congo to follow earlier precedents of passive peacekeeping, for practical and theoretical reasons. The government was keen to limit the possibility of Canadian casualties. This largely explains Diefenbaker's initial reticence; he mistakenly assumed the UN would ask Canada for combat forces. His change in attitude is attributable to the subsequent clarification of the UN's request: Canada was asked to contribute only non-combat personnel. The government also placed restrictions on where army and air force personnel could serve within the Congo, to further reduce the chance of casualties.

At first, the idea that a peacekeeping mission would use force, especially when dispatched to an intra-state conflict such as the Congo, was almost inconceivable to Canadian diplomats. For example, when Hammarskjöld raised the prospect of more forceful ONUC intervention on behalf of Baluba refugees, Charles Ritchie expressed reservations as to the appropriateness and legality of such an initiative, a position that was subsequently supported by the Legal Division at External Affairs. When ONUC ultimately did use force, Ottawa was noticeably uncomfortable. Ambassadors Ritchie and Tremblay consistently counselled both Hammarskjöld and U Thant to exercise restraint as successive enabling resolutions passed by the Security Council increased the prospect that ONUC would be involved in fighting. Although in the third round of hostilities Howard Green eventually became reconciled to what seemed an inevitable confrontation between ONUC and the Katanga gendarmerie, Canadian diplomats in New York continued to press for a peaceful resolution to the Katangan secession. They had little choice once cabinet refused to authorize an intervention in the Advisory Committee that would have approved a UN plan entailing increased risk of confrontation with Katangese forces. National Defence was no less concerned about the use of force. Significantly, when ONUC's air unit was supplemented with fighter and light bomber aircraft in advance of the third round in Katanga, the military was no longer willing to provide an air commander – a position consistently filled by a Canadian officer since ONUC's inception. While Canada publicly supported the secretary-general following the final round of fighting in Katanga, some at External Affairs privately expressed concerns, especially regarding ONUC's "offensive" thrust to Jadotville. This muscular version of peacekeeping was not hailed as a welcome innovation.

The differing views within Ottawa on the use of force highlight the various bureaucratic and administrative components involved in the decisionmaking process on questions related to peacekeeping and Canada's Congo policy. Conflicting views between divisions at External Affairs on a proposed course of action were not uncommon. The European Division, for example, was generally more sympathetic to Belgian perspectives on colonial questions than were the other divisions. The views of the Defence Liaison, African and Middle Eastern, and United Nations Divisions were all taken into account. The views of the latter, largely under the leadership of Geoffrey Murray, were especially significant. Howard Green's role, as secretary of state for external relations throughout much of the Congo crisis, was crucial and accounts for the predominance of the United Nations Division in policy making on this issue. Green's interest in all things UN and his predisposition to carefully consider Canada's developing relations with newly independent nations in Africa and Asia are key factors to take into account when explaining Canada's support of ONUC and Congo policy generally. Green was also an able proponent of his department's interests and views, never shying away from pressing his opinion on Prime Minister Diefenbaker and his other cabinet colleagues.

The relationship between External Affairs and National Defence was generally cooperative. Joint submissions to cabinet, on significant issues related to ONUC, were not uncommon, though most questions related to the peacekeeping mission were settled at the ministerial level, after the initial decision to participate was taken. Occasionally, there were differences between the two departments. In ONUC's last two years, National Defence was forced to stretch military resources to their limits in order to meet financial objectives of the Diefenbaker government's austerity program. In addition, ONUC drained the military of the very type of soldier it could least afford to provide: those who were bilingual, and those who had specialized training in military communications. As a result, National Defence was less able to meet requests forwarded by External Affairs. Recognizing this trend, officials at External Affairs began an internal process of prioritization – pressing National Defence only on the requests they considered most worthy. Yet, as was seen in the cases of the continued renewal of the Pisa-Leopoldville air lift, National Defence's decision not to reappoint an air commander, and the final effort to arrange military training for the Congolese forces, National

Defence sometimes refused to meet a request even when pressed to do so by External Affairs. In these instances, Green turned to Diefenbaker. The prime minister encouraged Douglas Harkness, his minister of national defence, to re-examine decisions but never to reverse them. Thus, on these relatively rare occasions, National Defence's position prevailed.

The prime minister and cabinet also shaped Congo policy. John Diefenbaker was prime minister for the majority of ONUC's duration. Lester Pearson became prime minister in the peacekeeping mission's final months, when few significant issues remained to be addressed. In the case of Diefenbaker, whenever a decision relating to the Congo or to ONUC could have serious political repercussions, it was considered in cabinet. Diefenbaker's views were critical here; he often swayed the final decision. Decisions to contribute forces to ONUC in the first place, to halt the dispatch of troops when political conditions in the Congo became too unstable, to restrict the area of operations for both RCAF and army personnel, to provide contributions to the secretary-general's Congo fund, to not provide food aid during the Kasai famine, and to oppose UN strategies that could lead to hostilities in Katanga were all taken at the cabinet level. Notably, there were times when officials at External Affairs cleverly attempted to work around cabinet decisions that rejected a departmental submission. In the case of food aid, funds were sought from within departmental sources so as not to require an addition to the estimates. And, on the question of UN policy in Katanga, instructions were issued to the Canadian ambassador to simply remain silent in the Advisory Committee meeting when this issue was raised. The prime minister also discussed the Congo situation with various world leaders: in bilateral summits with American presidents Eisenhower and Kennedy and British prime minister Macmillan, and during meetings of the Commonwealth prime ministers. Such occasions were never used to set Canadian Congo policy, but they did provide Diefenbaker with an opportunity to hear the views of other heads of government.

As might have been expected, public opinion was most often an explicit consideration when the Congo was discussed in cabinet, rather than at the departmental level. It is not, however, entirely clear how Diefenbaker and his colleagues determined what public opinion was. Some opinion polls were carried out in this period, but polling was not nearly as pervasive as it is today, leaving the historian at a distinct methodological disadvantage in trying to reconstruct with any real certainty what public opinion was on particular issues. Throughout this book, I have presented examples of letters from concerned citizens and interest groups sent to the prime minister and the secretary of state for external affairs, newspaper editorials, letters to newspaper editors, and interventions in the House of Commons. This was done to give voice to particular viewpoints that existed at that time and of which the government would have been aware; it is not my intent to suggest that these accurately reflected widespread views or were indicators of true public opinion. In fact, when deducing what public opinion was, Diefenbaker did not necessarily use any of these sources of public opinion, so readily available to himself and later for the historian. On the question of whether to provide food aid during the Kasai famine, for example, we saw that Diefenbaker simply ignored much of what was printed in the media and the many letters he received imploring him to send food to the Congo. If Diefenbaker did truly consider public opinion, he appears to have dismissed the letters and contemporary media as unrepresentative of most Canadians' views. This is significant because for the entire time Canadians were present in the Congo, no other issue caused as great a public reaction as did the famine. In any case, it is clear that even in cabinet public opinion was only one of many factors taken into account when decisions relating to the Congo were made. At the departmental level, public opinion rarely seems to have been a concern. One External Affairs departmental memo enumerated no less than ten major considerations in Canada's Congo policy – public opinion did not make the list.[7] Moreover, cabinet documents prepared by External Affairs and National Defence never emphasized public opinion as a significant matter. In some ways, this is not surprising: civil servants may be implicitly aware of the significance of opinion but will always be more concerned with policy.

There is no doubt as to the most important determinant in Canada's Congo policy: support for the United Nations and peacekeeping. Within the first month of the crisis, officials at External Affairs came to believe that the future of both peacekeeping and the institution itself would be at risk if the UN failed disastrously in the Congo. This view was only reaffirmed as the crisis wore on and was increasingly shaped by the politics of the Cold War. In his final speech to Parliament as secretary of state for external affairs, Howard Green said, "We have tried to keep tempers cool. We have tried to urge moderation, and I think we have been able to do quite a lot in that regard. Our policy in regard to the Congo has been throughout, and is today, to support the United Nations."[8]

For a middle power whose foreign policy rested on a tradition of multilateralism, the United Nations was an important institution to preserve. As Tom Keating has observed, "Canadian support for multilateralism has not been an altruistic commitment to international order but a means of meeting vitally important national objectives."[9] In its support of the United Nations and the practice of peacekeeping, Canada was serving its own self-interests. There is, therefore, a danger in overemphasizing the significance of altruism or public opinion as determinants in Canadian peacekeeping policy; doing so implies Canada peacekeeps primarily to reinforce our self-image and to preserve a national symbol. James Eayrs's satirical portrait of the Canadian peacekeeper as a "Sir Galahad, sword gleaming, white horse prancing, knight-errantry shining, rushing in to save lesser breeds from the consequences of their own miscalculations, greed, and stupidity,"[10] is in some ways still an apt critique of Canadian peacekeeping. But to understand fully the reasons why Canada was so committed to ONUC, Eayrs's altruistic image should be balanced by John Holmes's admonition to search out the element of calculation in the motivations for Canadian foreign policy. Canada's Congo policy was certainly shaped by both self-interest and pragmatism.

# Notes

## Introduction

1  H. Basil Robinson, *Diefenbaker's World: A Populist in Foreign Affairs* (Toronto: University of Toronto Press, 1989), 315.
2  George Clay, "Entire Cabinet of the Congo Lacks Single Day's Experience," *Globe and Mail*, 30 June 1960, 7.
3  Inis L. Claude, "United Nations' Use of Military Force," *Journal of Conflict Resolution* 7, 2 (June 1963): 126.
4  Alastair Buchan, "Concepts of Peacekeeping," in *Freedom and Change: Essays in Honour of L.B. Pearson*, ed. M.G. Fry (Toronto: McClelland and Stewart, 1975), 19. For an equal sense of ominous foreboding, see also Brian Urquhart, *A Life in Peace and War* (New York: W.W. Norton, 1987), 144.
5  Alan James, *Britain and the Congo Crisis, 1960-63* (London: Macmillan, 1996), 25.
6  Norman Hillmer, "Peacekeeping: Canadian Invention, Canadian Myth," in *Welfare States in Trouble*, ed. Sune Akerman and J.L. Granatstein (Uppsala, Sweden: Swedish Science Press, 1995), 161.
7  Paul Martin, *A Very Public Life*, vol. 2 (Toronto: Deneau, 1985), 178-214.
8  Harold Jacobson, "The Changing United Nations," in *Foreign Policy in the Sixties: The Issues and the Instruments*, ed. Roger Hilsman and Robert Good (Baltimore: Johns Hopkins University Press, 1965), 69-71.
9  Albert Legault, *The Authorization of Peacekeeping Operations in Terms of the Nature of the Conflict* (Paris: International Information Centre on Peacekeeping Operations, 1968), 6.
10  John Holmes, "Canadian External Policies since 1945," *International Journal* 18, 2 (1963): 140-42.
11  Geoffrey Murray, interview with author, Ottawa, 31 July 2003.
12  John Holmes, *The Better Part of Valour: Essays on Canadian Diplomacy* (Toronto: McClelland and Stewart, 1970), 8.
13  Geoffrey Pearson, "Canadian Attitudes towards Peacekeeping," in *Peacekeeping: Appraisals and Proposals*, ed. Henry Wiseman (Willowdale, ON: Pergamon Press, 1983), 121.
14  *Foreign Relations of the United States* [hereafter *FRUS*], *1961-1963*, vol. 13, doc. 420, Telegram from Secretary of State Rusk to the Department of State.
15  Kim Richard Nossal, "Analyzing the Domestic Sources of Canadian Foreign Policy," *International Journal* 39, 1 (1983-84): 1-22.
16  D.W. Middlemiss and J.J. Sokolsky, *Canadian Defence: Decisions and Determinants* (Toronto: Harcourt Brace Jovanovich, 1989), 120-21.
17  J.L. Granatstein, "Canada and Peacekeeping: Image and Reality," *Canadian Forum* 54, 263 (August 1974): 14-19. J.L. Granatstein, "Peacekeeping: Did Canada Make a Difference? And What Difference Did Peacekeeping Make to Canada?" in *Making a Difference?* ed. John English and Norman Hillmer (Toronto: Lester Publishing, 1992), 222-34. J.L. Granatstein, *Who Killed the Canadian Military?* (Toronto: HarperCollins, 2004).

18  This is an important finding in Kevin A. Spooner, "Canada, the Congo Crisis, and United Nations Peacekeeping, 1960-1964" (PhD diss., Carleton University, 2002).

19  John Hilliker, "The Politicians and the 'Pearsonalities': The Diefenbaker Government and the Conduct of Canadian External Relations," *Historical Papers* (1984): 152.

20  John Hilliker and Donald Barry, *Canada's Department of External Affairs*, vol. 2 (Montreal and Kingston: McGill-Queen's University Press, 1995), 148.

21  Geoffrey Murray, interview with author, Ottawa, 31 July 2003. William Barton, interview with author, Ottawa, 1 August 2003.

### Chapter 1: Prelude to Crisis

1  Adam Hochschild, *King Leopold's Ghost* (Boston and New York: Houghton Mifflin Company, 1999), 161-64. David Gibbs, *The Political Economy of Third World Intervention* (Chicago: University of Chicago Press, 1991), 43.

2  Wynfred Joshua suggests that the Société Générale de Belgique controlled, either indirectly or directly, some 70 percent of the Congolese economy. Wynfred Joshua, "Belgium's Role in the UN Peace-keeping Operation in the Congo," *Orbis* 11, 2 (1967): 415.

3  Hochschild, *King Leopold's Ghost*, 194. Library and Archives Canada [hereafter LAC], RG6, A-1, vol. 123, file 1888.

4  Gibbs, *The Political Economy of Third World Intervention*, 46-49.

5  Hochschild, *King Leopold's Ghost*, 277-79.

6  As quoted in Ernest W. Lefever, *Crisis in the Congo* (Washington, DC: Brookings Institution, 1965), 4.

7  Douglas Anglin, "Towards a Canadian Policy on Africa," *International Journal* 15, 4 (Autumn 1960): 293-94.

8  Ibid., 298-307.

9  Ibid., 299-300, 306.

10  LAC, RG20, vol. 60, file 19775 part 1: Letter Désy to Skelton, 5 August 1940; Letter Cranborne to Massey, 27 March 1941. LAC, RG20, vol. 329, file T11681: Memo Heasman to Newman, 27 November 1947.

11  Comparative statistics from Congolese sources place Canada in the top twenty importing and exporting countries; however, these statistics did not take into account the relatively large number of Canadian goods reaching the Congo via other nations (i.e., Canadian goods shipped to the Congo through Belgium, the United States, etc.). For this reason, Canadian statistics are a better indicator of the actual level of trade.

12  Anglin, "Towards a Canadian Policy on Africa," 294-97.

13  LAC, RG25, vol. 3270, file 6386-40 part 1: Summary of Despatch No. 279, 6 June 1955; Despatch No. 307, 8 June 1955. Aluminium Limited had become the parent company of the Aluminum Company of Canada in 1928; subsequent corporate name changes have included Alcan Aluminium Ltd. (1966) and Alcan Inc. (2001).

14  LAC, RG25, vol. 3270, file 6386-40 part 1, Letter 173 Turgeon to King, 5 April 1945.

15  LAC, RG25, vol. 7033, file 6386-40 parts 2 and 2.2, Background Paper on the Belgian Congo, 1956; Letter 142 Hébert to Léger, 21 February 1958.

16  LAC, RG25, vol. 7033, file 6386-40 part 2.2, Letter and memo Hébert to Reid, 8 January 1957.

17  LAC, RG25, vol. 7033, file 6386-40 part 2.2, Letter Reid to Hébert, 30 April 1957.

18  LAC, RG25, vol. 3270, file 6386-40 part 1, Memo Douglas to Pope, 8 June 1951.

19  LAC, RG25, vol. 3270, file 6386-40 part 1, Memo Brodie to Munro, 29 January 1952.

20  LAC, RG25, vol. 7033, file 6386-40 part 3, Memo Nyenhuis to Robertson, 1 June 1959.

21  LAC, RG25, vol. 7033, file 6386-40 part 3.2, Memo Nyenhuis to Robertson, 14 November 1959.

22  LAC, RG25, vol. 7033, file 6386-40 part 3.2, Memo Nyenhuis to Robertson, 8 October 1959.

23  LAC, RG25, vol. 7033, file 6386-40 part 3, Telegram Brussels to External Affairs [hereafter External], 8 January 1959; Letter Nyenhuis to Robertson, 8 January 1959; Memo by Glazebrook, 30 January 1959.

24  In the year prior to independence, administration of the Congo was dependent on some ten thousand Belgians. Harold Jacobson, "ONUC's Civilian Operation: State Preserving and

State Building," *World Politics* 17, 1 (1964): 79. See also Lefever, *Crisis in the Congo*, 6-8; Gibbs, *The Political Economy of Third World Intervention*, 73-76; Michel Struelens, *The United Nations in the Congo or O.N.U.C. and International Politics* (Brussels: Max Arnold, 1976), 18-19.

25 LAC, RG25, vol. 7033, file 6386-40 part 3, Memo Nyenhuis to Robertson, 1 June 1959.

26 Rosalyn Higgins, *United Nations Peacekeeping, 1946-1967: Documents and Commentary,* vol. 3 (Oxford: Oxford University Press, 1980), 9. Kalb also asserts that Kasavubu was a federalist who favoured considerable autonomy and was open to the idea of secession. Madeleine Kalb, *The Congo Cables* (New York: Macmillan, 1982), xxii.

27 Higgins, *United Nations Peacekeeping, 1946-1967,* 10. See also Kalb, *The Congo Cables,* xxiv. Colin Legum, Foreword and Notes to *Congo My Country*, by Patrice Lumumba (London: Pall Mall Press, 1962), xiii-xiv. Legum argues that Lumumba was not in favour of rejecting Belgian assistance outright; he wanted Belgium's co-operation but only if it was prepared to recognize that the Congo was truly independent.

28 LAC, RG25, vol. 5208, file 6386-40 part 5, Letter 368 Canadian Embassy, Brussels, to Robertson, 17 June 1960. *FRUS, 1958-1960*, vol. 14, doc. 97, Memorandum of Conversation between the Ambassador in Belgium (Burden) and Patrice Lumumba.

29 LAC, RG25, vol. 3270, file 6386-40 part 1, Letter and attached clipping Canadian Embassy, Brussels to Pearson, 23 January 1950.

30 LAC, RG25, vol. 3270, file 6386-40 part 1, Letter Ausman to Heeney, 3 April 1950; Letter Gibson-Smith to Director, Trade Commission Service, 25 January 1951. LAC, RG25, vol. 5208, file 6386-40 part 5, Memo European Div to Commonwealth Div, 6 June 1960.

31 LAC, RG25, vol. 7034, file 6386-B-40 part 1, Letter 388 Pierce to Robertson, 31 July 1959; Memo Commonwealth Div to Consular Div, 21 September 1959; Memo European Div to Personnel Div, 25 November 1959; Memo Robertson to Green, 22 March 1960. LAC, RG2, vol. 5937, Cabinet Documents 167/60 and 196/60. LAC, RG2, vol. 2746, Cabinet Conclusions, 30 June 1960.

32 LAC, RG25, vol. 5208, file 6386-40 part 4, Memo: The Belgian Congo, 10 March 1960; Letter Belgian Ambassador to Canada to Green, 19 April 1960.

33 John Schlegel, *The Deceptive Ash: Bilingualism and Canadian Policy in Africa: 1957-1971* (Washington, DC: University Press of America, 1978), 214.

34 Ibid., 216, 224-28.

35 Georges Abi-Saab, *The United Nations Operation in the Congo 1960-1964* (Oxford: Oxford University Press, 1978), 5-6.

36 Catherine Hoskyns, *The Congo since Independence* (London: Oxford University Press, 1965), 88.

37 By 4 August, the United States Air Force had evacuated 3,170 persons to Europe, including 55 Canadians. David W. Wainhouse, *International Peacekeeping at the Crossroads: National Support-Experience and Prospects* (Baltimore: Johns Hopkins University Press, 1973), 283.

38 LAC, RG 25, vol. 5209, file 6386-40 part 9, Letter Bull to Robertson, 4 August 1960.

39 "Revolt in Congo Spreads," *Halifax Chronicle-Herald*, 8 July 1960, 1. "Panic-Stricken Europeans Flee Congo Troop Bayonets," *Toronto Daily Star*, 8 July 1960, 1.

40 Brian Urquhart and Ernest Lefever both suggest the press exaggerated the extent of violence in the Congo. Brian Urquhart, *Hammarskjold* (New York: Alfred A. Knopf, 1972), 402-3. Lefever, *Crisis in the Congo*, 6.

41 As quoted in Gibbs, *The Political Economy of Third World Intervention*, 82.

42 LAC, RG 25, vol. 5209, file 6386-40 part 9, Letter Bull to Robertson, 4 August 1960. LAC, RG25, vol. 7034, file 6386-B-40 part 1, Letter Bull to Hughes, 1 August 1960.

43 A.A.J. van Bilsen, "Some Aspects of the Congo Problem," *International Affairs* 38, 1 (1962): 48. Michael Schatzberg is more blunt, suggesting that the Katangan secession "was a barely concealed attempt to dismember Zaire; Belgium accorded Tshombe every support except diplomatic recognition." Michael Schatzberg, *Mobutu or Chaos?* (New York: University Press of America, 1991), 11.

44 Andrew W. Cordier and Wilder Foote, *Public Papers of the Secretaries-General of the United Nations*, vol. 5, *Dag Hammarskjöld, 1960-1961* (New York: Columbia University Press, 1975), 19.

45  *FRUS, 1958-1960*, vol. 14, doc. 116, Telegram from the President's Assistant Staff Secretary (Eisenhower) to the Staff Secretary (Goodpaster), at Newport, Rhode Island; doc. 117, Memorandum of Telephone Conversation between President Eisenhower and Secretary of State Herter. Lefever argues that the United States could have mounted an intervention at this point but decided against it because "the political cost of direct aid was overestimated in Washington," as a result of the State Department's "oversensitivity to charges of 'neo-colonialism.'" Lefever, "The Limits of UN Intervention in the Third World," *The Review of Politics* 30, 1 (1968): 13.

46  Cordier and Foote, *Dag Hammarskjöld, 1960-1961*, 19.

## Chapter 2: Decision Time

1  Canadian Institute of Public Opinion (CIPO) Poll 283, July 1960. The following acknowledgment and disclaimer applies to this and all subsequent references to CIPO polls: "The data were collected by the Canadian Institute of Public Opinion (Gallup Poll). Codebook preparation and data cleaning were completed by the Carleton University Social Science Data Archives, under the auspices of the Machine Readable Archives Division of the Public Archives of Canada. These organizations provided the data but can not be held responsible for the analyses or interpretations presented nor for any problems with the data."

2  "Where Are the UN Police?" *Globe and Mail*, 12 July 1960, 6. "Pour une action plus efficace de l'ONU au Congo" [For a more effective UN role in the Congo], *Le Devoir*, 19 July 1960, 4.

3  Canada, House of Commons, *Debates*, 12 July 1960: 6101.

4  LAC, RG25, vol. 5208, file 6386-40 part 5, Memo Defence Liaison [hereafter DL] (1) to UN Div: Congo – Role of the United Nations, 12 July 1960.

5  Alan James, *Britain and the Congo Crisis, 1960-63* (London: Macmillan, 1996), 43.

6  LAC, RG25, vol. 5208, file 6386-40 parts 5 and 6, Memo UN Div to Arnold Smith: Congo, 12 July 1960; Memo: Situation in the Congo, 13 July 1960.

7  LAC, RG25, vol. 5208, file 6386-40 parts 5-7, Telegram Brussels to External: Congo, 16 July 1960; Memo Commonwealth Div to Robertson: Ghana, the Congo, Katanga, and Canada, 14 July 1960; Memo for Minister: Political Situation in the Congo, 12 July 1960.

8  Helmut Sonnenfeldt, "The Soviet Union and China: Where They Stood in 1960," in *Footnotes to the Congo Story*, ed. Helen Kitchen (New York: Walker and Company, 1967), 27.

9  LAC, RG25, vol. 5208, file 6386-40 parts 5 and 6: Telegram Brussels to External: Congo, 12 July 1960; Telegram Brussels to External: Congo Foreign Policy, 13 July 1960. Directorate of History and Heritage, Department of National Defence [hereafter DHH], file 491C.023 (D4), Director of Military Intelligence [hereafter DMI] Memo: Appreciation of Situation in Congo Republic, 14 July 1960.

10  LAC, RG25, vol. 5208, file 6386-40 part 5, Telegram Geneva to External: UN Action in Belgian Congo, 12 July 1960; Telegram Permanent Mission, New York [hereafter PERMISNY] to External: Disorders in Congo, 12 July 1960.

11  LAC, RG25, vol. 5208, file 6386-40 parts 5 and 6, Telegram PERMISNY to External: Disorders in Congo, 12 July 1960; Telegram 910 PERMISNY to External: Disorders in Congo, 13 July 1960.

12  As quoted in Brian Urquhart, *Ralph Bunche: An American Odyssey* (New York: W.W. Norton, 1993), 311.

13  LAC, RG25, vol. 5208, file 6386-40 part 6, Telegram 915 PERMISNY to External: Disorders in Congo, 13 July 1960; Memo Robertson to Green, 13 July 1960; Memo for Minister: Congo, 13 July 1960.

14  Ralph Bunche, "The United Nations Operation in the Congo," in *From Collective Security to Preventive Diplomacy*, ed. Joel Larus (New York: John Wiley and Sons, 1965), 411.

15  Leon Gordenker, *The UN Secretary-General and the Maintenance of Peace* (New York: Columbia University Press, 1967), 246.

16  John Holmes, "The United Nations in the Congo," *International Journal* 16, 1 (1960-61): 8.

17  Andrew W. Cordier and Wilder Foote, *Public Papers of the Secretaries-General of the United Nations*, vol. 5, *Dag Hammarskjöld, 1960-1961* (New York: Columbia University Press, 1975), 23. See also D.W. Bowett, *United Nations Forces* (London: Stevens and Sons, 1964), 186.

18 Cordier and Foote, *Dag Hammarskjöld, 1960-1961*, 25-26. See also Ernest Lefever, "U.S. Policy, the UN and the Congo," *Orbis* 11, 2 (Summer 1967): 397.

19 Cordier and Foote, *Dag Hammarskjöld, 1960-1961*, 26. *FRUS, 1958-1960*, vol. 14, doc. 131, Telegram from the Mission at the United Nations to the Department of State. See also Indar Jit Rikhye, "United Nations Peacekeeping Operations and India," *India Quarterly* 41, 3-4 (July-December 1985): 310.

20 Herbert Nicholas, "An Appraisal," in *International Military Forces: The Question of Peacekeeping in an Armed and Disarming World*, ed. Lincoln Bloomfield (Boston: Little, Brown, 1964), 119.

21 Resolution 143 (1960) July 14. *In favour:* Argentina, Ceylon, Ecuador, Italy, Poland, Tunisia, Union of Soviet Socialist Republics, United States; *against:* none; *abstentions:* China, France, United Kingdom.

22 Cordier and Foote, *Dag Hammarskjöld, 1960-1961*, 26.

23 Peter Calvocoressi, *World Order and New States* (London: Chatto and Windus, 1962), 92. See also Georges Abi-Saab, *The United Nations Operation in the Congo 1960-1964* (Oxford: Oxford University Press, 1978), 15, 20.

24 Brian Urquhart, "Peacekeeping: A View from the Operational Centre," in *Peacekeeping: Appraisals and Proposals*, ed. Henry Wiseman (Toronto: Pergamon Press, 1983), 165. See also Indar Jit Rikhye, *The Theory and Practice of Peacekeeping* (London: Hurst, 1984), 88.

25 LAC, RG25, vol. 5208, file 6386-40 part 6, Memo Robertson to Green, 13 July 1960; Memo by G.S. Murray, 13 July 1960; Telegram 911 PERMISNY to External: Disorders in Congo, 13 July 1960.

26 H. Basil Robinson, *Diefenbaker's World: A Populist in Foreign Affairs* (Toronto: University of Toronto Press, 1989), 148.

27 LAC, RG25, vol. 5208, file 6386-40 part 6, Memo from the Office of the Secretary of State for External Affairs [hereafter SSEA], 13 July 1960.

28 "Bataillon canadien prêt à partir à la demande de l'ONU" [Canadian battalion ready to leave at the UN's request], *Le Devoir*, 13 July 1960, 2. "Canada Aid 'Not Likely,'" *Montreal Gazette*, 13 July 1960, 1. "Our Troops Set – But Not Likely to Go," *Winnipeg Free Press*, 13 July 1960, 1. "La contribution du Canada au Congo dépendra de l'ONU" [Canada's contribution to the Congo depends on the UN], *Le Devoir*, 14 July 1960, 3.

29 Robinson, *Diefenbaker's World*, 148. This view, that Diefenbaker ruled out combat forces from the outset but remained open to the idea that Canada might later contribute administrative or support personnel, was reiterated by Robinson in a conversation with the author. Robinson also noted that he had become ill immediately after the initial request, so his recollection of the subsequent sequence of events relating to the UN's requests for assistance is uncertain. H. Basil Robinson, phone interview with author, 31 July 2003.

30 G. Ann Livingstone, "Canada's Policy and Attitudes Towards United Nations Peacekeeping, 1956-1964, with Specific Reference to Participation in the Forces Sent to Egypt (1956), the Congo (1960) and Cyprus (1964)" (PhD diss., Keele University, 1995), 185. John P. Schlegel, *The Deceptive Ash: Bilingualism and Canadian Policy in Africa: 1957-1971* (Washington, DC: University Press of America, 1978), 227, fn 95.

31 Canada, House of Commons, *Debates*, 13 July 1960: 6179.

32 "Canada to Aid Congo Only If UN in Charge," *Globe and Mail*, 13 July 1960, 1.

33 LAC, RG25, vol. 5208, file 6386-40 part 6, Telegram PERMISNY to External: Canadian Contribution to Congo, 14 July 1960.

34 LAC, RG25, vol. 5208, file 6386-40 part 6, Memo Robertson to Green, 14 July 1960. J.L. Granatstein refers to Ottawa dispatches that reported Ralph Bunche in Leopoldville saying Canada would be expected to send paratroopers. He notes that the government doubted the accuracy of the reports, in response to calls for action in the conservative press. It turns out that the news stories were based on a leaked private conversation between General Alexander and Bunche, in which they only *theoretically* discussed the possibility of using bilingual paratroopers for rescue operations. Thus, the reports were inaccurate. J.L. Granatstein, "Canada: Peacekeeper," in *Peacekeeping: International Challenge and Canadian Response* (Lindsay, ON: Canadian Institute of International Affairs, 1968), 155-56. LAC, RG25, vol. 5219, file 6386-C-40 part 1, Memo for Minister: Congo: Canadian Contribution, 20 July 1960.

35  LAC, RG25, vol. 5208, file 6386-40 part 6, Memo Robertson to Green, 14 July 1960.

36  LAC, RG2, vol. 2747, Cabinet Conclusions, 14 July 1960, paras. 4-5.

37  Canada, House of Commons, *Debates*, 14 July 1960: 6273-74.

38  LAC, RG25, vol. 5208, file 6386-40 part 6, Memo for Minister: Congo, 14 July 1960; Outgoing Message External to PERMISNY: Congo, 14 July 1960.

39  Canada, House of Commons, *Debates*, 14 July 1960: 6296.

40  "Canada's Defense Duty," *Globe and Mail*, 14 July 1960, 6.

41  John G. Diefenbaker, *One Canada*, vol. 2 (Toronto: Macmillan, 1976), 129.

42  "The UN's Congo Force," *Halifax Chronicle-Herald*, 15 July 1960, 4.

43  LAC, RG25, vol. 5208, file 6386-40 part 6, Telegram NATOPARIS to External, 14 July 1960.

44  LAC, RG25, vol. 5208, file 6386-40 part 6, Telegram PRETORIA to External, 14 July 1960; Telegram 1817, Washington, DC [hereafter WASHDC] to External, 14 July 1960; Telegram 1825 WASHDC to External, 14 July 1960. *FRUS, 1958-1960*, vol. 14, doc. 140, Memorandum of Discussion at the 452nd Meeting of the National Security Council; doc. 149, Memorandum from the Director of Intelligence and Research (Cumming) to Secretary of State Herter. The Americans had nonetheless taken military precautions against Soviet intervention. The US aircraft carrier *Wasp* was quietly stationed near the Congolese coast and the American ambassador was reportedly given authority to order the ship to catapult its planes if necessary. See David W. Wainhouse, *International Peacekeeping at the Crossroads: National Support-Experience and Prospects* (Baltimore: Johns Hopkins University Press, 1973), 282. Stephen R. Weissman, *American Foreign Policy in the Congo 1960-1964* (Ithaca, NY: Cornell University Press, 1974), 279.

45  LAC, RG25, vol. 5208, file 6386-40, part 6, Telegram External to Brussels, 14 July 1960.

46  "Soviet Issues Warning," *Globe and Mail*, 16 July 1960, 1. "Mr. K. Brinksman," *Globe and Mail*, 16 July 1960, 6. "Mr. K. Fuels the Cold War," *Toronto Daily Star*, 16 July 1960, 4.

47  LAC, RG25, vol. 5219, file 6386-C-40 part 1, Memo for the Under Secretary of State for External Affairs [hereafter USSEA]: Conversation with the Belgian Ambassador concerning Congo situation, 20 July 1960. *FRUS, 1958-1960*, vol. 14, doc. 128, Memorandum of Conversation.

48  The Americans faced a similar challenge. Hamilton Armstrong suggests the United States tried to balance a tradition that favoured independence movements with the interests of its NATO allies. He found it did so "without remarkable success." Hamilton F. Armstrong, "U.N. on Trial," *Foreign Affairs* 39, 3 (1961): 397.

49  LAC, RG25, vol. 5219, file 6386-C-40 part 1, Memo Robertson to Green, 20 July 1960.

50  Alan James suggests that there was little likelihood of "massive intervention" by the Soviets, given the very serious logistical limitations they would have faced in any attempt to intervene directly in the Congo and that this would have been viewed as "most unlikely" even in 1960. He adds, however, that without ONUC "there might well have been much greater pressure on the Soviet Union to intervene and [it] might have felt less well placed to resist it." Alan James, *The Politics of Peacekeeping* (London: Chatto and Windus, 1969), 362-63. Alan James, "Peacekeeping and the Parties," in *The United Nations and Peacekeeping: Results, Limitations, and Prospects*, ed. Indar Jit Rikhye (Basingstoke, UK: Macmillan / International Peace Academy, 1990), 129.

51  J.L. Granatstein, "Canada and Peacekeeping: Myth and Reality," *The Canadian Forum* 54, 263 (August 1974): 16. J.L. Granatstein, "Peacekeeping: Did Canada Make a Difference? And What Difference Did Peacekeeping Make to Canada?" in *Making a Difference?* ed. John English and Norman Hillmer (Toronto: Lester Publishing, 1992), 229.

52  Weissman, *American Foreign Policy in the Congo*, 53. Schatzberg concurs that "Western policy makers" believed there was "much to fear" from perceived Soviet intentions. Michael Schatzberg, *Mobutu or Chaos?* (New York: University Press of America, 1991), 14.

53  Diefenbaker, *One Canada*, 126.

54  Cordier and Foote, *Dag Hammarskjöld, 1960-1961*, 28-32.

55  Ibid., 33-34.

56  *FRUS, 1958-1960*, vol. 14, doc. 124, Memorandum of Telephone Conversation between Secretary of State Herter and the Representative at the United Nations (Lodge). Although the UN does not seem to have explicitly said so in its communications with Ritchie at this point, Brian Urquhart maintains that only Canada could have provided the required bilingual

personnel and that "it was for this compelling reason that Canadian units had been included in the force." Brian Urquhart, *Hammarskjold* (New York: Alfred A. Knopf, 1972), 433.

57  LAC, RG25, vol. 5208, file 6386-40 part 6, Telegram 943 and 944 PERMISNY to External, 15 July 1960.

58  LAC, RG25, vol. 5208, file 6386-40 part 6, Memo: Assistance for Congo, 15 July 1960.

59  Granatstein, "Canada: Peacekeeper," 155.

60  LAC, RG2, vol. 2747, Cabinet Conclusions, 16 July 1960. "Canada to Send Food for Congo," *Winnipeg Free Press*, 18 July 1960, 2. "Canada in the Congo," *Halifax Chronicle-Herald*, 27 July 1960, 4.

61  Donal O'Carroll, "Ireland's UN Peacekeeping Experience 1958-1995," in *Peacekeeping 1815 to Today*, ed. Serge Bernier (Ottawa: International Commission of Military History, 1995), 530.

62  LAC, RG25, vol. 5208, file 6386-40 part 7, Memo Robertson to Green, 18 July 1960.

63  DHH, file 112.1.003 (D9), Memo from DGPO [director-general of plans and operations]: UN Forces in the Congo, 18 July 1960.

64  DHH, file 112.1.003 (D9), Memo from DGPO: UN Forces in the Congo, 18 July 1960.

65  Granatstein, "Canada: Peacekeeper," 155. LAC, RG25, vol. 5208, file 6386-40 part 7, Memo Robertson to Green, 19 July 1960. LAC, RG25, vol. 5219, file 6386-C-40 part 1, Memo Robertson to Green, 19 July 1960.

66  Because of mechanical difficulties with a number of planes sent to transport von Horn, the commander's arrival was significantly delayed until 18 July. This helps to explain the ambiguity in the UN requests of Canada. Even after his arrival, von Horn had difficulty determining requirements because a lack of communications made it difficult to contact his contingents. Maj. Gen. Carl von Horn, *Soldiering for Peace* (London: Cassell, 1966), 131-36. Lincoln P. Bloomfield, "Headquarters Field Relations: Some Notes on the Beginning and End of ONUC," *International Organization* 17 (1963): 379. Wainhouse, *International Peacekeeping at the Crossroads*, 289.

67  LAC, RG2, vol. 2747, Cabinet Conclusions, 19 July 1960. LAC, RG2, vol. 5937, Cabinet Document 228/60.

68  LAC, RG2, vol. 2747, Cabinet Conclusions, 19 July 1960. LAC, RG2, vol. 5937, Cabinet Documents 228/60, 236/60, 238/60.

69  LAC, RG25, vol. 5219, file 6386-C-40 part 1, Memo for Minister: Congo: UN Role, 19 July 1960.

70  LAC, RG25, vol. 5219, file 6386-C-40 part 1, Memo: DL (1) to UN Div: Congo – Provision of Canadian Signallers, 20 July 1960. DHH, file 112.1.003 (D9), Memo: Special Meeting of Heads of Branches, 20 July 1960; Memo: Possible Canadian Contribution to UN Forces in Congo Republic, Synopsis No. 3 Events up to 0900 Hrs 21 Jul 60, 21 July 1960 [my emphasis].

71  DHH, file 112.1.003 (D9), Memo: Telephone Conversation – CGS [chief of the general staff]/ DGPO/D Sigs 0900 Hrs 21 Jul 60, 21 July 1960.

72  DHH, file 112.1.003 (D9), Telegram PERMISNY to External: Congo: UN Force; Memo: Telephone Conversation – CGS, Brigadier Bishop, DGPO, Col. Clement, D Sigs, Maj. Gen. Alexander, U.S. to SSG Labouisse, 21 July 1960; Memo: Telephone Conversation – CGS/ DGPO/D Sigs 0900 Hrs 21 Jul 60, 21 July 1960. LAC, RG25, vol. 5219, file 6386-C-40 part 1, Memo DL (1) Div to UN Div: Congo – Provision of Canadian Signallers, 21 July 1960. Lincoln Bloomfield highlights the seriousness of the shortage of French-speaking peacekeepers, noting that by December 1960 there were still only six bilingual personnel at ONUC HQ out of a staff composed from twenty-nine countries. Bloomfield, "Headquarters-Field Relations," 381.

73  LAC, RG2, vol. 2747, Cabinet Conclusions, 21 July 1960.

74  "Canada's Chance to Serve U.N.," *Toronto Daily Star*, 20 July 1960, 3. "Green Hedges on Congo," *Winnipeg Free Press*, 20 July 1960, 1. "Green Mum on Bunche Statement," *Montreal Gazette*, 21 July 1960, 4. "Canadians May Be Sent," *Winnipeg Free Press*, 21 July 1960, 15. "More Canadians May Go to Congo," *Halifax Chronicle-Herald*, 21 July 1960, 1.

75  DHH, file 112.1.003 (D9), Memo DGPO: Joint Study – Army/External Affairs, 25 July 1960; Notes of Conversation Brigadier Bishop/Colonel Clement, 26 July 1960; Memo: Signals for

Congo Republic, 26 July 1960. LAC, RG25, file 6386-C-40 part 1, Memo: UN Div to File: Congo: United Nations' Request for Signals and Logistics Support. United Nations Archives [hereafter UNA], S-0209-0003-11, United Nations Operations in the Congo [hereafter ONUC] – records on foreign countries, Canada – correspondence, cables, etc., untitled and unsigned memo dated 25 July 1960.

76  Fred Gaffen suggests that it was Lt. Col. J.A. Berthiaume who had "managed with the connivance of some members of the RCAF to circumvent this restriction and airlift the Tunisian contingent to Kasai province and its capital Luluabourg." Fred Gaffen, *In the Eye of the Storm: A History of Canadian Peacekeeping* (Toronto: Deneau and Wayne, 1987), 233-34.

77  LAC, RG25, vol. 5208, file 6386-40 part 7, Memo UN Div to DL (1): Congo: Development of UN Force, 22 July 1960. LAC, RG25, vol. 5219, file 6386-C-40 part 1, Memo for Minister: Congo: Use of RCAF aircraft, 21 July 1960; Memo for Minister: Congo: Use of RCAF aircraft, 23 July 1960. LAC, RG25, vol. 5209, file 6386-40 part 8, Telegram PERMISNY to External: Congo: Use of RCAF Aircraft, 23 July 1960.

78  LAC, RG25, vol. 5219, file 6386-C-40 part 1, Memo Green to Robertson: Congo – Modification of the Use of the RCAF North Stars, 23 July 1960; Letter Pearkes to Green, 25 July 1960; Letter Green to Pearkes, 27 July 1960; Memo for Minister: Congo: Use of RCAF Aircraft, 30 July 1960. LAC, RG25, vol. 5209, file 6386-40 part 8, Memo UN Div to USSEA: Use of RCAF Aircraft on Pisa-Leopoldville Airlift, 27 July 1960. LAC, RG25, vol. 5219, file 6386-C-40 part 2, Letter Green to Pearkes, 4 August 1960.

79  Resolution 145 (1960) July 22. *In favour:* Argentina, Ceylon, China, Ecuador, France, Italy, Poland, Tunisia, Union of Soviet Socialist Republics, United Kingdom, United States; *against:* none; *abstentions:* none.

80  Catherine Hoskyns, *The Congo since Independence: January 1960-December 1961* (London: Oxford University Press, 1965), 150-52, 155. Jack Citrin, *UN Peacekeeping Activities: A Case Study in Organizational Task Expansion*, Monograph Series in World Affairs 3.1 (Denver: University of Denver, 1965-66), 40.

81  As quoted in Cordier and Foote, *Dag Hammarskjöld, 1960-1961*, 45.

82  Rosalyn Higgins, *United Nations Peacekeeping, 1946-1967: Documents and Commentary* (Oxford: Oxford University Press, 1980), 88.

83  DHH, file 112.1.003 (D9), Memo: Possible Canadian Contribution to UN Forces in Congo Republic, Synopsis No. 6 Events up to 1400 Hrs, 25 July 1960; Memo: Possible Canadian Contribution to UN Forces in Congo Republic, Synopsis No. 7 Events up to 1400 Hrs, 26 July 1960; Memo: Vice Admiral DeWolf RCN to CGS: Use of *Bonaventure* in Support of Congo Operations, 26 July 1960. DHH, file 112.1.003 (D9), vol. 2, Letter CGS to Minister of the Department of National Defence [hereafter MDND]: Concentration of Personnel and Equipment Earmarked for Service – Congo Republic, 25 July 1960.

84  LAC, RG25, vol. 5225, file 6386-D-40 part 1, Memo for Prime Minister: Visit of Prime Minister Lumumba of the Republic of the Congo, 29 July 1960; Memorandum for the USSEA, 27 July 1960. *FRUS, 1958-1960*, vol. 14, doc. 153, Memorandum of Conversation. Dwight D. Eisenhower Library, Christian A. Herter Papers, 1957-1961, box 13, CAH Telephone Calls, 7/1/60-8/31/60, Memorandum of Telephone Conversation with Canadian SSEA, 25 July 1960. "Lumumba Invites Canadians," *Winnipeg Free Press*, 26 July 1960, 1.

85  LAC, RG25, vol. 5225, file 6386-D-40 part 1, Memo for Prime Minister: Visit of Prime Minister Lumumba of the Republic of the Congo, 29 July 1960; Memorandum for the USSEA, 27 July 1960. Kaplan suggests the Belgians believed Lumumba had been received in the United States "as if he had been the King of the Belgians himself" and that this considerably coloured Belgian views of US policy. Lawrence Kaplan, "The United States, Belgium, and the Congo Crisis of 1960," *The Review of Politics* 29, 2 (1967): 246.

86  LAC, RG25, vol. 5225, file 6386-D-40 part 1, Memo for the Prime Minister, 29 July 1960; Memo Commonwealth Div to Smith: Possible Visit of Patrice Lumumba to Ottawa, 22 July 1960. LAC, RG25, vol. 5209, file 6386-40 part 8, Telegram PERMISNY to External: Congo – Visit of Prime Minister Lumumba to Canada, 27 July 1960.

87  "Le premier ministre Lumumba affirme à Montréal ..." [Prime Minister Lumumba declares in Montreal], *Le Devoir*, 30 July 1960, 13. "Lumumba Here: Belgians Said Behind Riots," *Montreal Gazette*, 30 July 1960, 1.

88 LAC, RG25, vol. 5225, file 6386-D-40 part 1, Telegram WASHDC to External: Visit of Congolese Prime Minister, 28 July 1960; Memo for Minister: Conversations with Mr. Lumumba, 1 August 1960; Memo Robertson to Green, 1 August 1960. Geoffrey Murray, interview with author, Ottawa, 31 July 2003. Negative assessments were not reserved for Lumumba alone. A Congolese ordnance officer by the name of Captain Mawoso accompanied Lumumba on his visit to Ottawa. Cadieux described him as "a sincere, but somewhat inarticulate and limited individual. He spoke without resentment, but I have the impression that he would describe in the same smiling fashion a fire that destroyed his house or a flood that had eliminated a number of villages." LAC, RG25, vol. 5225, file 6386-D-40 part 1, Memo for the USSEA, 30 July 1960.

89 LAC, RG25, vol. 5225, file 6386-D-40 part 1, Memo Robertson to Green, 1 August 1960; Memorandum from Information Division to Commonwealth Division, 2 August 1960. Kalb notes that Lumumba was willing to meet with Aroutunian for some thirty-five minutes, even though he decided to cut his Ottawa trip short once he failed to obtain direct bilateral assistance. Madeleine Kalb, *The Congo Cables* (New York: Macmillan, 1982), 41.

90 Higgins, *United Nations Peacekeeping, 1946-1967*, 127.

91 LAC, RG25, vol. 5225, 6386-D-40 part 1, Memo PERMISNY to USSEA, 3 December 1960; Telegram Leopoldville to External, 3 October 1960.

92 Diefenbaker, *One Canada*, 128. Charles Lynch spins a rather legendary tale of Green's reaction to the Congolese request for women. Lynch suggests, "Green, a prim and proper man with a minimal knowledge of the world outside Canada and no knowledge at all of Africa, sent back word that the Canadian government did not deal in such matters. One of Green's aides, in delivering the reply, let slip on the sly that maybe the distinguished guests could try the By Ward Market, the hangout for hookers, just two blocks down the street." The veracity of this particular account is questionable given Lynch's patently false report of Lumumba's later death, which he suggests happened at the hands of an angry Leopoldville mob that tore him limb from limb. A more reliable source, diplomat George Ignatieff, suggests that Green misunderstood Lumumba's request for "girls" and sent stenographers; when it became clear that Lumumba actually wanted prostitutes, "arrangements were made to meet the wishes of the Congolese prime minister the following night." Accountants at External Affairs reportedly charged the expense as "flowers." Charles Lynch, *You Can't Print THAT!* (Edmonton: Hurtig, 1983), 188-90; George Ignatieff, *The Making of a Peacemonger* (Toronto: University of Toronto Press, 1985), 191.

93 LAC, RG2, vol. 2747, Cabinet Conclusions, 28 July 1960. DHH, file 112.1.003 (D9), Telegram PERMISNY to External: Congo: UN Force, 28 July 1960. As late as 25 July, Green was still forcefully denying to the Canadian press any and all rumours that Canada had plans to send troops to the Congo; see, for example, "No Congo Force: Green Denies Rumor Canada Sending 300-800 Troops," *Winnipeg Free Press*, 25 July 1960, 1.

94 LAC, RG2, vol. 2747, Cabinet Conclusions, 28 July 1960. LAC, RG2, vol. 5937, Cabinet Document 243/60. LAC, RG25, vol. 5209, file 6386-40, part 8, Memo Robertson to Green, 27 July 1960.

95 Diefenbaker Canada Centre [hereafter DCC], file MG1/XII/C/114, Memo from Office of the Judge Advocate General: Dispatch of Canadian Forces to Congo, 25 July 1960. LAC, RG2, vol. 2747, Cabinet Conclusions, 30 July 1960. LAC, RG25, vol. 5219, file 6386-C-40, part 1, Memo SSEA to USSEA: Canadian Contribution to the UN Emergency Force [hereafter UNEF] in the Congo Republic, 28 July 1960.

96 Canada, House of Commons, *Debates*, 1 August 1960: 7327-48. LAC, RG2, vol. 2747, Cabinet Conclusions, 5 August 1960.

97 Sean M. Maloney, *Canada and UN Peacekeeping: Cold War by Other Means, 1945-1970* (St. Catharines, ON: Vanwell, 2002), 127.

**Chapter 3: Deployment**

1 LAC, RG25, vol. 5209, file 6386-40 part 9, Bull to USSEA, 5 August 1960. Alexander's attempts to disarm the Force Publique are outlined in greater detail in Catherine Hoskyns, *The Congo since Independence: January 1960-December 1961* (London: Oxford University Press, 1965), 133-39.

2   LAC, RG25, vol. 5209, file 6386-40 part 9, Letter Bull to USSEA, 5 August 1960. The many logistical difficulties ONUC encountered at deployment are addressed by Lincoln P. Bloomfield, "Headquarters-Field Relations: Some Notes on the Beginning and End of ONUC," *International Organization* 17 (1963): 376-89, and Edward H. Bowman and James E. Fanning, "The Logistics of a UN Military Force," *International Organization* 17 (1963): 355-76.

3   LAC, RG25, vol. 5209, file 6386-40 part 9, Letter Bull to Hughes, 1 August 1960.

4   DHH, file 410.Congo (D1), Memo: Organisation Canadian Forces – Congo Republic, 2 August 1960.

5   DHH, file 112.1.003 (D9), vol. 2, Telegram Canadian Army [hereafter CANARMY] to Central Command [hereafter CENCOM]: Canadian Soldiers Congo, 4 August 1960.

6   This was a newer version of the AN/GRC-26 sets used and available in Canada. See John S. Moir, ed., *History of the Royal Canadian Corps of Signals, 1903-1961* (Ottawa: Corps Committee, Royal Canadian Corps of Signals, 1962), 315. DHH, file 112.1.003 (D9), vol. 2, Telegram CANARMY to CENCOM: Canadian Soldiers Congo, 4 August 1960. LAC, RG58, vol. 278, file 1750-64-6, Extract from the Minutes of a Meeting of the Treasury Board [T.B. 568585], 5 August 1960.

7   DHH, file 112.1.003 (D9), Transcript of Telephone Conversation, 29 July 1960.

8   DHH, file 112.1.003 (D9), Memo to Col. A. Mendelsohn, 29 July 1960. DHH, file 112.1.003 (D9), Memo: Possible Canadian Contribution to UN Forces in Congo Republic Synopsis No. 9 Events up to 1400 Hrs, 29 July 1960.

9   LAC, RG25, vol. 5219, file 6386-C-40 part 3, Memo Mendelsohn to Army Headquarters [hereafter AHQ], 2 August 1960; Memo Mendelsohn to AHQ, 4 August 1960.

10  The proposed communications net covered Leopoldville (HQ ONUC), Libenge (HQ Liberian Task Force), Goma (HQ Irish Sector), Stanleyville (HQ Ethiopian Brigade), Luluabourg (HQ Tunisian Brigade), Matadi (HQ Moroccan Brigade), Coquilhatville (HQ Independent Moroccan Coy), Inongo (HQ Guinea Brigade) and eventually two stations in Katanga.

11  DHH, file 112.1.003 (D9), vol. 2, Memo: Cote to D Sigs: Preliminary Report: UN Comm Requirements, 2 August 1960.

12  LAC, RG24, vol. 18482, War Diaries CDN HQ UNEF in Congo and No. 57 Canadian Signal Squadron, August 1960. "UN Force Receives Side Arms," *Montreal Gazette*, 5 August 1960, 1.

13  March notes that ONUC "involved almost every long-range transport aircraft that the RCAF had available at the time. Only essential transport runs were maintained throughout North America and Europe." William March, "The Royal Canadian Air Force and Peacekeeping," in *Peacekeeping 1815 to Today*, ed. Serge Bernier (Ottawa: International Commission of Military History, 1995), 471. See also David W. Wainhouse, *International Peacekeeping at the Crossroads: National Support – Experience and Prospects* (Baltimore: Johns Hopkins University Press, 1973), 284. J.L. Granatstein, "Canada and Peacekeeping: Image and Reality," *The Canadian Forum* 54, 263 (1974): 16.

14  LAC, RG24, vol. 21484, file 2137.3 part 1, Telegram External to PERMISNY: Text of Proposed Reply to SecGens note 15/7 concerning Sigs and Log Support, 12 August 1960. DHH, file 112.1.003 (D9), vol. 2, Letter CGS to MDND: Employment – 57 Signal Squadron – Congo, 5 August 1960. LAC, RG25, file 6386-C-40 part 2, Memo DL (1) to UN Div: Congo – Formal Reply to the UN Regarding Canadian Contribution to the UN Forces, 11 August 1960.

15  LAC, RG25, vol. 5209, file 6386-40 part 10, Letter Bull to USSEA, 19 August 1960. LAC, RG25, vol. 5209, file 6386-40 part 9, Letter Bull to USSEA: Comments on Political Situation in the Congo Republic, 5 August 1960. Ralph Bunche, "The United Nations Operation in the Congo," in *From Collective Security to Preventive Diplomacy*, ed. Joel Larus (New York: John Wiley and Sons, 1965), 412.

16  Colin Legum, Foreword and Notes to *Congo My Country*, by Patrice Lumumba (London: Pall Mall Press, 1962), xv.

17  United Nations, Department of Public Information, *The Blue Helmets: A Review of United Nations Peace-keeping*, 3rd ed. (New York: United Nations Department of Public Information, 1996), 179-80. Jones suggests these two principles were "basic to Hammarskjold's concept of how the peacekeeping operation should be conducted." Goronwy J. Jones, *The United Nations and the Domestic Jurisdiction of States* (Cardiff: University of Wales Press / Welsh Centre for International Affairs, 1979), 128.

18  Wynfred Joshua, "Belgium's Role in the UN Peacekeeping Operation in the Congo," *Orbis* 11, 2 (1967): 437. David Gibbs, "Dag Hammarskjöld, the United Nations, and the Congo Crisis of 1960-1: A Reinterpretation," *The Journal of Modern African Studies* 31, 1 (1993): 165-66.

19  LAC, RG25, vol. 5219, file 6386-C-40 part 2, Memo for Minister: Congo: Problem of Katanga, 2 August 1960. LAC, RG24, vol. 21484, file 2137.3 part 1, Telegram PERMISNY to External: Congo, 4 August 1960.

20  Brian Urquhart, *Ralph Bunche: An American Odyssey* (New York and London: W.W. Norton, 1993), 324. Bunche, "The United Nations Operation in the Congo," 417.

21  Peter Calvocoressi, *World Order and New States* (London: Chatto and Windus, 1962), 85-86. D.W. Bowett, *United Nations Forces* (London: Stevens and Sons, 1964), 155, 207. Michael Harbottle, *The Blue Berets: The Story of The United Nations Peacekeeping Forces* (London: Leo Cooper, 1971), 53.

22  LAC, RG25, vol. 5219, file 6386-C-40 part 2, Memo for Minister: Congo: Debate in the House on August 1, 8 August 1960; Memo for Minister: Withdrawal of Belgian Troops from the Congo, 6 August 1960; *FRUS, 1958-1960*, vol. 14, doc. 123, Telegram from the Mission at the United Nations to the Department of State.

23  Canada, House of Commons, *Debates*, 8 August 1960: 7747.

24  Resolution 146 (1960), 9 August. *In favour:* Argentina, Ceylon, China, Ecuador, Poland, Tunisia, Union of Soviet Socialist Republics, United Kingdom, United States; *against:* none; *abstentions:* France, Italy.

25  Herbert Nicholas, "UN Peace Forces and the Changing Globe: The Lessons of Suez and Congo," *International Organization* 17 (1963): 331-32.

26  Jane Boulden, *The United Nations and Mandate Enforcement: Congo, Somalia and Bosnia* (Kingston: Centre for International Relations, Queen's University / Institut Québécois des Hautes Études Internationales, Université Laval, 1999), 29-30.

27  Mona Gagnon, "Peace Forces and the Veto: The Relevance of Consent," *International Organization* 21, 4 (Autumn 1967): 821.

28  Wainhouse, *International Peacekeeping at the Crossroads*, 270.

29  Franck and Carey note the prohibition against intervention was maintained by Resolution 146 because the council had not yet explicitly approved enforcement action under Article 41 or 42 of Chapter VII. Thomas M. Franck and John Carey, *The Legal Aspects of the United Nations Action in the Congo*, ed. Lyman M. Tondel Jr. (Dobbs Ferry, NY: Oceana Publications/ Association of the Bar of the City of New York, 1963), 20.

30  Brian Urquhart, *Hammarskjold* (New York: Alfred A. Knopf, 1972), 429-30. David Gibbs suggests that many Belgian financiers believed Hammarskjöld conspired against them, not with them, using ONUC to weaken Union Minière in favour of Swedish economic interests. Gibbs, "Dag Hammarskjöld, the United Nations, and the Congo Crisis of 1960-1," 171-73.

31  Bunche, "The United Nations Operation in the Congo," 417.

32  As quoted in Madeleine G. Kalb, *The Congo Cables* (New York: Macmillan, 1982), 49-50.

33  Alan James, "Peacekeeping and the Parties," in *The United Nations and Peacekeeping: Results, Limitations, and Prospects*, ed. Indar Jit Rikhye (Basingstoke, UK: Macmillan / International Peace Academy, 1990), 133.

34  LAC, RG25, vol. 5219, file 6386-C-40 part 3, Letter Wood to USSEA: Congo – UN Relations, 18 August 1960.

35  Andrew W. Cordier and Wilder Foote, *Public Papers of the Secretaries-General of the United Nations*, vol. 5, *Dag Hammarskjöld, 1960-1961* (New York: Columbia University Press, 1975), 82-90; Hoskyns, *The Congo since Independence*, 173.

36  LAC, RG25, vol. 5219, file 6386-C-40 part 3, Letter FR Miller to USSEA: United Nations Force – Congo: Restriction on Canadian Forces, 15 August 1960. DHH, file 112.1.003 (D9), vol. 2, Telegram CANARMY to ONUC Leopoldville, 19 August 1960.

37  Hoskyns, *The Congo since Independence*, 193-95; United Nations, *The Blue Helmets*, 181.

38  LAC, RG25, vol. 5209, file 6386-40 part 10.2, Telegram WASHDC to External: Congo, 30 August 1960. *FRUS, 1958-1960*, vol. 14, doc. 173, Telegram from the Department of State to the Embassy in the Congo; doc. 178, Telegram from the Embassy in the Congo to the Department of State.

39   David Gibbs, "Secrecy and International Relations," *Journal of Peace Research* 32 (May 1995): 220. David Gibbs, *The Political Economy of Third World Intervention* (Chicago: University of Chicago Press, 1991), 91.

40   LAC, RG25, vol. 5209, file 6386-40 part 10.2, Telegram Brussels to External: Congo – Communist Infiltration, 31 August 1960; Telegram Brussels to External: Congo, 31 August 1960. LAC, RG25, vol. 5209, file 6386-40 part 10, Letter Bull to USSEA: Comments on the Political Situation in the Congo Republic, 19 August 1960.

41   DHH, file 112.1.003 (D9), vol. 2, Letter to Mendelsohn, 2 August 1960.

42   Canadian Communications and Electronics Museum [hereafter CCEM], box 137, Article: The Royal Canadian Signals in the Congo by Col. H.W.C. Stethem and Capt. R. Fournier, undated.

43   CCEM, box 137, Article: The Royal Canadian Signals in the Congo by Col. H.W.C. Stethem and Capt. R. Fournier, undated. Fred Gaffen, *In the Eye of the Storm: A History of Canadian Peacekeeping* (Toronto: Deneau and Wayne, 1987), 235.

44   CCEM, box 137, Article: The Royal Canadian Signals in the Congo by Col. H.W.C. Stethem and Capt. R. Fournier, undated. Gaffen, *In the Eye of the Storm*, 221.

45   J.P.R.E. Beauregard, "UN Operations in the Congo, 1960-1964," *Canadian Defence Quarterly* (August 1989): 27. Wainhouse, *International Peacekeeping at the Crossroads*, 308. LAC, RG24, vol. 21484, file 2137.3 part 1, Memo: Canadian Contribution to UN Forces in the Congo Republic, Synopsis No. 13, 12 August 1960.

46   CCEM, box 137, Article: The Royal Canadian Signals in the Congo by Col. H.W.C. Stethem and Capt. R. Fournier, undated.

47   Indar Jit Rikhye, "Preparation and Training of UN Peacekeeping Forces," in *Peace-Keeping: Experience and Evaluation (The Oslo Papers)*, ed. Per Frydenberg (Oslo: Norwegian Institute of International Affairs, 1964), 190.

48   LAC, RG24, vol. 18482, War Diary, CDN HQ UNEF in Congo, August 1960.

49   LAC, RG25, vol. 5219, file 6386-C-40 part 3, Wood to USSEA, 20 August 1960. LAC, RG 24, vol. 18482, War Diary – No. 57 Canadian Signal Squadron, August 1960. Gaffen, *In the Eye of the Storm*, 224-25. "UN Troops at Airport Get Orders to Shoot," *Globe and Mail*, 19 August 1960, 1.

50   LAC, RG25, vol. 5219, file 6386-C-40 part 3, Letter Hammarskjöld to Congolese Ambassador to the U.N., 18 August 1960. LAC, RG25, vol. 5209, file 6386-40 part 10, Telegram PERMISNY to External, 19 August 1960. DCC, file MG1/VI/(845 Congo), Copy of Letter: Secretary-General to Government of Republic of Congo, 18 August 1960.

51   DCC, file MG1/XII/C/114, Memo for Prime Minister by USSEA, 18 August 1960. "Diefenbaker Alters View on Gravity of Incidents," *Globe and Mail*, 19 August 1960, 1. LAC, RG25, vol. 5209, file 6386-40 part 10, Memo Robertson to Diefenbaker, 18 August 1960. DCC, file MG/VII/A/543, vol. 65, Press Release No. 63 Department of External Affairs, 18 August 1960. "Dag Meets Green on Incident," *Halifax Chronicle-Herald*, 19 August 1960, 1, 6.

52   "Canadian Troops Attacked," *Halifax Chronicle-Herald*, 19 August 1960, 1. "Sauvage attaque des Congolais contre des soldats canadiens," *Le Devoir*, 19 August 1960, 1. "A Time for Coolness," *Globe and Mail*, 19 August 1960, 6. "Matter for the UN," *Halifax Chronicle-Herald*, 23 August 1960, 4. "Let's Not 'Bring the Boys Home,'" *Toronto Daily Star*, 19 August 1960, 3.

53   LAC, RG25, vol. 5219, file 6386-C-40 part 3, Letter Robertson to Clark, 24 August 1960; Memo Robertson to Diefenbaker, 22 August 1960. Maj. Gen. Carl von Horn, *Soldiering for Peace* (London: Cassell, 1966), 188-89. LAC, RG25, vol. 5209, file 6386-40 part 10, Telegram PERMISNY to External: Congo, 19 August 1960.

54   LAC, RG25, vol. 5219, file 6386-C-40 part 3, Telegram PERMISNY to External, 21 August 1960. "UN Denies Charges against Its Troops," *Globe and Mail*, 20 August 1960, 1.

55   LAC, RG25, vol. 5209, file 6386-40 part 10, PERMISNY to External, 21 August 1960. Madeleine Kalb suggests that Mobutu often took it upon himself to "patch things up with the United Nations after Lumumba had made a particularly outrageous statement" and cites this apology for the N'Djili incident as a notable example. Kalb, *The Congo Cables*, 93. "Lumumba Apologizes to Canada," *Globe and Mail*, 22 August 1960, 1.

56   LAC, RG25, vol. 5219, file 6386-C-40 part 3, Letter Wood to USSEA: Congo Attitude to Non-African UN Troops, 18 August 1960. Kalb, *The Congo Cables*, 51.

57 DHH, file 144.9.009 (D30), Memo Mendelsohn to AHQ, 29 August 1960. LAC, RG25, vol. 5209, file 6386-40 part 10.2, Letter PERMISNY to USSEA, 29 August 1960. RG24, vol. 18482, War Diary – No. 57 Canadian Signal Squadron, August 1960. "PM Protests Latest Attack," *Globe and Mail*, 29 August 1960, 1. Gaffen, *In the Eye of the Storm*, 225-26. "Corporal Hero, Says Injured Canadian," *Halifax Chronicle-Herald*, 31 August 1960, 1. DHH, file 144.9.009 (D30), Memo: Incident Involving Canadian Personnel, 29 August 1960.

58 LAC, RG25, vol. 5209, file 6386-40 part 10.2, Outgoing Message External to PERMISNY, 27 August 1960; Outgoing Message External to PERMISNY: New Incident Involving Canadian Service Personnel, 27 August 1960. Gaffen, *In the Eye of the Storm*, 226. "No Direct Reply from Lumumba," *Halifax Chronicle-Herald*, 1 September 1960, 2.

59 LAC, RG25, vol. 5209, file 6386-40 part 10, Telegram PERMISNY to External, 19 August 1960. LAC, RG25, vol. 5209, file 6386-40 part 10.2, Telegram Dublin to External: Congo, 25 August 1960.

60 LAC, RG25, vol. 5209, file 6386-40 part 11, PERMISNY to External, 2 September 1960. LAC, RG25, vol. 5219, file 6386-C-40 part 3, Letter Wood to USSEA, 20 August 1960. LAC, RG24, vol. 21485, file 2137.3 part 2, Report on Conversation at UNHQ between Rikhye and Speedie, 23 August 1960.

61 LAC, RG25, vol. 5209, file 6386-40 part 10, Telegram PERMISNY to External, 19 August 1960. LAC, RG25, vol. 5219, file 6386-C-40 part 4, Memo by Cadieux, 27 August 1960; Letter Wood to USSEA: Incidents in Stanleyville, 2 September 1960.

62 LAC, RG25, vol. 5219, file 6386-C-40 part 2, Telegram PERMISNY to External, 8 August 1960; Memo Robertson to Green, 8 August 1960. LAC, RG24, vol. 21484, file 2137.3 part 1, Telegram PERMISNY to External: Congo, 8 August 1960. UNA, S-0209-0003-11, ONUC – records on foreign countries, Canada – correspondence, cables, etc., untitled and unsigned memo dated 8 August 1960.

63 LAC, RG25, vol. 5209, file 6386-40 part 10, Telegram PERMISNY to External, 15 August 1960; Dispatch Moscow to SSEA: Congo, 16 August 1960; Telegram BGRAD to External, 16 August 1960.

64 LAC, RG25, vol. 5209, file 6386-40 part 10.2, Despatch Moscow to External, 23 August 1960; LAC, RG25, vol. 5219, file 6386-C-40 part 3, Memo Robertson to Diefenbaker, 22 August 1960.

65 LAC, RG25, vol. 5219, file 6386-C-40 part 3, Memo Robertson to Diefenbaker, 22 August 1960; Telegram PERMISNY to External: Congo: Security Council References to Canadian Troops, 21 August 1960. Brian Urquhart, *Hammarskjold*, 453.

66 LAC, RG25, vol. 5219, file 6386-C-40 part 3, Robertson to Diefenbaker, 25 August 1960.

67 LAC, RG25, vol. 5209, file 6386-40 part 11.2, Telegram PERMISNY to External, 15 September 1960. LAC, RG2, vol. 2747, Cabinet Conclusions, 17 August 1960.

68 LAC, RG24, vol. 21484, file 2137.3 part 1, Memo: Congo Operations – RCAF Participation [Chief of Air Staff to MDND], 9 August 1960; Memo: Canadian Contribution to UN Forces in the Congo Republic, Synopsis No. 13, 12 August 1960. LAC, RG25, vol. 5219, file 6386-C-40 part 2, Memo Robertson to Green, 9 August 1960; Memo Pearkes to Green, 11 August 1960.

69 LAC, RG24, vol. 21484, file 2137.3 part 1, Telegram PERMISNY to External: Congo – UN Use of Caribou Aircraft, 18 August 1960. "Mixup Stalls RCAF Craft for Congo," *Montreal Gazette*, 9 September 1960, 1. The Canadian government was guilty of placing the diplomatic cart before the horse. Precedent established that no nation had the right to insist on the inclusion of its forces in a peacekeeping mission. Although the Canadian government did not quite go this far, it was certainly premature to announce the acquisition of the Caribou for service in ONUC prior to consultations with the UN Secretariat on the appropriateness and suitability of such a contribution. On the development of this precedent, see Wainhouse, *International Peacekeeping at the Crossroads*, 558.

70 LAC, RG25, vol. 5219, file 6386-C-40 part 4, Memo DL to Cadieux, 30 August 1960; Memo Murray to Robertson, 14 September 1960. LAC, RG24, vol. 21485, file 2137.3 part 2, Telegram PERMISNY to External: Congo Caribou Aircraft, 2 September 1960. DHH, file 112.1.009 (D21), vol. 4, *Aide Mémoire*: Notes on Congo, Meeting with Col. Mendelsohn, 12 September 1960. UNA, S-0209-0003-16, ONUC – records on foreign countries, Canada, vol. 1 – ONUC

military assistance, Note for file by Labouisse, 29 August 1960. UNA, S-0791-0045-10, UN Operation in the Congo, Force Commander, 3310/2/Ops – Canadian Troops – Personnel, Telegram Cordier to SG and von Horn, 14 August 1960.

71   LAC, RG24, vol. 21484, file 2137.3 part 1, Memo: Possible Canadian Contribution to UN Forces in the Congo Republic Synopsis No. 10, 2 August 1960; Memo: Canadian Contribution to UN Forces in the Congo Republic Synopsis No. 11, 3 August 1960. DHH, file 75/380, Press Release: Canada to Operate Congo Air Operations, 2 August 1960. LAC, RG24, vol. 3022, file 895-8/115, Organisation Order 8.13, 2 August 1960.

72   In August 1960, Canadians occupied all of the positions at the United Nations Air Transport Force. By November, von Horn anticipated Canadians would still hold four of thirteen positions. Coughlin underlines the RCAF's experience as the UN's only airlift in the Middle East as the reason why Canadians were asked to play such a key role in the Air Transport Force. T.G. Coughlin, "The UN and the RCAF," *Roundel* 16, 10 (December 1964): 6. LAC, RG24, vol. 3022, file 895-8/115, Letter and Attached Charts Von Horn to UN HQ (New York), 23 August 1960. Gaffen, *In the Eye of the Storm*, 222-23.

73   DCC, file MG1/VI/R/52(107/G411Conf), Telegram Accra to External: Ghana and Congo, 2 August 1960; Outgoing Message External to Accra: Message for Nkrumah, 29 August 1960. DCC, file MG1/XII/C/114, Memo for Prime Minister: Crisis in Congo and the Role of Ghana, 1 August 1960. LAC, RG25, vol. 5219, file 6386-C-40 part 2, Memo Robertson to Green, 4 August 1960; Letter Pearkes to Diefenbaker, 9 August 1960. LAC, RG2, vol. 2747, Cabinet Conclusions, 12 August 1960.

74   LAC, RG25, vol. 5219, file 6386-C-40 part 3, Memo Robertson to Diefenbaker, 24 August 1960. LAC, RG25, vol. 5209, file 6386-40 part 10, Outgoing Message External to PERMISNY: Congo – Training of *Force Publique*, 12 August 1960. LAC, RG25, vol. 5209, file 6386-40 part 9, Letter USSEA to Chairman, Chiefs of Staff [hereafter CCOS]: United Nations Operations in the Congo – Canadian Participation, 3 August 1960. DHH, file 112.1.003 (D9), vol. 2, Letter CGS to MDND: Provision of Additional Officers: United Nations Operations in the Congo, 6 August 1960. LAC, RG25, vol. 2747, Cabinet Conclusions, 17 August 1960. UNA, S-0209-0003-12, ONUC – records on foreign countries, Canada – correspondence, cables, etc., Memo for file dated 23 August 1960.

75   E.M. Miller, "Legal Aspects of the U.N. Action in the Congo," *American Journal of International Law* 55, 1 (1961): 18.

76   Brady Lee, "Peacekeeping, the Congo, and Zones of Peace," *Peace Review* 9, 2 (June 1997): 189. Jones, *The United Nations and the Domestic Jurisdiction of States*, 131.

77   Alan James, *The Politics of Peacekeeping* (London: Chatto and Windus, 1969), 359.

78   Carole Collins, "The Cold War Comes to Africa: Cordier and the 1960 Congo Crisis," *Journal of International Affairs* 47, 1 (1993): 246. Collins is equally damning of Hammarskjöld, suggesting that both he and Cordier "were willing to undermine any leader, like Lumumba, whom they thought served Soviet aims in the Congo" (255). This interpretation is echoed in the work of David Gibbs, who suggests ONUC "intervened extensively in the politics of the country, thereby not conforming to the popular image of a passive 'peace-keeping' force." Gibbs, "Dag Hammarskjöld, the United Nations, and the Congo Crisis of 1960-1," 163.

79   Marion McVitty, "An Approach to Development of United Nations Peacekeeping Machinery Based on the Significance of UNEF and ONUC Experience," in *Legal and Political Problems of World Order*, ed. S.H. Mendlovitz (New York: Fund for Education Concerning World Peace through World Law, 1962), 337. Other authors, in their interpretations of this incident, are also forgiving of Cordier's actions. See Jones, *The United Nations and the Domestic Jurisdiction of States*, 132, and Nicholas, "UN Peace Forces and the Changing Globe," 332.

80   As quoted in James, "Peacekeeping and the Parties," 142-43.

81   LAC, RG25, vol. 5219, file 6386-C-40 part 2, Memo for Minister: Congo: Advisory Committee for Secretary-General, 4 August 1960. LAC, RG25, vol. 5219, file 6386-C-40 part 3, Memo for Prime Minister: Congo: Soviet Complaints about Canadian Contingent, 22 August 1960; Memo for Prime Minister: Advisory Committee for Congo Force, 24 August 1960. S.J. Michalak, "Peacekeeping and the UN: The Problem of Responsibility," *International*

*Studies Quarterly* 11, 4 (December 1967): 301-2, 308. LAC, RG24, vol. 21485, file 2137.3 part 2, Telegram External to PERMISNY: Congo Advisory Committee, 24 August 1960.

82 LAC, RG24, vol. 21485, file 2137.3 part 2, Telegram External to PERMISNY: UN Force in Congo, 26 August 1960. Alan James, *Britain and the Congo Crisis, 1960-1963* (London: Macmillan, 1996), 187n.

83 DCC, file MG1/VI/(845 Congo), Letter Delta Committee of the Communist Party of Canada to Diefenbaker, 6 August 1960; Letter Gallagher (Canadian Council of Churches) to Diefenbaker, 7 August 1960. LAC, RG25, vol. 5209, file 6386-40 part 10, Letter V.M. McFaul to Diefenbaker, 11 August 1960 [emphasis in original]; Letter E.L. Knott to Diefenbaker, 16 August 1960; Letter C.B. McNair to Green: Katanga, 18 August 1960.

84 DCC, file MG1/VI/(845 Congo), Telegram Blair to Diefenbaker, 29 August 1960; Letter Jones to Diefenbaker, 29 August 1960; Telegram Madden to Diefenbaker, 30 August 1960; Letter Barker to Diefenbaker, 5 September 1960. LAC, RG25, vol. 5209, file 6386-40 part 11, Letter Critchell to Green, 29 August 1960 [emphasis in original].

85 DCC, file MG1/VI/(845 Congo), Letter Riaskowsky to Diefenbaker, 30 August 1960. DCC, file MG1/XII/C/114, Memo to Prime Minister from Professor Maxwell Cohen, 30 August 1960. LAC, RG25, file 6386-40 part 11, Letter Green to Critchell, 12 September 1960.

## Chapter 4: Constitutional Crisis

1 Thomas Franck, "United Nations Law in Africa: The Congo Operation as a Case Study," *Law and Contemporary Problems* 27 (Autumn 1962): 650-52.

2 LAC, RG25, vol. 5220, file 6386-C-40 part 5, Despatch Leopoldville to SSEA: Political Situation, 31 October 1960.

3 Madeleine Kalb, *The Congo Cables* (New York: Macmillan, 1982), 375. Ernest Lefever, "US Policy, the UN and the Congo," *Orbis* 11, 2 (Summer 1967): 398-99. Michael Schatzberg, *Mobutu or Chaos?* (New York: University Press of America, 1991), 21. See also Lawrence Devlin, *Chief of Station, Congo: A Memoir of 1960-7* (New York: PublicAffairs, 2007).

4 LAC, RG25, vol. 5209, file 6386-40 part 11, Telegram PERMISNY to External: Advisory Committee on Congo, 2 September 1960; Memo Legal Div to Sicotte: Legality of the Operations of the UN Forces in the Congo, 13 September 1960.

5 LAC, RG25, vol. 5219, file 6386-C-40 part 4, Memo for USSEA: Congo: United Nations Military Operation, 14 September 1960.

6 LAC, RG25, vol. 5220, file 6386-C-40 part 5, Letter Murray to Ritchie, 16 September 1960.

7 LAC, RG2, vol. 2747, Cabinet Conclusions, 14 September 1960. Ultimately, the UN Secretariat agreed to make use of at least two of the Caribou in UNEF, as replacements for two Dakotas serving there. LAC, RG25, vol. 5220, file 6386-C-40 part 5, Letter Barton to Campbell, 23 September 1960.

8 Draft Tunisian-Ceylonese sponsored resolution. *In favour:* Argentina, Ceylon, China, Ecuador, Italy, Tunisia, United Kingdom, United States; *against:* Poland, Union of Soviet Socialist Republics; *abstentions:* France.

9 LAC, RG25, vol. 5220, file 6386-C-40 part 5, Telegram 1457 PERMISNY to External: Congo – Security Council, 15 September, 1960; Telegram 1459 PERMISNY to External: Congo – Security Council, 15 September 1960; Telegram PERMISNY to External: Congo: Security Council, 16 September 1960.

10 General Assembly Resolution 1474 (ES-IV), 20 September 1960. *In favour:* Afghanistan, Argentina, Australia, Austria, Belgium, Brazil, Burma, Cambodia, Canada, Ceylon, Chile, China, Colombia, Costa Rica, Cuba, Denmark, Dominican Republic, Ecuador, El Salvador, Ethiopia, Federation of Malaya, Finland, Ghana, Greece, Guatemala, Guinea, Haiti, Honduras, Iceland, India, Indonesia, Iran, Iraq, Ireland, Israel, Italy, Japan, Jordan, Laos, Lebanon, Liberia, Libya, Luxembourg, Mexico, Morocco, Nepal, Netherlands, New Zealand, Nicaragua, Norway, Pakistan, Panama, Paraguay, Peru, Philippines, Portugal, Saudi Arabia, Spain, Sudan, Sweden, Thailand, Tunisia, Turkey, United Arab Republic, United Kingdom, United States, Uruguay, Venezuela, Yemen, Yugoslavia; *against:* none; *abstentions:* Albania, Bulgaria, Byelorussian SSR, Czechoslovakia, France, Hungary, Poland, Romania, Ukrainian SSR, Union of South Africa, Union of Soviet Socialist Republics.

11  Jane Boulden, *The United Nations and Mandate Enforcement: Congo, Somalia, and Bosnia* (Kingston: Centre for International Relations, Queen's University / Institut Québécois des Hautes Études Internationales, Université Laval, 1999), 30. D.W. Bowett, *United Nations Forces* (London: Stevens and Sons, 1964), 161. Leon Gordenker, *The UN Secretary-General and the Maintenance of Peace* (New York: Columbia University Press, 1967), 274.

12  LAC, RG25, vol. 5220, file 6386-C-40 part 5, Outgoing Message External to PERMISNY: Congo Emergency Session, 17 September 1960; Statement by Canadian Delegation to Emergency Session of General Assembly on the Congo, 17 September 1960; Telegram PERMISNY to External: Congo: Emergency Special Session of the UN General Assembly, 17 September 1960.

13  LAC, RG2, vol. 5937, Cabinet Document 296.60, Memo to Cabinet: Instruction for Canadian Delegation to 15th Session of General Assembly of UN, 16 September 1960.

14  Raymond Rodgers, "The PM at the UN: An Assessment," *Saturday Night*, 29 October 1960, 23.

15  LAC, RG25, vol. 5210, file 6386-40 part 12, Summary Record of PM Conversation with President Eisenhower (September 27, 1960), 1 October 1960. *FRUS, 1958-1960*, vol. 2, doc. 194, Memorandum of a Conversation, Waldorf Towers, New York, September 27, 1960, 2:45 p.m. Eisenhower's memoirs suggest that Diefenbaker's remarks about Menon's views applied to the president's speech – in fact, they applied to Diefenbaker's own speech. Denis Smith and Basil Robinson both discuss Diefenbaker's speech to the General Assembly and largely confirm Menon's interpretation of it. Robinson recounts the tortuous experience of preparing countless drafts of the speech, attempting to meet Diefenbaker's desire to take a hard line against the Soviets. Smith observes, "Against the advice of his officials, who preferred a constructive and moderate speech in the Pearson tradition, Diefenbaker wanted fireworks." Denis Smith, *Rogue Tory: The Life and Legend of John G. Diefenbaker* (Toronto: Macfarlane Walter and Ross, 1995), 373. H. Basil Robinson, *Diefenbaker's World: A Populist in Foreign Affairs* (Toronto: University of Toronto Press, 1989), 151-56. Dwight D. Eisenhower, *Waging Peace, 1956-1961* (New York: Doubleday, 1965), 585.

16  LAC, RG25, vol. 5210, file 6386-40 part 12, Report on Guinea Reception 1 October 1960 by J.A. Berthiaume (Lt. Col.), 2 October 1960; Telegram Leopoldville to External, 10 October 1960. LAC, RG25, vol. 5225, file 6386-D-40 part 1, Telegram Leopoldville to External: Congo – Lumumba Statement at Guinea Reception, 3 October 1960; Telegram Leopoldville to External: Lumumba Speeches, 5 October 1960.

17  LAC, RG24, vol. 18482, War Diary – No. 57 Canadian Signal Squadron, September, Letter Pariseau to Bindoff, 19 September 1960.

18  DHH, file 112.1.009 (D21), vol. 4, Letter Vice-Chief of the General Staff [hereafter VCGS] to CGS: Organization – Canadian Forces in the Congo, 14 September 1960. LAC, RG25, vol. 5220, file 6386-C-40 part 5, Outgoing Message External to PERMISNY: Congo – Canadian Army Commander, 17 October 1960.

19  LAC, RG25, vol. 5220, file 6386-C-40 part 5, Telegram Canadian Delegation in New York [hereafter CANDELNY] to External: UN Forces in Congo, 18 October 1960; Letter CCOS to USSEA: Communications Between Military Contingents in the Congo and National Governments, 31 October 1960; Letter USSEA to CCOS: UN Forces in the Congo, Communications between National Contingents and their Governments, 28 October 1960. DHH, file 112.1.003 (D9), vol. 2, Command Instructions for the Commander, Canadian Army Forces, UNOC, 17 October 1960. LAC, RG25, vol. 5220, file 6386-C-40 part 6, Outgoing Message External to PERMISNY: United Nations Forces in the Congo, 3 November 1960. DHH, file 112.1.009 (D21), vol. 4, Letter CGS to Smith, CO 57th, 31 October 1960. Documentary evidence at the UN suggests the Ethiopian contingent was the country at the centre of this controversy. UNA, S-0787-0015-03, UNOC – Force Commander, Personnel FC/3061 – Signals and Communications.

20  LAC, RG24, vol. 18482, War Diary – No. 57 Canadian Signal Squadron, October, Unit Orders, 12 October 1960. On the issue of contingents communicating with their home governments see also Indar Jit Rikhye, Michael Harbottle, and Bjørn Egge, *The Thin Blue Line: International Peacekeeping and Its Future* (New Haven, CT, and London: Yale University Press, 1974), 85,

and D. Colwyn Williams, "Origins and Practices of Peacekeeping," *The Future of UN Peace-keeping: A Policy Paper of the United Nations Association in Canada* (Toronto: United Nations Association in Canada, 1965), 18.

21 LAC, RG25, vol. 5220, file 6386-C-40 part 5, Telegram Leopoldville to External: Training of Congo Army, 6 October 1960; Numbered Letter Leopoldville to USSEA: Training of Congolese Officers, 13 October 1960; Despatch Leopoldville to SSEA: Return of the Belgians, 28 October 1960.

22 LAC, RG25, vol. 5210, file 6386-40 part 12, Telegram Leopoldville to External: Congo, 13 October 1960. LAC, RG24, vol. 18842, War Diary – No. 57 Canadian Signal Squadron, October, Unit Orders, 4 October 1960. LAC, RG25, vol. 5220, file 6386-C-40 part 5, Telegram Leopoldville to External: Congo Political Situation, 25 October 1960. LAC, RG25, vol. 5210, file 6386-40 part 13, Telegram Leopoldville to External: UN Day Parade, 25 October 1960.

23 LAC, RG25, vol. 5225, file 6386-H-40 part 1, Telegram PERMISNY to External: Congo and General Assembly Appeal for Funds, 21 September 1960; Memo for the Prime Minister: Congo – General Assembly Appeal for Funds, 22 September 1960; Letter Donald Fleming to SSEA, 11 October 1960. LAC, RG25, vol. 5210, file 6386-40 part 12, Memo for the Minister: International Financial Aid to the Republic of the Congo, 3 October 1960. LAC, RG2, vol. 2747, Cabinet Conclusions, 20 October 1960.

24 LAC, RG25, vol. 5220, file 6386-C-40 part 5, Outgoing Message External to CANDELNY: Advisory Committee on Congo, 12 October 1960.

25 LAC, RG25, vol. 5220, file 6386-C-40 part 6, Telegram CANDELNY to External: Advisory Committee on Congo – Conciliation Commission, 15 November 1960; Outgoing Message External to CANDELNY: Advisory Committee on Congo – Conciliation Commission, 16 November 1960.

26 LAC, RG25, vol. 5220, file 6386-C-40 part 5, Memo for the Minister: Congo – Use of RCAF North Star Aircraft, 24 October 1960; Letter Green to Harkness, 24 October 1960; Letter Harkness to Green, 27 October 1960. LAC, RG25, vol. 5220, file 6386-C-40 part 6, Letter Vaughan (UN) to Speedie, 10 November 1960; Telegram PERMISNY to External: Congo: Use of RCAF North Star Aircraft, 7 November 1960; Memo for Minister: Congo – Use of RCAF North Star Aircraft, 16 November 1960. LAC, RG25, vol. 5221, file 6386-C-40 part 7, Letter Green to Harkness, 21 November 1960.

27 The UN Secretariat was not convinced by the Baluba explanation. The Irish report of the incident asserted that the UN peacekeepers were not mistaken for Katangan gendarmerie. LAC, RG25, vol. 5220, file 6386-C-40 part 6, Telegram Leopoldville to External: Ambush of Irish Patrol, 12 November 1960. LAC, RG25, vol. 5221, file 6386-C-40 part 7, Memo UN Div to USSEA: Congo, 29 November 1960. LAC, RG2, vol. 2747, Cabinet Conclusions, 10 November 1960.

28 LAC, RG25, vol. 5221, file 6386-C-40 part 7, Notes by DL (1): Notes on the Position of Canadian Troops in the Congo, 24 November 1960; Memo for Minister: Position of Canadian Troops in the Congo, 24 November 1960; Telegram Leopoldville to External: Fighting between Armée Nationale Congolaise [hereafter ANC] and UN Troops in Leopoldville, 22 November 1960. LAC, RG25, vol. 5221, file 6386-C-40 part 8, Letter Col. Smith to CGS, 24 November 1960. DHH, file 90/336, box 1, Dumont-Bayliss interview with J. Berthiaume. DCC, file MG1/VI/(845 Congo), Letter from Unknown Authors in 3 Communities to Diefenbaker, 23 November 1960 [emphasis in original].

29 LAC, RG25, vol. 5221, file 6386-C-40 part 7, Notes on United Nations Military Operations in the Congo, 28 November 1960; Memo DL (1) to File: Congo – Strength and Deployment of Canadian Contingent, 13 December 1960; Letter USSEA to Harkness, 1 December 1960; Letter Harkness to Green, 28 November 1960. LAC, RG25, vol. 5220, file 6386-C-40 part 6, Telegram PERMISNY to External: Congo: UN Request for Assistance, 17 November 1960. UNA, S-0209-0003-12, ONUC – records on foreign countries, Canada – correspondence, cables, etc., Note for file by G.C. Bowitz, 15 November 1960.

30 LAC, RG25, vol. 5221, file 6386-C-40 part 8, Letter P.D. Smith to General Clark, 19 December 1960. Walter Dorn and David Bell, "Intelligence and Peacekeeping: The UN Operation in

the Congo 1960-1964," in *Peacekeeping 1815 to Today*. ed. Serge Bernier (Ottawa: International Commission of Military History, 1995), 581, 587.

31 LAC, RG25, vol. 5210, file 6386-40 part 14, Summary of a Letter Written to CGS by CO 57 Independent Signal Squadron, 8 December 1960. LAC, RG25, vol. 5221, file 6386-C-40 part 8, Memo DL (1) Div to Glazebrook: Congo – Reported Withdrawal of Senior Canadian Officer, 20 December 1960. On Rikhye's early efforts to have Berthiaume removed from ONUC HQ, see Indar Jit Rikhye, *Military Adviser to the Secretary-General: U.N. Peacekeeping and the Congo Crisis* (London: Hurst, 1993), 63.

32 LAC, RG24, vol. 21485, file 2137.3 part 4, Letter CGS to CCOS: Lt. Col. Berthiaume – Transfer from ONUC to UNTSO, 11 January 1961; Letter USSEA to CCOS: Lt. Col. Berthiaume – Transfer from ONUC to UNTSO, 30 January 1961. DHH, file 90/336, box 3, part 46, Telegram MacEoin to Bunche, undated. LAC, RG25, vol. 5221, file 6386-C-40 part 9, Outgoing Message External to PERMISNY: Col. Berthiaume – Transfer from ONUC to UNTSO, 19 January 1961.

33 LAC, RG25, vol. 5221, file 6386-C-40 part 8, Memo DL (1) Div to Glazebrook: Congo – Reported Withdrawal of Senior Canadian Officer, 20 December 1960. LAC, RG25, vol. 5221, file 6386-C-40 part 9, Outgoing Message External to PERMISNY: Col. Berthiaume – Transfer from ONUC to UNTSO, 19 January 1961. DHH, file 90/336, box 1, part 3, Memo J.A. Berthiaume to DMI: HQ ONUC: Status of Canadian Officers, 1 August 1961.

34 DHH, file 90/336, box 1, part 3, Memo J.A. Berthiaume to DMI: HQ ONUC: Status of Canadian Officers, 1 August 1961. "Congo Duty Finished for Canadian Officer," *Montreal Gazette*, 14 February 1961, 2. LAC, RG25, vol. 5221, file 6386-C-40 part 8, Memo DL (1) Div to Glazebrook: Congo – Reported Withdrawal of Senior Canadian Officer, 20 December 1960. LAC, RG25, vol. 5222, file 6386-C-40 part 12, Memo DL (1) Div to Glazebrook: Activities of Col. Berthiaume in the Congo, 3 March 1961. DHH, file 90/336, box 1, Dumont-Bayliss interview with J. Berthiaume, 12 September 1990.

35 LAC, RG25, vol. 5220, file 6386-C-40 part 6, Memo J.D. Foote to D. Stansfield: Notes on the Congo, 4 November 1960; Telegram Leopoldville to External: Departure of President Kasavubu for New York, 7 November 1960. LAC, RG25, vol. 5221, file 6386-C-40 part 8, Despatch Leopoldville to SSEA: The Political Situation in the Congo, 22 November 1960.

36 LAC, RG25, vol. 5220, file 6386-C-40 part 6, Numbered Letter Leopoldville to USSEA: Conversation with Col. Mobutu, 10 November 1960; Memo J.D. Foote to D. Stansfield: Notes on the Congo, 4 November 1960. LAC, RG25, vol. 5221, file 6386-C-40 part 7, Telegram Leopoldville to External: Conversation with General Rikhye, 21 November 1960.

37 LAC, RG25, vol. 5221, file 6386-C-40 part 8, Despatch Leopoldville to SSEA: The Political Situation in the Congo, 22 November 1960. LAC, RG25, vol. 5221, file 6386-C-40 part 7, Telegram Leopoldville to External: Conversation with General Rikhye, 21 November 1960.

38 LAC, RG25, vol. 5210, file 6386-40 part 12, Summary Record of Prime Minister's Conversation with President Eisenhower September 27, 1960, 1 October 1960. LAC, RG25, vol. 5220, file 6386-C-40 part 6, Memo UN Div to USSEA: Congo: Credentials of Kasavubu's Delegation, 8 November 1960.

39 LAC, RG25, vol. 5220, file 6386-C-40 part 6, Memo UN Div to USSEA: Recent Developments at the General Assembly, 15 November 1960; Memo UN Div to USSEA: Congo: Credentials of Kasavubu's Delegation, 16 November 1960; Memo for UN Div: Congo: Credentials of Kasavubu's Delegation, 17 November 1960; US *Aide Mémoire* delivered to Minister: Congo, 17 November 1960; Letter and Attached Message UK High Commissioner to SSEA, 17 November 1960; Telegram CANDELNY to External: 15th UN General Assembly: Congolese Credentials, 17 November 1960. LAC, RG25, vol. 5210, file 6386-40 part 13, Telegram WASHDC to External: Congo, 17 November 1960. *FRUS, 1958-1960*, vol. 14, doc. 264, Telegram from the Mission at the United Nations to the Department of State. Stephen R. Weissman, *American Foreign Policy in the Congo, 1960-1964* (Ithaca, NY: Cornell University Press, 1974), 106-7.

40 General Assembly Resolution 1498 (XV), 22 November 1960. *In favour:* Argentina, Australia, Austria, Belgium, Bolivia, Brazil, Cameroon, Chad, Chile, China, Columbia, Congo (Brazzaville), Costa Rica, Cyprus, Dahomey, Denmark, Dominican Republic, Ecuador, El Salvador, France, Gabon, Greece, Guatemala, Haiti, Honduras, Iceland, Italy, Ivory Coast, Japan, Jordan, Laos, Luxembourg, Madagascar, Mexico, Nepal, Netherlands, New Zealand,

Nicaragua, Niger, Norway, Panama, Paraguay, Peru, Philippines, Portugal, Senegal, Spain, Thailand, Turkey, Union of South Africa, United Kingdom, United States, Uruguay; *against:* Afghanistan, Albania, Bulgaria, Byelorussian SSR, Ceylon, Cuba, Czechoslovakia, Ghana, Guinea, Hungary, India, Indonesia, Iraq, Mali, Morocco, Poland, Romania, Saudi Arabia, Togo, Ukrainian SSR, Union of Soviet Socialist Republics, United Arab Republic, Yemen, Yugoslavia; *abstentions:* Burma, Cambodia, Canada, Central African Republic, Ethiopia, Federation of Malaya, Finland, Iran, Ireland, Israel, Lebanon, Liberia, Libya, Pakistan, Somalia, Sudan, Sweden, Tunisia, Venezuela.

41  LAC, RG25, vol. 5220, file 6386-C-40 part 6, Memo for Minister: Congo: Kasavubu Credentials, 17 November 1960; Memo SSEA to USSEA: Congo Credentials, 18 November 1960. LAC, RG25, vol. 5221, file 6386-C-40 part 7, Telegram Leopoldville to External, 29 November 1960.

42  LAC, RG25, vol. 5225, file 6386-H-40 part 1, Memo for Minister: Costs of UN Activities in the Congo – July to December 1960. LAC, RG25, vol. 5225, file 6386-H-40 part 1, Outgoing Message External to PERMISNY: Financing of ONUC, 31 August 1960 [emphasis in original]. Peter V. Bishop, "Canada's Policy on the Financing of U.N. Peace-keeping Operations," *International Journal* 20, 4 (Autumn 1965): 464-68.

43  LAC, RG25, vol. 5210, file 6386-40 part 14, Outgoing Message External to CANDELNY: Fifth Committee Congo Financing, 29 November 1960.

44  LAC, RG25, vol. 5225, file 6386-H-40 part 1, Letter USSEA to Deputy Minister, Department of National Defence: United Nations Operations in the Congo, 6 October 1960. LAC, RG25, vol. 5210, file 6386-40 part 14, Memo to Cabinet: Financing of the UN Congo Operations, 29 November 1960; Memo for USSEA: Financing UN operations in the Congo, 2 December 1960. DCC, file MG1/XII/C/114, Typewritten Note: Airlift to Congo, 3 December 1960.

45  Catherine Hoskyns, *The Congo since Independence: January 1960-December 1961* (London: Oxford University Press, 1965), 266-67.

46  DHH, file 90/336, box 1, Dumont-Bayliss interview with J. Berthiaume, 12 September 1990.

47  Hoskyns, *The Congo since Independence*, 267. A more recent account of Lumumba's assassination discusses Lumumba's capture by Mobutu's forces and emphasizes the decision by von Horn and Dayal, confirmed by UN HQ, to stop Ghanaian peacekeepers near to where Lumumba was arrested from intervening. Ludo de Witte, *The Assassination of Lumumba*, trans. Ann Wright and Renée Fenby (London and New York: Verso, 2001), 51-57. United Nations culpability in Lumumba's fate is debated by Brian Urquhart and Ludo De Witte in an exchange that appeared in the *New York Review*, 4 October 2001, 4-7; 20 December 2001, 103-5; and 14 February 2002, 49-50.

48  Thomas M. Franck and John Carey, *The Legal Aspects of the United Nations Action in the Congo*, ed. Lyman M. Tondel Jr. (Dobbs Ferry, NY: Oceana Publications/The Association of the Bar of the City of New York, 1963), 26.

49  LAC, RG25, vol. 5210, file 6386-40 part 14, Telegram Leopoldville to External: Situation in Stanleyville, 10 December 1960; Memo: Situation in the Congo, 9 December 1960; Memo African Section to USSEA: Situation in the Congo, 9 December 1960. LAC, RG25, vol. 5221, file 6386-C-40 part 7, Telegram External to PERMISNY: Position in Congo, 9 December 1960. LAC, RG24, vol. 18482, War Diary – No. 57 Canadian Signal Squadron, December, Telegram Stanleyville Detachment to 57th Leopoldville, 1 December 1960.

50  Canada received a telegram, dated 13 December and signed by Gizenga, informing the government of the installation of the Stanleyville government. Robertson advised Diefenbaker, "We do not propose to reply to Mr. Gizenga's message." LAC, RG25, vol. 5210, file 6386-40 part 15, Memo for Prime Minister, 15 December 1960.

51  The RCAF did, in fact, develop emergency evacuation plans for Canadians in the Congo. LAC, RG25, vol. 5221, file 6386-C-40 part 7, Telegram PERMISNY to External: Congo, 13 December 1960; Memo DL (1) to File: Number and Location of Canadian Civilians in the Congo, 13 December 1960.

52  DCC, file MG1/VI/(845 Congo), Telegram King to JGD, 6 December 1960; Letter Congress of Canadian Women to Diefenbaker, 29 December 1960. LAC, RG25, vol. 5211, file 6386-40 parts 16 and 16.2, Letter Alicia Humphries to Diefenbaker, 22 January 1961. "Problems of Lumumba's Arrest," *Montreal Gazette*, 3 December 1960, 6. "Is This the End for Lumumba?" *Toronto Daily Star*, 3 December 1960, 6.

53  LAC, RG25, vol. 5210, file 6386-40 part 14, Outgoing Message External to PERMISNY: Congo Trends, 5 December 1960.

54  LAC, RG25, vol. 5221, file 6386-C-40 part 7, Telegram PERMISNY to External: Congo Trends, 9 December 1960; Memo African Section to Ignatieff: Situation in the Congo, 9 December 1960. LAC, RG25, vol. 5210, file 6386-40 part 15, Telegram PERMISNY to External: Congo, 14 December 1960.

55  LAC, RG25, vol. 5221, file 6386-C-40 part 7, Memo UN Div to USSEA: Congo at the UN, 14 December 1960.

56  LAC, RG25, vol. 5221, file 6386-C-40 part 7, Memo UN Div to USSEA: Congo at the UN, 14 December 1960. LAC, RG25, vol. 5221, file 6386-C-40 part 8, Memo: UN Div to USSEA: Congo at the United Nations, 16 December 1960; US *Aide Mémoire*, 16 December 1960. Andrew W. Cordier and Wilder Foote, *Public Papers of the Secretaries-General of the United Nations*, vol. 5, *Dag Hammarskjöld, 1960-1961* (New York: Columbia University Press, 1975), 271.

57  LAC, RG25, vol. 5221, file 6386-C-40 part 8, Memo UN Div to Ignatieff: Congo Debate, 19 December 1960; Memo for Minister: Congo Debate, December 1960; Memo UN Div to USSEA: Congo Debate, 19 December 1960.

58  LAC, RG25, vol. 5221, file 6386-C-40 part 8, Telegram CANDELNY to External: Item 85 – Situation in the Republic of Congo, 20 December 1960; Memo for Minister: Congo Debate, 20 December 1960.

59  LAC, RG25, vol. 5221, file 6386-C-40 part 9, Numbered Letter Leopoldville to USSEA: Some Local Views about the Congo, 5 January 1961. LAC, RG25, vol. 5211, file 6386-40 parts 16 and 16.2, Summary of Letter from Leopoldville: Views about the UN and the Congo by Actors in the Drama, 12 January 1961.

60  LAC, MG32, B13, vol. 10, file 6, NATO Long Term Planning: Canadian position, no date; "Howard Green Needles NATO," *Toronto Daily Star*, 19 December 1960, 6.

61  LAC, RG25, vol. 5211, file 6386-40 parts 16 and 16.2, Memo for the Minister: Request for NATO Support of Belgium's Congo Activities, 12 January 1961; Outgoing Message External to NATOPARIS: Belgian Policy in the Congo, 20 January 1961. LAC, RG25, vol. 5221, file 6386-C-40 part 9, Memo European Div to USSEA: Request for NATO Support of Belgium's Congo Activities, 18 January 1961; Memo DL (1) to USSEA: Request for NATO Support for Belgium's Congo Activities, 16 January 1961.

62  LAC, RG25, vol. 5221, file 6386-C-40 part 9, Telegram Brussels to External: Congo, 12 January 1961; Telegram Brussels to External: Congo, 26 January 1961. LAC, RG25, vol. 5211, file 6386-40 parts 16 and 16.2, Outgoing Message External to NATOPARIS: Congo PAC Meeting January 24, 20 January 1961; Outgoing Message External to NATOPARIS: Belgian Policy in the Congo, 20 January 1961.

63  Hoskyns, *The Congo since Independence*, 307. De Witte, *The Assassination of Lumumba*, 79.

64  LAC, RG25, vol. 5221, file 6386-C-40 part 9, Telegram PERMISNY to External: Congo Advisory Committee, 23 January 1961.

65  LAC, RG25, vol. 5221, file 6386-C-40 part 9, Minutes of UN Advisory Committee on Congo, 20 January 1961; Telegram PERMISNY to External: Congo Advisory Committee, 23 January 1961. Canada, House of Commons, *Debates*, 19 January 1961: 1217.

66  LAC, RG25, vol. 5221, file 6386-C-40 part 9, Telegram PERMISNY to External: Congo Advisory Committee, 23 January 1961. LAC, RG25, vol. 5211, file 6386-40 parts 16 and 16.2, Memo for the Minister: Recommendations of Congo Advisory Committee for Release of Mr. Lumumba, 25 January 1961; Outgoing Message External to PERMISNY: Congo Advisory Committee, 26 January 1961.

67  LAC, RG25, vol. 5221, file 6386-C-40 part 7, Memo UN Div to USSEA: United Nations Commander in the Congo, 30 November 1960; Memo UN Div to USSEA: Congo Situation, 2 December 1960. DHH, file 90/336, box 3, part 48, Memo Supreme Commander to Ambassador Dayal, 10 December 1960.

68  LAC, RG25, vol. 5221, file 6386-C-40 part 8, Memo for Minister: Congo – Report from Col. Berthiaume, 24 December 1960; Memo UN Div to USSEA: Congo: Canadian Worries about United Nations Operations, 27 December 1960; Memo for Minister: Congo: Canadian Views about Current United Nations Operations, 28 December 1960; Memo for Minister: Congo:

Canadian Views about United Nations Operations, 29 December 1960. LAC, RG25, vol. 5221, file 6386-C-40 part 9, Memo African and Middle Eastern Div [hereafter AMED] to UN Div: Congo and the United Nations, 18 January 1961; Memo AMED to USSEA: Congo and UN Officials, 20 January 1961; Memo DL (1) to USSEA: Congo and UN Officials, 23 January 1961. The Defence Liaison division subsequently supported the African and Middle Eastern Division's view that Canada should not publicly support or criticize Dayal but should privately give advice to Hammarskjöld on the "proper role of his representative in the Congo."

69 LAC, RG25, vol. 5221, file 6386-C-40 part 8, Outgoing Message External to PERMISNY: Congo: Canadian Views about Current Operations, 29 December 1960; Telegram PERMISNY to External: Congo: Canadian Views about Current UN Operations, 30 December 1960.

70 LAC, RG25, vol. 5220, file 6386-C-40 part 5, Letter CCOS to USSEA: RCAF Personnel for the Congo, 14 October 1960. LAC, RG25, vol. 5220, file 6386-C-40 part 6, Memo for MDND: United Nations Request for Assistance in the Congo, 18 November 1960. LAC, RG2, vol. 2747, Cabinet Conclusions, 25 November 1960.

71 LAC, RG25, vol. 5211, file 6386-40 parts 17 and 17.2, Memo for File: Famine Situation South Kasai Congo, 1 February 1961. DCC, file MG1/VI/(802/C749), Letter Waterworth to Diefenbaker, 24 January 1961; Class Set of 31 Letters to Diefenbaker, 1 February 1961; Telegram to Diefenbaker, 16 January 1961.

72 "Famine Sweeps Kasai," *Globe and Mail*, 29 December 1960, 1. "Food for Congo," *Toronto Daily Star*, 23 January 1961, 6. "Too Selfish?" *Toronto Daily Star*, 26 January 1961, 6. "Relieving the Congo Famine," *Montreal Gazette*, 27 January 1961, 6.

73 LAC, RG25, vol. 5211, file 6386-40 parts 16 and 16.2, Memo to the Minister: Famine in the Congo – FAO Appeal, 16 January 1961. LAC, RG25, vol. 5211, file 6386-40 parts 17 and 17.2, Letter USSEA to Director-General External Aid Office: Famine Relief in South Kasai Province, 2 February 1961; Letter USSEA to W.S. Stanbury, 15 February 1961. LAC, RG2, vol. 6178, Cabinet Document 22.61, Memo to Cabinet: Famine in the Congo, 20 January 1961. LAC, RG2, vol. 6176, Cabinet Conclusions, 26 and 31 January 1961.

74 LAC, RG25, vol. 5221, file 6386-C-40 part 9, Memo for Minister: Congo – Possible Question in the House, 27 January 1961; Memo for Prime Minister: Congo: Withdrawal of Contingents from UN Force, 25 January 1961; Telegram ME15 External to PERMISNY: Congo: Suggested Complaint about UAR Activity, 20 January 1961. LAC, RG25, vol. 5211, file 6386-40 parts 16 and 16.2, Memo for the Minister: Congo: Suggested Complaint about Activity of UAR, 20 January 1961.

75 LAC, RG2, vol. 6178, Cabinet Document 17.61, Memo to Cabinet: Additional Canadian Army Staff Officers for Congo, 17 January 1961. LAC, RG25, vol. 5221, file 6386-C-40 part 9, Memo for Minister: Congo – Request for Assistance, 19 January 1961; Memo SSEA to Ignatieff: Congo – Request for Assistance, 23 January 1961. LAC, RG24, vol. 18482, War Diary – No. 57 Canadian Signal Squadron, January, Telegram 57th Leopoldville to CANARMY, 9 January 1961. LAC, RG2, vol. 6176, Cabinet Conclusions, 31 January 1961.

76 Kalb, *The Congo Cables*, 375-76. Lefever concurs that Kennedy, in comparison with Eisenhower, supported "more vigorous UN measures." Lefever, "US Policy, the UN and the Congo," 401. Likewise, Weissman interprets January 1961 as a time of transition in American policy; see Weissman, *American Foreign Policy in the Congo 1960-1964*, 284.

77 LAC, RG25, vol. 5221, file 6386-C-40 part 10, US *Aide Mémoire*, Cover Memo and Statement by Dean Rusk: United States Policy on the Congo, 7 February 1961; Memo for Minister: US Approach to Congo Problem, 6 February 1961; Outgoing Message External to PERMISNY, 6 February 1961. The new American approach is outlined in a 1 February 1961 memorandum from Secretary of State Dean Rusk to President Kennedy, *FRUS, 1961-1963*, vol. 20, doc. 17.

78 LAC, RG25, vol. 5221, file 6386-C-40 part 10, Telegram NATOPARIS to External: Congo, 9 February 1961. LAC, RG25, vol. 5211, files 6386-40 parts 17 and 17.2, Outgoing Message External to NATOPARIS: Congo, 14 February 1961. Alan James, *Britain and the Congo Crisis, 1960-63* (London: Macmillan, 1996), 50. On Belgium's opposition to the US initiative, see also Wynfred Joshua, "Belgium's Role in the Peace-keeping Operation in the Congo," *Orbis* 11, 2 (1967): 426-27.

**Chapter 5: Continued Chaos**

1  As quoted in Catherine Hoskyns, *The Congo since Independence: January 1960 – December 1961* (London: Oxford University Press, 1965), 315. See also A.A.J. van Bilsen, "Some Aspects of the Congo Problem," *International Affairs* 38, 1 (1962): 50.

2  LAC, RG25, vol. 5211, file 6386-40 parts 17 and 17.2, Summary of Meeting, 10 February 1961; Notes on the Congo by Brigadier R.M. Bishop, 13 February 1961; Memo for Minister: United Kingdom Policy, 2 February 1961.

3  Andrew W. Cordier and Wilder Foote, *Public Papers of the Secretaries-General of the United Nations*, vol. 5, *Dag Hammarskjöld 1960-61* (New York: Columbia University Press, 1975), 332-36.

4  Canada, House of Commons, *Debates*, 13 February 1961: 1971. LAC, RG25, vol. 5221, file 6386-C-40 part 10, Telegram PERMISNY to External: Congo, 14 February 1961. *FRUS, 1961-1963*, vol. 20, doc. 30, Telegram from the Department of State to the Embassy in the Congo.

5  "The Afro-Asian Plan," *Halifax Chronicle-Herald*, 21 February 1961, 4. "Congo Crisis Creates New Opportunity," *Montreal Gazette*, 22 February 1961, 6. "Africans in City to Mourn," *Montreal Gazette*, 14 February 1961, 1. "Lament for Lumumba," *Toronto Daily Star*, 14 February 1961, 6.

6  LAC, RG25, vol. 5212, file 6386-40 part 20, Letter Mackenzie to Green, 13 February 1961. DCC, file MG1/VI/(845 Congo), Letter Miskew to Diefenbaker, 14 February 1961. LAC, RG25, vol. 5211, file 6386-40 parts 17 and 17.2, Telegram Young Communist League to Green, 14 February 1961.

7  LAC, RG2, vol. 6176, Cabinet Conclusions, 16 February 1961. LAC, RG25, vol. 5221, file 6386-C-40 part 10, Telegram PERMISNY to External: Congo, 16 February 1961.

8  Canada, House of Commons, *Debates*, 14 February 1961: 2012. LAC, RG25, vol. 5221, file 6386-C-40 part 10, Memo: Current Developments in Congo Situation, 17 February 1961; Memo for USSEA: The Situation in the Congo, 16 February 1961.

9  Soviet Draft Resolution. *In favour:* Union of Soviet Socialist Republics; *against:* Chile, China, Ecuador, France, Liberia, Turkey, United Kingdom, United States; *abstentions:* Ceylon, United Arab Republic.

10  Security Council Resolution 161 (1961), 21 February 1961. *In favour:* Ceylon, Chile, China, Ecuador, Liberia, Turkey, United Arab Republic, United Kingdom, United States; *against:* none; *abstentions:* France, Union of Soviet Socialist Republics.

11  LAC, RG25, vol. 5222, file 6386-C-40 part 11, Memo for Minister: Congo: Security Council Debate, 21 February 1961. Prime Minister Diefenbaker and President Kennedy met in Washington on 20 February and received a briefing on the American assessment of the Congo situation and related activity at the UN. An American memorandum of the conversation suggests Diefenbaker and Howard Green were "in complete sympathy with United States purposes." *FRUS, 1961-1963*, vol. 13, doc. 418, Memorandum of Conversation.

12  A number of scholars maintain that this resolution did not change ONUC into an enforcement action, in spite of its authorization to use force. Others highlight ways in which the mandate was expanded, bringing it ever closer to an enforcement action. Some, however, do interpret the resolution as authorizing enforcement action. See Jane Boulden, *The United Nations and Mandate Enforcement: Congo, Somalia, and Bosnia* (Kingston: Centre for International Relations, Queen's University / Institut Québécois des Hautes Études Internationales, Université Laval, 1999), 33. D.W. Bowett, *United Nations Forces* (London: Stevens and Sons, 1964), 163-65. Paul Diehl, *International Peacekeeping* (Baltimore: Johns Hopkins University Press, 1994), 51. Jack Citrin, *UN Peacekeeping Activities. A Case Study in Organizational Task Expansion*, Monograph Series in World Affairs 3.1 (Denver: University of Denver, 1965-66), 40-41. Alan James, *The Politics of Peacekeeping* (London: Chatto and Windus, 1969), 414. Goronwy J. Jones, *The United Nations and the Domestic Jurisdiction of States* (Cardiff: University of Wales Press / Welsh Centre for International Affairs, 1979), 134-35. Anthony Parsons, *From Cold War to Hot Peace: UN Interventions, 1947-1994* (London: Michael Joseph, 1995), 87.

13  LAC, RG25, vol. 5211, file 6386-40 part 18, Memo: The Congo, 24 February 1961. Canada, House of Commons, *Debates*, 23 February 1961: 2337-38. LAC, RG25, vol. 5211, file 6386-40

parts 17 and 17.2, Message from Duncan Sandys, Commonwealth Secretary: Congo, 17 February 1961. Alan James, *Britain and the Congo Crisis, 1960-63* (London: Macmillan, 1996), 88-89.

14  LAC, RG25, vol. 5222, file 6386-C-40 part 11, Telegram PERMISNY to External: Congo Advisory Committee Meeting 22 February 1961, 23 February 1961; Telegram PERMISNY to External: Congo Advisory Committee, 25 February 1961.

15  LAC, RG25, vol. 5222, file 6386-C-40 part 11, Telegram PERMISNY to External: Congo Advisory Committee, 25 February 1961; Outgoing Message External to PERMISNY: Congo: Implementation of Security Council Resolution, 24 February 1961; Memo UN Div to Ignatieff: Congo: Implementation of Security Council Resolution, 23 February 1961; Telegram PERMISNY to External: Congo Advisory Committee Meeting 22 February 1961, 23 February 1961.

16  LAC, RG25, vol. 5221, file 6386-C-40 part 10, Memo DL (1) to USSEA: Congo – Strength and Development of Canadian Contingent, 17 February 1961. LAC, RG25, vol. 5222, file 6386-C-40 part 11, Despatch SSEA to PERMISNY: UN Airlift-Replacement of North Star Aircraft, 23 February 1961; Memo for Minister: Congo – Use of RCAF North Star Aircraft, 20 February 1961; Letter Harkness to Green, 24 February 1961.

17  LAC, RG25, vol. 5221, file 6386-C-40 part 10, Memo DL (1) to USSEA: Congo – Strength and Development of Canadian Contingent, 17 February 1961. LAC, RG25, vol. 5222, file 6386-C-40 part 11, Telegram Leopoldville to External: Incident between ANC and ONUC, 28 February 1961; Telegram PERMISNY to External: Congo, 28 February 1961. LAC, RG24, vol. 18483, War Diary – No. 57 Canadian Signal Squadron, Diary Entry, 27 February 1961. LAC, RG25, vol. 5222, file 6386-C-40 part 12, Telegram Leopoldville to External: Incident Involving ANC and Canadian Soldiers, 2 March 1961. Canada, House of Commons, *Debates*, 27 February 1961: 2445.

18  LAC, RG25, vol. 5222, file 6386-C-40 part 12, Outgoing Message External to PERMISNY: Congo – Matadi Incident, 9 March 1961; Outgoing Message External to PERMISNY: Congo – Matadi Incident, 13 March 1961. LAC, RG24, vol. 18483, War Diary – No. 57 Canadian Signal Squadron, Statement of Captain Belanger, 8 March 1961; Statement of Sgt Wood, 8 March 1961; Statement of Sgt Harris, 8 March 1961; Statement of Signaller Bates, 8 March 1961; Report: Matadi Action (4 March 1961), 10 March 1961; Extracts of Statements by Signaller Janules and Signaller Beggs, 10 March 1961.

19  LAC, RG25, vol. 5222, file 6386-C-40 part 12, Outgoing Message External to PERMISNY: Congo – Matadi Incident, 13 March 1961.

20  LAC, RG25, vol. 5222, file 6386-C-40 part 12, Outgoing Message External to PERMISNY: Congo – Matadi Incident, 13 March 1961; Telegram Leopoldville to External: Congo – Matadi Incident, 7 March 1961; Telegram Leopoldville to External: Congo – Matadi Incident, 8 March 1961; Outgoing Message External to Leopoldville, PERMISNY: Congo – Matadi, 5 March 1961.

21  DHH, file 73/1223 part 461, Memo and Related Correspondence, Judge Advocate General to CCOS, 28 February 1961. LAC, RG24, vol. 18483, War Diary – No. 57 Canadian Signal Squadron, Telegram 57th Leopoldville to CANARMY, 2 March 1961; Diary Entry, 1 March 1961. LAC, RG25, vol. 5222, file 6386-C-40 part 12, Telegram PERMISNY to External: Congo: Orders to UN Troops re Surrender of Personal Weapons, 3 March 1961.

22  LAC, RG25, vol. 5212, file 6386-40 parts 19 and 19.2, Memo for the Minister: Canadian Position Concerning Use of Force by UN in the Congo, 7 March 1961. LAC, RG25, vol. 5222, file 6386-C-40 part 12, Telegram ME74 External to PERMISNY: Possible Use of Force by UN in Congo, 7 March 1961.

23  LAC, RG25, vol. 5211, file 6386-40 part 18, Memo for the Minister: Implications for the Belgians of Certain Clauses of the Security Council Resolution, 24 February 1961; Memo for the Minister: Congo Questions Affecting Belgium – Guidance for NATO discussion, 25 February 1961.

24  LAC, RG25, vol. 5212, file 6386-40 parts 19 and 19.2, Memo European Div to AMED: Advisory Committee on the Congo: Belgian Request for Information, 8 March 1961; Memo AMED to USSEA: Advisory Committee on the Congo – Belgian Request for Information, 10 March 1961. LAC, RG25, vol. 5222, file 6386-C-40 part 12, Memo for Minister: Advisory

Committee on Congo: Belgian Request for Information, 15 March 1961; Telegram Brussels to External: Congo, 10 March 1961; Telegram Brussels to External: Congo, 13 March 1961. LAC, RG25, vol. 5222, file 6386-C-40 part 13, Telegram CANDELNY to External: Congo – Belgian Request for Information, 27 March 1961. LAC, RG25, vol. 5212, file 6386-40 part 20, Memo AMED to USSEA: Advisory Committee on the Congo: Belgian Request for Information, 22 March 1961; DEA Outgoing Message External to Brussels: Approach to Belgian Government, 28 March 1961; Telegram Brussels to External: Matadi, 30 March 1961.

25  DCC, file MG1/XII/C/110.3, Notes for a Statement by Prime Minister: Congo, 14 March 1961; Notes on Conversation with Macmillan at Chequers, 10 March 1961. DCC, file MG1/XII/C/110.2, Press Conference Transcript: Bryce and Murray, 8 March 1961. DCC, file MG1/XII/C/110.4, Press Conference Transcript: Bryce, 15 March 1961. DCC, file MG1/XII/C/114, Typewritten Notes, 16 March 1961. LAC, RG25, vol. 5211, file 6386-40 part 18, Notes for Possible Statement by Prime Minister at Prime Ministers' Meeting, 24 February 1961. LAC, RG25, vol. 5212, file 6386-40 parts 19 and 19.2, Memo: Notes of Interview with Mr. R. Dayal, 12 March 1961 (approximately); Memo for the Prime Minister: Congo: Visit of Mr. Dayal, 12 March 1961.

26  LAC, RG25, vol. 5222, file 6386-C-40 part 12, Telegram PERMISNY to External: Congo Advisory Committee Meeting – 13 March 1961, 14 March 1961.

27  General Assembly Resolution 1599 (XV), 15 April 1961. *In favour:* Afghanistan, Albania, Austria, Bulgaria, Burma, Byelorussian SSR, Cambodia, Canada, Ceylon, Chad, China, Congo (Brazzaville), Cuba, Cyprus, Czechoslovakia, Dahomey, Denmark, Ecuador, Ethiopia, Federation of Malaya, Finland, Gabon, Ghana, Guinea, Hungary, Iceland, India, Indonesia, Iran, Iraq, Ireland, Israel, Ivory Coast, Jordan, Lebanon, Liberia, Libya, Madagascar, Mali, Morocco, Nicaragua, Niger, Nigeria, Norway, Poland, Romania, Saudi Arabia, Senegal, Somalia, Sudan, Sweden, Togo, Tunisia, Turkey, Ukrainian SSR, Union of Soviet Socialist Republics, United Arab Republic, Upper Volta, Venezuela, Yemen, Yugoslavia; *against:* Belgium, Nepal, Portugal, Union of South Africa, Uruguay; *abstentions:* Argentina, Australia, Bolivia, Brazil, Cameroon, Central African Republic, Chile, Colombia, Congo (Leopoldville), Costa Rica, Dominican Republic, El Salvador, France, Greece, Guatemala, Haiti, Honduras, Italy, Japan, Laos, Luxembourg, Mexico, Netherlands, New Zealand, Pakistan, Panama, Paraguay, Peru, Philippines, Spain, Thailand, United Kingdom, United States.

28  General Assembly Resolution 1601 (XV), 15 April 1961. *In favour:* Afghanistan, Austria, Bolivia, Brazil, Burma, Cambodia, Canada, Ceylon, Chile, Colombia, Denmark, Ecuador, Ethiopia, Federation of Malaya, Finland, Ghana, Guinea, Iceland, India, Indonesia, Iran, Iraq, Ireland, Jordan, Lebanon, Liberia, Libya, Mali, Mexico, Morocco, Nepal, New Zealand, Nigeria, Norway, Panama, Saudi Arabia, Senegal, Sudan, Sweden, Togo, Tunisia, United Arab Republic, Venezuela, Yemen, Yugoslavia; *against:* Congo (Leopoldville), Portugal, Spain; *abstentions:* Albania, Argentina, Australia, Belgium, Bulgaria, Byelorussian SSR, Cameroon, Central African Republic, Chad, China, Congo (Brazzaville), Costa Rica, Cuba, Cyprus, Czechoslovakia, Dahomey, Dominican Republic, El Salvador, France, Gabon, Greece, Guatemala, Haiti, Honduras, Hungary, Israel, Italy, Ivory Coast, Japan, Laos, Luxembourg, Madagascar, Netherlands, Nicaragua, Niger, Pakistan, Paraguay, Poland, Romania, Somalia, Thailand, Turkey, Ukrainian SSR, Union of South Africa, Union of Soviet Socialist Republics, United Kingdom, United States, Upper Volta, Uruguay.

29  LAC, RG25, vol. 5222, file 6386-C-40 part 13, Telegram CANDELNY to External: Congo, 4 April 1961; Telegram External to CANDELNY: Congo Resolutions in UN General Assembly, 11 April 1961; Memo for Minister: Assembly Resolutions on Congo, 13 April 1961.

30  LAC, RG25, vol. 5226, file 6386-L-40 part 1, Memo European Div to AMED: Belgium and the Congo, 28 March 1961.

31  LAC, RG25, vol. 5222, file 6386-C-40 part 13, Telegram Brussels to External: Belgian Request for Information – Congo Advisory Committee, 5 April 1961; Telegram PERMISNY to External: Congo Advisory Committee – Belgian Request for Information, 10 April 1961; Memo for Minister: Belgian Request for Information on Advisory Committee Discussion, 12 April 1961.

32  LAC, RG24, vol. 7169, file 2-5081-7 part 1, Minutes of meeting, 6 April 1961. LAC, RG25, vol. 5223, file 6386-C-40 part 14, Letter Ross Campbell to USSEA: United Nations Financing

– Congo, 15 April 1961. LAC, RG25, vol. 5225, file 6386-H-40 part 2, Memo for the Minister: United Nations Financing, 15 April 1961; Memo for the Minister: Canadian Government's Assessment for the Congo Ad Hoc Account for 1961, 5 June 1961.

33 LAC, RG25, vol. 5222, file 6386-C-40 part 12, Telegram Leopoldville to External: Dayal's Return to Congo, 22 March 1961; Telegram External to PERMISNY: Proposed Return of Dayal to Congo, 23 March 1961; Memo UN Div to USSEA: Dayal's Return to the Congo, 24 March 1961. LAC, RG25, vol. 5222, file 6386-C-40 part 13, Telegram PERMISNY to External: Return of Dayal to Congo, 28 March 1961. LAC, RG25, vol. 5223, file 6386-C-40 part 14, Memo UN Div to AMED: Congo: Appointment of Mr. Dayal, 24 April 1961.

34 LAC, RG24, vol. 18483, War Diary – No. 57 Canadian Signal Squadron, Statement by K.R. Carleton Regarding Incident En Route to Zongo Falls, 3 April 1961; Diary Entries, April 1961. LAC, RG25, vol. 5222, file 6386-C-40 part 13, Outgoing Message External to PERMISNY: Congo: Arrest of Canadian Servicemen, 4 April 1961; Telegram Leopoldville to External: Incident Involving Five Canadian Soldiers, 4 April 1961.

35 LAC, RG24, vol. 18483, War Diary – No. 57 Canadian Signal Squadron, Diary Entry, April 1961; Memo: Incident 16 April 1961 – Summary, 16 April 1961; Monthly Report to Surgeon General CFMS, 2 June 1961.

36 LAC, RG24, vol. 18483, War Diary – No. 57 Canadian Signal Squadron, Telegram 57th to CANARMY, 10 April 1961; Telegram ONUC Stanleyville to ONUC Leopoldville, 12 April 1961; Report on Stanleyville Incident on 8-9 April 1961, 14 April 1961.

37 LAC, RG25, vol. 5222, file 6386-C-40 part 13, Memo for Minister: United Nations Request for Air Lift Assistance, 11 April 1961; Letter Green to Harkness, 11 April 1961; Telegram PERMISNY to External: Congo: Enquiry re RCAF Assistance in Airlift Indian Troops from Dar to Kamina, 14 April 1961; Telegram Leopoldville to External: UN Request for RCAF Planes, 13 April 1961. LAC, RG25, vol. 5223, file 6386-C-40 part 14, Letter CCOS to USSEA: Congo: Request for Assistance, 17 April 1961; Outgoing Message: Congo: Request for Assistance, 21 April 1961; Telegram PERMISNY to External: Congo – UN Request for Assistance – Canadian Observers, 4 May 1961.

38 DHH, file 73/1223, part 461, Memo Acting Chief of the Air Staff to CCOS: Congo – UN Request for Assistance, 31 May 1961. LAC, RG25, vol. 5223, file 6386-C-40 part 14, Letter CCOS to USSEA: UN Request for Assistance – Congo and Attached Biography of H.A. Morrison, 30 May 1961. LAC, RG25, vol. 5223, file 6386-C-40 part 15, Letter CCOS to USSEA: Congo – UN Request for Assistance, 27 June 1961.

39 LAC, RG25, vol. 5223, file 6386-C-40 part 15, Telegram PERMISNY to External: Congo: UN Request for Assistance, 29 June 1961; Letter CCOS to USSEA: Congo: Request for Assistance, 12 July 1961.

40 Canada, House of Commons, *Debates*, 8 May 1961: 4501; 9 May 1961: 4539-41.

41 LAC, RG25, vol. 5223, file 6386-C-40 part 14, Telegram External to PERMISNY: Congo – Situation of Canadian Troops, 15 May 1961; Telegram External to PERMISNY: Canadian Troops – Return to Matadi, 16 May 1961; PERMISNY to External: Canadian Troops – Return to Matadi, 19 May 1961; PERMISNY to External: Canadian Troops – Return to Matadi, 17 May 1961.

42 LAC, RG25, vol. 5223, file 6386-C-40 part 14, Numbered Letter Leopoldville to USSEA: Canadian Troops – Return to Matadi, 25 May 1961. LAC, RG25, vol. 5223, file 6386-C-40 part 15, Memo to Prime Minister: Answer to Possible Question in the House – Return of UN Troops to Matadi, 14 June 1961; Telegram PERMISNY to External: Canadian Troops: Return to Matadi, 13 June 1961; Outgoing Message External to PERMISNY: Congo, 16 June 1961. LAC, RG24, vol. 18483, War Diary – No. 57 Canadian Signal Squadron, Minutes of No. 57 Canadian Signal Unit Staff Meeting, 16 June 1961.

43 LAC, RG25, vol. 5213, file 6386-40 part 23, Minutes of Meeting with Col. Paul Smith Held May 30, 1961, 5 June 1961.

44 LAC, RG25, vol. 5223, file 6386-C-40 part 14, Note for File, 26 April 1961 (approximately); Memo for Minister: UN Agreement with President Kasavubu: Advisory Committee Meeting This Afternoon, 26 April 1961. LAC, RG25, vol. 5212, file 6386-40 part 21, Outgoing Message: UN Agreement with Kasavubu, 26 April 1961.

45  LAC, RG25, vol. 5222, file 6386-C-40 part 13, Telegram Leopoldville to External: Call on President Kasavubu, 5 April 1961. DCC, file MG1/VIII/2386(845/C749), Memo AMED to Robinson: Telegram from Baluba Chiefs and Telegram from General Committee of CONAKAT [Confédération des Associations du Katanga], 9 May 1961; Katangan Press Release, 2 May 1961. LAC, RG25, vol. 5213, file 6386-40 part 22, Memo for the Minister: *Aide Mémoire* from the Government of Katanga, 1 May 1961. LAC, RG25, vol. 5212, file 6386-40 part 21, Memo: Status of the Canadian Acting Consul-General in Leopoldville, 25 April 1961. LAC, RG25, vol. 5213, file 6386-40 part 24, Memo for Minister: Recent Developments in the Congo, 28 July 1961.

46  LAC, RG25, vol. 5223, file 6386-C-40 part 14, Telegram Leopoldville to External: Dayal's Return, 18 May 1961; Telegram Leopoldville to External: Dayal's Return, 21 May 1961; Telegram Leopoldville to External: Dayal Return, 24 May 1961. Rajeshwar Dayal, *Mission for Hammarskjold: The Congo Crisis* (Princeton, NJ: Princeton University Press, 1976), 258, 261.

47  LAC, RG25, vol. 5222, file 6386-C-40 part 13, Telegram External to Leopoldville: Training of Congolese Army, 5 April 1961; Memo Campbell to DL (1): Training of Congolese Army, 7 April 1961. LAC, RG24, vol. 5086, file 3445-34/73, Memo: Telephone Conversation – Colonel Parker – Lt. Col. Speedie 1130 hours 3 May 1961: Training of the ANC, 3 May 1961. LAC, RG25, vol. 5223, file 6386-C-40 part 15, Letter USSEA to CCOS and Attached Telegram: Training of Congolese Army, 27 June 1961; Telegram Leopoldville to External: Follow Up on Visit to General Mobutu, 19 June 1961.

48  LAC, RG25, vol. 5223, file 6386-C-40 part 15, Memo: United Nations Operation in the Congo: A Case Study of the Political Control of United Nations Peace-keeping Forces, 8 June 1961. LAC, RG25, vol. 5213, file 6386-40 part 23, Memo: Congo, 9 June 1961; Memo: Draft Articles for Commentary for Sixteenth Session, 14 July 1961.

### Chapter 6: The Challenge of Katanga

1  LAC, RG25, vol. 5213, file 6386-40 part 25, Memo for Minister: Recent Developments in the Congo, 18 August 1961. LAC, RG25, vol. 5213, file 6386-40 part 24, Memo for Prime Minister: Congratulatory Message to New Congolese Prime Minister, 8 August 1961. DCC, file MG1/VII/2327(840/C749), Telegram External to Leopoldville: Congratulations to Prime Minister Adoula, 11 August 1961.

2  DCC, file MG1/VI/8858.A (845 Congo), Telegram 57th to CANARMY, 16 August 1961. LAC, RG25, vol. 5213, file 6386-40 part 25, Memo for Minister: Current Situation in the Congo, 6 September 1961; Telegram Leopoldville to External: Courtesy Call on Prime Minister Adoula, 25 August 1961; Memo for Minister: Current Situation in the Congo, 6 September 1961. Catherine Hoskyns, *The Congo since Independence: January 1960-December 1961* (London: Oxford University Press, 1965), 400.

3  Indar Jit Rikhye, Michael Harbottle, and Bjørn Egge, *The Thin Blue Line: International Peacekeeping and Its Future* (New Haven, CT, and London: Yale University Press, 1974), 779.

4  LAC, RG25, vol. 5213, file 6386-40 part 25, Memo for Minister: Rioting in Katanga: Report of Threats Against Canadian Captain, 7 September 1961.

5  LAC, RG25, vol. 5223, file 6386-C-40 part 15, Telegram 57th Canadian Signal Unit to CANARMY, 1 September 1961; Memo for Minister: Canadian Participation in UN Congo Operations, 13 September 1961; Telegram CANARMY to 57th Canadian Signal Unit: For Stetham from CGS, 19 September 1961. Gaffen, in his account of this incident, suggests "Côté had followed the dictates of his conscience rather than those of his superiors in the UN force. Officials at External Affairs believed he should have acted as instructed. Colleagues in the force there were more understanding." The evidence contradicts this interpretation. The highest-ranking officials at both External Affairs and National Defence expressed concern about Côté's instructions and ONUC's actions. Fred Gaffen, *In the Eye of the Storm* (Toronto: Deneau and Wayne, 1987), 237.

6  LAC, RG25, vol. 5213, file 6386-40 part 25, Telegram PERMISNY to External: Congo-Katanga-SecGen's Views, 7 September 1961; Outgoing Message External to PERMISNY: Sec-Gen's Views on Katanga, 12 September 1961. Brian Urquhart, *Hammarskjold* (New York: Alfred A. Knopf, 1972), 560.

7 United Nations, *The Blue Helmets*, 3rd ed. (New York: United Nations Department of Public Information, 1996), 191. Michael N. Harbottle, *The Blue Berets: The Story of the United Nations Peacekeeping Forces* (London: Leo Cooper, 1971), 64. LAC, RG25, vol. 5223, file 6386-C-40 part 15, Memo for Minister: UN Clash in Katanga, 13 September 1961. LAC, RG25, vol. 5213, file 6386-40 part 25, Memo for Mr. Campbell: Katanga, 15 September 1961. See William J. Durch, *The Evolution of UN Peacekeeping: Case Studies and Comparative Analysis* (New York: St. Martin's Press, 1993), 341; Stanley Meisler, "Crisis in Katanga," in *Soldiers for Peace*, ed. Barbara Benton (New York: Facts on File, 1996), 110; and Rikhye, Harbottle, and Egge, *The Thin Blue Line*, 79-80.

8 This single jet menaced ONUC forces and gave the Katangese gendarmerie air superiority because, at this point, ONUC had no offensive aircraft at all. The CIA front company Seven Seas Airlines had delivered three Fouga Magisters to Katanga early in 1961, even though this was not consistent with official US policy. See Michael Schatzberg, *Mobutu or Chaos?* (New York: University Press of America, 1991), 12; David W. Wainhouse, *International Peacekeeping at the Crossroads: National Support – Experience and Prospects* (Baltimore: Johns Hopkins University Press, 1973), 297; and *FRUS, 1961-1963*, vol. 20, doc. 31, Telegram from the Department of State to the Consulate in Elisabethville.

9 DHH, file 144.9.009 (D43), vol. 1, Memo: Report on the Operation Undertaken to Capture the Katangese Ministers of State, 15 September 1961; Memo: Report on the Situation in Elisabethville, 22 September 1961.

10 LAC, RG24, vol. 18483, War Diary – No. 57 Canadian Signal Squadron, Report on the Albertville "Flare Up," 22 September 1961. LAC, RG25, vol. 5213, file 6386-40 part 25, Memo for Minister: Telephone Conversation – Colonel Stetham, Congo, 18 September 1961.

11 LAC, RG25, vol. 5213, file 6386-40 part 25, Telegram 255 Leopoldville to External: Katanga Situation, 17 September 1961. *FRUS, 1961-1963*, vol. 20, doc. 112, Telegram from the Department of State to the Embassy in the Congo. Alan James, *Britain and the Congo Crisis, 1960-63* (London: Macmillan, 1996), 105.

12 LAC, RG25, vol. 5214, file 6386-40 part 26, Memo for the Prime Minister: The Congo, 20 September 1961; Message from Duncan Sandys to Howard Green, 22 September 1961. LAC, RG25, vol. 5223, file 6386-C-40 part 16, Despatch Leopoldville to SSEA: Background on UN September 13 Operations in Katanga, 10 November 1961. James, *Britain and the Congo Crisis*, 108-11. See also O'Brien's own full account of events: Conor Cruise O'Brien, *To Katanga and Back* (New York: Grosset and Dunlap, 1962), and Donald Harman Akenson, *Conor: A Biography of Conor Cruise O'Brien*, vol. 1 (Montreal and Kingston: McGill-Queen's University Press, 1994), 175-81.

13 LAC, RG25, vol. 5223, file 6386-C-40 part 16, Outgoing Message External to PERMISNY: Congo, 21 September 1961. LAC, RG25, vol. 5214, file 6386-40 part 26, Outgoing Message External to PERMISNY: The Congo, 20 September 1961; Outgoing Message External to PERMISNY: Congo Advisory Committee, 11 October 1961.

14 LAC, RG25, vol. 5223, file 6386-C-40 part 16, Memo to Minister: Congo: UN Request for Assistance, 22 September 1961; Memo for Minister: Congo – UN Request for Canadian Transport Planes and Crews, 22 September 1961. LAC, RG2, vol. 6177, Cabinet Conclusions, 23 September 1961. LAC, RG24, vol. 21485, file 2137.3 part 5, Memo Chief of Air Staff to Minister National Defence, 25 September 1961.

15 LAC, RG2, vol. 6177, Cabinet Conclusions, 23 September 1961. "U.N. Uses Force," *Halifax Chronicle-Herald*, 15 September 1961, 4. "The U.N. Stake in Katanga," *Toronto Daily Star*, 15 September 1961, 6. "The Congo Is Integrated at Last," *Montreal Gazette*, 15 September 1961, 6. "U.N. Action in Katanga Condemned," *Halifax Chronicle-Herald*, 18 September 1961, 4. Canadian Institute of Public Opinion (CIPO) Poll 291, September 1961.

16 LAC, RG25, vol. 5223, file 6386-C-40 part 16, Memo for Minister: UN Operations in Katanga, 18 October 1961; Memo for Minister: Congo: UN Request for Assistance, 17 October 1961; Letter Green to Harkness, 17 October 1961; Letter Harkness to Green, 25 October 1961; Letter Green to Harkness, 2 November 1961; Memo Ross Campbell to DL (1): Congo: UN Request for Assistance, 3 November 1961; Letter Harkness to Green, 6 November 1961. LAC, RG2, vol. 6177, Cabinet Conclusions, 23 October 1961. *FRUS, 1961-1963*, vol. 20, doc. 117, Telegram from the Department of State to the Embassy in the Congo; doc. 120

National Security Action Memorandum No. 97. UNA, S-0209-0003-13, ONUC – records on foreign countries, Canada – correspondence, cables, etc., Memo Bowitz to Bunche, 30 October 1961.

17  LAC, RG25, vol. 5223, file 6386-C-40 part 17, Memo for Minister: Incidents Involving Canadians in the Congo, 28 November 1961; Letter CCOS to USSEA, 18 December 1961. LAC, RG2, vol. 6177, Cabinet Conclusions, 20 November 1961. LAC, RG25, vol. 5224, file 6386-C-40 part 18, Telegram PERMISNY to External: Congo: RCAF Airlift, 24 January 1962; Numbered Letter Leopoldville to USSEA: Congo: RCAF Airlift, 18 January 1962.

18  J.L. Granatstein and David Bercuson, *War and Peacekeeping* (Toronto: Key Porter, 1991), 221. LAC, RG25, vol. 5223, file 6386-C-40 part 17, Letter CCOS to USSEA: Assistance for the UN in the Congo, 29 November 1961; Outgoing Message External to PERMISNY: Congo – UN Enquiry re: Assistance, 4 December 1961. LAC, RG24, vol. 3022, file 895-8/115, Memo Chief of Air Staff to Vice Chief of Air Staff, 24 October 1961.

19  LAC, RG25, vol. 5223, file 6386-C-40 part 16, Memo: Cousineau to Stephens: Colonel Stetham's Reports, 25 October 1961.

20  LAC, RG25, vol. 5223, file 6386-C-40 part 16, Memo to Minister: Congo: UN Request for Assistance, 22 September 1961; Memo DL (1) to USSEA: Request for Military Advisers and Instructors for the Congo, 5 October 1961. LAC, RG24, vol. 5086, file 3445-34/73, Memo Directorate of Military Operations and Plans [hereafter DMOP] to DGPO: Training Assistance for ANC – Congo, 18 September 1961; Letter CGS to MDND (through CCOS): Instructors for the Congo, 15 November 1961. LAC, RG25, vol. 5214, file 6386-40 part 27, Telegram Leopoldville to External: UN Request for Military Advisers and Instructors for Congo, 7 November 1961; Memo for Minister: Congo – Request for Military Training Assistance, 9 November 1961. LAC, RG25, vol. 5226, file 6386-M-40 parts 1 and 2; Memo for Minister: Congo – Request for Military Training Assistance, 21 November 1961.

21  John Stoessinger, "The Payments Dispute," *The Future of UN Peace-Keeping Operations: A Policy Paper of the United Nations Association in Canada*, ed. Willson Woodside (Toronto: United Nations Association in Canada, 1965), 24.

22  LAC, RG25, vol. 5225, file 6386-H-40 part 2, Memo for Minister: Financing of the Congo Operations, 25 October 1961. LAC, RG25, vol. 5224, file 6386-C-40 part 19, Report: UNOC Estimated Costs and Financing, 15 April 1962. William Barton, interview with author, Ottawa, 1 August 2003.

23  United Nations, *The Blue Helmets*, 192-93; LAC, RG25, vol. 5214, file 6386-40 part 27, Memo for the Minister: Security Council Meeting on the Congo, 10 November 1961; Memo for the Minister: The Congo, 3 November 1961. LAC, RG25, vol. 5223, file 6386-C-40 part 16, Telegram CANDELNY to External: Minister Call on SecGen, 16 November 1961.

24  Brian Urquhart, *Ralph Bunche: An American Odyssey* (New York and London: W.W. Norton, 1993), 348.

25  LAC, RG25, vol. 5224, file 6386-C-40 part 18, Telegram PERMISNY to External: Congo – Sec-Gen's Views, 18 January 1962. LAC, RG25, vol. 5215, file 6386-40 part 30, Memo AMED to USSEA: U Thant's Conduct of Congo Affairs, 7 March 1962.

26  Security Council Resolution 169 (1961), 24 November 1961. *In favour:* Ceylon, Chile, China, Ecuador, Liberia, Turkey, United Arab Republic, Union of Soviet Socialist Republics, United States; *against:* none; *abstentions:* France, United Kingdom.

27  LAC, RG25, vol. 5214, file 6386-40 part 28, Outgoing Message External to CANDELNY: Congo, 22 November 1961. LAC, RG25, vol. 5223, file 6386-C-40 part 17, Memo for Minister: Killing of Thirteen Italian Officers in the Congo, 29 November 1961. American policy in advance of this round of Security Council diplomacy was laid out in an 11 November 1961 memorandum from Secretary of State Rusk to President Kennedy: *FRUS, 1961-1963*, vol. 20, doc. 140.

28  LAC, RG25, vol. 5214, file 6386-40 part 28, Memo for Minister: Situation in the Congo, 6 December 1961. Meisler, "Crisis in Katanga," 114. By this point, Conor Cruise O'Brien had departed the Congo under a cloud of controversy over his handling of ONUC hostilities in Katanga. O'Brien presents a spirited defence of his actions and a scathing interpretation of the role of his superiors in his biography *To Katanga and Back*. Ritchie's critical view of

O'Brien was no doubt shaped in part by his friendship with the Irish representative to the UN, Freddie Boland. Boland went so far as to exclude O'Brien from a dinner party held to discuss the Congo crisis and attended by Ritchie and UN luminaries such as Bunche, Sir Patrick Dean, and General MacEoin, on the grounds that O'Brien was "not quite the right colour," as quoted in Akenson, *Conor: A Biography of Conor Cruise O'Brien*, 179.

29 LAC, RG25, vol. 5214, file 6386-40 part 28, Memo to Minister: Situation in the Congo, 6 December 1961; Memo for Prime Minister: The Congo, 14 December 1961. LAC, RG25, vol. 5223, file 6386-C-40 part 17, Cover Letter and Message Harold Macmillan to Diefenbaker, 14 December 1961; Telegram Leopoldville to External: Cease Fire in Katanga, 13 December 1961; Memo UN Div to AMED: United Nations Operation in Katanga, 15 December 1961. *FRUS, 1961-1963*, vol. 20, doc. 143, Telegram from the Mission to the United Nations to the Department of State. Both Joshua and Lefever comment on the strength of United States support for U Thant, regardless of pleas from its European allies. Wynfred Joshua, "Belgium's Role in the UN Peace-keeping Operation in the Congo," *Orbis* 11, 2 (1967): 432. Ernest Lefever, "U.S. Policy, the UN and the Congo," *Orbis* 11, 2 (1967): 403. Stephen R. Weissman, *American Foreign Policy in the Congo, 1960-1964* (Ithaca, NY, and London: Cornell University Press, 1974), 163-64.

30 Alistair Horne, *Macmillan, 1957-1986*, vol. 2 (London: Macmillan, 1989), 401-4. See also James, *Britain and the Congo Crisis*, 149-51.

31 LAC, RG25, vol. 5214, file 6386-40 part 28, Memo for Prime Minister: The Congo, 14 December 1961. LAC, RG25, vol. 5214, file 6386-40 part 29, Memo for Minister: Situation in Katanga, 16 December 1961. LAC, RG25, vol. 5223, file 6386-C-40 part 17, Memo UN Div to AMED: United Nations Operation in Katanga, 15 December 1961. LAC, RG2, vol. 6177, Cabinet Conclusions, 7 December 1961. "Canada Supports UN Acts," *Halifax Chronicle-Herald*, 15 December 1961, 1. "Canada Backs U.S. Stand on Katanga," *Halifax Chronicle-Herald*, 18 December 1961, 3. "Some UN Actions in the Congo 'Not Very Wise' But Canada Backs Operation – Green," *Halifax Chronicle-Herald*, 19 December 1961, 3. LAC, MG32, B13, vol. 10, file 6, "Item I – Review of the International Situation, The Congo."

32 LAC, RG25, vol. 5214, file 6386-40 part 28, Outgoing Message External to PERMISNY: Congo Advisory Committee, 15 December 1961. LAC, RG25, vol. 5214, file 6386-40 part 29, Memo for Minister: Situation in Katanga, 16 December 1961. LAC, RG25, vol. 5226, file 6386-P-40 part 1, Letter Bullock to Green, 19 December 1961. DCC, file MG1/VI/(845 Congo), Letter E. Tate to Diefenbaker, 15 December 1961; Letter M. Brown to Diefenbaker, 15 December 1961. "The UN in Katanga," *Halifax Chronicle-Herald*, 15 December 1961, 4. "The Struggle in Katanga," *Halifax Chronicle-Herald*, 16 December 1961, 4. "Tragic Events in Katanga," *Halifax Chronicle-Herald*, 22 December 1961, 4. "Critical of UN Actions in Katanga," *Montreal Gazette*, 12 December 1961, 6. "Objects to Use of Canadians in U.N. Force in Congo," *Montreal Gazette*, 14 December 1961, 6. "Savagery in Katanga," *Toronto Daily Star*, 13 December 1961, 4. "Splits Within and Without the Congo," *Montreal Gazette*, 15 December 1961, 6. "Little Force for a Big Job," *Montreal Gazette*, 7 December 1961, 6. "U.N.'s Role in Congo Changes," *Montreal Gazette*, 9 December 1961, 6. "Britain and Katanga," *Globe and Mail*, 8 December 1961, 6. "Dubious U.K. Policy in Congo," *Toronto Daily Star*, 8 December 1961, 6. "Canada Is on the Right Side," *Toronto Daily Star*, 16 December 1961, 6.

33 LAC, RG25, vol. 5224, file 6386-C-40 part 18, Numbered Letter Leopoldville to USSEA: Conduct of UN Troops during December Fighting in Elisabethville, 16 January 1962. United Nations, *The Blue Helmets*, 193. Ralph Bunche, "The United Nations Operation in the Congo," in *From Collective Security to Preventive Diplomacy*, ed. Joel Larus (New York: John Wiley and Sons, 1965), 418. Rikhye, Harbottle, and Egge, *The Thin Blue Line*, 81. Meisler, "Crisis in Katanga," 116.

34 LAC, RG25, vol. 5223, file 6386-C-40 part 17, Letter Harkness to Green, 7 December 1961; Memo UN Div to USSEA: Congo Replacement for A/C Morrison, 13 December 1961; Letter Green to Harkness, 18 December 1961.

35 LAC, RG25, vol. 5223, file 6386-C-40 part 17, Letter Harkness to Green, 20 December 1961. LAC, RG25, vol. 5214, file 6386-40 part 29, Memo UN Div to USSEA: Canadian Military Assistance to the UN in the Congo, 3 January 1962. LAC, RG25, vol. 5224, file 6386-C-40

part 18, Memo SSEA to Ignatieff, Campbell DL (1), European Div and Attached Telegram, 5 January 1962; Memo Robinson to USSEA: Replacement for Air Commodore Morrison, 11 January 1962; Memo for Prime Minister: Congo – Replacement for A/C Morrison as UN Air Commander, 8 January 1962; Memo from Prime Minister to Robinson, 10 January 1962.

36  DCC, file MG1/XII/F/215, Memo to Prime Minister from CCOS: Canadian Assistance to Establish an Officers' Training School in Congo, 27 December 1961; Memo for Prime Minister: Congo – Request for Military Training Assistance, 27 December 1961. LAC, RG2, vol. 6177, Cabinet Conclusions, 28 December 1961.

37  LAC, RG25, vol. 5214, file 6386-40 part 29, Memo UN Div to USSEA: Canadian Military Assistant to the UN in the Congo, 3 January 1962; Memo AMED to Mr. Ignatieff: UN Request for French-speaking Officers, 10 January 1962; Memo Campbell to USSEA: UN Request for Military Advisers and Instructors for the Congo, 26 January 1962. LAC, RG2, vol. 6189, Cabinet Document 39.62, UN Request for Military Advisers and Instructors for the Congo, 23 January 1962; Cabinet Document 35.62, Military Training Assistance to the Congo, 17 January 1962. LAC, RG2, vol. 6192, Cabinet Conclusions, 26 January 1962.

38  United Nations, *The Blue Helmets*, 193. LAC, RG25, vol. 5215, file 6386-40 part 30, Outgoing Message External to PERMISNY: Congo, 20 February 1962. LAC, RG25, vol. 5224, file 6386-C-40 part 18, Telegram PERMISNY to External: Congo, 14 February 1962.

39  LAC, RG25, vol. 5215, file 6386-40 part 30, Memo for Minister: The Situation in the Congo, 2 March 1962; Memo AMED to Ignatieff: Congo: UN Intentions in Katanga, 19 April 1962.

40  LAC, RG25, vol. 5226, file 6386-O-40 part 1, Numbered Letter USSEA to Leopoldville: Communist Block Embassies in Leopoldville, 30 January 1962; Numbered Letter Leopoldville to USSEA: Lunch with Soviet Colleagues, 1 February 1962; Numbered Letter Leopoldville to USSEA: Communist Block Embassies in Leopoldville, 23 February 1962. The two shortest telegrams in the Congo files demonstrated a rare example of Ottawa reciprocating humour. When asked if an official from External Affairs could visit Leopoldville, Gauvin replied "No objections. Mr. Cousineau very welcome. Even more welcome if he could manage to bring two fresh salmons packed in dry ice." When Ottawa asked the UN for permission and the Secretariat nixed the idea, External Affairs wired back, "No Cousineau No Salmon"; LAC, RG25, vol. 5224, file 6386-C-40 part 19, Telegram Leopoldville to External: Visit of Departmental Officer, 15 March 1962; Outgoing Message External to Leopoldville: Visit of Departmental Officer, 15 March 1962.

41  LAC, RG25, vol. 5215, file 6386-40 part 30, Numbered Letter Leopoldville to USSEA: Incident Involving Mr. Bomboko, 9 February 1962.

42  LAC, RG25, vol. 5224, file 6386-C-40 part 18, Outgoing Message External to PERMISNY: Possible Appointment of General Burns as Commander in Chief of ONUC, 5 February 1962; Telegram PERMISNY to External: Following for Minister from Ritchie, 13 February 1962.

43  LAC, RG25, vol. 5224, file 6386-C-40 part 18, Telegram PERMISNY to External: Congo – UN Request for Assistance, 16 February 1962; Memo DL (1) to USSEA: Congo – UN Request for 2 additional Signal Detachments, 19 February 1962. LAC, RG25, vol. 5224, file 6386-C-40 part 19, Letter CCOS to USSEA: Congo – UN Request for 2 additional Signal Detachments, 11 April 1962; Outgoing Message External to PERMISNY: Congo: UN Request for Assistance, 13 April 1962; Memo for Minister: Congo: UN Request for Two Additional Signal Detachments, 31 March 1962. LAC, RG2, vol. 6189, Cabinet Document 106.62, 15 March 1962.

44  LAC, RG25, vol. 5224, file 6386-C-40 part 19, Letter USSEA to CCOS: Congo: UN Request for Assistance, 12 March 1962; Outgoing Message External to PERMISNY: Congo, 8 March 1962; Letter CCOS to USSEA: UN Request for Assistance – Congo, 20 March 1962; Letter USSEA to CCOS: Congo: UN Request for Assistance, 28 March 1962. Walter Dorn and David Bell, "Intelligence and Peacekeeping: The UN Operation in the Congo 1960-1964," in *Peacekeeping 1815 to Today*, ed. Serge Bernier (Ottawa: International Commission of Military History, 1995), 582-83.

45  LAC, RG25, vol. 5224, file 6386-C-40 part 19, Telegram PERMISNY to External: Congo: ONUC Forces Direct External Communications, 5 April 1962; Notes for Mr. A.R. Menzies: ONUC – Direct External Communications, 10 April 1962; Letter A.R. Menzies to W.H. Barton: External Communications with UN Contingents in the Congo, 25 April 1962.

46  LAC, RG24, vol. 7169, file 2-5081-6 part 15, Telegram PERMISNY to External: Provision of Instructors for Congolese Army, 2 February 1962; Telegram External to PERMISNY: Provision of Instructors for Congolese Army, 10 February 1962. LAC, RG25, vol. 5215, file 6386-40 part 30, Memo for Minister: Provision of Officers for the Congolese Army, 3 February 1962; Memo for Minister: Provision of French-speaking Officers to the Congo, 23 February 1962. LAC, RG25, vol. 5226, file 6386-M-40 part 1, Memo: UN Request for Fifteen French-speaking Officers to Train Congolese Army, 5 February 1962. UNA, S-0209-0003-14, ONUC – records on foreign countries, Canada – correspondence, cables, etc., Letter Burns to Bunche, 22 February 1962; Letter Bunche to Burns, 2 March 1962. Canada, House of Commons, *Debates*, 29 January 1962: 304-5.

47  LAC, RG24, vol. 7169, file 2-5081-6 part 15, Telegram Leopoldville to External: Training of Congolese Army, 24 February 1962. LAC, RG25, vol. 5215, file 6386-40 part 30, Telegram Leopoldville to External: Training of Congolese Army, 12 March 1962; Memo AMED to DL (1) Div: Training of Congolese Army, 22 March 1962; Memo DL (1) Div to USSEA: Training of Congolese Army, 23 March 1962. LAC, RG25, vol. 5226, file 6386-N-40 part 1, Memo AMED to DL (1): Provision of Instructors for the Congolese Army, 9 April 1962.

48  LAC, RG25, vol. 5224, file 6386-C-40 part 20, Memo for Minister: Congo – UN Requests for Assistance, 24 August 1962; Letter DL (1) to Gauvin, 6 July 1962; Letter Gauvin to Menzies, 31 August 1962.

49  LAC, RG25, vol. 5224, file 6386-C-40 part 19, Memo AMED to DL (1): Congo – UN Request for Assistance, 8 May 1962; Letter USSEA to CCOS, 9 May 1962; Memo DL (1) to USSEA: Congo – Canadian Participation in Joint Reconciliation Commission, 6 June 1962. LAC, RG25, vol. 5224, file 6386-C-40 part 20, Telegram Leopoldville to External: UN Request for Assistance, 5 July 1962; Telegram Leopoldville to External: UN Request for Assistance, 7 July 1962; Memo for Minister: Congo – UN Requests for Assistance, 12 July 1962; Memo for Minister: Congo – UN Requests for Assistance, 24 August 1962. LAC, RG25, vol. 5215, file 6386-40 part 32, Memo AMED to DL (1) Div: Canadian Role in UN Operations in the Congo, 18 July 1962. LAC, RG24, vol. 7169, file 2-5081-6 part 16, Telegram PERMISNY to External: Congo: UN Request for Assistance, 9 May 1962; Telegram External to PERMISNY: Congo: UN Request for Assistance, 1 June 1962.

50  LAC, RG24, vol. 7169, file 2-5081-6 part 16, Telegram External to PERMISNY: Congo – Extension of RCAF airlift, 4 June 1962. LAC, RG25, vol. 5224, file 6386-C-40 part 20, Letter CCOS to USSEA, 13 July 1962. The monetary exchange crises facing Diefenbaker are addressed by Denis Smith in *Rogue Tory: The Life and Legend of John G. Diefenbaker* (Toronto: Macfarlane Walter and Ross, 1995), 437-39, 442-45.

51  LAC, RG25, vol. 5224, file 6386-C-40 part 20, Memo for Minister: Canadian Airlift to the Congo, 17 July 1962.

52  DHH, file 73/1223, part 463, Note CCOS to Chief of the Air Staff, July 1962; Letter USSEA to CCOS, 20 July 1962. LAC, RG25, vol. 5224, file 6386-C-40 part 20, Memo DL (1) to Ross Campbell: Provision of RCAF Air Transport for UN Operations, 15 August 1962; Memo for Prime Minister: Canadian Airlift to Congo, 16 August 1962; Outgoing Message External to PERMISNY: Congo – RCAF Airlift, 17 August 1962; Memo SSEA to Ross Campbell: Canadian Airlift to the Congo, 1 September 1962.

53  LAC, RG25, vol. 5226, file 6386-J-40 part 1, Memo for Minister: Establishment of Diplomatic Relations with the Congo (Leo), 4 June 1962; Numbered Letter Leopoldville to USSEA: Presentation of Letter of Introduction, 13 July 1962.

54  *FRUS, 1961-1963*, vol. 20, doc. 241, Message from Prime Minister Macmillan to President Kennedy. LAC, RG25, vol. 5215, file 6386-40 part 32, Memo for Minister: The Congo, 27 July 1962. James, *Britain and the Congo Crisis*, 172-76.

55  LAC, RG25, vol. 5215, file 6386-40 part 32, Outgoing Message External to PERMISNY: Congo – Use of Force in Katanga, 19 July 1962; Memo for Minister: The Congo, 11 July 1962; Outgoing Message External to PERMISNY: Congo Advisory Committee Meeting, 28 July 1962; Minutes of Advisory Committee on Congo, 31 July 1962. The Americans believed the views of India, Ireland, Nigeria, Ethiopia, and Malaya expressed during the 31 July meeting of the Advisory Committee would be the most important to consider. *FRUS, 1961-1963*, vol. 20, doc. 267, Record of Understanding.

56  LAC, RG25, vol. 5215, file 6386-40 part 32, Memo for Minister: Plan for National Reconciliation in the Congo, 15 August 1962; Memo: British Policy in the Congo, 13 August 1962; Memo for AMED: Congo, 14 August 1962; Memo for Minister: Plan for National Reconciliation in the Congo, 15 August 1962. See also James, *Britain and the Congo Crisis,* 181-83.

57  LAC, RG25, vol. 5215, file 6386-40 part 32, Memo for AMED: Congo, 14 August 1962; Memo: The Congo, 24 August 1962. LAC, RG25, vol. 5216, file 6386-40 part 34, Memo for Minister: Possible Question in the House on the Congo, 8 November 1962. LAC, RG24, vol. 7169, file 2-5081-6 part 16, Telegram PERMISNY to External: Plan for National Reconciliation, 17 August 1962; Telegram Leopoldville to External: Interview with Gardiner, 30 August 1962. Peyton Lyon, *Canada in World Affairs, 1961-1963* (Toronto: Canadian Institute of International Affairs, 1968), 323, 324.

58  See James, *Britain and the Congo Crisis,* 171. James suggests, "Coming out against the United States' anti-Katangan line would also have deeply offended the Commonwealth's Afro-Asian members, and of the older, white, members, Canada would certainly have been upset." As seen here, evidence suggests Canada initially shared some of the British concerns about sanctions, but support for the United Nations became a paramount consideration. By January 1963, the African and Middle Eastern Division was already rewriting history in a memo that suggested Canada had fully supported the U Thant Plan. LAC, MG32, B13, vol. 9, Memo AMED to SSEA: External Affairs Debate – Congo, 23 January 1963.

59  LAC, RG24, vol. 7169, file 2-5081-6 part 17, Telegram Leopoldville to External: Implementation of UN Plan, 5 October 1962. LAC, RG25, vol. 5216, file 6386-40 part 33, Memo: The Congo Situation, 27 September 1962.

60  LAC, RG25, vol. 5216, file 6386-40 part 34, Memo for the Minister: The Congo, 19 October 1962; Memo for the Prime Minister: The Congo, 19 October 1962; Memo from SSEA: The Congo, 23 October 1962; Memo to the Cabinet: The Situation in the Congo, 25 October 1962; Outgoing Message External to PERMISNY: Congo Advisory Committee, 6 November 1962. LAC, RG2, vol. 6193, Cabinet Conclusions, 30 October 1962.

61  LAC, RG25, vol. 5216, file 6386-40 part 35, Memo for Minister: The Congo: Possible Question in the House, 29 November 1962; Memo for Minister: The Congo, 17 December 1962. Canada, House of Commons, *Debates,* 12 December 1962: 2580-81.

62  DCC, file MG1/XII/C/291, Notes: Bahamas Meetings – December 21-22, 1962: Specific Points Discussed with President Kennedy at Luncheon Meeting, 21 December 1962. LAC, RG25, vol. 5216, file 6386-40 part 35, Memo for Minister: British Policy on the Congo, 28 December 1962. *FRUS, 1961-1963,* vol. 20, doc. 372, Memorandum of Conversation; doc. 378, Memorandum of Conversation. James, *Britain and the Congo Crisis,* 189.

63  LAC, RG24, vol. 7169, file 2-5081-6 part 17, Telegram PERMISNY to External: Congo Operations – Code Intercept, 5 November 1962. LAC, RG24, vol. 21487, file 2137.3 part 9, Telegram PERMISNY to External: Congo: Standby Signals Detachments, 12 November 1962. LAC, RG25, vol. 5225, file 6386-D-40 part 2, Memo AMED to Economic Div: Possible Supply of NAPALM Bombs to ONUC, 16 November 1962. *FRUS, 1961-1963,* vol. 20, doc. 327, Memorandum from the Undersecretary of State for Political Affairs (McGhee) to the President's Deputy Special Assistant for National Security Affairs (Kaysen).

64  LAC, RG25, vol. 5224, file 6386-C-40 part 21, Letter USSEA to CCOS: Congo – Employment of Personnel from Canadian Contingent, 19 October 1962. LAC, RG25, vol. 5216, file 6386-40 part 34, Memo DL (1) Div to AMED: Congo: Employment of Canadian Contingent, 16 October 1962. DHH, file 112.3M2.003 (D15), Report P.S. Cooper to VCGS: Congo – Canadian Officers at HQ ONUC, 23 October 1962. LAC, RG24, vol. 21487, file 2137.3 part 9, Letter Raymont to SO/Admin: UN Requests and Review of Congo Establishment Canadian Officers, HQ ONUC, 7 December 1962; Numbered Letter USSEA to PERMISNY: Canadian Contingent – ONUC, 9 January 1963.

65  LAC, RG25, vol. 5224, file 6386-C-40 part 19, Letter CCOS to USSEA: UN Request for Assistance – Congo, 20 March 1962. LAC, RG24, vol. 21487, file 2137.3 part 9, Letter CGS to CCOS: Military Assistant to Chief of Staff ONUC, 4 January 1963. LAC, RG25, vol. 5224, file 6386-C-40 part 21, Memo DL (1) to USSEA: Congo: UN Requests for Assistance, 14 December 1962; Letter CCOS to USSEA, 4 January 1963; Memo for Minister: Congo: UN Requests for Assistance, 7 January 1963.

66  Urquhart, *Ralph Bunche*, 356-57. Bunche, "The United Nations Operation in the Congo," 419. LAC, RG24, vol. 7169, file 2-5081-6 part 17, Telegram Leopoldville to External: The Third Round Has Started, 29 December 1962. The repatriation of Indian troops became necessary when hostilities broke out on the Chinese-Indian border. Gauvin's impression that this was a significant factor in the UN's decision to engage the gendarmerie is shared by several scholars. See Durch, *The Evolution of UN Peacekeeping*, 344; Alan James, *The Politics of Peacekeeping* (London: Chatto and Windus, 1969), 420; Francis Parakatil, *India and United Nations Peacekeeping* (New Delhi: S. Chand, 1975), 124.

67  DCC, file MG1/VI/8858.A (845 Congo), Memo for Mr. Dier and Attached Letters Amory to Robertson and Home to Green, 2 January 1963. LAC, RG25, vol. 5216, file 6386-40 part 36, Memo for USSEA: Congo, 2 January 1963; Memo for Prime Minister: Congo, 3 January 1963. LAC, RG24, vol. 7169, file 2-5081-6 part 17, Telegram Leopoldville to External: Third Round Phase Two – Hawks Versus Doves, 3 January 1963. Urquhart, *Ralph Bunche*, 357. Harlan Cleveland, "The UN in the Congo: Three Questions," in *Footnotes to the Congo Story*, ed. Helen Kitchen (New York: Walker and Company, 1967), 69.

68  This controversy specifically, and the implications of ONUC's actions for Katangan secession more generally, are addressed by a number of authors. See Mona Gagnon, "Peace Forces and the Veto: The Relevance of Consent," *International Organization* 21, 4 (Autumn 1967): 828-35; James, *The Politics of Peacekeeping*, 421; Goronwy J. Jones, *The United Nations and the Domestic Jurisdiction of States* (Cardiff: University of Wales Press / Welsh Centre for International Affairs, 1979), 140; Brian Urquhart, "United Nations Peace Forces and the Changing United Nations: An Institutional Perspective," *International Organization* 17 (1963): 349. Urquhart, *Ralph Bunche*, 359. UNA, S-0370-0003-09, UN Undersecretary-General for Special Political Affairs (1958-72: Bunche), Congo, Letter Sherry to Bunche, 8 January 1963.

69  LAC, RG25, vol. 5224, file 6386-C-40 part 21, Memo DL (1) to Bow: Canadian Armed Forces in Katanga, 10 January 1963. A.E. King, "UN Commander Honours Canadian Signal Unit in Congo," *Canadian Army Journal* 17, 1 (1963): 93.

70  LAC, RG25, vol. 5216, file 6386-40 part 36, Memo DL (1) to Ross Campbell: UN Action in Katanga, 8 January 1963; Memo UN Div to Ross Campbell: United Nations Action in Katanga, 9 January 1963; Memo AMED to Ross Campbell: United Nations Action in Katanga, 11 January 1963. *FRUS, 1961-1963*, vol. 20, doc. 402, Telegram from Embassy in the Congo to Department of State. Murray's views on the legitimacy of the UN's actions in the Congo were repeated elsewhere. See G.S. Murray, "United Nations Peace-Keeping and Problems of Political Control," *International Journal* 18, 4 (Autumn 1963): 454.

### Chapter 7: Preparing for Withdrawal

1  Ernest Lefever, "US Policy, the UN and the Congo," *Orbis* 11, 2 (1967): 407. Weissman bluntly suggests the Greene plan was a UN "cover" for Western military aid. Stephen R. Weissman, *American Foreign Policy in the Congo 1960-1964* (Ithaca, NY: Cornell University Press, 1974), 213.

2  LAC, RG24, vol. 21487, file 2137.3 part 9, Telegram Leopoldville to External: Mobutu's visit and Request, 23 November 1962; Letter Administration to Coordinator Joint Staff: Congolese Armed Forces: Re-organization and Retraining, 23 November 1962; Letter CCOS to USSEA, 28 November 1962. LAC, RG25, vol. 5226, file 6386-M-40 part 2, Memo to Minister: Congo – Requests for Military Training Assistance, 5 December 1962. *FRUS, 1961-1963*, vol. 20, doc. 415, Memorandum from Secretary of State Rusk to President Kennedy.

3  LAC, RG25, vol. 5216, file 6386-40 part 36, Memo UN Div to DL (1) Div: Congo: ANC Retraining and Re-organization, 25 January 1963. LAC, RG24, vol. 7169, file 2-5081-6 part 18, Telegram External to PERMISNY: Congo: ANC Retraining and Reorganization Scheme, 1 February 1963.

4  LAC, RG24, vol. 7169, file 2-5081-6 part 18, Telegram PERMISNY to External: Congo Advisory Cttee 73rd Meeting March 20, 21 March 1963. LAC, RG25, vol. 5224, file 6386-C-40 part 22, Minutes Congo Advisory Cttee, 1 March 1963. LAC, RG25, vol. 5217, file 6386-40 part 37, Memo for Minister: Training the Congolese Armed Forces, 8 April 1963. *FRUS, 1961-1963*, vol. 20, doc. 421, Information Memorandum from Assistant Secretary of State for African Affairs (Williams) to Secretary of State Rusk.

5  LAC, RG24, vol. 21487, file 2137.3 part 10, Telegram PERMISNY to External: Congo: ANC Retraining Plan, 28 March 1963. LAC, RG25, vol. 5217, file 6386-40 part 37, Memo AMED to Ross Campbell: Congo: ANC training, 28 March 1963. LAC, RG25, vol. 5224, file 6386-C-40 part 22, Telegram PERMISNY to External: Congo: ANC Retraining Scheme, 4 April 1963.

6  LAC, RG24, vol. 21487, file 2137.3 part 10, Telegram External to PERMISNY: Congo: ANC Training, 15 April 1963. LAC, RG25, vol. 5217, file 6386-40 part 37, Telegram PERMISNY to External: Congo Advisory Cttee Meeting, 24 April 1963. LAC, RG25, vol. 5217, file 6386-40 part 38, Memo: Prime Minister's Visit to London May 1-4, 1963, 29 April 1963. LAC, RG24, vol. 7169, file 2-5081-6 part 18, Telegram Leopoldville to External: ANC, 5 May 1963. United Nations, *Yearbook of the United Nations 1963* (New York: Office of Public Information, United Nations, 1963), 4-5.

7  Rosalyn Higgins, *United Nations Peacekeeping, 1946-1967: Documents and Commentary*, vol. 3 (Oxford: Oxford University Press, 1980), 361. Joshua asserts, "At no time did the Secretary-General object to Belgium's bilateral arms aid. In fact, in private conversations he indicated his approval." Wynfred Joshua, "Belgium's Role in the UN Peace-keeping Operation in the Congo," *Orbis* 11, 2 (1967): 436.

8  LAC, RG25, vol. 5217, file 6386-40 part 38, Memo for Minister: Request for Canadian Assistance in Training the Congolese Army, 8 May 1963; Memo SSEA to AMED: Training the Congolese Army Request for Canadian Assistance, 10 May 1963. LAC, RG25, vol. 5226, file 6386-N-40 part 1, Letter SSEA to MDND: Request for Assistance in Training the Congolese Army, 16 May 1963. LAC, RG24, vol. 21487, file 2137.3 part 11, Letter CGS to CCOS: Congo – Provision of Training Coordinator, 22 May 1963.

9  LAC, RG25, vol. 5224, file 6386-C-40 part 22, Telegram WASHDC to External: Congo: ANC Retraining Scheme, 5 June 1963. LAC, RG24, vol. 21487, file 2137.3 part 11, Telegram Brussels to External: ANC Training, 19 June 1963; Telegram Brussels to External: Congo: ANC Training, 27 June 1963; Telegram Leopoldville to External: ANC Training, 2 July 1963. *FRUS, 1961-1963*, vol. 20, doc. 423, Memorandum of Conversation. Gary Harman, interview with author, Ottawa, 31 July 2003.

10 LAC, RG24, vol. 21487, file 2137.3 part 11, Telegram External to Brussels: Congo: ANC Training, 25 June 1963; Letter CGS to CCOS: Congo: Assistance in Training the ANC, 8 July 1963; Memo: Congo: Assistance in Training the ANC, 30 July 1963. LAC, RG25, vol. 5226, file 6386-N-40 part 1, Telegram WASHDC to External: Congo: ANC Retraining Scheme, 11 July 1963; Memo to Minister: Congo: Request for Canadian Assistance in Training the Armed Forces, 23 July 1963. LAC, RG25, vol. 5217, file 6386-40 part 38, Memo A.D. Rowe to Hicks: Congo: ANC Training, 27 August 1963. *FRUS, 1961-1963*, vol. 20, doc. 424, Memorandum from the Acting Department of State Executive Secretary (McKesson) to the President's Special Assistant for National Security Affairs (Bundy).

11 DHH, file 73/1223 part 1081, Letter Martin to Hellyer: Canadian Assistance in Training the Congolese Armed Forces, 31 October 1963; Letter CCOS to CGS: Canadian Assistance in Training of Congolese Armed Forces, 5 November 1963. LAC, RG24, vol. 21487, file 2137.3 part 12, Letter Hellyer to Martin, 6 November 1963; Telegram External to Leopoldville: Request for Canadian Participation in ANC Training, 25 November 1963; Telegram Brussels to External: Request for Canadian Participation ANC Training, 28 November 1963; Telegram WASHDC to External: Congo: ANC Retraining, 29 November 1963. LAC, RG25, vol. 10648, file 21-14-6-ONUC-5 part 1, Letter W.M. Wood to Collins: Congo: ANC Training, 15 October 1963. *FRUS, 1961-1963*, vol. 20, doc. 430, Memorandum of Conversation.

12 LAC, RG25, vol. 5224, file 6386-C-40 part 21, Letter USSEA to CCOS: UN Request for Assistance, 18 January 1963; Memo DL (1) Div to Ross Campbell: Congo: UN Request for Assistance, 6 February 1963; Letter CCOS to USSEA: Congo – UN Request for Assistance, 12 February 1963; Letter CCOS to USSEA: Congo – UN Request for Assistance, 12 February 1963; Telegram PERMISNY to External: Congo: UN Request for Assistance, 27 February 1963. LAC, RG25, vol. 5224, file 6386-C-40 part 22, Outgoing Message External to PERMISNY: Congo Ops, 23 March 1963; Memo DL (1) to USSEA: Congo Ops, 29 March 1963; Letter CCOS to USSEA: Standby Signal Detachments for Congo, 31 May 1963. LAC, RG24, vol. 21487, file 2137.3

part 10, Memo Prepared by DMOP: Congo: Notes for Meeting 5 March 1963, 1 March 1963; Letter Vice-Admiral Rayner to CCOS: Congo: U.N. Request for Assistance, 6 March 1963; Letter CCOS to USSEA: UN Request for Assistance – Congo, 22 March 1963.

13 LAC, RG25, vol. 5224, file 6386-C-40 part 21, Letter Col. Moore (PERMISNY) to Colonel Parker [DMOP, DND HQ], 21 January 1963; Letter Moore to Parker, 23 January 1963. LAC, RG25, vol. 5224, file 6386-C-40 part 22, Letter Purves to USSEA: UN Request for Assistance – Congo; Helicopter Pilots and Ground Crew, 7 March 1963; Telegram PERMISNY to External: Congo: Reduction of UN Forces, 17 April 1963; Telegram PERMISNY to External: Congo: Reduction of UN Forces, 6 May 1963; Telegram PERMISNY to External: Congo: Reduction UN Forces, 17 July 1963. LAC, RG24, vol. 21487, file 2137.3 part 11, Letter CCOS to MDND: Standby Signal Detachment for the Congo, 23 May 1963. LAC, RG24, vol. 7169, file 2-5081-6 part 18, Telegram PERMISNY to External: Military Planning Congo Operation, 31 January 1963. LAC, RG25, vol. 5217, file 6386-40 part 37, Memo DL (1) to File: Congo: ANC Training and Re-organization Scheme, 7 March 1963. LAC, RG25, vol. 21487, file 2137.3 part 12, Letter Walsh to CCOS: Future Establishment 57 Canadian Signal Unit ONUC, 28 October 1963.

14 LAC, RG24, vol. 21487, file 2137.3 part 11, Telegram External to PERMISNY: Congo: Withdrawal of ONUC, 9 August 1963. LAC, RG25, vol. 5217, file 6386-40 part 38, Memo SSEA to AMED: United Nations Military Force in the Congo, 31 August 1963; Memo for Minister: Withdrawal of ONUC, 13 August 1963.

15 General Assembly Resolution 1885 (XVIII). *In favour:* Afghanistan, Algeria, Australia, Austria, Belgium, Burundi, Cambodia, Cameroon, Canada, Central African Republic, Ceylon, Chad, Chile, China, Congo (Brazzaville), Congo (Leopoldville), Costa Rica, Cyprus, Dahomey, Denmark, Dominican Republic, Ecuador, El Salvador, Ethiopia, Finland, Gabon, Ghana, Greece, Guatemala, Guinea, Honduras, Iceland, India, Indonesia, Iran, Ireland, Israel, Italy, Ivory Coast, Jamaica, Japan, Laos, Lebanon, Liberia, Libya, Luxembourg, Malaysia, Mauritania, Mexico, Nepal, Netherlands, New Zealand, Nicaragua, Niger, Nigeria, Norway, Pakistan, Philippines, Rwanda, Senegal, Sierra Leone, Somalia, Sudan, Sweden, Tanganyika, Thailand, Togo, Trinidad and Tobago, Tunisia, Turkey, Uganda, United Kingdom, United States, Upper Volta, Uruguay, Venezuela; *against:* Albania, Bulgaria, Byelorussian SSR, Cuba, Czechoslovakia, Hungary, Mongolia, Poland, Romania, Ukrainian SSR, Union of Soviet Socialist Republics; *abstentions:* Argentina, Brazil, Burma, Colombia, France, Iraq, Jordan, Kuwait, Madagascar, Mali, Panama, Paraguay, Peru, Portugal, Saudi Arabia, Spain, Syria, United Arab Republic, Yemen, Yugoslavia.

16 LAC, RG24, vol. 21487, file 2137.3, part 11, Telegram PERMISNY to External: Congo: Withdrawal of ONUC, 27 August 1963; Telegram PERMISNY to External: Withdrawal of ONUC, 10 September 1963; Letter Martin to Hellyer, 31 October 1963. LAC, RG25, vol. 5217, file 6386-40 part 38, Letter Hellyer to Martin, 31 August 1963. DHH, file 73/1223 part 1081, Letter CCOS to MDND, 29 August 1963. United Nations, *Yearbook of the United Nations 1964* (New York: Office of Public Information, United Nations, 1964), 6, 578.

17 LAC, RG25, vol. 10648, file 21-14-6-ONUC-5 part 1, Telegram PERMISNY to External: ONUC – Request for Assistance Air Commander, 6 November 1963; Letter CCOS to USSEA: ONUC – Air Commander, 6 December 1963; Letter Menzies to Hicks, 13 December 1963; Memo DL (1) Div to Ross Campbell: Notes for Briefing of Brigadier Dextraze, 27 November 1963. LAC, RG24, vol. 21487, file 2137.3 part 11, Letter CGS to CCOS: Provision of a Brigadier as Chief of Staff to ONUC, 18 October 1963; Letter CCOS to Minister, 22 October 1963. DHH, file 73/1223 part 1081, Letter USSEA to CCOS, 8 October 1963; Letter CCOS to USSEA, 25 October 1963.

18 LAC, RG24, vol. 21487, file 2137.3 part 12, Numbered Letter Leopoldville to USSEA: United Nations Forces Commander in the Congo, 3 January 1964. DHH, file 112.1.003 (D21), vol. 3, Letter Dextraze to CGS, 2 June 1964; Telegram Osorio Tafall to Secretary-General and Ralph Bunche, 2 June 1964. LAC, RG24, vol. 7169, file 2-5081-6 part 19, Numbered Letter Leopoldville to USSEA: Staff Relations – ONUC, 21 February 1964.

19 DHH, file 144.9.009 (D57), PRO: United Nations Force Commander Honours Canadian Signal Unit in Congo, 10 April 1963.

20  LAC, RG25, vol. 10646, file 21-14-6-ONUC-2, Letter and Attached from Secretary-General, 12 February 1964. DHH, file 144.9.009 (D65), Recommendation for Award in Peacetime: Joseph Lessard, 27 February 1964; Recommendation for Award in Peacetime: Paul Mayer, 27 February 1964; Recommendation for Award in Peacetime: J. Dextraze, 27 February 1964. For a complete, detailed account of the rescue operations see DHH, file 144.9.009 (D38), Operation Jadex One, A Chronological Account of the Rescue Operations in Kwilu Province (24 January to 3 February 1964), 25 February 1964.

21  DHH, file 144.9.009 (D49), Telegram 57th to CANARMY, 1 January 1964. LAC, RG24, vol. 21487, file 2137.3 part 12, Telegram PERMISNY to External: Congo – Continuation of UNOC, 6 February 1964; Letter USSEA to CCOS: UN Congo Operations – Preparation for Withdrawal, 16 March 1964.

22  LAC, RG24, vol. 21487, file 2137.3 part 12, Telegram External to PERMISNY: ONUC – Canadian Signals and Nigerian Police Force, 27 April 1964; Letter CGS to CCOS: ONUC Repatriation, 21 May 1964; Letter CGS to CCOS: Request for Employment Lt. Col. P.A. Mayer: Special Duties – Congo, 23 June 1964; Telegram PERMISNY to External: ONUC – Message from the Secretary-General to the Government of Canada, 2 July 1964. LAC, RG24, vol. 18488, War Diary – No. 57 Canadian Signal Squadron, Diary Entry, June 1964. CCEM, box 137, Directorate of Public Relations Press Release, 30 June 1964.

23  Howard Green, "Perilous Times in the Congo," *Victoria Colonist*, 26 June 1964, 44.

### Conclusion

1  Senate of Canada, Standing Committee on Foreign Affairs, *Meeting New Challenges: Canada's Response to a New Generation of Peacekeeping* (Ottawa: Government of Canada, 1993).

2  Canada's World, "The Canada's World Poll, 2008," 31, http://www.igloo.org/canadasworld.

3  J.L. Granatstein and Sean Maloney are the two most vocal proponents of this view. See J.L. Granatstein, *Whose War Is It? How Canada Can Survive in the Post-9/11 World* (Toronto: HarperCollins, 2007); Sean Maloney, "From Myth to Reality Check; From Peacekeeping to Stabilization," *Policy Options* 26, 7 (September 2005): 40-46.

4  J.L. Granatstein, "Canada and Peacekeeping: Image and Reality," *The Canadian Forum* 54, 263 (1974): 14-19.

5  Norman Hillmer and J.L. Granatstein, *Empire to Umpire: Canada and the World to the 1990s* (Toronto: Copp Clark Longman, 1994), 350.

6  See Sean Maloney, "The Horror! The Horror! Canada and UN Operations in the Congo, 1960-1963," in *Canada and UN Peacekeeping: Cold War by Other Means, 1945-1970* (St. Catharines, ON: Vanwell, 2002).

7  LAC, RG25, vol. 5213, file 6386-40 part 23, Memo: Congo, 9 June 1961.

8  As quoted in Peyton Lyon, *Canada in World Affairs, 1961-1963* (Toronto: Canadian Institute of International Affairs, 1968), 325.

9  Tom Keating, *Canada and World Order: The Multilateralist Tradition in Canadian Foreign Policy* (Toronto: McClelland and Stewart, 1993), 18.

10  James Eayrs, "Military Policy and Middle-Power," in *Canada's Role as a Middle Power*, ed. J. King Gordon (Toronto: Canadian Institute of International Affairs, 1966), 81.

# Bibliography

**Primary Sources**

Archives

*Canadian Communications and Electronics Museum, CFB Kingston*
Files

*Diefenbaker Canada Centre, University of Saskatchewan, Saskatoon*
John G. Diefenbaker papers

*Directorate of History and Heritage, Department of National Defence Headquarters, Ottawa*
Files and historical reports

*Dwight D. Eisenhower Library, Abilene, Kansas*
Christian A. Herter Papers

*Library and Archives Canada, Ottawa*
*Government Archives Division*
 Cabinet (RG2)
 Secretary of State (RG6)
 Justice (RG13)
 Finance (RG19)
 Trade and Commerce (RG20)
 Department of National Defence (RG24)
 Department of Foreign Affairs (RG25)
 Auditor General (RG58)
*Manuscript Division*
 J. King Gordon
 Howard Green
 Douglas Harkness
 Lester Pearson
 Norman Robertson
 H. Basil Robinson

*National Archives and Records Administration, United States*
General Records of the Department of State

*United Nations Archives, New York*
Files

**Interviews, Correspondence, and Private Papers**
William Barton
Ivan Burch
Bill Carr
Lloyd Carr
E. Foubert
Brian Hanly
Gary Harman
Ian Hetman
Geoffrey Murray
Wally Pokotylo
H. Basil Robinson
Ken Smith
Bob Terry
Edward Thornhill
Thomas White

**Newspapers and Periodicals, 1960-64**
*Canadian Army Journal*
*Canadian Business*
*Canadian Commentator*
*The Canadian Forum*
*Canadian Labour*
*The Chronicle-Herald* (Halifax)
*Commercial Intelligence Journal*
*Le Devoir*
*External Affairs*
*The Financial Post*
*Foreign Trade*
*The Globe and Mail*
*Maclean's*
*The Montreal Gazette*
*Saturday Night*
*Toronto Daily Star*
*Victoria Colonist*
*Winnipeg Free Press*

**Other Sources**
Abi-Saab, Georges. *The United Nations Operation in the Congo 1960-1964.* Oxford: Oxford University Press, 1978.
Akenson, Donald Harman. *Conor: A Biography of Conor Cruise O'Brien.* Montreal and Kingston: McGill-Queen's University Press, 1994.
Alexander, H.T. *African Tightrope.* London: Pall Mall Press, 1965.
Anglin, Douglas G. "Towards a Canadian Policy on Africa." *International Journal* 15, 4 (Autumn 1960): 290-310.
Armstrong, Hamilton Fish. "U.N. on Trial." *Foreign Affairs* 39, 3 (1961): 388-415.
Balsara, Nilufer. "Paying for Peace: Canada, the United Nations and the Financing of the Congo Peacekeeping Mission, 1960-1964." PhD diss., University of Toronto, 1999.
Barton, William H. *Who Will Pay for Peace? The U.N. Crisis.* Behind the Headlines Series 24, 5. Toronto: Canadian Institute of International Affairs, 1965.
Beauregard, J.P.R.E. "UN Operations in the Congo, 1960-1964." *Canadian Defence Quarterly* (August 1989): 27.
Benton, Barbara, ed. *Soldiers for Peace: Fifty Years of United Nations Peacekeeping.* New York: Facts on File, 1996.
Bernier, Serge, ed. *Peacekeeping 1815 to Today.* Ottawa: International Commission of Military History, 1995.

Bishop, Peter V. "Canada's Policy on the Financing of U.N. Peace-keeping Operations." *International Journal* 20, 4 (Autumn 1965): 463-83.

Bloomfield, Lincoln P. "Conflict Resolution: UN Nonfighting Forces." *Naval War College Review* 20, 9 (April 1968): 17-25.

–. "Headquarters Field Relations: Some Notes on the Beginning and End of ONUC." *International Organization* 17 (1963): 376-89.

–. "International Force in a Disarming – but Revolutionary – World." *International Organization* 17 (1963): 444-64.

–, ed. *International Military Forces: The Question of Peacekeeping in an Armed and Disarming World*. Boston: Little, Brown, 1964.

Boulden, Jane. *The United Nations and Mandate Enforcement: Congo, Somalia, and Bosnia*. Kingston: Centre for International Relations, Queen's University / Institut Québécois des Hautes Études Internationales, Université Laval, 1999.

Bowett, D.W. *United Nations Forces*. London: Stevens and Sons, 1964.

–. "United Nations Peacekeeping." *International Relations (London)* 3, 10 (November 1970): 756-65, 815.

Bowman, Edward H., and James E. Fanning. "The Logistics Problems of a UN Military Force." *International Organization* 17 (1963): 355-76.

Buchan, Alastair. "Concepts of Peacekeeping." In *Freedom and Change: Essays in Honour of L.B. Pearson*, edited by M.G. Fry, 16-25. Toronto: McClelland and Stewart, 1975.

Bunche, Ralph. "The United Nations Operation in the Congo." In *From Collective Security to Preventive Diplomacy*, edited by Joel Larus, 409-23. New York: John Wiley and Sons, 1965.

Burns, Arthur Lee, and Nina Heathcote. *Peacekeeping by U.N. Forces*. London: Pall Mall Press, 1963.

Calvocoressi, Peter. *World Order and New States*. London: Chatto and Windus, 1962.

Canada. House of Commons. *Debates*. 1960-1964.

–. Standing Committee on National Defence and Veterans Affairs. *The Dilemmas of a Committed Peacekeeper: Canada and the Renewal of Peacekeeping*. 1993.

Canada. Senate. *Debates*. 1960-1964.

–. Standing Committee on Foreign Affairs. *Meeting New Challenges, Canada's Response to a New Generation of Peacekeeping: Report of the Standing Committee on Foreign Affairs*. 1993.

Canada's World. "The Canada's World Poll, 2008." http://www.igloo.org/canadasworld (accessed 28 October 2008).

Citrin, Jack. *UN Peacekeeping Activities: A Case Study in Organizational Task Expansion*. Monograph Series in World Affairs 3.1. Denver: University of Denver, 1965-66.

Claude, Inis L. "The United Nations and the Use of Force." *International Conciliation* 532 (March 1961): 325-84.

–. "United Nations' Use of Military Force." *Journal of Conflict Resolution* 7, 2 (June 1963): 117-29.

Cleveland, Harlan. "The UN in the Congo: Three Questions." In *Footnotes to the Congo Story*, edited by Helen Kitchen, 69-76. New York: Walker and Company, 1967.

Collins, Carole. "The Cold War Comes to Africa: Cordier and the 1960 Congo Crisis." *Journal of International Affairs* 47, 1 (1993): 243-69.

–. "Fatally Flawed Mediation: Cordier and the Congo Crisis of 1960." *Africa Today* 39, 3 (1992): 5-22.

Cordier, Andrew W., and Wilder Foote, eds. *Dag Hammarskjöld, 1958-1960*. Vol. 4 of *Public Papers of the Secretary-General of the United Nations*. New York: Columbia University Press, 1974.

–, eds. *Dag Hammarskjöld, 1960-1961*. Vol. 5 of *Public Papers of the Secretary-General of the United Nations*. New York: Columbia University Press, 1975.

Cordier, Andrew W., and Max Harrelson, eds. *U Thant, 1961-1964*. Vol. 6 of *Public Papers of the Secretary-General of the United Nations*. New York: Columbia University Press, 1976.

Dayal, Rajeshwar. *Mission for Hammarskjold: The Congo Crisis*. Princeton, NJ: Princeton University Press, 1976.

De Witte, Ludo. *The Assassination of Lumumba*. Translated by Ann Wright and Renée Fenby. London and New York: Verso, 2001.

Devlin, Lawrence. *Chief of Station, Congo: A Memoir of 1960-67.* New York: Public Affairs, 2007.

Dicks, H.V. "National Loyalty, Identity and the International Soldier." *International Organization* 17 (Spring 1963): 425-43.

Diefenbaker, John G. *One Canada.* 3 vols. Toronto: Macmillan, 1975, 1976, 1977.

Diehl, Paul F. *International Peacekeeping.* Baltimore: Johns Hopkins University Press, 1994.

Dorn, A. Walter, and David F.H. Bell. "Intelligence and Peacekeeping: The UN Operation in the Congo 1960-1964." In *Peacekeeping 1815 to Today,* edited by Serge Bernier, 579-91. Ottawa: International Commission of Military History, 1995.

Durch, William J., ed. *The Evolution of UN Peacekeeping: Case Studies and Comparative Analysis.* New York: St. Martin's Press, 1993.

Eayrs, James. "Canadian Policy and Opinion during the Suez Crisis." *International Journal* 12 (Spring 1957): 97-108.

–. "Military Policy and Middle Power: The Canadian Experience." In *Canada's Role as a Middle Power,* edited by J. King Gordon, 67-86. Toronto: Canadian Institute of International Affairs, 1966.

Eisenhower, Dwight D. *Waging Peace, 1956-1961.* New York: Doubleday, 1965.

English, John. *The Worldly Years: The Life of Lester Pearson, 1949-1972.* Toronto: Vintage Books, 1992.

English, John, and Norman Hillmer, eds. *Making a Difference? Canada's Foreign Policy in a Changing World Order.* Toronto: Lester Publishing, 1992.

Fairclough, Ellen. *Saturday's Child: Memoirs of Canada's First Female Cabinet Minister.* Toronto: University of Toronto Press, 1995.

Falk, Richard A., and Saul H. Mendlovitz, eds. *The Strategy of World Order.* Vol. 3. New York: World Law Fund, 1966.

Findlay, Trevor. *The Blue Helmets' First War? Use of Force by the UN in the Congo, 1960-1964.* Clementsport, NS: Canadian Peacekeeping Press, 1999.

Franck, Thomas M. "United Nations Law in Africa: The Congo Operation as a Case Study." *Law and Contemporary Problems* 27 (Autumn 1962): 632-52.

Franck, Thomas M., and John Carey. *The Legal Aspects of the United Nations Action in the Congo,* edited by Lyman M. Tondel Jr. Dobbs Ferry, NY: Oceana Publications / Association of the Bar of the City of New York, 1963.

Gaffen, Fred. *In the Eye of the Storm: A History of Canadian Peacekeeping.* Toronto: Deneau and Wayne, 1987.

Gagnon, Mona H. "Peace Forces and the Veto: The Relevance of Consent." *International Organization* 21, 4 (Autumn 1967): 812-36.

Gardam, John. *The Canadian Peacekeeper.* Burnstown, ON: General Store Publishing House, 1992.

Gibbs, David N. "Dag Hammarskjöld, the United Nations, and the Congo Crisis of 1960-1: A Reinterpretation." *Journal of Modern African Studies* 31, 1 (1993): 163-74.

–. *The Political Economy of Third World Intervention.* Chicago: University of Chicago Press, 1991.

–. "Secrecy and International Relations." *Journal of Peace Research* 32 (May 1995): 213-28.

Goldblatt, Murray. "The Long Frustrating Quest for a Peacekeeping Formula." *International Perspectives* (July/August 1972): 13-18.

Gordenker, Leon. *The UN Secretary-General and the Maintenance of Peace.* New York: Columbia University Press, 1967.

Gordon, Donald. "Canada as Peace-keeper." In *Canada's Role as a Middle Power,* edited by J. King Gordon, 51-66. Toronto: Canadian Institute of International Affairs, 1966.

Gordon, J. King, ed. *Canada's Role as a Middle Power.* Toronto: Canadian Institute of International Affairs, 1966.

–. "Prospects for Peacekeeping." *International Journal* 25, 2 (Spring 1970): 370-87.

–. *The United Nations in the Congo.* Carnegie Endowment for International Peace, 1962.

Granatstein, J.L. "Canada: Peacekeeper, a Survey of Canada's Participation in Peacekeeping Operations." In *Peacekeeping: International Challenge and Canadian Response,* 93-187. Toronto: Canadian Institute of International Relations, 1968.

–. "Canada and Peacekeeping: Image and Reality." *Canadian Forum* 54, 263 (1974): 14-19.

–. "Peacekeeping: Did Canada Make a Difference? And What Difference Did Peacekeeping Make to Canada?" In *Making a Difference?* edited by John English and Norman Hillmer, 222-36. Toronto: Lester Publishing, 1992.

–. "Peacekeeping Is Our Profession?" *International Journal* 25 (Spring 1970): 414-19.

–. "War and Peacekeeping: 'The Military History of an Unmilitary People.'" *Beaver* 74, 6 (1994-95): 41-53.

–. *Who Killed the Canadian Military?* Toronto: HarperCollins, 2004.

–. *Whose War Is It? How Canada Can Survive in the Post-9/11 World.* Toronto: HarperCollins, 2007.

Granatstein, J.L., and David Bercuson. *War and Peacekeeping.* Toronto: Key Porter, 1991.

Hammarskjöld, Dag. *Markings.* New York: Alfred A. Knopf, 1964.

Harbottle, Michael N. *The Blue Berets: The Story of the United Nations Peacekeeping Forces.* London: Leo Cooper, 1971.

Higgins, Rosalyn. *United Nations Peacekeeping 1946-1967.* Vol. 3. Oxford: Oxford University Press, 1980.

Hill, Roger J. *Command and Control Problems of the UN and Similar Peacekeeping Forces.* Ottawa: Department of National Defence, 1968.

Hilliker, John. "The Politicians and the 'Pearsonalities': The Diefenbaker Government and the Conduct of Canadian External Relations." *Historical Papers* 19, 1 (1984): 152-67.

Hilliker, John, and Donald Barry. *Coming of Age, 1946-1968.* Vol. 2 of *Canada's Department of External Affairs.* Montreal and Kingston: McGill-Queen's University Press, 1995.

Hillmer, Norman. "Canadian Peacekeeping and the Road Back to 1945." In *Canada e Italia: Prospettive di Co-operazione,* edited by Fabrizio Ghilardi, 145-59. Pisa and Milan: Centro Interuniversitario di Studi sul Canada, 1994.

–. "Canadian Peacekeeping: New and Old." In *Peacekeeping 1815 to Today,* edited by Serge Bernier, 539-48. Ottawa: International Commission of Military History, 1995.

–. "Mike Was Right: The Pearson Impulse in Canadian Peacekeeping." Paper presented at the Lester B. Pearson Canadian International Training Centre, public fora on Peacekeeping and the Canadian Future: A Canadian Commitment. Halifax, Montreal, Ottawa, Toronto, Winnipeg, Calgary, and Victoria, September-October 2000.

–. "Peacekeeping: Canadian Invention, Canadian Myth." In *Welfare States in Trouble,* edited by Sune Akerman and J.L. Granatstein, 159-70. Uppsala, Sweden: Swedish Science Press, 1995.

–. "Peacemakers, Blessed and Otherwise." *Canadian Defence Quarterly* 19, 1 (Summer 1989): 55-58.

Hillmer, Norman, and J.L. Granatstein. *Empire to Umpire: Canada and the World to the 1990s.* Toronto: Copp Clark Longman, 1994.

Hillmer, Norman, and Bill Rawling. "United Nations Peacekeeping Operations." In *We Stand on Guard: An Illustrated History of the Canadian Army,* edited by John Marteinson, 450-89. Montreal: Tormont, 1992.

Hochschild, Adam. *King Leopold's Ghost.* Boston and New York: Houghton Mifflin, 1999.

Holmes, John. *The Better Part of Valour: Essays on Canadian Diplomacy.* Toronto: McClelland and Stewart, 1970.

–. "Canada's Role in the United Nations." *Air University Review* 18, 4 (1967): 18-27.

–. "Canadian External Policies since 1945." *International Journal* 18, 2 (1963): 136-47.

–. "The United Nations in the Congo." *International Journal* 16, 1 (1960-61): 1-16.

Holsti, Ole R. "Public Opinion and Foreign Policy: Challenges to the Almond-Lippmann Consensus Merson Series; Research Programs and Debates." *International Studies Quarterly* 36 (1992): 439-66.

Horne, Alistair. *Macmillan, 1957-1986.* London: Macmillan, 1989.

Hoskyns, Catherine. *The Congo since Independence: January 1960-December 1961.* London: Oxford University Press, 1965.

Ignatieff, George. *The Making of a Peacemonger: The Memoirs of George Ignatieff.* Toronto: University of Toronto Press, 1985.

Jacobson, Harold. "The Changing United Nations." In *Foreign Policy in the Sixties: The Issues and the Instruments*, edited by Roger Hilsman and Robert Good, 67-89. Baltimore: Johns Hopkins University Press, 1965.

–. "ONUC's Civilian Operation: State Preserving and State Building." *World Politics* 17, 1 (1964): 75-107.

James, Alan. *Britain and the Congo Crisis, 1960-1963*. London: Macmillan, 1996.

–. *Keeping the Peace in the Cyprus Crisis of 1963-64*. Basingstoke, UK: Palgrave Macmillan, 2002.

–. "Peacekeeping and the Parties." In *The United Nations and Peacekeeping: Results, Limitations, and Prospects*, edited by Indar Jit Rikhye, 125-46. Basingstoke, UK: Macmillan / International Peace Academy, 1990.

–. *Peacekeeping in International Politics*. London: Macmillan/International Institute for Strategic Studies, 1990.

–. *The Politics of Peacekeeping*. London: Chatto and Windus, 1969.

–. *The Role of Force in International Order and United Nations Peace-Keeping*. Ditchley Paper 20. Ditchley Park, UK: Ditchley Foundation, 1969.

–. "UN Action for Peace. II. Law and Order Forces." *The World Today* 18, 12 (December 1962): 503-13.

–. "The United Nations: Broker, Big Brother or Buffer?" In *The United Nations and the Quest for Peace*, edited by Anthony Parsons and Alan James, 18-34. Cardiff: Welsh Centre for International Affairs, 1986.

Janson, Jacques, and Pauline Dumont-Bayliss. "Sans Tambour ni Trompette!–Le Contingent des Forces Canadiennes au Congo: une Discrétion Source d'Efficacité." *Canadian Defence Quarterly* 22, 1 (August 1992): 12-16.

Jockel, Joseph T. *Canada and International Peacekeeping*. Toronto and Washington: Canadian Institute of Strategic Studies / Center for Strategic and International Studies, 1994.

Jones, Goronwy J. *The United Nations and the Domestic Jurisdiction of States*. Cardiff: University of Wales Press / Welsh Centre for International Affairs, 1979.

Joshua, Wynfred. "Belgium's Role in the UN Peace-keeping Operation in the Congo." *Orbis* 11, 2 (1967): 414-39.

Kalb, Madeleine. *The Congo Cables*. New York: Macmillan, 1982.

Kaplan, Lawrence S. "The United States, Belgium, and the Congo Crisis of 1960." *The Review of Politics* 29, 2 (1967): 239-56.

Kasoff, Mark J., and Christine Gesell, eds. *Peacekeeping as an Expression of Canadian Values: Proceedings from the 8th annual Redding Symposium*. Bowling Green, OH: Canadian Studies Center at Bowling Green State University, 1995.

Keating, Tom. *Canada and World Order: The Multilateralist Tradition in Canadian Foreign Policy*. Toronto: McClelland and Stewart, 1993.

King, A.E. "UN Commander Honours Canadian Signal Unit in Congo." *Canadian Army Journal* 17, 1 (1963): 92-96.

Kitchen, Helen, ed. *Footnotes to the Congo Story*. New York: Walker and Company, 1967.

Konczacki, Janina M. "William G. Stairs and the Occupation of Katanga: A Forgotten Episode in the 'Scramble' for Africa." *Dalhousie Review* 66, 3 (1986): 243-55.

Lee, Brady. "Peacekeeping, the Congo, and Zones of Peace." *Peace Review* 9, 2 (June 1997): 189-91.

Lefever, Ernest W. *Crisis in the Congo*. Washington, DC: Brookings Institution, 1965.

–. "The Limits of UN Intervention in the Third World." *The Review of Politics* 30, 1 (1968): 3-19.

–. "Reining in the U.N." *Foreign Affairs* 72, 3 (Summer 1993): 17-20.

–. *Uncertain Mandate: Politics of the U.N. Congo Operation*. Baltimore: Johns Hopkins University Press, 1967.

–. *United Nations Peacekeeping in the Congo: An Appraisal*. Washington, DC: Brookings Institution, 1964.

–. *United Nations Peacekeeping in the Congo, 1960-1964: An Analysis of Political, Executive and Military Control*. Vols. 1-4. Washington, DC: Brookings Institution, 1966.

–. "US Policy, the UN and the Congo." *Orbis* 11, 2 (Summer 1967): 394-413.

Legault, Albert. *The Authorization of Peacekeeping Operations in Terms of the Nature of the Conflict*. Paris: International Information Centre on Peacekeeping Operations, 1968.

Lenarcic, David A. "Meeting Each Other Halfway: The Departments of National Defence and External Affairs during the Congo Peacekeeping Mission, 1960-64." YCISS Occasional Paper Number 37. CDISP Special Issue Number 1. 1996.

–. "Peacekeeping, 1965: The Canadian Military's Viewpoint." *Canadian Military History* 5, 1 (1996): 105-9.

Livingstone, G. Ann. "Canada's Policy and Attitudes towards United Nations Peacekeeping, 1956-1964, with Specific Reference to Participation in the Forces Sent to Egypt (1956), the Congo (1960) and Cyprus (1964)." PhD diss., Keele University, 1995.

Lumumba, Patrice. *Congo My Country*. London: Pall Mall Press, 1962.

Lynch, Charles. *You Can't Print THAT!* Edmonton: Hurtig, 1983.

Lyon, Peyton V. *Canada in World Affairs, 1961-1963*. Toronto: Oxford University Press, 1968.

–. "Letter to the Editor." *Canadian Forum* 54, 645 (October 1974): 34-35.

Maloney, Sean M. *Canada and UN Peacekeeping: Cold War by Other Means, 1945-1970*. St. Catharines, ON: Vanwell, 2002.

–. "From Myth to Reality Check: From Peacekeeping to Stabilization." *Policy Options* 26, 7 (September 2005): 40-46.

March, William. "The Royal Canadian Air Force and Peacekeeping." In *Peacekeeping 1815 to Today*, edited by Serge Bernier, 467-77. Ottawa: International Commission of Military History, 1995.

Martelli, George. *Experiment in World Government: An Account of the United Nations Operation in the Congo 1960-1964*. London: Johnson Publications, 1966.

–. *Leopold to Lumumba*. London: Chapman and Hall, 1962.

Martin, Paul. *Canada and the Quest for Peace*. New York: Columbia University Press, 1967.

–. *A Very Public Life*. Vol. 2. Toronto: Deneau, 1985.

Martin, Pierre, and Michel Fortmann. "Canadian Public Opinion and Peacekeeping in a Turbulent World." *International Journal* 50, 2 (Spring 1995): 370-400.

Matthews, Robert O. "Africa in Canadian Affairs." *International Journal* 26 (Winter 1970-71): 122-50.

McVitty, Marion H. "An Approach to Development of United Nations Peacekeeping Machinery Based on the Significance of UNEF and ONUC Experience." In *Legal and Political Problems of World Order*, edited by S.H. Mendlovitz, 335-51. New York: Fund for Education Concerning World Peace through World Law, 1962.

Meisler, Stanley. "Crisis in Katanga." In *Soldiers for Peace*, edited by Barbara Benton, 110-19. New York: Facts on File, 1996.

Merriam, Alan P. *Congo: Background to Conflict*. Evanston, IL: Northwestern University Press, 1961.

Michalak, S.J. "Peacekeeping and the UN: The Problem of Responsibility." *International Studies Quarterly* 11, 4 (December 1967): 301-19.

Middlemiss, D.W., and J.J. Sokolsky. *Canadian Defence: Decisions and Determinants*. Toronto: Harcourt Brace Jovanovich, 1989.

Miller, E.M. "Legal Aspects of the U.N. Action in the Congo." *American Journal of International Law* 55, 1 (1961): 1-28.

Moir, John S., ed. *History of the Royal Canadian Corps of Signals, 1903-1961*. Ottawa: Corps Committee, Royal Canadian Corps of Signals, 1962.

Moskos, Charles C. *Peace Soldiers: The Sociology of a UN Military Force*. Chicago: University of Chicago Press, 1976.

Murray, G.S. "United Nations Peace-Keeping and Problems of Political Control." *International Journal* 18, 4 (Autumn 1963): 442-57.

Nicholas, Herbert. "An Appraisal." In *International Military Forces: The Question of Peacekeeping in an Armed and Disarming World*, edited by Lincoln Bloomfield, 105-25. Boston: Little, Brown, 1964.

–. "UN Peace Forces and the Changing Globe: Lessons of Suez and Congo." *International Organization* 17 (1963): 321-37.

Nimer, Benjamin. *The United Nations Force in the Congo: A Political Analysis*. Washington, DC: George Washington University, 1966.

Nkrumah, Kwame. *Challenge of the Congo*. New York: International Publishers, 1967.

Nossal, Kim Richard. "Analyzing the Domestic Sources of Canadian Foreign Policy." *International Journal* 39 (Winter 1983/84): 1-22.

O'Brien, Conor Cruise. *To Katanga and Back*. New York: Grosset and Dunlap, 1962.

O'Carroll, Donal. "Ireland's UN Peacekeeping Experience 1958-1995." In *Peacekeeping 1815 to Today*, edited by Serge Bernier, 528-38. Ottawa: International Commission of Military History, 1995.

Parakatil, Francis. *India and United Nations Peacekeeping*. New Delhi: S. Chand, 1975.

Parsons, Anthony. *From Cold War to Hot Peace: UN Interventions, 1947-1994*. London: Michael Joseph, 1995.

Pearson, Geoffrey. "Canadian Attitudes towards Peacekeeping." In *Peacekeeping: Appraisals and Proposals*, edited by Henry Wiseman, 118-29. Willowdale, ON: Pergamon Press, 1983.

–. *Seize the Day: Lester B. Pearson and Crisis Diplomacy*. Ottawa: Carleton University Press, 1993.

Pearson, Lester. "Keeping the Peace." *Survival* 6, 4 (1964): 150-58.

–. *Mike: The Memoirs of the Right Honourable Lester B. Pearson, 1957-1968*. Vol. 3. Edited by John A. Munro and Alex I. Inglis. Toronto: University of Toronto Press, 1975.

Pradhan, Ram Chandra. *The United Nations and the Congo Crisis*. New Delhi: MANAS Publications, 1975.

Rikhye, Indar Jit. *Military Adviser to the Secretary-General: U.N. Peacekeeping and the Congo Crisis*. London: Hurst, 1993.

–. "Peacekeeping and Peacemaking." In *Peacekeeping: Appraisals and Proposals*, edited by Henry Wiseman, 5-18. Toronto: Pergamon Press, 1983.

–. "Preparation and Training of UN Peacekeeping Forces." In *Peace-Keeping: Experience and Evaluation (The Oslo Papers)*, edited by Per Frydenberg, 183-97. Oslo: Norwegian Institute of International Affairs, 1964.

–. *The Theory and Practice of Peacekeeping*. London: Hurst, 1984.

–. "United Nations Peacekeeping Operations and India." *India Quarterly* 41, 3-4 (July-December 1985): 303-19.

Rikhye, Indar Jit, Michael Harbottle, and Bjørn Egge. *The Thin Blue Line: International Peacekeeping and Its Future*. New Haven, CT, and London: Yale University Press, 1974.

Rikhye, I.J., and Kjell Skjelsbaek, eds. *The United Nations and Peacekeeping: Results, Limitations, and Prospects*. Basingstoke, UK: Macmillan/International Peace Academy, 1990.

Ritchie, Charles. *Diplomatic Passport*. Toronto: Macmillan, 1981.

Robinson, H. Basil. *Diefenbaker's World: A Populist in Foreign Affairs*. Toronto: University of Toronto Press, 1989.

Schatzberg, Michael. "Military Intervention and the Myth of Collective Security: The Case of Zaire." *Journal of Modern African Studies* 27 (June 1989): 315-40.

–. *Mobutu or Chaos?* New York: University Press of America, 1991.

Schlegel, John P. *The Deceptive Ash: Bilingualism and Canadian Policy in Africa: 1957-1971*. Washington, DC: University Press of America, 1978.

Schwar, Harriet Dashiell, ed. *Foreign Relations of the United States, 1958-1960, Africa*. Vol. 14. Washington, DC: State Department, 1992.

–, ed. *Foreign Relations of the United States, 1961-1963, Congo Crisis*. Vol. 20. Washington, DC: State Department, 1994.

Smith, Denis. *Rogue Tory: The Life and Legend of John G. Diefenbaker*. Toronto: MacFarlane Walter and Ross, 1995.

Sonnenfeldt, Helmut. "The Soviet Union and China: Where They Stood in 1960." In *Footnotes to the Congo Story*, edited by Helen Kitchen, 25-34. New York: Walker and Company, 1967.

Spooner, Kevin. "Canada, the Congo Crisis, and United Nations Peacekeeping, 1960-1964." PhD diss., Carleton University, 2002.

–. "The Origins of Canadian Participation in the United Nations Operation in the Congo, 1960." MA thesis, Carleton University, 1995.

Stethem, H.W.C., and R. Fournier. "Signal Squadron in the Congo." *Canadian Army Journal* 17, 2 (1963): 110-20.

Stoessinger, John. "The Payments Dispute." In *The Future of UN Peace-keeping Operations: A Policy Paper of the United Nations Association in Canada*, edited by Willson Woodside, 22-31. Toronto: United Nations Association in Canada, 1965.

Streulens, Michel. *The United Nations in the Congo or O.N.U.C. and International Politics.* Brussels: Max Arnold, 1976.

Taylor, Alastair, David Cox, and J.L. Granatstein. *Peacekeeping: International Challenge and Canadian Response.* Toronto: Canadian Institute of International Affairs, 1968.

Thornhill, Edward. *From Buggies ... to Jets.* Winnipeg: Edward Thornhill, 1997.

United Nations. *The Blue Helmets.* 3rd ed. New York: United Nations Department of Public Information, 1996.

–. *The United Nations and the Congo: Some Salient Facts.* New York: United Nations, 1963.

–. *Yearbook of the United Nations, 1960-1964.* New York: United Nations Office of Public Information, 1961, 1962, 1963, 1964, 1965.

Urquhart, Brian. *Hammarskjold.* New York: Alfred A. Knopf, 1972.

–. *A Life in Peace and War.* New York and London: W.W. Norton, 1987.

–. "Peacekeeping: A View from the Operational Center." In *Peacekeeping: Appraisals and Proposals*, edited by Henry Wiseman, 161-72. Toronto: Pergamon Press, 1983.

–. *Ralph Bunche: An American Odyssey.* New York and London: W.W. Norton, 1993.

–. "United Nations Peace Forces and the Changing United Nations: An Institutional Perspective." *International Organization* 17 (1963): 338-54.

–. "A UN Perspective." In *International Military Forces: The Question of Peacekeeping in an Armed and Disarming World*, edited by Lincoln Bloomfield, 126-44. Boston: Little, Brown, 1964.

Van Bilsen, A.A.J. "Some Aspects of the Congo Problem." *International Affairs* 38, 1 (1962): 41-52.

von Horn, Maj. Gen. Carl. *Soldiering for Peace.* London: Cassell, 1966.

Wainhouse, David W. *International Peace Observation.* Baltimore: Johns Hopkins University Press, 1966.

–. *International Peacekeeping at the Crossroads: National Support – Experience and Prospects.* Baltimore: Johns Hopkins University Press, 1973.

Weissman, Stephen R. *American Foreign Policy in the Congo 1960-1964.* Ithaca, NY: Cornell University Press, 1974.

Williams, D. Colwyn. "Origins and Practices of Peacekeeping." In *The Future of UN Peace-Keeping: A Policy Paper of the United Nations Association in Canada*, edited by Willson Woodside, 10-20. Toronto: United Nations Association in Canada, 1965.

Wiseman, Henry, ed. *Peacekeeping: Appraisals and Proposals.* Toronto: Pergamon Press, 1983.

Woodside, Willson, ed. *The Future of UN Peace-Keeping: A Policy Paper of the United Nations Association in Canada.* Toronto: United Nations Association in Canada, 1965.

Worthington, Peter. *Looking for Trouble: A Journalist's Life ... and Then Some.* Toronto: Key Porter, 1984.

# Index

*Note:* "t" after a page number indicates a table.

**A**BAKO. *See* Association Culturelle des Ressortissants de Bas-Congo (ABAKO)
Abbas, Mekki, 152, 156, 159
Adoula, Cyrille: establishment of Adoula government, 162; and Katanga, 194, 195; meeting about ANC training, 206; request for peacekeepers to remain, 208; requests for officer instructors, 181, 187, 204-6; on Resolution 1474 (ES-IV), 203
Advisory Committee. *See* United Nations (UN), Advisory Committee
Africa: Afro-Asian bloc, 149-50, 202; Canadian relations with, 14, 26; internal politics of, 88
aid: bilateral aid, 56, 58, 201, 212; Canada's budget for African aid, 25-26; financial aid, 73, 103, 114, 128, 161, 220; food aid, 35, 48-49, 64, 85, 128-30, 220, 221
air commander position, 179-81
aircraft: C119s (aircraft), 168, 170; Caribou aircraft, 85, 86, 96-97, 235n69, 237n7; Fouga Magister jet trainer, 165, 249n8; North Star aircraft, 52, 53-54, 85; seizure of, 170; use of long-range transport aircraft, 232n13; Yukon turbo-prop (aircraft), 170. *See also* Royal Canadian Air Force (RCAF)
Albertville, 165-66
Alexander, Henry T. (Maj. Gen.): arrival of, 63; on Canadian combat forces, 227n34; on Ghanaian training proposal, 87; and need for signallers, 51-52; on white troops, 59
Aluminum Limited, 16, 224n13

ANC. *See* Armée Nationale Congolaise (ANC)
Anglo-Belgian-Indian Rubber Company, 12
Argue, Hazen (MP), 39
Armée Nationale Congolaise (ANC): coup by, 94-95; disarmament of, 135; incident of 2 April, 152-53; and Joseph Mobutu, 122; and Matadi incident, 143-44; and Nathaniel Welbeck incident, 106; training of, 102, 160, 172, 181, 186, 197, 201-6, 212, 216; transport of, 72. *See also* Force Publique
Armstrong, Hamilton, 228n48
Aroutunian, Amasasp, 45-46, 58, 61. *See also* Soviet Union
Articles. *See under* United Nations (UN), Charter
Association Culturelle des Ressortissants de Bas-Congo (ABAKO), 21-22
Ausman, L.H., 24
austerity program, 188, 189-90, 219

**B**aluba people: ambush of Irish peacekeepers, 105, 239n27; Baluba refugees, 218; massacre of, 89, 95-96; secession of South Kasai, 72; and South Kasai famine, 128-29
Barriefield (ON), 55, 64, 65
Barry, Donald, 9
Barton, William, 9-10, 173, 186
Belanger, G.E. (Capt.), 143-44
Belgium: administration of Congo, 224n24; assistance of Joseph Mobutu, 122; Belgian Congo, 20-21; Canada-Belgian relations, 121-23, 147-48; and Communism, 23-24, 43-45, 72-73;

concern over Canadian opinions, 69; and the Congo, 12-13; and the Congo Crisis, 45; criticism of United States, 132; and Hammarskjöld, 233n30; Lumumba on, 56-57; and Lumumba's overseas visits, 56, 230n85; military intervention by, 28; and NATO policy on the Congo, 216; Paul Henri Spaak, 205; Pierre Wigny, 55, 122-23; relations with, 150; request for information, 147-48; requests to Canada, 25; support of Katanga, 68; timeline for independence, 22; withdrawal of troops, 36, 68-69, 71; and World War II, 17

Bell, David, 185

Berlin Conference of 1884-85, 12

Berthiaume, J.A. (Lt. Col.): arrest of Lumumba, 216; and efforts to locate Lumumba, 115-16; and Guinean reception, 100; on Indian officers, 108-9; and Kasai airlift, 230n76; and Mobutu, 109-10; and Nathaniel Welbeck incident, 106; removal of, 107-9, 157; secondment from UNTSO, 41; von Horn's comments on, 127

bilateral agreements, 203-4, 212

bilateral aid, 56, 58, 201, 212. *See also* aid

bilingualism: C Pro C detachment, 75; and Congo Crisis, 218; and inclusion of Canada, 52, 228n56; and "One Canada" mindset, 39; shortage of bilingual peacekeepers, 229n72

Bindoff, R.C. (Maj.), 65, 101

Birchall (Air Comm.), 190

Bishop, Peter, 114

Bishop, R.M. (Brig.), 51-52

Blair, Robert, 92

Boland, Freddie, 250n28

Bomboko, Justin: and Berthiaume, 157; on Canada, 191, 203; described, 67; diplomatic incident with Mr. Weidman, 183-84; on Kasavubu, 110; and Lovanium University parliament, 162; and Lumumba, 123; meeting with Col. Smith, 144-45; and Nathaniel Welbeck, 105; protest to, 81

Bone (Signaller), 80

Bouffard (Maj.), 105-6

Boulden, Jane, 70

Britain. *See* United Kingdom

Brodie, A.B., 20

Bull, Roger, 27, 28, 63, 64, 67

Bullock, W.J.W., 178

Bunche, Ralph: on Canadian combat forces, 227n34; and Caribou aircraft, 86; on Congolese, 82; and Congolese

independence, 26, 27-28; on Congolese officials, 67; on entry into Jadotville, 199; and military intervention, 34-35; and N'Djili incident, 77, 79; negotiations in Katanga, 68; request for force commander position, 184; request for officer instructors, 186-87; requests for assistance, 33-34. *See also* United Nations (UN)

Burden, William, 23

Burns, E.L.M. (Gen.), 180, 184, 186

Bussieres (Capt.), 166

**C**119s (aircraft), 168, 170. *See also* aircraft

Cadieux, Marcel, 45, 196, 231n88

Calvocoressi, Peter, 36

Campbell, H.L. (A/M), 10

Campbell, Ross, 113, 187, 190, 193, 199-200

Canada: national identity, 214; national self-image of, 46; national sovereignty, 203; political history of, 1-2; potential involvement of, 37-43; reputation of, 7

Canadian Armed Forces
– austerity program, 188, 189-90, 219
– Canadian contingent in ONUC: activities in the Congo, 100-2; arrival of, 73-81; and espionage, 106-7; evacuation plans for, 241n51; increase in size of, 106; and peacekeeping, 214; preparations to send units, 64-65; quartering of, 73; reputation of, 158, 197; restrictions on deployment, 64-65, 67, 71; services provided by signallers, 74
– meeting of heads of branches, 51
– National Survival Plan, 50
– units of: 2nd Batallion, Royal Canadian Regiment, 32, 38; 426 Transport Squadron, 190; Canadian HQ, ONUC, 64, 101; Canadian Provost Corps (C Pro C), 75; Royal 22e Regiment, 51, 74; Royal Canadian Corps of Signals, 50. *See also* 57th Signal Squadron
– *See also* National Defence, Department of; Royal Canadian Air Force (RCAF)

Canadian Council of Churches, 91

Canadian government
– Cabinet: and Canadian involvement, 41, 48, 50; consideration of ONUC, 97; and decision making, 220; and Katanga, 194-95; and Pisa-Leopoldville airlift, 52
– Diefenbaker government: decisions of, 61-62; resolution in support of participation in ONUC, 60-61

– Finance, Department of, 103, 173
– foreign policy: and Afro-Asian bloc, 149-50; and Congo Crisis, 8, 148-52; considerations of, 8, 161; diplomatic relations with the Congo, 13-19, 191; External Affairs directives, 99; formal response of, 66; francophone influence in, 25-26; funding of ONUC, 114-15; of John Diefenbaker, 2; on Kasavubu, 104, 118; and moralism, 214, 215; relationship with Belgium, 16-17; speech to General Assembly, 120; statement on Congo Crisis policy, 99 (*see also* Diefenbaker, John; External Affairs, Department of; Pearson, Lester B.)
– *See also* National Defence, Department of
Carey, John, 233n29
Caribou aircraft, 85, 86, 96-97, 235n69, 237n7. *See also* aircraft
Carpenter, F.S. (Air Comm.), 65, 73, 86
Carr, W.K. (Grp. Capt.), 87, 100, 125
Central Intelligence Agency (CIA), 44, 95, 249n8. *See also* United States
Chambers, Robert, 78
Chand, Dewan Prem (Maj. Gen.), 198
Chapman (Air Comm.), 155
*Chronicle-Herald*: on attacks on peacekeepers, 77; on Canadian involvement, 43, 53; on Congo Crisis, 27; on foreign aid, 49; on Katanga, 168-69; on Patrice Lumumba's death, 136. *See also* newspapers
Churchill, Gordon, 25, 105
Clark, S.F. (Lt. Gen.), 10, 50, 52, 53, 77, 88, 107
Clay, George, 3
Clement, J.B. (Col.), 51-52
Cohen, Maxwell, 92
Cold War: and Canadian actions, 62; Canadian attempt at neutrality, 7, 113, 120; Canadian attempt at objectivity, 215-16; and Canadian involvement, 217; and Congo, 6-7, 33, 43-46, 47; and Lumumba, 111; politics of, 5; and Security Council meetings, 55; and UN, 98-100
Collins, Carole, 89, 236n78
colonialism, 18. *See also* decolonization
combat forces, 39, 41, 45, 218
Commonwealth Communication System, 74
Commonwealth Division, 14. *See also* External Affairs, Department of
Commonwealth Prime Ministers' Conferences, London, 14, 148

communications difficulties, 199
communications net, 232n10
Communism: Communist Party of Canada, 91, 136; and the Congo, 23-24, 29-30, 33, 43-46, 118; and Lumumba, 23-24, 46, 56-57, 72; "Lunch with Soviet Colleagues," 183; penetration of Africa, 60
conciliation commission, 103-4
Confédération des Associations du Katanga (CONAKAT), 28
Congo. *See* Democratic Republic of Congo (DRC)
Congo Advisory Committee. *See* United Nations (UN), Advisory Committee
Congo Reform Association, 13
Congolese Jeunesse movement, 210
Congress of Canadian Women, 117
consent, principle of, 4
Co-operative Commonwealth Federation, 39
Cordier, Andrew: appointment of, 84; attempts to oust Lumumba, 89, 236n78; on Berthiaume, 108; on communications with home governments, 101; on evacuation of peacekeepers, 117; negotiations with Congolese government, 95; orders of, 89, 98; replacement of, 94; and use of RCAF aircraft, 54. *See also* United Nations (UN)
Côté, Mario, 163-64, 248n5
Coughlin, T.G., 236n72
Credentials committee, 112-13. *See also* United Nations (UN)
Critchell, C., 92
Cumont, C.P. (Gen.), 28

Daigle, R.C. (Maj.), 73
Dayal, Rajeshwar: appointment of, 90; arrival of, 94; and Berthiaume, 109; and Congolese, 102, 145; on Congolese politicians, 121; criticisms of, 144-45; and death of Lumumba, 241n47; and Diefenbaker, 148-49; and Mobutu coup, 95; removal of, 125-27, 242n68; return to Congo, 152, 159. *See also* Opération des Nations Unies au Congo (ONUC)
De Witte, Ludo, 123
decolonization: and Belgian intervention, 28; and Belgium, 45; and Canadian foreign policy, 217-18; and ONUC personnel, 47; and UN, 6-7; views on, 17-19
Democratic Republic of Congo (DRC): Adoula government, 162-63; bilateral

assistance, 203; College of Commissioners, 95; Congo Reform Association, 13; constitutional crisis, 94-133, 158-59, 162; governmental interregnum, 94; history of, 3; Ileo government, 134; independence of, 21-22, 25-30; Kitona Declaration, 182; Leopoldville government, 118, 123, 162-63; Mobutu coup, 94-95, 213; Mouvement National Congolais, 23; political developments in, 67-73, 89-91, 100-3, 110-11, 158-60, 182-84, 191-96; political divisions of, 110; political parties, 21; Stanleyville government, 117, 118, 122, 123, 137, 158; and trade, 15-16; understanding of UN, 67-68
demonstrations, 67, 163, 167
*Le Devoir,* 31, 38-39, 77. *See also* newspapers
DeWolf, H.G. (V. Adm.), 10, 56
Dextraze, J.A. (Brig.), 209-11
Diefenbaker, John: and Africa, 14; background of, 1-2, 9; on Belgians, 69; on Canadian involvement, 31, 38, 39-43, 48; on Congo policy, 148; criticism of Soviet Union, 216; decision-making process of, 220; foreign policy of, 2, 9; on funding of ONUC, 114-15; and Katanga, 194-95; letter of protest, 76; and Lumumba's visit, 57-58; meeting with Eisenhower, 238n15; "one Canada" vision, 39, 218; on Pisa-Leopoldville airlift, 190; on public opinion, 129; reasons behind involvement, 215; speech to General Assembly, 100, 238n15; on Stanleyville attack, 81; and UN requests for assistance, 227n29; on use of force, 156; on use of North Star aircraft, 54. *See also* Canadian government
disarmament, 63, 135, 184
Domaine de la Couronne, 12
Dorn, Walter, 185
Douglas, R.F. (Wing Com.), 19-20
Dulles, Allen, 44
Dumont-Bayliss, Pauline, 109
Dunlap, C.R. (A/M), 10
Dupuy, Pierre, 26

Eayrs, James, 221
education, 17, 20, 22
eight-power resolution, 119-20
Eisenhower, Dwight, 29, 72, 238n15. *See also* United States
Elisabethville, 70-71, 165, 197-98
English, 75
equipment, 67

espionage, 106-7, 130, 171, 185
Ethiopian contingent, 154, 238n19
evacuation plans, 241n51
External Affairs, Department of: and Africa, 14-15, 122; and air commander position, 180; assessment of UN needs, 50; and Belgian Congo, 25; on Canadian involvement, 37; and Caribou aircraft, 85; comic relief in, 183, 252n40; Commonwealth Division, 14; considerations in Canada's Congo policy, 221; consultations on involvement, 31-33, 53; on decolonization, 17-19; differences between divisions, 219; and espionage, 107; evaluation of UN requests, 50, 188; and financial pressure, 192; and funding of ONUC, 173; and Greene Plan, 205; Howard Green's role in, 9-10; on Kasavubu delegation, 111-13; and Katanga, 33, 167, 174, 176, 177, 194-95, 199; and Mario Côté incident, 248n5; and napalm bombs, 196; on officer transfers, 88; and ONUC chain of command, 126-27; on ONUC deployment, 182; and Operation Morthor, 166-67; and Paul Martin, 6, 31, 204, 205; and Pisa-Leopoldville airlift, 190; on request for officer instructors, 181, 187; on request for ONUC HQ staff, 185; on requests for personnel, 207; review of Congo policy, 118; and revisions to ONUC instructions, 95-96; on security of peacekeepers, 81; structure of, 10; trade with Congo, 15-16; on UN intervention, 103-4; and use of force, 218-19; views of, 148; on withdrawal of Canadian troops, 211; working process of, 220. *See also* Gauvin, Michel; Murray, Geoffrey; Ritchie, Charles; Robertson, Norman; Robinson, Basil

February 1960 conference, 22
57th Signal Squadron: amalgamation with Canadian HQ, 101; change of command, 188, 210; complement of, 141; detachments of, 74; dispatch to Matadi, 156-57; Elisabethville detachment, 165; formation of, 64-65; incidents with Congolese, 152-53; Matadi detachment, 143; praise of, 199; reduction of, 212; repatriation of, 207; 2nd Brigade, 51; on use of force, 145-46; withdrawal of, 211
Finance, Department of, 103, 173. *See also* Canadian government

financial aid, 73, 103, 114, 128, 161, 220. *See also* aid

financial pressure, 191-92

Fleming, Donald, 103

food aid, 35, 48-49, 64, 85, 128-30, 220, 221. *See also* aid

Food Services section, 75

force, use of: and Congo Crisis, 218-19; disagreements on, 68; External Affairs on, 218-19; and Katanga, 192; and Leopoldville and Matadi incidents, 145; ONUC preparations, 196; in peace-keeping, 162-200; and Security Council Resolution 161 (1961), 138-39, 138-41, 244n10, 244n12; and Security Council Resolution 169 (1961), 175; and self-defence, 141, 143, 145-46, 156

Force Publique: disarmament of, 63; mutiny of, 26-27, 44; and race relations, 19-20; training plan, 87-88. *See also* Armée Nationale Congolaise (ANC)

Ford, Robert, 83

foreign aid, 26, 48-49, 85, 129

foreign officers, 163

foreign policy. *See* Canadian government, foreign policy

foreign soldiers. *See* mercenaries

Fouga Magister jet trainer, 165, 249n8

426 Transport Squadron, 190

Franck, Thomas, 233n29

Freddy (Capt.), 24

French. *See* bilingualism

frugality, 114

Gaffen, Fred, 230n76, 248n5

Gagnon, Mona, 70

Gardiner, Robert, 158, 198, 199. *See also* Opération des Nations Unies au Congo (ONUC)

Gates, Thomas, 44

Gauvin, Michel: and Adoula, 162-63; attacks on peacekeepers, 143; briefing of, 134-35; on Brigadier Raja, 179; on Canadian instructors, 160; on Dayal, 152; on decision to engage gendarmerie, 198, 255n66; establishment of embassy, 191, "Lunch with Soviet Colleagues," 183; and Matadi incident, 145; on Operation Morthor, 166, 167; and U Thant Plan, 194; on UN requests, 154-55, 188. *See also* External Affairs, Department of

Gavel (Corp.), 80

General Assembly. *See* United Nations (UN), General Assembly

Ghana, 87-88, 105, 116, 241n47

Gibbs, David, 72, 233n30, 236n78

Gibson-Smith, W., 24

Gizenga, Antoine: hostilities with Mobutu, 155; and Kasavubu, 158; requests for military assistance, 29; and Soviet Union, 136, 138; Stanleyville government, 117, 137, 162-63, 241n50; and Tananarive conference, 149

*Globe and Mail,* 40, 42, 44, 77, 128. *See also* newspapers

Granatstein, J.L.: on American supply of transport, 66; on Diefenbaker, 48; on public opinion, 8, 214-15; on public pressure, 46

Green, D.G. (Col.), 210, 211

Green, Howard: background of, 9-10; and Canada's role, 7; on Canadian involvement, 42, 53, 59, 231n93; on Canadians instructing ANC, 160; and Congolese request for women, 59, 231n89; and diplomatic ties to DRC, 25; and espionage, 130; and evacuation of troops, 117; on Hammarskjöld, 69; and Kasavubu, 113; and Katanga, 167, 174, 177-78, 194, 196; letter of protest, 76; and Lumumba, 56, 59, 124, 135, 231n89; and NATO, 121-22, 132; on ONUC, 151, 184, 212-13; on Pisa-Leopoldville airlift, 105, 190; requests for signal personnel, 106; on Resolution 161 (1961), 139; role of, 219; and sanctions, 193; and South Kasai famine, 129; on Soviet Union, 137; on UN Congo policy, 221; on UN requests, 168, 170; and use of North Star aircraft, 54; on white troops, 59. *See also* External Affairs, Department of

Greene Plan, 201-6, 255n1

Guebre, Kebbede (Lt. Gen.), 199, 210

Guha (Brig.), 197

Guimond, B.J. (Lt. Col.), 65

Guinean reception, 100

Gullion, Edmund, 166, 177, 198, 211

Hamilton, W.S. (Col.), 188, 210

Hammarskjöld, Dag: advice on Dayal, 242n60, and Advisory Committee, 90-91, 140; background of, 10-11; and Canadian involvement, 39, 40-41, 83-84, 86; and conduct of peacekeeping operations, 232n17; and Congolese independence, 26, 27-28; death of, 166; and evacuation of ONUC, 119; formal reply to, 66; and intervention, 5; and Kasavubu, 149; and Katanga,

164-65; letter of protest from, 76; and Lumumba, 57, 116, 123-24; negotiations with Tshombé, 70-71; and ONUC command, 125-27; and Operation Morthor, 166; plans of, 34-35, 40-41; requests for personnel, 47-48, 50-51, 53; and Security Council, 55; and Soviet Union, 236n78; and Stanleyville incident, 82; training plans, 88. *See also* United Nations (UN)

Hampson, George, 121

Harkness, Douglas: air commander position, 179-80; appointment of, 104; background information on, 10; and RCAF commitment to the UN, 104-5; request for officer instructors, 187; requests for signal personnel, 106, 184; response to UN requests, 169-70; on use of force, 145. *See also* National Defence, Department of

Harman, Gary, 204

Hébert, Charles, 16, 18-19

Hellyer, Paul, 204, 205, 207. *See also* National Defence, Department of

Hennemeyer, Robert, 43-44

Herridge, Herbert (MP), 61

Herter, Christian, 29, 45, 56, 69

Hilliker, John, 9

Hillmer, Norman, 6, 214-15

Hochschild, Adam, 12-13

Holmes, John, 7, 222

Home (Lord), 196

Horn, Max, 15-16

Hoskyns, Catherine, 115, 123, 163

Humphries, Alicia, 117

hydroelectricity projects, 16

Ignatieff, George, 231n92

Ileo, Joseph, 121, 134, 158, 162

immunization, 50, 51, 55, 64, 65

incidents: of 2 April, 152-53; ambush of Irish peacekeepers, 105, 239n27; 5 December roadblock, 176; Leopoldville (15 April), 153; Leopoldville (26 February), 143; massacre of Italians, 175; Nathaniel Welbeck incident, 105-6; Stanleyville (8 April), 154; Yukon incident, 170

independence, 21-22, 25-30

India, 102, 198, 255n66. *See also* Dayal, Rajeshwar; Opération des Nations Unies au Congo (ONUC), national preferences at HQ

Inga Project, 16

intelligence work, 171, 185

intervention, prohibition of, 70, 233n29

Irish peacekeepers, 105, 239n27

Ironsi, Thomas Aguiyu (Maj. Gen.), 209-11

Iyassu (Gen.), 172

Jadotville, 165, 182-83, 198

James, Alan: on British position, 32, 132, 139, 191; on Canada's concerns, 254n58; on Congo, 5; on Soviet intervention, 228n50; on United Kingdom, 139

Janssens, Emile (Lt. Gen.), 26-27

Jha, C.S., 140-41

Johnson (Lt. Col.), 64

Johnson, David, 83

Jones, Goronwy, 232n17

Joshua, Wynfred, 224n2

Kalb, Madeleine, 131, 225n26, 231n89, 234n55

Kaldager, Christian (Maj. Gen.), 209

Kalonji, Albert, 72

Kamina, 68, 69, 165

Kanza, Thomas, 54-55

Kaplan, Lawrence, 230n85

Kasai: famine in, 128-30, 221; Kasai airlift, 230n76; and Katanga, 174; Port-Francqui, 155; secession of South Kasai, 72

Kasavubu, Joseph: and ABAKO, 21-22; background of, 22-23; Canadian opinion on, 216; and conciliation committee, 104; coup by, 89; and Dayal, 159; delegation to UN, 111-13, 240n40; formation of Ileo government, 134; Kalb on, 225n26; on Katanga, 158-59; political position of (in 1960), 110; requests for assistance, 44; and Tananarive conference, 149

Katanga, 162-200; action against, 158-59; and Adoula government, 163; attack by, 197-98; casualties in, 179; debate over entry of ONUC, 68; development of, 12-13; and Fouga Magister aircraft, 165, 249n8; and Hammarskjöld, 164; hostilities in, 197-200; independence of, 28-29; and Kasai, 174; Operation Morthor, 165-67; secession of, 32-33, 225n43; and U Thant Plan, 192; UN discussions on, 191; UN presence in, 71; Union Minière du Haut Katanga, 12-13, 68, 194-95, 198; and use of force, 218. *See also* Tshombé, Moïse

Keating, Tom, 221

Kennedy, John F.: Congo policy of, 131-33, 243n76; meeting on ANC training, 204-5, 206; NATO meeting,

195; and Prime Minister Macmillan, 166, 191. *See also* United States

Kettani, Ben Hammou (Gen.), 107. *See also* Opération des Nations Unies au Congo (ONUC)

Khiari, Mahmoud, 174. *See also* Opération des Nations Unies au Congo (ONUC)

Khrushchev, Nikita, 33, 44, 99-100. *See also* Soviet Union

King, H. (Maj.), 41

Kinshasa, 11. *See also* Leopoldville

Kipushi, 182-83, 198

Kitona, 68, 69

Kitona Declaration, 182

Kolwezi, 182-83

Kuznetsov, Vasily, 55, 83-84. *See also* Soviet Union

Labouisse, Henry, 52

labour tax, 12

Laurendeau, André, 31

Lefever, Ernest, 226n45, 243n76

Léger, Jules, 43, 132

Legum, Colin, 67, 225n27

Leopold II (King), 12-13

Leopoldville: arrival of peacekeepers, 64; Belgian invasion of, 28; demonstrations in, 67; incident of 15 April, 153; incident of 26 February, 141, 143; and Kasavubu, 110; Leopoldville government, 118, 123, 162-63; Mendelsohn on, 65; as ONUC HQ location, 52. *See also* Pisa-Leopoldville airlift

Lessard, J.A. (Sgt.), 210

Linner, Sture (ONUC Officer-in-Charge), 167

Livingstone, Ann, 39

Lodge, Henry Cabot, 48, 69

*London Observer*, 3. *See also* newspapers

Lulua people, 72

Lumumba, Patrice: arrest of, 115-21, 123-25; attack on Katanga, 89; attacks on, 67; background of, 23; and Belgium, 56-57, 225n27; on Canada, 59, 100, 217; and Communism, 44; death of, 135, 138, 241n47, 246n28; demands of supporters, 116; on history of Congo, 13; meeting with Aroutunian, 58, 61, 231n89; on N'Djili incident, 78-79; and ONUC, 68; opinion of UN, 58; political position of (in 1960), 111; and racism, 70-71; release of, 119-20, 132; requests for assistance, 44; and Soviet Union, 46, 71-73, 83; visit to Canada, 56-59, 231n88; visit to United States, 230n85

Lundula, Victor (Gen.), 82, 154

Lynch, Charles, 231n92

MacEoin, Sean (Gen.): appointment of, 107, 127; and Berthiaume, 107-8, 109; complaint to, 163; and Matadi incident, 144, 145; on risk of hostilities, 155, 156; strategic plans of, 169; on use of force, 143, 145-46. *See also* Opération des Nations Unies au Congo (ONUC)

MacKinnon, James, 15-16

Macmillan, Harold, 166, 177, 191, 195. *See also* United Kingdom

MacNaughton, J.W., 31-32, 37

Madden, John, 92

"Mallard" operation, 55

Maloney, Sean, 62

mandate enforcement, 8

March, William, 232n13

Marois, J.J.B.L. (Capt.), 80

Martin, Paul, 6, 31, 204, 205. *See also* External Affairs, Department of

Matadi incident, 143-45

Mawoso (Capt.), 231n88

Mayer, P.A. (Lt. Col.), 210, 211

McFaul, V., 91

McNair, Bronson, 91

McVitty, Marion, 89

Mendelsohn, Albert (Col.), 64-65, 73, 86, 96-97, 101, 158

Menon, Krishna, 100, 238n15

mercenaries: in Katanga, 5, 174-75, 177, 182, 191, 196, 198; and Operation Rumpunch, 163, 165, 167-68; and Resolution 161 (1961), 138

Michel, Serge, 73

Middlemiss, D.W., 8

Military Committee of the Joint Reconciliation Commission, 189

Military Information Branch, 185

military intervention, request for, 34

Miller, Frank R. (Air Chief Marshal), 10, 31, 71

mining, 12-13, 68, 194-95, 198

missionaries, 13-14, 116, 210

mistaken identity, 2, 82, 105, 170, 239n27

Mobutu, Joseph: and ANC training, 102, 187, 201, 204-5; on Canadian instructors, 160; and capture of Lumumba, 241n47; and Dayal, 159; first coup by, 94-95; and Greene Plan, 205; political position of (in 1960), 110-11; second coup by, 213; and UN, 79, 234n55. *See also* Armée Nationale Congolaise (ANC)

Mobutu Sese Seko, 11. *See also* Mobutu, Joseph

Montreal, 57

*Montreal Gazette:* on Berthiaume, 109; on Katanga, 168; on Lumumba, 57, 117, 136; on South Kasai famine, 129; on standby batallion, 38. *See also* newspapers

moralism, 214, 215

Morel, Edmund, 13

Morozov, Platon Dmitrievich, 137. *See also* Soviet Union

Morrison, H.A. (Air Comm.), 155, 170, 179-81

Morthor, Operation, 165-66, 168

Mouvement National Congolais, 23

multilateralism, 221

Munongo, Godefroid, 68, 164

Murray, Geoffrey: and Advisory Committee, 140; on air commander position, 180; on Canada, 7; on Dayal, 152; on debate in General Assembly, 119; on Howard Green, 9; on Katanga, 199; and Lumumba's visit, 57; on Mendelsohn's briefings, 96-97; role of, 219. *See also* External Affairs, Department of

names, use of, 11

napalm bombs, 196

National Defence, Department of: and air commander position, 171, 179-81; and austerity program, 188, 189-90, 219; availability of bilingual officers, 172, 181; and Canadian instructors, 160, 181, 187; on Canadian involvement, 37; consultations on involvement, 31-32, 53; Douglas Harkness's role, 10; on espionage, 107; and Greene Plan, 204, 205; and Mendelsohn briefings, 96-97; officer transfers, 88; and ONUC HQ, 130-31, 185; and Paul Hellyer, 204, 205, 207; and Pisa-Leopoldville airlift, 189-90; and role of Canadian peacekeepers, 96-97; status of Canadian officers, 197; and UN requests, 49-50, 127-28, 154-55, 184, 188-90, 206-7, 209, 219-20; and use of force, 218-19. *See also* Canadian Armed Forces; Canadian government; Harkness, Douglas; Pearkes, George

National Survival Plan, 50

NATO: American initiative, 132; Belgian position, 69, 122; and Canada, 62, 122-23; and combat forces, 49; and Greene Plan, 202; meeting in Bahamas, 195; Paris NATO meeting, 178; policy on the Congo, 216

N'Djili incident, 75-79, 77, 82-83; Mobutu's apology, 234n55

neo-colonialism, 47, 226n45. *See also* decolonization

neutrality, 4, 5, 109

*New York Herald Tribune,* 24. *See also* newspapers

newspapers: and Canadian involvement, 38-39, 53; on the Congo, 31; coverage of post-independence events, 27; *Le Devoir,* 31, 38-39, 77; *Globe and Mail,* 40, 42, 44, 77, 128; *London Observer,* 3; *Montreal Gazette,* 38, 57, 109, 117, 129, 136, 168; *New York Herald Tribune,* 24; *Pravda,* 83; *Victoria Colonist,* 212; *Winnipeg Free Press,* 38, 53. *See also* Chronicle-Herald; Toronto Daily Star

Nigeria, 156-57, 211

night clubs, 153

Nkrumah, Kwame, 87-88

Normandin (Maj.), 189

Noronha, Reggie (Brig.), 198

North Atlantic Council meeting, 121

North Star aircraft: arrival of, 64; controversy over use, 53-54; and Pisa-Leopoldville airlift, 52, 65-66, 85, 87; replacement of, 141, 170. *See also* aircraft

Nossal, Kim Richard, 8

Nwokedi, Francis, 158

Nyenhuis, K., 20-21

O'Brien, Conor Cruise, 163, 166, 176, 250n28

"one Canada" mindset, 39, 218. *See also* bilingualism; Diefenbaker, John

Opération des Nations Unies au Congo (ONUC): air commander position, 209; and Belgian advisers, 163-64; brigade HQ, 52; Canada's motivation for involvement, 215; Canadian contribution to, 2, 85-89, 96-97, 104-10, 141-47, 152-58, 168-72, 184-90, 196-97, 206-12; Canadian representation at HQ, 74-75, 107-8, 197, 216; Canadian role in, 180; communication needs of, 52; communication with home governments, 67, 101-2, 156-57, 171, 185-86, 238n19; composition of, 5, 35-36, 47-49, 55, 130-31, 142(t); cost of, 114, 140, 151; deployment of, 45, 63-93; evacuation of units, 116-17; financing of, 113-15, 151-52, 173-74; force reductions, 207; and formative principles, 4-5; funding of, 208; importance of, 149; and

Kasavubu, 158-59; and Katanga, 169, 176, 198; key principles of, 46-47; and Kitona Declaration, 182; lack of co-operation in, 165; level of force, 6-7; Mendelsohn on, 96-97; Military Information Branch, 185; national preferences at HQ, 97, 108-9, 125, 189; Operation Morthor, 165-66, 168; Operation Rumpunch, 163; options for Katanga, 174; organization and operation of, 125-27; political intervention of, 236n78; RCAF contribution, 87, 104-5; requirements of, 59, 65; and Resolution 146 (1960), 70; revision of instructions, 95-96; role of, 67-73, 70, 138-41; role of commander, 126-27; withdrawal of, 201-13; withdrawal of national forces, 130. *See also* Canadian Armed Forces; Dayal, Rajeshwar; Royal Canadian Air Force (RCAF); United Nations (UN)
Orientale province, 111
Osorio-Tafall, Bibiano (ONUC officer-in-charge), 210

paratroopers, 227n34
Pariseau, J.J.B. (Capt.), 80, 81, 101
peace enforcement, 7
peacekeepers: concerns for safety of, 118-19; dispatch of, 31-62; safety of, 155-56, 211. *See also* Canadian Armed Forces, Canadian contingent in ONUC; Opération des Nations Unies au Congo (ONUC)
peacekeeping: Canadian financial policy on, 113-14; history of, 5-6; and national identity, 214; and politics, 134-61; redefinition of, 7-8; UN division on, 161; and use of force, 162-200
peacemaking, 7
Pearkes, George: on Canadian troops, 97; and deployment, 67, 71; recommendations for involvement, 59; *Toronto Daily Star* on, 53; on training plans, 88; use of aircraft, 54, 85-86; on white troops, 59. *See also* National Defence, Department of
Pearson, Geoffroy, 7
Pearson, Lester B.: on Canadian involvement, 41; on creation of ONUC Advisory Committee, 90; election of, 204; and foreign affairs, 9; political history of, 1; on sanctions on Katanga, 195; on Suez Crisis, 5; UN address, 208. *See also* Canadian government
phone system, 74

Pierce, Sydney, 23, 122, 147
Pisa-Leopoldville airlift: and austerity program, 189-90; and Cabinet, 52; details of, 50-51; extension of, 104-5, 141; and North Star aircraft, 85, 87. *See also* aircraft; Royal Canadian Air Force (RCAF)
Plan of National Reconciliation, 192-94, 254n58
political differences, bridging of, 7
political parties, 21
Port-Francqui (Kasai), 155
*Pravda*, 83. *See also* newspapers; Soviet Union
press: and Canadian involvement, 39; on Caribou aircraft, 86; and Hammarskjöld's death, 167. *See also* newspapers
prostitutes, 59, 231n89
public opinion: and Communism, 46; to Congo Crisis, 31, 91-92; government consideration of, 220-21; on Katanga, 178-79; on Lumumba's arrest, 117; on Lumumba's death, 136-37; on peacekeeping, 39, 214-15; and policy, 8; public pressure, 46; on South Kasai famine, 128-29; and UN requests, 168-69

Quebec secessionist movement, 178

race relations: and Advisory Committee, 90-91; and ANC, 144; as Belgian colony, 13; in Congo, 19-23; and Congo Crisis, 27-28; and Congolese independence, 26-29; European exodus from Congo, 27; and Katangan independence, 29; and N'Djili incident, 79; orders on identification by country, 102; terms for Congolese, 153; and UN forces, 70; and white troops, 37, 79, 81-82
radio sets, 52, 64, 74
Raja (Brig.), 179. *See also* Opération des Nations Unies au Congo (ONUC)
Rayner, H.S. (V. Adm.), 10
RCAF. *See* Royal Canadian Air Force (RCAF)
recreational opportunities, 153
"Red Danger Reported in Congo," 31
Reid, Escott, 18-19, 89
repair shop, 74
Republic of Zaire, 11. *See also* Democratic Republic of Congo (DRC)
rescue operations, 210
Resolutions, General Assembly. *See under* United Nations (UN), General Assembly

Resolutions, Security Council. *See under*
United Nations (UN), Security
Council
Rich (Capt.), 165
Rikhye, Indar Jit (Brig.): and air commander position, 180; attempts to remove,
125-27; and Berthiaume, 107-9; on
Canadian unit, 207; on communication with home governments, 185-86;
on Congolese, 82; and Mobutu, 102;
on N'Djili incident, 77; request for
intelligence officer, 107; request for
officer instructors, 181; use of English,
75. *See also* Opération des Nations
Unies au Congo (ONUC)
riots, 20, 21-22, 27
Ritchie, Charles: and Advisory Committee,
124, 140; background of, 32; and
Belgium, 150-51; on Canada and NATO,
120; and Canadian involvement, 40,
47; on Hammarskjöld, 84; meetings
with Hammarskjöld, 125-27, 149; and
offers of assistance, 34; and ONUC, 38,
95-96; on Resolution 161 (1961), 138;
and safety of peacekeepers, 118-19;
and Soviet Union, 137; on treatment
of Canadians, 81; on treatment of
Lumumba, 124; on use of force, 218;
and use of North Star aircraft, 54. *See
also* External Affairs, Department of
Robertson, Norman: on American
initiative, 131; background of, 10; on
Belgian policy, 118; on Belgian troops,
69; on Canadian involvement, 37-38;
on Canadian representation to Congo,
25; on financial contributions to UN
Congo fund, 103; and Katanga, 33; on
Lumumba, 58; and ONUC, 45, 60; and
Pisa-Leopoldville airlift, 190; on UN
requests, 188. *See also* External Affairs,
Department of
Robinson, Basil: and Canadian involve-
ment, 39, 48; on John Diefenbaker, 2,
38, 227n29, 238n15. *See also* External
'Affairs, Department of
Rothschild, Robert, 147, 150-51. *See also*
Belgium
Royal 22e Regiment, 51, 74
Royal Canadian Air Force (RCAF):
evacuation plans, 241n51; Pisa-
Leopoldville airlift, 50-51, 85, 87,
104-5, 141, 189-90; provision of air
commander, 219; requests from UN,
127-28, 155, 169, 188, 206; use of
long-range transport aircraft, 232n13.
*See also* aircraft

Royal Canadian Corps of Signals, 50. *See
also* Canadian Armed Forces; 57th
Signal Squadron
rubber policy, 12, 13
Rumpunch, Operation, 163
Rusk, Dean, 7

Salumu, Bernard, 58
sanctions, 191-93, 195, 254n58
Sandys, Duncan, 139, 167
Schatzberg, Michael, 225n43, 228n52
Scheyven, Louis, 45
Schlegel, John, 25-26, 39
Sechelt Conservative Association, 92
2nd Batalion, Royal Canadian Regiment,
32, 38
Security Council. *See* United Nations (UN),
Security Council
Seven Seas Airlines, 249n8
sexual activity, 153
Slim, Mongi, 36
Smith, Denis, 238n15
Smith, P.D. (Col.): assessment of Congo
situation, 157; on Berthiaume, 107-8;
on Canadian personnel, 130-31; on
Canadian position at ONUC HQ,
107-8; debriefing of, 157-58; and
incident with ANC, 153; and Matadi
incident, 143-46; orders on chain of
command, 101; requested intelligence
operation, 106-7; on Stanleyville
incident, 154
Smith, Sidney, 9
Sobolev, Arkadiy, 36. *See also* Soviet Union
Société Générale de Belgique, 13, 224n2.
*See also* Belgium
La Société Internationale Forestière et
Minière du Congo (FORMINIERE), 13
Sokolsky, J.J., 8
South Kasai, 72, 128-30. *See also* Kasai
Soviet Union: and Aroutunian, 45-46,
58, 61; attack on Hammarskjöld,
216; Canadian criticism of, 120; on
Canadian participation, 83-84, 98; on
Congo Crisis, 33; Congolese requests
to, 44; and Gizenga regime, 136, 137;
and Khrushchev, 33, 44, 99-100; and
Kuznetsov, 83-84; and Lumumba,
71-73, 83; and NATO involvement, 45;
on ONUC composition, 55; *Pravda*, 83;
pressure to intervene, 228n50; response
to Lumumba's death, 136, 137; and
Sobolev, 36; Soviet Draft Resolution,
138, 244n9; and Western policy
makers, 228n52; and witchcraft
course, 24

Spaak, Paul Henri, 205. *See also* Belgium
Special Commonwealth African Assistance Plan, 14
Speedie (Lt. Col.), 107, 160
St. Laurent, Louis, 1
standby battalion, 32, 38
Stanley, Henry, 12
Stanleyville: and Gizenga regime, 137, 162-63; and Lumumba, 115-16, and ONUC, 52, 74, 100, 116, 127, 154, 232n10; Stanleyville government, 117, 118, 122, 123, 137, 158, 241n50; Stanleyville incidents, 80-83, 154
Stetham, H.W.C. (Col.), 157, 162, 163-64, 165, 171, 188
Stevens, G.R., 15
Stubbs (Capt.), 154
Sudanese peacekeepers, 143-44, 145
Suez Crisis, 5
supplies, 50-51. *See also* Pisa-Leopoldville airlift
Swedish peacekeepers, 70-71, 79, 82

Tananarive conference, 149
Taschereau, J.C.A.A. (Capt.), 75-76, 77
technical assistance, requests for, 27-28, 34
terms, use of, 11
Timberlake, Clare, 35, 95. *See also* United States
*Toronto Daily Star:* on Canadian involvement, 53; on Congo Crisis, 27; on Howard Green, 121-22; on Katanga, 168, 179; on letter of protest, 77; on Lumumba, 117, 136; on Nikita Khrushchev, 44; on South Kasai famine, 128. *See also* newspapers
trade, 15-17, 224n11
"trans-Atlantic French-speaking" country, 35, 37, 38, 41
transit camp, 155
Tremblay, Paul, 103, 192, 198, 201-3, 218. *See also* External Affairs, Department of
Tshombé, Moïse, 28-29, 32-33, 68, 176, 182, 198. *See also* Katanga
the Tunisian resolution, 36
Turgeon, William, 17
24 November resolution. *See* United Nations (UN), Security Council, Resolution 169 (1961)
21 February resolution. *See* United Nations (UN), Security Council, Resolution 161 (1961)

U Thant: as acting secretary-general, 174-75; and air commander position, 180; background of, 11; and bilateral military assistance, 203-4; and Congo Crisis, 191; and Greene Plan, 202-3; and Katanga, 195; and military offensive, 200; and ONUC, 198; request for officer instructors, 181, 186; request for signal personnel, 184; U Thant Plan, 192-94, 254n58; withdrawal of ONUC, 207-8, 211. *See also* United Nations (UN)
Union Minière du Haut Katanga, 12-13, 68, 194-95, 198. *See also* Katanga
United Arab Republic (UAR) contingent, 130
United Kingdom: British trade with Congo, 15-16; and death of Dag Hammarskjöld, 167; on foreign involvement in Congo, 32; and Harold Macmillan, 166, 177, 191, 195; and Katanga, 176-78, 191-93, 195-96; on Resolution 161 (1961), 139
United Nations (UN)
– Advisory Committee: and Belgian withdrawal, 150-51; on bilateral assistance, 203; Canadian tactics in, 217; and Charles Ritchie, 140; and conciliation committee, 104; creation of, 90-91; and Dag Hammarskjöld, 164; functioning of, 124; and funding, 173; and Greene Plan, 202; and Kasavubu delegation, 112-13; and Katanga, 192, 194; and Lumumba's arrest, 123-24; request for officer instructors, 181; and revisions to ONUC instructions, 95-96; and U Thant, 175; and use of force, 146; withdrawal of ONUC, 208
– and Canada: reputation in, 14; support of, 221
– Charter: Article 25, 68, 70; Article 49, 68, 70; Article 99, 35; and peacekeeping, 3-4
– diplomacy: Congolese requests to UN, 27-29; history of peacekeeping, 3; and Joseph Mobutu regime, 95; in New York, 81-85, 97-100, 103-4, 111-15; relations between states, 6; response to Congo Crisis, 33-37; role in the Congo, 60
– financial position of, 173, 208
– General Assembly: Canada's voting pattern, 216; Credentials committee, 112-13; Fifteenth regular session, 99-100; Fifth (Budgetary) Committee, 114; meeting of 17 September, 98; Resolution 1474 (ES-IV), 98, 103, 203, 237n10; Resolution 1498 (XV), 113,

240n40; Resolution 1583 (XV), 151; Resolution 1599 (XV), 149-50, 246n27; Resolution 1601 (XV), 150, 246n28; Resolution 1620 (XV), 151-52; Resolution 1732 (XVI), 173; Resolution 1885 (XVIII), 208, 257n15; Uniting for Peace Resolution, 4, 98
– requests to Canada: for aircraft, 154, 168; consultations on Canadian involvement, 53; for cryptographer, 196; for force commander (officer to fill position), 184; for intelligence officers, 107, 171; for logistics personnel, 47-48, 49, 51, 52, 64, 155, 211; for military police, 188; for mobile photo-developing unit, 188; for napalm bombs, 196; for officer instructors, 172, 181, 186-87, 206; for ONUC HQ staff, 130, 185, 189, 206; for RCAF personnel, 127-28, 155, 169, 188, 206; for signal personnel, 47-48, 49-53, 106, 184, 196, 207; for UNEF aircraft, 38
– Security Council: draft Tunisian-Ceylon sponsored resolution, 98, 237n8; meetings of, 35-36, 54-55, 98, 119; Resolution 143 (1960), 68, 69; Resolution 145 (1960), 55, 68, 230n79; Resolution 146 (1960), 70, 233n29; Resolution 161 (1961), 138-41, 244n10, 244n12; Resolution 169 (1961), 175; Western Resolution, 119-20
– United Nations Air Transport Force, 87, 236n72
– United Nations Emergency Force (UNEF): and Caribou aircraft, 237n7; and consent, 4; operations of, 36; personnel from, 51
– United Nations Truce Supervisory Organization (UNTSO), 34; secondment of officers, 48; use of personnel, 40-41
– *See also* Hammarskjöld, Dag; Opération des Nations Unies au Congo (ONUC); U Thant
United Nations Division: and air commander position, 180; on Kasavubu delegation, 111-13. *See also* External Affairs, Department of
United States: and Advisory Committee, 253n55; Bureau of African Affairs, 14-15; and Canada's role, 7; Central Intelligence Agency (CIA), 44, 95, 249n8; Clare Timberlake, 35, 95; on Communists, 43-44; Dwight Eisenhower, 29, 72, 238n15; financial support, 211; on foreign involvement, 32; foreign policy, 46; and independence movements, 228n48; and intervention, 226n45; John F. Kennedy's Congo Policy, 131-33; and Kasavubu delegation, 111-13; on Katanga, 176-78; and Lumumba, 56-57, 72, 230n85; and Mobutu, 95; and ONUC funding, 208; and Operation Morthor, 166; request for military assistance from, 29; on Soviet comments, 98; and Soviet intervention, 228n44; and training program, 204-6; transport of peacekeepers, 66; and U Thant Plan, 192-93; and UN, 119-20; and use of force, 196; *Wasp* (US aircraft carrier), 228n44
Uniting for Peace Resolution, 4, 98. *See also* United Nations (UN), General Assembly
Urquhart, Brian: beating of (incident), 176; on Canadian involvement, 228n56; on Dag Hammarskjöld, 164; on events in Congo, 179, 198, 225n40; on race, 27; on security council, 37; on U Thant, 174. *See also* Opération des Nations Unies au Congo (ONUC)

*Victoria Colonist,* 212. *See also* newspapers
von Horn, Carl (Gen.): appointment of, 48; on Caribou aircraft, 86; criticisms of, 125; and death of Lumumba, 241n47; delay in arrival of, 63, 229n66; departure of, 107; deployment of forces, 53; on N'Djili incident, 77; and Stanleyville attack, 80; transfer of UNTSO officers, 40; and UN Air Transport Force, 87, 236n72. *See also* Opération des Nations Unies au Congo (ONUC)

Wainhouse, David, 75
Walsh, G. (Lt. Gen.), 10, 186
*Wasp* (US aircraft carrier), 228n44
Waterworth, Florence, 128
weaponry, 65, 156-57, 196
Weidman, Mr., 183
Weissman, Stephen, 46, 176, 255n1
Welbeck incident, 105-6, 157
Welbeck, Nathaniel, 105-6
Western Resolution, 119-20. *See also* United Nations (UN)
Wieschhoff, Hans, 34
Wigny, Pierre, 55, 122-23. *See also* Belgium
Williams, Bruce, 87
*Winnipeg Free Press,* 38, 53. *See also* newspapers

witchcraft, 24
Wood, William Mackenzie, 79, 82-83, 95, 102, 110-11
Woodside, Willson, 129
World War II, 17
Worthington, Peter, 100

Yukon turbo-prop (aircraft), 170. *See also* aircraft

Zorin, Valerian, 98. *See also* Soviet Union